Y0-BCR-748

J. M. HODGES LIBRARY
WHARTON COUNTY JUNIOR COLLEGE
WHARTON, TEXAS

# Fitting Yourself for Business

## FOURTH EDITION

Elizabeth Gregg MacGibbon
*Author of "Manners in Business"*

33632

### GREGG PUBLISHING DIVISION
*McGraw-Hill Book Company*

*New York*
*Chicago*
*Dallas*
*Corte Madera, Calif.*
*Toronto*
*London*

FITTING YOURSELF FOR BUSINESS, FOURTH EDITION

Copyright © 1961 by McGraw-Hill Book Company, Inc.

Copyright, 1955, 1947, 1941, by McGraw-Hill Book Company,

Inc. All rights reserved. This book, or parts thereof, may not

be reproduced in any form without permission of the publishers.

LIBRARY OF CONGRESS CATALOG NO. 61-9467

7 8 9 MP–61 9 8 7

44538

Published by Gregg Publishing Division

McGraw-Hill Book Company

Printed in the United States of America

650, 19
m174f
4th. ed.

33632

*To my son*

GREGG LINVILLE MacGIBBON

*whose beginning experiences in business*
*provided invaluable material for this book*

# Preface

Someone has said, "Going to work is a shock, but not going is a greater one." *Fitting Yourself for Business,* Fourth Edition was written to help beginners in business to face up to and survive both shocks. Since the advent of its first edition, there have been ups and downs in the employment picture. In subsequent editions, *Fitting Yourself for Business* has endeavored to present these changes to students nearing graduation and to prepare them for the conditions they were about to meet. At times when jobs were scarce the prospect was gloomy for up-coming employees; at other times the situation looked dark for employers, when there were not enough workers available to meet their needs.

However, there is no use now in looking back on those days when the low birth rate of the depression years, (the thirties), resulted in there being too few employees for office jobs eighteen years later. For, since 1958, when the "war babies" began graduating from high school, there has been what would formerly have been considered an ample supply of new "help" to man the nation's offices. Government estimates on births show the following:

Young persons reaching 18 years of age
1960................. 2.6 million
1965................. 3.8 million

with the number entering the labor market estimated to drop somewhat after 1965.

Ironically, although young people in greater numbers than ever are approaching employment, the expansion of business has absorbed more and more workers until there is now a definite shortage of office employees. The resulting problem—how to get more work out of fewer people—is being met by employers in two ways. First, by employee training programs, and second, by automation.

Because they are having to hire young men and women who are not prepared to do the work which must be done, training programs for incoming employees have been set up by innumerable large companies. In small firms the new recruits can be trained on the job. There is a bulletin on training programs put out by the International Association of Personnel Women, whose president is associated with the Pet Milk Company of St. Louis. This report gives a brief résumé of the training programs of 44 companies which employ up to 5,000 or more persons. The list of employers reads like a *Who's Who* of American Business, and the listing of the material used in the training programs of these companies is impressive. Furthermore, in this report, complete training programs are offered, on loan, to other companies who likewise find it necessary to train typists, stenographers, business machine and switchboard operators. Some courses take 16 weeks to complete, while others are as brief as a four-session refresher course for secretaries, covering telephone technique, typing shortcuts, mail and letters, spelling, grammar, punctuation, and secretarial personality. Judging by the pamphlets and books recommended by the Association of Personnel Women, there is an acute demand for material to use in this important work of making qualified employees out of the "hands" available.

But the 44 companies referred to in this report constitute only a fraction of the innumerable firms which have found it necessary to pay employees while they learn what to do and how to do it. In addition to employer-sponsored courses, many of the business machine manufacturers, such as the IBM, maintain training schools to which purchasers and lessees of their equipment may send employees for specific training in the use of these machines.

While the training of new employees is certain to produce a greater output of work, this alone has not solved the employers' problem, nor does it appear likely to do so. Automation, or the employment of machines to take over the work formerly done by hand, is, in many instances, proving to be the answer. Perhaps "mechanization" is a better word than automation. By whatever name we call it, machines are now used to take the drudgery out of many tasks, and speed up the work. So successful is this innovation that more machines are being invented, and business is rapidly installing them in order to get along with fewer clerks, typists and stenographers.

Let's see how and where mechanization is replacing office workers.

Instead of dictating to stenographers and secretaries, as formerly, many businessmen are now converting to dictating machines, with typists doing the typing from records or discs. Also, more and more medium-size and large offices are using photographic machines, as well as electrically-driven multilith machines, to do copy work which was formerly done by typists. This speeds up the work and requires fewer typists. Bank bookkeeping, now practically all done by machine, is learned through on-the-job training. In banks and insurance companies where millions, if not billions, of checks have to be handled annually, mechanization has probably reached its highest point. In a metropolitan bank which services all its numerous branches electronically, I visited the business machine room where $250,000 worth of machines were in operation. Only a few persons were about, to handle the equipment. I was relieved to learn that the machines had to be told what to do; hence there would always be need for *some* human brains!

There are degrees of automation—ranging from the key punch machine to the costly computer. While banks and insurance companies would like to hire key punch operators, it seems they are scarce. Students who can type 45 to 50 words per minute are ready to be taught key punch operation which pays around $250 a month to start. A supervisor of key punch work can earn as much as $450. Faster work is done by the better operators, and natural ability, concentration, and, in some cases, educational background, play a part in how far one can go in this technological field. The top job, head of the machine room, pays $13,000 annually, and is usually held by a man. Girls with college degrees in mathematics or economics appear to be best suited to progress in handling machine equipment, but this does not rule out the high school graduate who has a mechanical flair.

Obviously, the job set-up for the business beginner has changed greatly in recent years. Where business once hoped that the recent graduate applying for his or her first job would know something about routine clerical work, filing and hand bookkeeping, if not typing and shorthand, it now seems willing to settle for mere willingness to go to work. While knowledge of shorthand and typing is still an entree to desirable starting positions, these skills are no longer the only opening wedge. Instead of being "choosey," and asking the nervous young applicant, "What can you *do?*", the employer or his representative now welcome the totally untrained beginner with open arms, as a possible trainee. Today's training programs and automation are helping not only the harried employer, but the hopeful beginner who wishes to try his hand at office work.

But a word of caution. Beginners should not be deluded by the eagerness of business to start them at good-paying jobs. Mere presence in the office scene will not keep even the most decorative employee there for long. Competition still exists among workers; and supervisors are there to spot those who merit promotions and dispense with the services of the lazy and the indifferent. Although little may be required of the new employee, success, as always, depends to a great extent upon his eagerness to learn, his attention to detail, and good old fashioned "stick-to-it-iveness."

ELIZABETH GREGG MacGIBBON

# Contents

# CHAPTER 1

# Planning for a Career

From early childhood, most boys and many girls count on working as soon as they leave school. This is a natural and an inevitable plan. Ours is a business country, made up of factories, farms, banks, stores, offices, shops, and services of all kinds. It is as a nation of business enterprises and business people that we have made a unique and outstanding contribution to the world. In fact, Americans seem to have what might be called a *genius* for business, and the United States is recognized as the leading business nation of the world.

To support yourself and get started in life, you will go to work in some capacity, doubtless in business. You will have considerable choice as to fields, and you may prepare in school for a beginning job in the field you prefer. After that, you will be on your own. Right now, you probably express your ambition in general terms, as, "Believe me, I'm going to get a job as soon as I graduate." And you will. There is no need for you to feel nervous about what lies ahead—getting your first job and making good in it. These things can be taken in your stride. What you should do now is to learn the fundamental facts about business and see, in advance, your probable starting point.

Actually, business will not be altogether new to you. All your life you have been exposed to it—ever since you spent your first coin for a candy bar or an ice-cream cone. The corner grocery, the barbershop, the drugstore (especially the soda fountain), the movie theater, the filling station, and the bicycle shop are typical business enterprises in America. In these casual, everyday contacts with business, you have been a "consumer"—buying the goods and services provided by others.

## KINDS OF BUSINESS

It is not the purpose of this book to trace the history of business from its early beginning as a one-man factory or store in the colonies to the

I

present nationwide, highly productive form of organization—the corporation. However, if you are to see, in their proper place, the various office positions in which you are most likely to start, you should be familiar with the *kinds* of business that make up the American system of private enterprise. While there are many different types of business, they can be grouped under three main divisions, based on their functions. These are:

1. PRODUCTION
   Manufacturers, making goods to be sold; farmers, producing foodstuffs

2. DISTRIBUTION
   Sales organizations, as retail stores, wholesalers, and brokers; railroads, truck lines, and shipping companies engaged in transporting goods to be sold

3. SERVICE
   All finance, including banks; hotels, restaurants; barbershops, beauty parlors; laundries, dry cleaners, and thousands of small service establishments providing daily conveniences to those who produce and distribute; the professions, as doctors, lawyers, dentists, architects, engineers, teachers, clergymen; advertising, which brings buyer and seller together; *personnel and office occupations, which are found in all kinds of business*

Now that you have taken a brief over-all look at what constitutes business, let's consider where you belong in this vast, complex system. As well as being a consumer, you will, within the next year or so, be on the other side of the picture. For when you go to work, you will produce, sell, or work in the service section of business. To find the place where you will do your best work and be happiest requires considerable planning.

## PLAN YOUR BUSINESS CAREER

You may say, "Why do I need a plan? I can get a job as soon as I'm through school. In fact, I already have one lined up." Such a statement shows your need for a plan. If you take just any job offered you, with no thought of where it leads, you may waste precious months, even years, before you find it leads nowhere. Or you may, after a trial period, find yourself totally unsuited to the work, in temperament or physical qualifications, and even in skills. True, you can quit and try something else, and quit and quit, and start again. But unless you have some idea as to where you are headed, your mistakes can exceed your progress.

*Reasons for Planning.* Suppose that a boy wanted to build a house or a boat. Would he start without a plan? He would want some sort of blueprint before he even bought the materials. Girls who have done some sewing know that they need instructions and a pattern by which to cut. A career plan is quite as necessary and can be almost as definite.

There is nothing very difficult about making a plan for your business life. Think of the plan you probably have right now for next year's vacation. Or the plan—call it a dream if you young women like—for your wedding, if, as, and when. And what young man doesn't plan for a car of his own no matter how remote the actual purchase seems? This sort of planning is fun. In fact, it's a very real part of your enjoyment in the things you are planning for. Planning your business life can be fun, too. It will give zest to every step you take.

However, your plan should be undertaken seriously—not merely in a spirit of fun. It may well be the most important thing you ever do. So, think your way into your plan. Have real reasons back of your choice of a career. And, above all, be sure it is *your* plan.

**Whose Plan Shall It Be?** Of course, your plan to be successful must be *your own*, not something your parents have wanted for you since you were small. Parents sometimes have a bad habit of settling their children's futures for them. Dad may have wanted to be a doctor but

Planning your career in business requires a blueprint or pattern just as does designing machinery or making a dress.

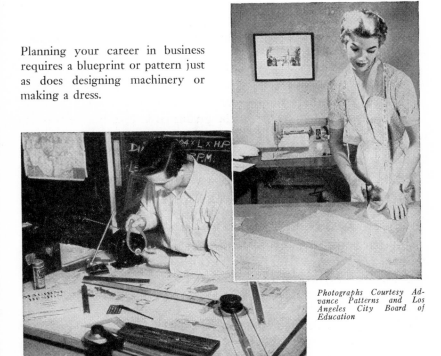

*Photographs Courtesy Advance Patterns and Los Angeles City Board of Education*

for financial reasons couldn't make the grade, so Junior must study medicine. Or perhaps Mother had a secret longing to become an actress, and so Jane, being so graceful and pretty, must go on the stage!

This is merely a way many parents have of compensating through their children for unfulfilled dreams of their own. If you have no talents along the lines suggested, you won't be in the least undutiful or disloyal if you hold firmly to your own ideas and preferences for your future. The first principle of success in any job is to like it for its own sake. It's a rare person who makes good in something for which he has no flair.

Again, there may be a store or a contracting business in the family. What more natural than a plan to have John or Harry take it over? Sometimes, when jobs are scarce, a family business is a godsend to sons and even to daughters. Often, as the younger generation progresses in the family field, everyone concerned is pleased and happy. John makes good, and Dad is proud. But when a young person with other interests and abilities is forced into a situation planned for him by his parents, discontent and failure may be the result.

Relatives other than parents can make wrong plans, too. I know a young man whose career was given a severe setback by his aunts' plan. At the time it looked wonderful. The two aunts were wealthy and were eager to give James the college education his parents could not finance. But they knew more about the stock market than they knew about vocational guidance. They had had much dealing with lawyers. The law was a highly respectable calling; their nephew was nice-looking and intelligent. Therefore, he should study law.

James was studious enough to be graduated in law, but he was shy and unable to speak in public. Even worse, he was totally unable to explain anything to anyone. These traits were so apparent in his social life that the aunts might have realized that James was not cut out to be a lawyer. No doubt, these negative qualities helped bring about James's rebellion after two years of the five-year law course. "I don't like law," he told his aunts. "There's nothing I'd hate more than being a lawyer."

Asked what he wanted to study, James's reply was, "Painting." The aunts were horrified, and James left college to follow his own plan as best he could. His struggle, and eventual success, is another story. My regret, and James's regret, is for those lost years.

## ADVANTAGES OF HAVING A PLAN

Nothing will whet your ambition so much as the plan you make for yourself. It will keep you striving against any and all odds. It will keep you alert, keen, and on your toes. Because it is your own plan, it will create in you the kind of discontent that will force you toward the job for which you are best suited and will keep you alive to the possibilities of promotion. It will not only help you to succeed faster, but it will help you to greater happiness in your work. Nothing is more important. When going to work each morning is equivalent to going to jail, something is wrong.

By making a plan for yourself, you already will have taken the first step on the road to success. Already you will stand out from the crowd. As you see your way more clearly, you will now and then shift your direction, to favor your plan. As you grow, your plan will grow. A survey of 10,000 people, young and old, showed that only one out of twenty ever had had any definite aim in life. Nearly all those who had achieved success stated they had had a definite goal and had done everything possible to reach it.

**Wishful Thinking Is Not Planning.** Of course, a plan should be something attainable, based on known facts and conditions. It would be only wishful thinking for a boy to say, on the day of his graduation, "I'm going to start in as a clerk in a gas and electric company. I shall be promoted every year until, in about ten or twelve years, I shall be in a very important position—making a big salary and headed for the presidency." Neither life nor business can be plotted in that definite fashion. What *can* be done is to take a good look at a number of fields; select the ones that seem most attractive; get information about them; size up oneself in relation to each of these fields; then, when possible, get a tryout job as a test. All these steps will be discussed shortly.

**It's a Man's World.** Before we list possible fields, a sad truth should be stated. For young men, the sky's the limit where planning is concerned. Once started, they can advance as far as ability, ambition, opportunity, and hard work will take them. But young women seldom have this chance. Possibly it's their own fault. But I have a suspicion they wouldn't have it any other way.

The difference between masculine and feminine planning shows up early. Boys plan for their lifework. But very often, if a girl is frank with herself, she premises her career plan with the condition, "If I don't marry, I'd like to . . . ." This would be a sorry old world if girls didn't dream of marriage, homes, and babies ahead of careers. Because hope for marriage springs eternal until young women are at least thirty, you find very few of them holding important executive positions. When you do meet them, almost without exception they are married and for one reason or another expect to continue working. Often they are widowed or divorced and have the responsibility of one or more children to support.

This is still a man's world and probably always will be. It is only since the invention of the typewriter and the telephone that women have come out of the kitchen and nursery into the business office. Men were tried out in the operation of both the typewriter and the telephone when these inventions first appeared, but they lacked the patience to handle the "new-fangled contraptions." Only then were young women called in. Their patience with detail gave them the jobs for keeps. In other words, they took over the office housekeeping, and as far as men are concerned, they can go on doing it.

Just as the lesser, detail jobs have fallen almost exclusively to women, so have the top office positions, administrative and managerial, gone to men. In spite of the large number of women now employed in the total labor market, there are still many employers who consider it a waste of time to train a smart girl for important executive work, since she may leave if she marries. In most cases, employers of office workers prefer not to use women in executive positions above those of office manager, personnel director, or head of the filing department.

*Girls Should Plan, Too.* It is just as important, however, for a girl to enter business in a field that attracts her as for her brother to do so. If she should work for only a few years, as she hopes, she will enjoy these years more if her work is interesting. To say that girls must choose between marriage and a career is not true. In such a choice, it is likely that they would all choose marriage. But it is a mistake for girls to count on not working after they marry. Look at your married friends and count the working wives, or make the same survey when on your first job. It may come as a shock to see that nearly all the young women around you have husbands and that many also have small children. In lunchroom and dressing-room conversations, the starry-eyed beginners will hear a lot about early breakfasts and getting the youngsters off to school. Sooner or later, they will learn a fact of present-day life—that, when living costs and taxes are high, it seems to take two pay checks to run a home.

Statistics are with the girls who plan to marry and to marry young. In 50 per cent of the marriages today, the bride is under twenty. The statistics [1] also show that married women in greater numbers than ever before have joined the labor force. In 1959 there were 23 million women working. *Over half* of these were married, with husband-and-wife teams representing three out of every ten families in the United States. Approximately 25 per cent of all the women working, when these figures were compiled, were single. Widows and divorced women

[1] *Working Women, Who Are They?* Fall 1959 statistics compiled by the Women's Division, Institute of Life Insurance, New York, N. Y.

account for another 16 per cent of the total number of employed women.

So, girls, don't be lukewarm about fields. Some career planning on your part, subject to its being a man's world, is good insurance. Although the statistics are against it, you *may* be lucky enough to retire from business when you marry, or when you add "Mother" to your title of Wife. Even so, you, like many another woman, may later return to work. The more you know and the higher you have gone before you quit, the better will be the job you can fill when you start again.

### ANALYZE YOURSELF

Before you can consider the fields listed later in this chapter, you need to know more about yourself. Many fields ideal for other people might not be your best choice. On the other hand, the right field for you would probably be undesirable for someone with different tastes and interests. The best way to get acquainted with yourself so as to match your tastes and interests to a field is to ask yourself a great many personal questions. The ones that follow are only a few to get you started. Write every question you can think of, and then answer all of them honestly. You'll learn things about yourself that you didn't know. Perhaps you haven't spent much time studying your personality and temperament, your mental and physical make-up, your interests and aptitudes. Now, in your search for a field where you will be most likely to succeed, you need to turn a searchlight on yourself.

Let's begin with the subjects you study in school. Ask yourself these questions:

1. In what school studies did I do well and have the most interest?
   a. Industrial-arts shops (for boys)
   b. Home economics (for girls)
   c. Mathematics
   d. Science
   e. Literature
   f. Drama
   g. Languages
   h. Social studies (history, civics, economics)
   i. Physical education
   j. R.O.T.C.

2. What outside activities do I enjoy most?
   a. Stage work and scene painting
   b. Photography club
   c. Spanish club (or other language club)

    *d.* Future Farmers of America and 4-H Clubs
    *e.* Art club
    *f.* Debating team
    *g.* Airplane-model club
    *h.* Groups, such as the YMCA, YWCA, YMI, YLI, and DeMolay

3. In which of the following do I do my best? When working
    *a.* With *things*, such as motors, furniture making, or fabrics
    *b.* With *people*, as in dramatics, on dance or entertainment committees, in clubs, or in sports
    *c.* With *facts* and ideas, as in writing or debating
    *d.* With *hands*, creatively, as in clay modeling, drawing, or painting

Now ask yourself as many personal questions as you can. Don't stop with the ones listed. See whether you can add a few.

1. Am I the rough-and-ready type, preferring outdoor work? Or—
2. Would I prefer working indoors?
3. Are my favorite sports those in which team play is important, such as football, baseball, basketball, or hockey? Or—
4. Do I like sports with individual performance, such as track, archery, tennis, golf, or fishing?
5. Am I good at organizing and directing the activities of other people? Or—
6. Do I prefer to let someone else take the responsibility while I do the work?
7. Do I perform well in a difficult situation? Or—
8. Do I easily become nervous and confused?
9. Do I like being in a crowd? Or—
10. Do I work better and feel happier when I am alone?
11. Am I fussy about having everything neat and in its place? Or—
12. Can I work in the midst of disorder?
13. Am I a person just bursting with ideas? Or—
14. Do I like detailed work with facts and figures?
15. Am I full of "pep and ginger"? Or—
16. Do I tire easily?
17. Do I stick with a task after starting it? Or—
18. Do I leave the job half finished?

When you have answered all these and your own questions, you may have met your real self for the first time.

## FIELDS OF WORK [2]

Before you can select a starting job—headed toward a career in business—let's look at the fields in which careers are to be found.

[2] Titles rearranged from United States Department of Commerce listing.

AGRICULTURE

COMMUNICATIONS AND PUBLIC
UTILITIES
Telephone and telegraph
Radio and television broadcasting
Utilities: electric and gas
Local public services

CONTRACT CONSTRUCTION

FINANCE, INSURANCE, AND REAL ESTATE
Banking
Security and commodity brokers,
dealers and exchanges
Insurance agents and combination
offices
Real estate

GOVERNMENT AND GOVERNMENT
ENTERPRISES
Federal (Washington, D. C.)
Federal (in 48 states)
State
County
Local or municipal

MANUFACTURING
Food and kindred products
Tobacco manufactures
Textile-mill products
Apparel, other finished fabrics
Lumber and timber basic products
Furniture and finished lumber
Paper and allied products
Printing and publishing
Chemicals and allied products
Products of petroleum and coal
Rubber products
Leather and leather products

Stone, clay, and glass products
Iron and steel and products
Nonferrous metals and products
Machinery (except electrical)
Electrical machinery
Transportation equipment, except
autos
Automobiles and auto equipment
Miscellaneous

SERVICES
Hotels and lodging places
Personal services
Commercial and trade schools and
employment agencies
Business services (not covered
elsewhere)
Miscellaneous repair services and
hand trades
Motion pictures
Amusement and recreation, except
motion pictures
Medical and health services
Legal services
Engineering, other professional
Educational services
Religious organizations

TRANSPORTATION
Railroads
Local railways and bus lines
Highway passenger transportation
Highway freight transportation
Water transportation
Air transportation (common car-
riers)
Pipe-line transportation
Services allied to transportation

WHOLESALE AND RETAIL TRADE

As you will note, manufacturing and service are the largest fields, yet every listing can be broken down into greater detail. For instance, under manufacturing, consider apparel. This includes all outerwear and underclothing manufactured for men, women, and children, also hats, shoes, hosiery, gloves, neckwear, and other accessories. Try another classification, such as automobiles and auto equipment. I leave you to make a list

of the many products turned out by factories in this group. Take a classification from services, such as miscellaneous repair services, and see
how many kinds of shops you can list under that general head.

### ANALYZE FIELDS IN RELATION TO YOURSELF

You have studied your interests and abilities and have looked over a
long list of occupational fields. Now select the fields that interest you
most. Then cut your first list as much as possible, and start analyzing the
fields in relation to yourself. Your objective is to *find the right field for
you.* It is likely to be a field that gives you an opportunity to do the
things you like to do, to make use of your talents and skills, and to take
responsibility.

On several sheets of paper, make an inventory of your main interests
as they relate to the fields you have chosen for further study. Here is
one way to do it.

## SELF-JOB INVENTORY

| You Like | Fields of Interest | Kinds of Work |
| --- | --- | --- |
| —outdoor work; to be with people; to work with your hands | Public utilities (gas and electric, telephone, or water company) | Lineman; surveying crew; meter reading; repair and installation crew |
| | Transportation (operations section) | Bus driver; brakeman; yardman; truck driver |
| —outdoor work; prefer to work alone | Government service | Postman; rural mail carrier; forestry service |
| | Construction | Carpenter; painter; electrician (apprenticeship usually required) |
| —mathematics and commercial subjects; prefer individual sports; like people, but work well alone | Any industry, service, or business firm | Bookkeeper; business-machine operator; typist or stenographer |
| —to draw; do stage work and sign painting; work with hands; prefer to be alone | Any business that uses creative services, as advertising agency or department store; teacher training; architects' office | Commercial artist; draftsman; interior decorator; art teacher; store display man |
| —English; public speaking; to be a class officer; on debating team; also cheerleader | Any manufacturing firm; wholesale company; retail store; real estate office; insurance company | Salesman or saleswoman |

So far so good. If your inventory shows fields that your interests and abilities seem to fit, the chances are you're on the right track. But if this "matchmaking" of yours shows that you and those fascinating fields are not made for each other—don't go into the "marriage." You would not be happy or successful and sooner or later would have to leave those fields. Admit your mistaken choice, and select another field or two for investigation—fields in which you are interested and for which you have basic aptitudes.

However, before you go further in finding your vocation, you should consider several other factors that will help you make a wise choice. These "yardsticks" have been so well described in a booklet, *Your Future Is What You Make It*,[3] that I shall quote directly from it.

Here are three yardsticks by which you can measure each vocational selection:

Contentment
Income
Opportunity

Both at this point and later in testing your choices, these yardsticks will guide your thinking.

### THE YARDSTICK OF CONTENTMENT

Perhaps your most important tool for measuring any vocational choice is the yardstick of contentment. If you like your work and can do it well—if you feel that it is an important service to others—if you take pride in it—then you will be more likely to gain recognition, to advance and to earn more.

Analyze the kind of work you've selected. Does it require travel—or will you be able to live at home? Is it constructive? Is it constantly changing—or is it routine? To one person the all-important thing is the farmer's contact with the outdoors and with growing things—to another, it is small-town friendliness or the stimulating challenge of the city.

### THE YARDSTICK OF INCOME

Now using the yardstick of income, investigate the average earnings for the occupation you have selected. Have you the ability and persistence to travel the hard road to above-average salaries? Or will you be content to accept less money for the satisfaction which the work will give you?

### THE YARDSTICK OF OPPORTUNITY

Another thing to consider is your chance of getting ahead. Is your chosen vocational field overcrowded? Does it continuously add to the nation's

---

[3] Published by the National Association of Manufacturers, 14 West 49th Street, New York 20, N. Y.

wealth and welfare—or is it the kind which produces items or services that are popular only when people have extra money to spend?

Apply this also to what you have to offer: Do you think you have outstanding talents in your chosen field or have you merely the minimum talents which will enable you to get along during the company's prosperous times only?

Is it a new occupational field? Is it one which is changing and expanding, where your chances for rapid advancement may be greater? Is it an older, well-established industry which might welcome fresh ideas?

### CONSIDER LOCATION, TOO

Location may be a very important factor to you in applying these yardsticks. Both average wages and living expenses vary widely in different sections of the country.

In large cities, income may be higher, but your expenses may rise in proportion. Higher income earners must also pay a much larger proportion in taxes.

In some communities, opportunities in the field you have chosen may be more limited and advancement slower, but living conditions may be more pleasant.

When all these yardstick tests have been passed by the field you are investigating, it must be good—that is, good for you. Now you are ready to begin reading about this field and examining it from every angle. Be a "Sam Spade" in digging out the facts.

### GET INFORMATION ABOUT FIELDS

In the example of transportation, which follows, young men will see how to secure information in their investigation of any field. Young women will find similar guidance by following the suggestions, given later, for studying the apparel field.

*Consult Family and Friends.* Let's suppose that some of you boys have put transportation high on your list of fields. Railroading was the first subdivision listed under transportation, so why not start there. This would be a sensible choice, for railroading is surely a man's business, with the top jobs always going to men. Since you want all the information you can get, first talk with any of your friends or relatives who work for railroads. They can answer many of your questions about the work and the kinds of jobs in this field.

*Consult School and Other Libraries.* Before you start the reading program I am about to recommend, it might be well to glance at the other subdivisions in this field—air lines, truck lines, bus lines, and water transportation. One of these might intrigue you more than "working on the railroad all the livelong day."

The modern library is one of the most valuable
sources of reference for those seeking career
information.

Your next source of information on any phase of transportation
should be the vocational counselor or the placement director of your
school. These faculty members can probably tell you what the beginning jobs and the employment requirements are in this or other fields of
your interest. The vocational books and magazines in your school library will supply background knowledge. For further information
about occupations, consult the reference room of your public library.
Trade journals and magazines are found in the magazine room. It will
pay you to spend some time looking through these periodicals, since
you may thus become interested in an occupation previously unknown
to you.

For those of you who live in or near New York, there is the Career
Library in *Mademoiselle's* College and Careers Department. *Mademoiselle* is the only one of the several magazines, edited especially for
young women, which pays attention to careers. However, you do not
have to go in person to this library in order to benefit from it, for if
you write to the Alumni Advisory Center of *Mademoiselle* they will

send you a list of their reprints and pamphlets on jobs of many kinds. As there is a small charge for these, it is best to know what is available and choose the subjects that interest you most.

By the time you have browsed through books and magazines in several libraries, you should have a sizable file of notes on the field of your search. The value of this preliminary reading is that it will help you to eliminate, if need be, any field that attracted you, and for which you thought you were suited. Transportation, for instance, may have been only a word to you when you began to study it. After learning something about railroading or the trucking business, how do you feel about going into this field? Has your reading on transportation made you eager to get into some phase of it? If so, keep on. But if your interest lags, or you find the details boring, my advice is to drop this field. Start reading up on another field or two where your interests and your personality traits seem to fit, going about it in much the same way as was suggested for transportation.

Obviously, the study of transportation was meant for our young men, since women usually go no further in that field than the position of private secretary. There are bright young women at information desks in airplane offices across the country, but I doubt whether there is advancement ahead for them. I might remark that there are also some not-so-bright girls giving out misinformation at such counters, like the one who told me my plane would fly at a height of 12,000 miles.

But there are natural fields for women, several of which will be discussed in the next chapter. One of the most outstanding of these is fashion, which quickly carries your interest to the field of apparel. If your likes and abilities indicate that you belong in this field, your reading would cover a wide range. You would need to study "the market" to learn something about the manufacture of women's clothing and accessories, about the sale of women's and girls' apparel through department stores and specialty shops, and about fashion design, buying exchanges, and fashion reporting. Somewhere in these many avenues—first through study and then through personal investigation—you will find the point from which to start your climb upward in the apparel or fashion fields.

But your investigation of the fashion field need not be at long distance. Visit your favorite department store; walk through the ready-to-wear sections and see how they are set up, featuring sports apparel, suits, coats, juvenile wear, and so forth. Your first job in this field would be as a sales person in one of these departments. You might start even further down, as a stock girl, learning merchandise at first hand.

**Go Direct to Business Firms.** When you have acquired all the information possible about your favorite field, you are ready to talk with someone directly connected with this type of business. In most cases, you will be looking into a field large and important enough so that you can go to the personnel department of a firm operating in that field. To illustrate, if you want to ask practical questions about railroading, it is probable that one or more of the big railroads have employment offices in your city, headed by men who will be glad to tell you something about careers in railroading.

Have your questions in good order before you go to such an interview. List them in a notebook, and write the answers briefly and rapidly during the conversation. This is the best opportunity you will have to find out things you need to know. First, you should ask about starting jobs. What kinds of jobs are they? Without putting salary questions first, it is all right for you to ask, "About what salary would I be paid at first if I started as a mail clerk or as a typist?" And I think—since you are seeking information only—you would be justified in asking, "What would my chances of advancement be?" Other questions will occur to you both before and during such an interview. Don't stay too long. Rise, thank the interviewer for his time and the information, and leave quickly—not by slow degrees.

When you make such calls, the reception you get will depend much on your attitude. This isn't the time to be a "big shot." Busy businessmen are usually willing to talk with serious-minded young people and to answer their questions because they are always looking for desirable future employees. But they are not looking for conversations with youngsters who want to start at the top and are primarily interested in present and future "big money." Frankly, business is fed up with beginners who expect to start their careers seated at desks bearing handsome name plates engraved with their names and titles. In these illusions, inspired no doubt by movie scenes, there is nothing on the desk but a telephone, and the young executive does nothing but give orders. In case you think this an exaggeration, read what the head of a New England shoe-manufacturing firm once told me. "Each June, our personnel manager is kept busy telling recent college graduates that there are no executive positions open to them in our organization. Most of these young men are quickly disposed of. They can't take the bitter truth that anyone coming in here and expecting to become an executive must first learn to make shoes. In fact, he would have to carry kegs of nails before he could even make shoes."

So, be careful, when you call on a personnel director, to show by your manner and your questions that you know you will have to start at or near the bottom. By your modest attitude, let the person interviewing you see that you are not seeking his job or that of the president of the company. Not just yet, anyway. Remember that you are *not* applying for a job *now*—only seeking information to help you decide whether this is the field where you wish to start. However, if you have finished school and are available for work immediately, you may be offered a job. You might be smart to take it and begin at once on the tryout type of job we shall discuss next. Now you are getting information on this field from a person who is well qualified to tell you where you can hope to begin and also how high you may be able to go, provided you prove to be qualified for this kind of work and adapted to it.

## NEXT—TRYOUT EXPERIENCE

Your next step is to test your plan by actually finding out whether you like the work you selected. All the reading and discussion will only give you, at best, a mental picture of a career or of a job in that field. And your dream could be very far from the reality. But actually doing some of the beginning work in the field of your choice will settle many questions for you. If you have been imagining yourself doing a type of work that does not even exist, or to which you could only advance after some years of apprenticeship, the sooner you find this out, the better. Or, while the starting spot may be just where you expected it to be, you may find the work something you are ill-equipped to do. But if you and the job "click," how fortunate for you! Months, and possibly years, of experimenting will have been by-passed, and you will be career-bound even sooner than you hoped.

There are several kinds of tryout experiences. Best-known is the summer vacation job. Maybe you have had such work in one or more vacations and already have tested some of your career ideas this way. Each year, in our country, two-fifths of the boys and one-fourth of the girls between fourteen and seventeen have jobs during the summer; between the ages of eighteen and nineteen, nearly 90 per cent of the boys and 60 per cent of the girls have jobs, although these figures include many who have left school for good and do not plan to attend college. Looking at these figures in another way, in 1959, for instance, the number of fourteen-to-nineteen-year-olds in the nation's labor force went up by over a million and a half in the months between May and August, and then went down again by a million and a third in August and September, as schools reopened.

A tryout job may be full time for a short period, as in the summer months, or it may be part time for an indefinite period. If your school sponsors a work-experience program, your part-time job will be part of your school training. Many of these jobs are in the school itself—such as working several hours a day in the school office or serving in the cafeteria. You are paid for such work, based on the local salary scale. Also, under such a program, all sorts of "out of school" [4] jobs are filled by students who work for private businesses several hours a day under work permits. Store jobs are among the most popular of these.

In New York City, a survey was conducted among 140 high school students who were in work-experience projects, to find out what they considered the most valuable things they had learned on their jobs. Here is the list in the order given by the student workers.

1. Punctuality and regularity
2. Honesty
3. How to work with people
4. Manners
5. Personal appearance
6. How to follow directions
7. How to meet people

If, in addition to learning something about the work, these beginners found out all these other things they need to know, they were lucky indeed.

*Junior Achievement—Practical Tryout.* Started over forty years ago, the Junior Achievement program has become a nationwide plan that gives teen-age boys and girls an advance sampling of business. Someone has called Junior Achievement, "big business on a small scale." Each fall semester, clear across our country, 4,000 or more new businesses are organized, carried on, and finally liquidated in May. These miniature businesses are set up and run by public and parochial high school students in their junior and senior years under the guidance of local businessmen. The students in each group decide the type of business they wish to start; then they sell stock at 50 cents a share, keep books, pay taxes, do banking, manufacture and sell goods. At the end of the school year, the students close the business. If they have made a profit, they pay back to their investors the 50 cents per share plus a percentage of the profit. If they have lost money, they have the unpleasant duty of explaining "why" to their stockholders. The one night a week spent at the headquarters of Junior Achievement, Inc., in his locality is of the greatest value to any young Achiever. I can think of no better way for a future businessman or businesswoman to learn the needs, problems, and procedures of business than under this program.

## MAKING GOOD USE OF YOUR TRYOUT EXPERIENCE

The tryout experience may be your means of finding out whether or not you really want to go into the field of your choice. Don't feel too

---

[4] Each state has its own laws governing the hours and other conditions under which minors can be employed, in conformity with the child-labor provisions of the Federal Fair Labor Standards Act.

bad if the test has negative results. Many a college student's well-laid plan has disappeared in confusion after its originator has tested it out during a summer vacation. For instance, college girls with high ideals and some study of sociology often think they want to go into social-service work. But a hot summer spent in a slum settlement house is enough to show them that the hardships of casework are not for them. How much better to find this out before spending years getting ready for this occupation!

For many boys who went direct from school into the armed services, the work to which they were assigned in the Army or the Navy served as a tryout. John Cox enrolled in an engineering school because of his road- and bridge-building experience with the army engineers. Other boys have chosen radio, transportation, or supply because of what they saw of these fields while working for Uncle Sam. But sometimes the trial experience in the service resulted negatively. Robert Hart, with department-store aspirations, worked in a Government warehouse and decided he didn't like merchandising in any form.

When your tryout experience justifies your choice of a field, you can begin making a career plan. Or perhaps it would be nearer the truth to say, "You can plan your first steps." At all stages, keep your plan flexible. Then you will find it easier to adjust your plan to conditions you did not anticipate. You will alter your plan every now and then, as unforeseen opportunities occur. But having some idea of your destination will keep you from going around in circles. You will be following an invisible arrow, pointed UP.

## TESTS MAY HELP YOU PLAN

Sometimes the making of a satisfactory career plan defies all the suggestions offered so far in this chapter. Or a tryout experience in work that attracted you may bring out unforeseen disadvantages, and you will decide that plan was not for you. This need not discourage you, for, by discovering early that your first choice was not your last, much valuable time will be saved. Instead of retracing your steps and making a more careful study of your interests and abilities, you might investigate whatever testing program your school sponsors. Today, many high schools, junior colleges, and private business schools give tests to their students in order to help them choose careers.

It is possible that you have taken some of these tests but have not thought of them in relation to your choice of a career. If so, ask your counselor for a summary of your tests and an interpretation of their value in connection with various occupations. Your counselor probably will explain to you that aptitude tests, coupled with interest tests, are only a means of helping you find the type of work in which you may reasonably expect to succeed. For the truth is that aptitude tests do not tell you the *exact* spot where you belong. It would be wonderful if a young person, wishing to plan his future, could take tests that would prove beyond a doubt the kind of work he should follow. But alas, it is not that simple. The most that any testing program can do is to show you a range of your abilities and interests, and point to one or more fields in which your chance for success would be good. This is very different from saying, "You should be a nurse," or, "The one thing you should do is train to be a civil engineer."

The tests listed below are the types most generally used.

| NAME | PURPOSE | SCOPE |
|---|---|---|
| Intelligence or Mental-Ability Test | To test reasoning ability—what you have to work with | Determines your intelligence in solving problems |
| Achievement Test | To test what you have learned about certain subjects | Shows extent of your general knowledge in use of words, arithmetic, reading ability, or certain other subjects taught in school |
| Aptitude Test | To predict how much ability you may show in certain areas of learning | Indicates the probability of your success in some activity in which you are as yet untrained, as mechanical comprehension |
| Interest Test | To indicate what you might like to do, by preference | Constitutes an inventory of your likes and dislikes of numerous activities. When checked against preferences of people successful in certain occupations, it indicates you may succeed in same field |
| Performance Test | To measure your ability in specific skills in which you have had training | Demonstrates the degree of skills acquired, as in shorthand and typing |

Let me issue another warning. Beware of taking too seriously those indications of talent that might better be developed as a hobby or a leisure-time pursuit than as a lifework. For example, many people have a degree of musical or artistic talent that is revealed in an interest test. But only an honest and skilled judge, as a teacher in that particular field, can say whether the talent is sufficient to justify the years of study and the large investment that would be required if the person were to have a career in music or art.

In the event that you have not taken any of the tests referred to here, ask your counselor whether, before you are graduated, you will be tested in school or elsewhere. Many schools arrange for their students to be given tests in the offices of their state employment services by the specially trained personnel there. Such tests consist of general aptitude tests developed by the United States Employment Service in co-operation with the various state employment offices "to indicate the abilities of persons who are without training or previous work experience and have not acquired skills." These, and the interest tests given young people about to enter the labor market, are similar to those given veterans by the Veterans' Counseling Service in offices maintained by the Veterans Administration in large city school departments and in colleges throughout the country. Vocational counseling by highly competent men and women is an important part of the service given veterans, many of whom have had little or no work experience before entering the armed services. In the offices of the state employment service, the testing program is strengthened by interviewers adding information as to local job opportunities and possible openings for trainees in the fields indicated by test results. I mention these two outstanding testing programs, hoping meanwhile that, if you need to take tests, you will not have to wait until you apply for work at your state employment service or become a veteran in need of a job.

## FIRST JOB AS TRYOUT EXPERIENCE

You may be one of those who, because he does not get a tryout job, has to consider his first job as a "test" experience. Often, this is the best thing that could happen to your plan. You have a much better chance of studying a business when you go into it as a full-time, permanent employee. Inside, even in a lowly job in a chosen field, you should be able to learn whether this is the kind of business in which you wish to spend the rest of your life. You might be a year finding that out. But it would be a year well spent—regardless of your decision. Someone has said, "It's not the first job that matters." Your first job may be experimental as to fields, or it may be merely a means of gaining needed experience. But your second job should be the one that represents thought and planning on your part.

Be sure you give that first job everything you have and get out of it everything there is in it for you. Even though your family and closest friends think you are making no headway, if you feel you are acquiring information and experience that are taking you in your charted direction, you can laugh at them all, for you are not like the planless person—a Mr. Micawber waiting for something good to turn up. You know where you are headed, and you are making strides in that direction. But for that little plan stored away in your mind, you might be just like many of your fellow workers, satisfied merely to have a job. You don't have to count on luck, though you may have it. That brain child of yours, that secret plan, is forcing you to study the jobs related to yours. It reminds you to watch for opportunities for which your training may have fitted you. It reminds you of the importance of adjusting yourself to the personalities about you, in order that you will be ready to advance when the time comes. You are not just holding a job. You have embarked on a business career.

Only to those of you who have a plan and seriously think you are not advancing in it sufficiently, do I say, "Make a change." And even then, make haste slowly. Sometimes those above you have plans for you of which you know nothing, plans which will open up a future beyond your fondest hopes.

Often, beginners are too impatient. They quit too soon. A man who heads one of the country's most important industries told me that twenty years ago he was ready to quit a job in which he had worked a year. He went to the president of the company and said, "I can't see any future here for myself." The president looked at him quizzically. "You haven't shown us yet that you're the man we are looking for to promote. But we're still hopeful. Maybe you can afford us a little longer if we can afford you. Why not wait a bit?"

Before we leave the subject of planning and begin to put our plans into action—a word to the young men. With world conditions as they are and are likely to be for some years to come, military service is apt to loom large in the life of every one of you. "How can I make a plan?" you may ask. Or, "What's the use of my planning?" These are natural questions when the only thing that seems certain is that you will go into one of the armed services. While the military prospect may discourage your career planning, it should not prevent your making a plan.

My advice is: *Have a definite, well-thought-out plan for your business life.* Even though you may not be able to start on it until your period of service is over, you can pick up your plan then. You will be much better off than if you return home with no idea of what you want to do or be. Also, many young men who have known where they were headed have been able to accomplish much in study while in the service, or have been employed in a type of work that had some carry-over into their civilian life. You, too, may be able to advance your career plan through the work you do while you are in uniform.

### CAREERS TO WHICH YOU MAY ASPIRE

In the next chapter, we shall study some careers in business that are suited to students graduating from high school, junior college, or private business school. You will be told once more that you must expect to start at the bottom. But how much more enjoyable it is in those lowly regions when there's a view! Run your eye over the list of careers that follow. Are some of these the ones to which you "matched" yourself earlier in this chapter?

| | |
|---|---|
| Accounting | Public utilities |
| Advertising and sales promotion | Publishing |
| Finance and banking | Purchasing |
| Industrial management | Radio and television |
| Insurance | Real estate |
| Investment | Research |
| Journalism | Restaurant and hotel management |
| Office management | Retailing |
| Personnel management | Sales and sales management |
| Private secretaryship | Statistical work |
| Public administration | Warehousing |
| Public relations | Wholesaling and brokerage |
| Public services | |

## TOPICS FOR DISCUSSION

1. What does it mean to be a "consumer"?
2. What are the three general kinds of business?
3. Name some of the businesses under each group.
4. All the various types of business that make up the American system of free enterprise are said to be grouped under three main divisions, based on their function. What do you understand "free enterprise" to be? What does "based on their function" mean?
5. Why do you think office occupations are classified under the service division of business?
6. Name four construction projects, such as home building, in which a plan is necessary. Who makes such plans?

7. Look into your own mind, and see how many different personal plans are now forming or are already well defined. Is a plan for your business life any less important to you than these personal plans? Is it any less indispensable to you than the home builder's plan is to him?
8. Are parents' career plans for their children necessarily right? Necessarily wrong? Why is it usually best to work out your own plan?
9. Discuss the difference between practical planning and wishful thinking. Is the latter the same thing as daydreaming?
10. Why should you ask yourself what studies you liked best in school and what interests you most outside the school? What connection do these have with your choice of a career? Illustrate.
11. Discuss the reasons why a young man's career plan is likely to be more definite than a young woman's. Do you think women could advance as far as men in the business world if they were willing to put careers ahead of personal plans for marriage and homemaking? If not, why not?
12. Discuss ways and means of getting career information, other than through your teachers. Is it advisable to put off opening your mental doors to such information until you are graduated and are ready to start looking for a job? If not, when should you start?
13. What is meant by "tryout experience"? Have you had any? If so, did such experience help you to find out what you were best suited for? If you have not had such experience, do you think that working during summer vacation or after school would help make your career plan more practical? Do you think such work, even though not actually in an office, would help you to secure an office position?
14. Assume that you have secured a beginning job. You now discover that it is not advancing you toward your goal. Of what value will your career plan be to you under these circumstances?

## ARE THESE STATEMENTS TRUE?

1. It does no good to plan. You have to take whatever job you can get.
2. If there is a family job available, it is a good idea to take it, even if it is not the kind of job in which you can do your best or be happiest.
3. Although railroading is known as a man's business, girls can rise just as high in it as boys can if they are bright and willing to work.
4. After you have selected a field in which you would like to work, you should read everything you can find about it in your school library and the public library.
5. Even though you are not happy in the job you got into by chance, you'd better stay with it and not try to plan something else.

## PROJECTS

1. Answer the questions on pages 7-8 about the school studies you like best and the things you do best. Then write what you have learned about your interests and abilities by asking yourself these questions.

2. Prepare a short paper discussing the importance your natural bent should play in the planning of your business life. Reread the part of this chapter that gives yardsticks for measuring your vocational choice. Write a short paragraph on each of the yardsticks—Contentment, Income, and Opportunity—based on how these will influence your choice of a career. Write another paragraph on Location if where you live and work is not important to you.

3. Answer the personal questions on page 8. Study your replies. What have you learned about yourself from this exercise? Make a further list of questions you should ask to get a better understanding of yourself.

4. Based on your answers to these questions, study the fields, and select one that might suit you. Now use the Self-Job Inventory given in this chapter to see whether the field and the job match you. If they do, make a tentative career plan.

5. Look up the biography of a nationally successful businessman. Write a brief paper showing how he developed his career plan, the obstacles he met, and what changes he had to make in his plan as he progressed through experience.

6. Write a 500-word paper on the work of Junior Achievement. If you have been or are a member of that group, use your own experience in describing the work done, and tell why you think this is a valuable try-out experience. If you are not an Achiever, get the information, and give your opinion of the value of this program.

# CHAPTER 2

# Careers in Business

From the careers listed in Chapter 1, we will select a few for further consideration. This is not, primarily, a book on careers. Rather, it was written to help the beginner in business get a job in an occupational field where he would have every opportunity to succeed. The mountain climber, standing at the foot of the peak he plans to ascend, is heartened when he can see his goal. Likewise, as the new employee gets glimpses of his goal, he will discover trails leading upward.

In case you have not looked up the word "career" in your dictionary, here is the definition given in *Webster's New Word Dictionary, College Edition.*

CAREER: One's advancement or achievement in a particular vocation; hence a lifework; profession; occupation.

You may think that selecting a lifework now is, to say the least, premature. For some students, who have not grown up mentally, it is. But for the serious-minded young man or woman, graduation means that the time for earning a living has arrived. For them, any study that will take a large part of the gamble out of job seeking, give a usable method of career planning, and help in the choice of a beginning job is well worth while. That is why the study of a few careers forms the basis of this chapter. The ones selected for presenting to you cannot include all those that you selected after taking your Self-Job Inventory. The chart at the end of this chapter, however, will cover still other careers and will show the starting jobs in each of them. Even more helpful should be the brief statement of personal qualifications for each position, the type of study necessary for progress, and the career possibilities.

***Beware the Glamour Jobs.*** Perhaps a word of caution should be inserted here. School placement offices and employment agencies say that almost all graduates want to go into the "glamour fields"—advertising, air lines, radio, and television. Obviously, all the hopefuls won't find jobs in those limited occupations. So, if you have been secretly dreaming of one of these, put it aside for the moment. Later, if you haven't become interested in a field with better possibilities, a tryout job in your dream field might make you more realistic. To illustrate: A business-school placement director told me of sending Alice M. on a summer stenographic job in an air-line office. Alice was thrilled because she longed for a career in that industry. But by the end of her temporary job, Alice was disillusioned. "Why," she told the placement office, "the correspondence was all about nuts and bolts. Not for me!" What a disappointment when she had expected romance in the airways. Similarly, many an aspiring lad stands behind the counter answering questions about flight schedules when he had other ideas about his place in commercial aviation.

## Accounting As a Career

As the career to be studied first, I have chosen accounting because it is a kind of work in which the opportunities for men and women are about equal. The first, and perhaps the only, "must" is that you must like to work with figures. If you were good in arithmetic in grammar school, and equally good in your high school algebra and geometry, you may find a career in accounting. In addition to a liking for mathematics, there are several personal qualities you need if you are to be successful as an accountant. You must be methodical and accurate, and have the ability to analyze figures. Much of the work of an accountant or auditor is verifying records kept by others. To be able to report to management, boards of directors, or stockholders on the correctness of a company's books, you must be able to analyze figures and report on what they mean. A sound knowledge of written English is helpful in preparing reports that are clear and concise. Sound health and good eyesight are also important.

Accounting is the youngest of the professions, with plenty of room at the top. The importance of complete and accurately kept accounting records has been constantly increasing. The efficient business executive today must know without delay all changes in the condition of his firm. He must have constantly at his command an array of facts and figures on which to base his decisions. Where shall he turn but to his book-keepers and accountants?

A continuance of positions in this field may be expected not only now but also for some time to come. For all firms, bookkeeping has been greatly complicated by Federal and state laws that require an enormous amount of statistical reporting. State and Federal income tax laws, sales and use taxes, the franchise tax, social security and unemployment insurance legislation, as well as numerous other enactments, require periodic reports that must be prepared by the accounting departments of virtually all businesses. This means more jobs for trained persons. And since these records have to be handled again in state and Federal offices, there are thousands of accounting jobs in civil service, as well as in private businesses. Accountants make good money and enjoy a position of respect in the business world and in their own communities. But the work is hard, requiring long hours in peak seasons. It is a career for the ambitious young person who is capable of setting his sights high and proceeding to his goal by study and hard work.

Of course, you will not begin as a full-fledged accountant. In fact, it will probably take some years of training and experience before you attain your ambition—and then only after considerable outside study at the college level. Your start may be no higher than assistant bookkeeper. Even to start there, you will need to know something about bookkeeping. If you plan a career in accounting, it is well to get as much training as possible while you are in school. Accounting begins where bookkeeping leaves off; so you would need to advance through several bookkeeping positions, taking on more and more responsibility, before you would be ready for accountancy.

There are two lines of advancement open to those who plan to go into accounting. One is in the private accounting field; the other is in public accounting. In all large businesses and many small ones, there is an accounting department where bookkeepers and accountants keep numerous records for the company and prepare its financial reports. This is called *private accounting* because the work is done only for the company by which you are employed. In private accounting, a beginner may start as a ledger clerk or as a payroll clerk before he becomes assistant bookkeeper. The steps up from there could be to full-charge bookkeeper (this usually in a small firm), then general bookkeeper or junior accountant.

With experience on the job and attendance at night classes in accounting, an alert young person can progress to the position of accountant, credit manager, or assistant auditor, at considerable increases in salary along the way. The next advance would be to such executive positions as comptroller, treasurer, or vice-president in charge of accounting. In the accounting field, there are excellent positions open to those who pass civil-service examinations in bookkeeping and accounting given by city, county, and state governments and the Federal Government. But these positions are not for beginners.

It is termed *public accounting* when one or more accountants have a business of their own in which they render professional accounting service to not one but many businesses. Before an accountant can open his own office, he must pass an examination given by the state board of accountancy in his state. Many states require accountants to pass the C.P.A. (Certified Public Accountant) examination before they can engage in practice. There are strict experience and educational requirements for permission to take this examination, and many top accountants do not have this "degree." Part of the preparation for the examination, however, can be obtained through working in the offices of certified public accountants, since these companies employ many young accountants.

A. C. Ernst, of the widely known accounting firm of Ernst and Ernst, has given valuable advice to young people who plan to enter the accounting field. He believes that, even though one expects to enter private practice as a C.P.A., the insight into business gained by working for an industrial or commercial firm for several years is invaluable. Mr. Ernst has explained that, as a junior in public accounting, one's work would be done under the observation of experienced men, and, as it was merited, an advance would be made up the ranks through semisenior, senior, supervisor, and then to executive.

The members of the staff in most public accounting organizations specialize in some particular branch, such as system work, taxes, retail store accounting, hotel accounting, or bank auditing. At the same time, the members of the staff maintain a familiarity with all branches of accountancy.

Before we leave accounting, another suggestion to those who are mathematically inclined. Bookkeeping and accounting work are to be found in virtually all types of business. When checking the business fields, you may have been especially attracted to one kind of manufacturing, yet your aptitude is definitely for figure work. There need be no conflict between these two, if you can get into the bookkeeping department of a manufacturing company whose kind of production interests you. There can be many different careers within a business organization, and there usually are. (To return to our study of railroading—here are some of the careers to be found there: accounting, management, traffic, freight, communications, operations—running the railroad—engineering, construction, and research.) You might go to the top in accounting in a manufacturing business. Or you might, after you were inside, see another kind of work you preferred and arrange to be transferred to that department. You remember the advice given earlier: "Keep your plan flexible."

## CAREERS IN MANAGEMENT

When you made an inventory of your personal assets—the things you do best—did you list the ability to organize and direct the work of others? If so, you may have in you the makings of a manager. Perhaps you noticed on our list of careers several that contained the word "management" in the title. There are said to be more than 400,000 business firms today that require managers. All sorts of managers—sales managers, hotel managers, comptrollers, personnel managers, production managers, and purchasing agents, to mention a few. A person must have executive ability to become a manager. Knowing how to do the work other people are to do under your direction is also essential. This technical knowledge can be obtained partly through outside study, but much of the know-how will be acquired by actually doing the work under a foreman or supervisor.

As in accounting, or any other top job, you don't start out as a manager. It may be a long, slow pull; but if you know where you're headed, and if you prepare for and work toward your objective, your chances of arriving are good. Here are a few of the lines of promotion leading to management jobs. The treasurer-comptroller usually starts as a bookkeeper, as you were told in our discussion of accounting. The production manager in a manufacturing plant may begin as a machine operator or factory clerk. Or, if he is an engineer by profession, he might begin as an engineering draftsman. From that start, he would progress as department foreman, general foreman, and superintendent. A purchasing agent often starts as a stock clerk, where he learns about merchandise as it comes to him for handling. His next job might be that of assistant purchasing agent, before he gets the highest job. Or he might come into this work from the accounting department of his company. A personnel manager sometimes starts as an interviewer, job analyst, or tester, though many have begun in small stores or factories. The personal qualities required of men who are to be successful managers are drive, friendliness, leadership, character, good judgment, the ability to express themselves, and—most important—*the ability to make decisions.*

**Don't Shun Manual Labor.** As you will have guessed from the lines of promotion sketched roughly above, many of the best managerial jobs are in large manufacturing plants where today a fourth of our nation's labor force is employed. A survey of 50 present business leaders in our country showed that the largest group, 11, began as workmen on production jobs. Of the remainder, 8 started as office clerks, 8 in the advertising or sales department, 4 as office boys, 4 as engineers, 3 as attorneys, and 2 as newspaper reporters, with the others coming up from accounting, geography, telegraphy, and bookkeeping. If you chose manufacturing of one kind or another as your field, by all means get a job in a factory, and learn the business from the ground up. You will need that knowledge, whether you progress in the factory end or in the office.

Fortunately, the idea that manual labor is something to be shunned, or ashamed of, is a thing of the past. But during the ten-to-twenty-year period when the white-collar job was glorified, that idea prevented many possible interesting careers. Often, a boy who would have made a good mechanic became, say, a dissatisfied bank clerk. All week he did work he hated, and on week ends he tinkered with a car or the house plumbing for fun. Shortly after World War II started in Europe, I attended a dinner in Philadelphia, sponsored by educators and vocational-guidance authorities, to consider how we could increase our nation's production if we were involved in the war. Several of the educators present admitted that they had been guilty of urging white-collar jobs on their students. Faced with the fact that we then did not have enough skilled and semiskilled workers to man our peacetime production, much less carry on a war effort, a rightabout-face was strongly recommended. Labor took its share of the blame, because, to protect its workers, it had discouraged apprenticeship programs. War plants and the high union wages they paid quickly removed the foolish idea that, to have social standing, a man must have a job where he could keep his hands clean.

In an interview granted while he was president of General Motors Corporation, the late William S. Knudsen said, "If I were twenty-one, I would be a mechanic. I would try hard to get work in a machine shop. If that failed, I would try for a job in a filling station or as an apprentice to an electrician or a plumber.... I would try to get some work to do with my hands." Mr. Knudsen came to this country from Denmark; a twenty-year-old youth who did not understand our language. Before he was thirty, he was made superintendent of the bicycle factory where he worked. He learned then to handle men. Speaking of this, Mr. Knudsen said: "The man who has been a mechanic has an advantage in the art of handling men. He has worked with such men himself; he knows their capacities and their limitations. He knows what makes a good boss and a bad boss."

In his day, Mr. Knudsen was young to be a manager. Now, the trend is toward youth in management, and progressive firms give tests to promising employees, looking for executive ability. Many of these companies scout graduating classes in search of students with good school records to whom they can give on-the-job training for jobs lead-ing up to management positions. A new club throughout the country, called the Young Presidents' Organization, now has five hundred mem-bers. To belong, a man has to have become president of his corporation before he is thirty-nine years old; his firm must have annual sales of $1 million or over and employ one hundred persons or more. Careers in management? Plenty of them.

## CAREERS WHERE WOMEN DO BEST

The management posts discussed above are most often filled by men. Women are found as managers of their own businesses, such as beauty parlors, tearooms or restaurants, knitting shops, and even grocery stores. They become buyers, department managers, and sales executives in re-tail stores, and a few women have gone to the very top as president or vice-president of specialty shops selling women's apparel. But in vir-tually all these cases where women have reached executive positions, the business is either manufacturing or selling a product to women. Beyond doubt, women are now making careers for themselves in fields where they compete with men, but the percentage of female top-notchers is as yet very small. Banking and insurance are fields where women are making strides, and where the prejudice against them in executive positions is rapidly breaking down.

When choosing a career, ambitious girls, it seems to me, make a mistake to fight their way into fields where the top jobs will always go to men. The "Men Only" listing is long, and includes oil companies, contracting and building, trucking and steamship lines, and, of course, our old friend the railroads. We should add iron and steel companies, public utilities, lumbering, and automotive manufacturing. There are many others that will occur to you. Unless a young woman cannot resist being a hand-maiden in such a business or is content to remain a private secretary, she should not start out in any business where the cards are so stacked against her. Instead, she should choose a field where women have already made considerable progress. The manufacture and sale of cos-metics, women's and children's apparel, processed foods, home furnish-ings, fabrics, and household appliances are a few of the businesses that are "naturals" for women.

Starting with an endowment of feminine knowledge, girls can take courses in home economics, either in school or in night classes, and increase their chances of advancement in fields already friendly to them. Instead of competing in a man's world, they will be smart to cash in on their femininity. I know it can be done, for I once organized and maintained a highly successful advertising agency of my own, based on

*Remington Rand Inc.*

The private secretary is one of the most important
persons in modern business—and the opportunities
for advancement are excellent.

the fact that I knew how to sell products and services to women, because, as a woman, I knew what women wanted. But I had first learned
advertising in department stores and furniture stores and had tested my
sales technique with words.

### CAREERS FOR SECRETARIES

There are some young women who refuse to settle for careers in
feminine fields. They relish the thought of pitting their brains against
the best masculine brains in a man's world and go right ahead with
career plans based entirely on their talents and interests. Thousands of
such young women are taking dictation, or holding even lesser jobs
than stenography in businesses on which they plan a siege. No one
suspects the existence of the career blueprints carefully hidden beneath
their competent curls.

*Secretarial Work an Opening Wedge.* Many girls know that secretarial work will give them an entree into certain businesses, so they

learn shorthand and typewriting. They begin as stenographers, or even as typists, if that is the best job open when they are ready. What these ambitious girls aim for is a toe hold in the kind of business where they want a career. They get in because they have skills to offer—and also have attractive personalities that enable them to get jobs in their selected fields. They have carefully planned this approach to their careers so that while they practice their skills they are also learning the things they need to know to progress in the business. A typical example of this is advertising agency work, where copy writers are made, not born. Such an aspirant may take executives' dictation for her first six months, biding her time. Then one day an emergency occurs that requires her to pinch-hit by producing her first piece of copy. She alone knows that for some months she has been studying English composition and copy writing in university extension classes two nights a week, preparing for this moment. Because she makes good in her first effort, she is called on frequently thereafter and gradually is relieved of secretarial duties in favor of writing copy. When the agency has an opening for a full-time copy writer, they know where to find one.

A second avenue of approach to the much-sought-after career in advertising is through the advertising department of a specialty shop or department store. Here, with a good background in English, with typing ability, and a flair for words, a young woman may acquire a basic knowledge of merchandising and copy writing. Shorthand would not necessarily help this girl get started—in fact, she would not need it. She might begin in sales, or as a stock clerk in ready-to-wear, and get her toe hold in advertising by preparing for the buyer the notes on department items to be advertised. This might bring her to the attention of the store's advertising department, and her transfer there as a copy girl might be next. In this job, she would pick up items from all the store departments and so learn about merchandise. Before long, she would be writing bits of descriptive copy for the store's large catalogue-type advertisements. Because of that "woman's know-how" referred to earlier, plus some experience, she is then in the enviable position of being able to advance through the advertising department to the top position of advertising manager or to enter agency work as a copy writer.

Advertising is only one of the fields young women are entering uninvited, through secretarial skills. Elsewhere in this book, you will read the story of a girl I have called Lenore Aitken, who got into radio as a secretary after her college degree had proved, in itself, inadequate to force the gate. Once in, with program ideas, before too long she was able to make a place for herself as a program director. Others, too, have penetrated radio, movie production, and television by the secretarial route. Publishing is another field where bright young women have started as stenographers, have become secretaries, and finally have arrived where they meant all along to land, as readers, assistant editors, and sometimes as editors.

A few of our most farsighted private business schools, recognizing the limitations placed on careers for women in general fields, are helping ambitious girls in ways not merely secretarial. For instance, when a student has analyzed herself and the fields, much as was done in Chapter 1, and has come up with a career preference, the school guides her toward this field. After the student has mastered the rudiments of shorthand and typewriting, the study of her chosen field begins. Toward the end of her course, she is given extensive training in the structure of the business she hopes to enter, in its special vocabulary, if one exists, and in other factors that will provide background. Then, when the student is ready for placement, an effort, usually successful, is made to send her as secretary to an executive high up in the field of her choice. Almost without exception, secretaries so placed advance into junior executive work, and often have secretaries of their own before too long.

**What Secretarial Work Is.** The number of secretaries who wage a campaign on the business world and capture a stronghold almost single-handed is small in proportion to the number who continue in important secretarial positions. No one word in the everyday business vocabulary is so misused as the word "secretary." Because so much glamour, good will, and success with a capital S have attached themselves to this word, all sorts of office workers assume the title. That is, they do so after hours, when no one is around to correct them. Mother tells all the neighbors that Jennie has got a job as secretary to a big businessman, when Jennie may be on her first job as a junior typist. The number of stenographers who tell their boy friends they are private secretaries is no greater than the number of straw bosses who, outside the office, refer casually to "my secretary." Both groups think to build up their own importance by associating themselves with an office function neither knows too much about. Such is the myth built up about being a secretary.

Let's see if we can clear up some of the confusion without robbing real secretaries of their well-earned glory, and without dampening the ambition of the many oncoming secretaries. In the first place, a secretary must be a *good* stenographer. When she gets to the top secretarial position, that of *executive* secretary, she may seldom, or never, use shorthand. But somewhere along the line she will have taken large amounts of dictation and learned the responsibilities connected with handling important correspondence. It is astonishing how many persons apply to employment agencies for positions as "secretary," saying they have been doing secretarial work. But when asked definite questions about their dictation and transcription speeds, they say, "Oh, I don't do shorthand," and proceed to tell how much more important their work was. All this may be true, but a secretary is, *first of all, a stenographer.*

Next, let's explore this matter of girls *starting* as private secretaries. In some instances they do, but the great majority of *real* secretaries started farther down the ladder. The young women who go direct from school to secretarial jobs are almost without exception those who have taken advanced secretarial training after graduating from high school or college. When these girls with a good general education have spent from nine months to two years studying shorthand, typewriting, and secretarial practice in a private business school or a collegiate school of business administration, they are technically ready to begin as secretaries. I say *technically* because before a person actually can do secretarial work in any organization she must know the policies and the problems of that firm and be at home in the routine of business generally. To acquire this knowledge, an internship is needed; and, in my belief, this can be got best by working first as a stenographer. Only when she has rounded out her preparation and training in this manner is the stenographer ready to assume the duties and responsibility of a secretary.

**Difference Between Secretary and Stenographer.** The vast difference between the work of a stenographer and that of a secretary is not always understood. The duties of a stenographer are confined largely to taking dictation and transcribing it. She may work in a stenographic pool where, under a supervisor, she is assigned to take the dictation of several executives, or she may work in a small office where she handles all the dictation from one or more persons and does other work, such as filing and answering the telephone. The secretary's job is distinguished from that of the stenographer in that the secretary has a closer personal contact with the executive and a knowledge of confidential business information. She spends less time at performing routine stenographic duties. She is given more frequent opportunity to exercise initiative and judgment. She is given important responsibilities and the authority to carry them out. Her salary is usually about 20 or 25 per cent higher than that of the stenographer, and the salary to which she can grow, even if she is not promoted into an executive job, is about twice that of the experienced stenographer.

A secretary becomes worthy of the title only when she has assumed some of the responsibilities of an executive—responsibilities that call for the exercise of initiative, judgment, imagination, and tact.

*Typical Activities of the Secretary.* The private secretary is really a manager. She must manage her time and often the time of her employer so that the necessary work is accomplished on schedule. The efficient secretary [1] can attend to the following demands in such rapid succession that they seem to be parts of a single activity.

Answer two telephone calls—one on the outside telephone line, which gives a message she must take down in shorthand, the other on the interoffice telephone, which asks for an address she must find while the line is held.

Finish transcribing a rush letter that is in her typewriter and requires three carbon copies.

Respond to the buzzer of her employer, for more dictation.

Find in the files a letter written a year ago, which he needs for that dictation.

Complete typing a report started yesterday and due the first thing tomorrow morning.

Turn away (courteously) an insistent caller for whom her employer cannot be interrupted.

Watch for a telegram on which an important deal depends.

Answer a question from an associate in the office who cannot go on with her work until she has assistance.

Remind her employer that he should go to a committee meeting in another fifteen minutes.

Catch up with the necessary filing of yesterday's correspondence.

Ask her employer when he can see his head clerk about a certain memorandum.

Tell her employer that his lawyer telephoned to say that he cannot make the desired appointment until next week.

If you are just starting your career, this list may have left you breathless. A really efficient secretary, however, could look down the list and mention another dozen items that she knows from experience might claim her attention at the very same time.

*Several Kinds of Secretaries.* The secretary described above is properly called a *private* secretary. Where her duties and contacts are more

[1] Frances A. Faunce and F. G. Nichols. *Secretarial Efficiency.* New York· McGraw-Hill Book Company, Inc., 1948.

with the outside world than within the organization where her boss is an executive, she is sometimes called a *public-relations*, or an *appointment*, secretary.

Important as her work is, the private secretary ranks below the *executive* secretary, who is really an executive assistant. Perhaps I should change pronouns here, because in organizations that prefer male secretaries (when they can get them), this young man's title is usually *executive* secretary. In many high-geared businesses, the executive secretary now uses a dictating machine or a voice-recording machine. The load of correspondence has lightened in these offices, since much of the business is carried on by telephone or teletype and later confirmed by memorandum. Or the correspondence between top executives is handled in many instances by the use of short, informal letters on personal stationery. These the secretary often types without dictation, or dictates them to a stenographer, for the executive to sign.

Dropping far down the line, we come to a job held today by many near beginners—that of the *steno-secretary*. A scarcity of experienced stenographers, coupled with the wish of some beginners to be called secretaries, has led to inexperienced girls starting as "secretaries." Regardless of the title on or off the job, these girls are only what might be called "second string" secretaries. Their work is to help a *real* secretary, and they are very lucky to get such a chance. I can think of no better spot from which to view and learn the work of the private secretary. A girl in such a junior position should try to get all the dictation and transcription experience possible, in the meantime relieving the real secretary, who is her boss, of much detail.

**Secretaries Who Go On and Up.** Many top-notch secretaries rise with their bosses. When an able young woman has worked as secretary to a promising junior executive, she often indirectly helps him to win promotion to higher positions in the company. Appreciation of this is shown by the secretary's going right on up with her boss, sometimes as his secretary and sometimes with a title of her own. I have in mind a publishing house where the assistant to the president is the woman who served as secretary to the same man when he was an editor in charge of the college textbook section. And there are outstanding women who have become secretary to the corporation after helping their bosses reach the heights. One such woman I know, in New York, is now such a secretary, but she still manages the stenographic pool, as she has for many years.

But before we leave this subject of the secretarial start, I want to tell you of three women working as assistant editors on magazines—all of whom began as secretaries. One, whom we shall call Amy Dunn, graduated from a commercial high school. Her first job was as secretary to a doctor. She says she was a medical secretary, but undoubtedly she learned the medical terms and work on that job, for she did not attend a school for medical secretaries. Her work with the doctor was fascinating to Amy, so much so that she wrote and had published two novels, both of which had medical backgrounds. The first doctor died, and she went on as secretary to another physician. Here she learned to do research work and got more practice in writing by preparing the papers her doctor-boss read at conventions.

Because of her growing interest in writing, Amy sought and got a position as secretary to an editor of a women's magazine. Within six weeks, she was made an apprentice reader. From there, Amy went on up, until today she is an associate editor at a five-figure salary. Her work is the final reading of manuscripts that have already passed the critical eye of three lesser editors. Oh yes, Amy's third novel has just been published and is receiving favorable comments. Certainly a successful secretary, who has gone places!

In the same magazine office where Amy works, I met another young woman, whom we shall call Mary Davis. Hers is a different kind of job —"laying out everything in the back of the book." Mary's title is assistant editor, and she does some editorial work, but her big job is arranging the page layouts, including the advertisements and the "continued" reading matter, for the last half of the magazine. Each page must look attractive, and everything must fit exactly, since the printers set up each page from her layout. And, of course, writers, advertisers, and editors must be pleased with the final result.

Miss Davis is a college graduate who spent four years preparing to teach, and then decided she'd rather do secretarial work. So, after a spell in a private business school, Mary put her shorthand and typing into action. When she went to the magazine as secretary, she was so good that before long she was put in charge of the reference library. Her present position—and it is truly a *position*—grew out of the library work, Mary says. Both jobs have this in common, infinite detail and great responsibility.

The third young woman was secretary to the managing editor of this same magazine. I don't know what her education is, but she would have had to be good to hold down such a secretaryship. But Nora (a nice name for her) wanted to get into editorial work, and being on the inside, she knew that a vacancy was coming up in a smaller magazine published by the company. Nora was interested in interior decorating, and the vacancy was to be in that department. So she took university courses at night and rounded out her knowledge of that subject. Needless to say, she was ready to step into the job of department editor the minute the outgoing editor walked out the door.

There is one more career I want to tell you about—that of Virginia Hughes. Let's leave the magazine publishing field and go to the foothills of the Sierra, in California. There, in the administration building of a tuberculosis sanitorium, you will meet Virginia, who is secretary to the superintendent and medical director. I have known Virginia since she graduated from high school at sixteen and took her commercial work in a private business school in San Francisco. Virginia was going places in secretarial work in San Francisco, had her own apartment and all that, but she didn't like being cooped up in a city. One summer, when vacationing in the foothills of California, she heard of a secretarial opening in a nearby sanitorium, and, presto, Virginia had a new job. "Hillview" is no ordinary hospital. It is owned and operated by fifteen California counties that send their tuberculosis patients there for treatment. The 10-acre property looks like a resort, with white cottages dotting the wide lawns, and native pines and oak trees blending into the landscape. But those screened-porch cottages house five hundred patients, and the village that has grown up about the "San" is home for several hundred employees.

It was into this setup that Virginia went as private secretary to the woman physician in charge. At first, one of her duties was to take from incoming patients, in shorthand, their medical histories. Virginia, in good health, had no fear of getting the disease. But before long, she was given more executive work, and one of her assistants took on this detail. When she realized the scope and size of her new job, Virginia told me, "This is the kind of job I've always wanted, but never dreamed I'd get." No doubt, Virginia's doctor-boss would say of her, "She's the kind of secretary I've always wanted, but never dreamed I'd get." For before Virginia took over, there had been a steady stream of city secretaries sent by metropolitan employment agencies. None had stayed over a month because they hated country living as much as Virginia had disliked city life. Virginia has been in the job six years, driving her car to work from the home she has bought, four miles from the "San." She has found contacts with the staff doctors and administrators stimulating, and the need for increasing her medical knowledge has broadened her education.

Now that you've met Virginia, let me share with you a letter describing her duties and responsibilities.

I don't know where to begin to tell you the details of my job. I think I should say first that I am not a medical secretary, but secretary to the superintendent and medical director. There are three girls in the office with me now. I handle all Dr. M's correspondence, and am in contact with all fifteen counties at all times, regarding the admission of patients. All the paper work in connection with discharges and admission is handled by one girl. That is tremendous, as everything has to be checked before it leaves the office. We handle all orders for medications (by that I mean special drugs for tuberculosis) and keep a running file of who is receiving what, and for how long. Another girl charts all laboratory work that is done daily, and does the filing. We also do all the medical dictation (primarily surgery). However, I don't do much of that any more, as it is done by dictaphone and one of my gals does that except for the really long complicated reports, or papers that are being written for medical journals.

There is quite a lot of what I suppose you would call executive work in the small details I handle every day, but they are too numerous to try to mention. I don't take much medical dictation any more, except for our general medical and surgical conference (every other Monday), when we sit all day and review cases, probably discussing an average of 150 cases each time. On that I take the notes, type them up on Tuesday, and then we give all necessary orders from that for drugs, surgery, and treatment. The boss lady calls it the rat race, and believe me it is. Today I spent several hours making up the list for next Monday. Then too, I take the minutes of the monthly board meeting. We, doctor and I, meet with a representative of each county, here, every other month. On alternate months, we travel to the different counties.

These stories of secretarial careers, selected from hundreds, should be proof, if proof were needed, that, starting as a secretary, a bright girl can go almost anywhere she wishes. And she does wish to go far—collectively and individually. To have the work of secretaries recognized professionally, the National Secretaries Association, with 13,000 members, got educators and high management officials interested in setting up standards for secretaries. The result is a twelve-hour examination, given once a year to secretaries all over the country who can qualify to take it. Those who pass the examination are given C.P.S. certificates—meaning certified professional secretary. The first of these examinations was given in 1951, when 62 secretaries were certified. In 1952, certificates were awarded to 123 secretaries; in 1959, to 245. As a result of their proved ability, many of the "certified" secretaries have been promoted by their employers, offered new jobs and honors, and received substantial raises in pay. Since a secretary must be twenty-five years of age and have worked several years before she can take these examinations, I am only suggesting to beginners that you may wish—someday—to add these initials to your diplomas. If you want to know more about "What Is a C.P.S.?" [2] I recommend an excellent article with this title, written by Dr. Estelle L. Popham, of New York University, formerly the dean of the Institute for Certifying Secretaries.

*Male Secretaries in Demand.* In case you young men have been bored by the "raves" over secretarial careers for women, listen to the raves of employers who want male stenographers and secretaries, but can't get them. For some years, there has been a strong demand in certain businesses for young men who know shorthand and typing, and who will start as secretaries, learn the business through taking dictation, and be promoted into executive positions. Schools in Ohio, New York, and California, and employment agencies everywhere, have told me they cannot begin to supply the demand for male stenographers. A call will come from a manufacturing plant for fifteen young men for office work, and a school is lucky if it has even one to send. Furthermore, these positions, once filled, are soon vacant because of the prompt promotions given these fortunate beginners.

It is hard to understand why, with hordes of young men prodded by inclination and their parents to desire white-collar jobs, there should be this blind spot regarding the possibilities of the stenographic start. Some boys regard stenography as a "sissy" occupation; others hesitate to enter classes that are 95 per cent feminine and, because girls of their age are quicker, soon become discouraged.

Railroad, oil, steel, air-line, mining, construction, and engineering companies head the list of those that express a preference for men secretaries when they are available. It is not only because of the logical line of promotion of informed male employees into junior executive positions, with vistas ahead, that these businesses like to employ men in stenographic work. There are often times when the secretary must travel with an executive, and to tell Tom to be ready to go to Washington with his chief tomorrow night is less complicated than to tell Margery the same thing.

But take a second look at the type of firms listed as especially interested in the male secretary. You will see that they are all technical or at least semitechnical in character. The proverbial masculine understanding of and liking for technical subjects, not to mention an education in them in some instances, give young men a break here. There is no doubt about the promotional possibilities growing out of a secretarial start. I recall that at one time every executive in the San Francisco office

---

[2] Estelle L. Popham. *Today's Secretary.* June, 1953.

of the Southern Pacific Company had started as a secretary, and two directors of the Standard Oil Company of California, including the first vice-president, had begun in that capacity.

While the demand for male secretaries is a definite one, it is limited because of the exceptionally high requirements. When the educational, character, personality, and appearance requirements have been met, the male applicant will need to be better at typing, taking dictation, and transcribing, because he will start at a higher level and a higher salary than can his feminine competitor. He won't have to start in a centralized department to get a chance at a secretarial job, nor would he be hired there. He will start as stenographer or even as secretary.

### COURT REPORTING A CAREER

Another field not exclusively masculine, but one where a top man can really go places with shorthand, is that of court reporter or general reporter. This is one of the least crowded professions for men, and a well-paying one. But for either men or women, court reporting takes not only great accuracy in shorthand but speed, and I mean *speed*—not only speed in taking notes but speed in transcription. Court reporting is not a place where one starts, but something to plan for and work up to over the years. Young women, as well as young men, may aspire to and train for this important work. For the ambitious young person who is willing to study and practice after hours, a career as court reporter is a goal worth working toward.

*Requirements Are High.* The business beginner with an eye on eventual court reporting should, as a first step, acquire a shorthand speed of 120 words per minute before leaving school. Several years' work in an exacting stenographic or secretarial job where speed and accuracy become well established, is the second step. There are private business schools where a person with court reporting aspirations can study nights or on a part-time basis while holding down a good bread-and-butter job. There are instances, however, where records in both manual and machine shorthand have been set by young men and women who have studied and practiced at home.

When one's shorthand and transcription speeds have reached the requirement for beginning court reporting (around 200 words per minute in shorthand and 30 words per minute in transcription), qualifying examinations can be taken. In some states a registration examination is given which, when passed, means that the reporter can go to work. But before a reporter can work in Federal courts he must pass a United States Civil Service Examination. Also, the National Shorthand Reporters Association conducts tests for those who wish to qualify for a Certificate of Merit—at speeds of 240, 260 and 280 words per minute.

Many court reporters are appointed by the judge for whom they work, and hold tenure for life. Others work for a Federal or state agency and are assigned to civil and criminal cases. Some reporters are employed by other reporters, or work on a free-lance basis, covering conventions, hearings and so forth.

Court reporting is highly responsible work and requires an active, attentive and receptive mind. Every word spoken in court or conference must be accurately recorded. Knowledge of legal terms and court procedures is essential. Mastery of English, and the ability to spell and to punctuate are indispensable. Often the shorthand notes taken in court are not transcribed until they are needed, which may be weeks, months, and even years later; in other cases, however, the notes of the court or the convention are required at once. Sometimes a reporter reads his notes to a dictating machine, and the transcription is then prepared by a transcriber.

A competent beginning reporter can earn from $4,000 to $6,000 a year, while an expert can make from $8,000 to $12,000.

*Reporting with Machine Shorthand.* In addition to shorthand, which, as you well know, is a manual skill, there is another method of taking dictation known as stenotypy, or machine shorthand. While stenotypy has entered many an office, its chief function is the reporting of conventions, state and Federal hearings, speeches in any type of meeting, and court reporting. Notes are taken easily, with the operator always up with the speaker. The speed is unbelievable—many operators doing 200 to 250 words a minute.

This method is taught primarily in schools operated by the manufacturers of the stenotype machine. Probably, the reason that high schools and private business schools do not teach it is because an operator has to buy her own machine. Or perhaps we should say "his" machine, since many stenotype operators are men. This comparatively new way of taking dictation is fast and accurate, and one of its greatest advantages is the ease with which one operator can read another operator's notes. I shall not explain stenotypy except to say that the notes are taken as printed words, not syllables, and that it is phonetic. Because of this, with a little training, a nonoperator can read notes and transcribe them, thus releasing the stenotype secretary for more executive-assistant work. Notes can be filed, remain in the files for years, be taken out later as needed, and then be transcribed by someone who never saw them before. To transcribe from stenotype notes, an operator should be able to type from 50 to 60 words a minute.

## CAREERS IN FILING

Bright young women who know how to type but have not studied shorthand are discovering that filing has career possibilities. The personal qualifications required of a beginning filing clerk who is to advance are orderliness, patience, accuracy, and the ability to take responsibility. Girls who have these qualifications and who are not easily bored by the recurring round of small tasks necessary to filing may look forward to progressing from file clerk to assistant supervisor, then to file supervisor or executive in charge of both the files and the file clerks. Beyond this, there are some really outstanding occupations, such as that of systematizer or analyst. This specialist services or analyzes filing departments, reorganizes them, or installs new systems of filing.

Then, too, the obscure but ambitious filing clerk may one day become a teacher of filing in a commercial high school, a private business school, or a university. The field is almost exclusively feminine, since filing is a housekeeping job filled with details that require unlimited patience and perseverance—a gift that most women possess. Sometimes, the position of file clerk is a "singleton"; that is, one person is in charge of specialized or technical files, such as legal or subject files, or a combination of business library and the files. On the other hand, the beginner may be one of several file clerks working under a highly trained file supervisor.

*Specialized Filing.* Law offices are especially dependent on their files and afford excellent opportunity for file clerks who have intelligence as well as good educational background. In one large law office, recent college graduates are given preference as file clerks provided they have graduated with honors. The reason is that in these positions high intelligence is considered more important even than training or experience. This office employs five persons in the filing department to service fifty practicing attorneys. When employing a new file clerk, the office manager takes great care to choose a young woman with an excellent memory, keen powers of observation, and a love of detail. Personality and a good appearance are also considered important, because the file clerks are in constant direct contact with the lawyers.

The head of the filing department in this particular firm believes that it takes a person with a high I.Q. to remember the general contents of the papers already in the files and to familiarize herself anew each week with from 4,000 to 5,000 new papers that come into the department to be filed. It is true that the file supervisor classifies and marks for the proper files all incoming material. But she expects the clerk who files them to learn the contents of each paper. All this is necessary to save the time of high-priced attorneys.

To illustrate, it often happens that several lawyers are working on the same case. One attorney will call for certain papers, but they are not in the files at the time. The file clerk working on the assignment must know which of the other lawyers has those particular papers and must be able to report back promptly as to just when he will be through with them. Again, a lawyer will call for a paper by name, saying, "Get me the agreement made between the Gray Company and the First National Bank on April 24, 1937." The file clerk must know which of the parties mentioned is a client of the firm, and just where that agreement is to be found in the files. Filing a dull job? Not in that office or in hundreds like it, where the files are the heart of the business.

Filing has become so important as a specialized occupation that women engaged in it have organized filing associations in New York, Boston, Philadelphia, and Chicago. The New York organization now bears the name of Records Management Association of New York, while its monthly magazine is the *Record*.

***Government Files Are Vast.*** My records do not show the number of file supervisors and other top executives who work on the extensive Government files. But they do show the total number of "mail and file" clerks employed by the Federal Government in 1957.[3] In that year, a total of 30,881 women were working in that capacity; 9,439 in Washington, D. C., and 21,442 throughout the country. Presumably, the file clerks working outside Washington are, for the most part, employed in the record depositories in New York, St. Louis, Chicago, Dallas, Denver, Boston, Kansas City, San Francisco, Seattle and Atlanta. In 1953, the Federal records filed in the archives in Washington, the "center" in Arlington, Virginia, and the above-mentioned cities, occupied 25 million cubic feet of space. No doubt that space has been considerably increased by now. However, beginning about 1954 the Government undertook a gigantic housecleaning aimed at reducing this mountain of records. Much outdated and useless material was destroyed and a strict control was put into effect to keep down the creation of new records, such as the 25 carbon copies that cluttered the files of every department to which they were sent. Wayne C. Grover, archivist of the United States, who then headed the Federal Records Council, was in charge of this cleaning out. His announced purpose was to end what he called "the slipshod, meaningless and magpie hoarding of records."

[3] *Occupations of Federal White-Collar Workers.* Pamphlet 56-1 issued by the Employment Statistics Office, U. S. Civil Service Commission.

Once when I was speaking to a group of employees in one Government department in Washington, I was given a glimpse of what was doubtless a small section of the Government files. After I had lunched with the supervisors of the stenographers and the file clerks who composed my audience, these two young women showed me the files of their department. I looked out over literally acres of filing cabinets, and I must confess that I wondered how anyone could ever find anything in such a vast system.

## CAREERS IN GOVERNMENT WORK

A chapter on careers in business is not complete without some statement about possible careers in the business of the Federal Government. I am told by friends and acquaintances who work in the various departments in Washington that advancement through civil service comes about much as it does in private business. The top officials and division chiefs in many of the departments are career employees who have worked themselves up from the rank and file after years of hard work and much planning. Many of them have worked during the day and attended college at night, since education plays an important part in their plans for advancement. I was interested to learn that the only woman who was ever a division chief in the central office of the Civil Service Commission in Washington was first employed there as a stenographer. When she was offered a supervisory job, she accepted it with reluctance and fear, but her success as a supervisor led to more and more responsible work.

The last time I was in Washington, D. C., I sat in the Senate Gallery one morning waiting for the Senate to convene, and fell into conversation with a young woman sitting next to me. She was "between jobs" in Government service and visiting the Senate for the first time in years. This young woman told me she had first taken a Grade 3 examination as a stenographer eleven years previously. She had progressed until now she was a Grade 6 at an annual salary of $5,390. "I haven't used my shorthand in years," she told me. In her last job, which had "folded" when the department was "done away with," she was supervising 35 who took dictation from the higher-ups. My chance acquaintance said that by the time the stenographers' letters came to her they had been sent to the dictator to see if they made sense, and to several other persons who read them for other reasons. Yet when she received the letters they were so full of misspelled words and garbled meaning that often they had to be retyped. It is not hard to see why this "6" with whom I talked was a supervisor. However, she was worried about finding another spot as a "6," since, as she told me, out of every twenty-five office workers in Washington there is only one Grade 6.

*One Young Man's Career Plan.* During this same visit to Washington, I met Philip Howe, a young man with a plan, who was well launched on a Government career. I asked him how he got started, and his reply is interesting. In 1948, while in college, he took a summer job as a typist in the Civil Service Commission. While he was working there, a vacancy occurred on the staff of the Commission's monthly magazine, the *Bulletin*. Because he had worked on his college paper, Philip was qualified to step into this job, and it proved to be an opening wedge. Since this was a permanent position, and Philip had now decided on a career in Government service, he did not return to college in the fall. His plan was to specialize in "public relations," and before many months he saw his opportunity. While working in the offices of the Civil Service Commission, Philip observed that there was no over-all co-ordinated plan for handling foreign visitors who came to the department seeking information about personnel administration. After much thought and his boss's approval, Philip worked out a program whereby all foreign guests are sent to the proper agencies and given the precise information and training they wish. In other words, from a hit-and-miss situation, this young man organized a complete program for improving one of the important services in the department where he works. Philip's career plan interested me especially, because it showed that even in a huge Government organization, someone with an *idea* can create a special job for himself. With his present foothold and his alertness to opportunity, Philip's plan is certain to keep him moving UP.

Sorry to bring you down from the heights. *Your* career is still in the future. Soon—almost in the present—you will be seeking your first job. More important to you, today, is the question, "Where can I begin?" That is what we shall talk about next. Regardless of how much room there is at the top, I assure you there are many good starting points. On the following pages, you will find a Beginning-Job Chart for Recent Graduates. At a glance, you can see the requirements for these jobs, what the duties are, and where the career possibilities lead. Let's look them over together.

BEGINNING-JOB CHART FOR

| Job Title | Where Work Performed | Duties and Responsibilities | Personal Requirements |
|---|---|---|---|
| Bookkeeper | Business and industrial firms of all kinds | Operates business machines; keeps financial records; prepares payroll; some typing | Sense of responsibility; dependability; neatness; accuracy; mind for figures |
| Dentist's and Doctor's Assistant | Dentists' and doctors' offices | Assists with patients; makes appointments and receives patients; answers telephone; keeps books and sends out bills; some typing | Pleasant manner and a way with people; neat appearance; good memory for faces and names helpful |
| Drafting (architectural, engineering) | Engineering firms in steel, oil, metal trades; architectural and construction firms | Mechanical and architectural drawing; tracings; detailing from plans, designs, or sketches; skill and speed important | Precise mind; well-developed reasoning powers; accuracy; neatness; sense of detail |
| General Clerk | Banks; insurance companies; manufacturing firms of all types; hotels, business offices of all kinds | Files orders, memos, correspondence; operates reproduction machines; some switchboard work or typing | Work well with others; follow directions; alertness and dependability; methodical and like detail |
| Government Office Worker | Federal, state, and local government offices | Work same as in most business clerical jobs; stenography, typing, bookkeeping, depending on function of department | Ability to follow directions; get along with others; assume responsibility |

## RECENT GRADUATES

| Education and Training | Starting Job | Preparation for Advancement | Career Possibilities |
|---|---|---|---|
| H.S.G.* or jr. college; bookkeeping training; typing; knowledge of stenography helpful | Usually as assistant bookkeeper; often combined with stenography and typing in small offices | Extra classes in accounting; sometimes on-job training sufficient | Cost accounting, auditing, purchasing, C.P.A., depending on area of accountancy that appeals |
| H.S.G. or jr. college; typing or knowledge of bookkeeping helpful; formal medical training sometimes necessary | Occasionally trained by doctor; large offices specialize in bookkeeping, appointments, etc. | Night-school courses if available, or learn with laboratory equipment in dental office | Medical secretary with extra shorthand; dental technician; laboratory or hospital technician |
| H.S.G. specializing in mechanical drawing; vocational H.S. best, or 2-year technical course at jr. college or college; formal training required; mathematical ability, drawing, and lettering skill essential | Junior draftsman doing tracings and details to test and perfect technique | On-job training important; outside courses will help; promotion possible in large firms if needed background is acquired | Partner in firm; graduate architects or engineers advance; draftsman can be dead-end job |
| H.S.G. desirable; commercial courses an aid; typing essential; some bookkeeping and knowledge of business machines helpful; learning on job possible | Varies with each employer; all skills used | Girls have better chances with typing skill; men can see which area in the business appeals and take night courses for the next step up | Can be dead-end job; may be steppingstone to other departments, sales, purchasing, etc. |
| H.S.G. or better; the more skills and education, the more chance of advancement | Depends on department assigned to and job applied for; see first- and second-class post office for information on civil-service examinations | Automatic raises; promotional examinations to next bracket | Once in agency or department of your choice, advancement through examinations and opportunity; if Federal Government, may work in Washington, D. C. or in states |

* High school graduate.

## BEGINNING-JOB CHART FOR

| Job Title | Where Work Performed | Duties and Responsibilities | Personal Requirements |
|---|---|---|---|
| Voice-Machine Transcriber | Most jobs in larger firms having transcription departments | Transcribing letters from voice machines; must be excellent typist; daily record of production shown by number of lines typed | Good hand-mind co-ordination; good hearing; background in English; ability to stand production pressure |
| Mail Clerk | Large industrial and business firms; banks; insurance companies | Delivers incoming mail to departments; picks up outgoing mail; operates stamp meter machine; buys and keeps records of stamps; acts as message center; duties similar to office boy in small offices | Pleasant disposition; willingness to do routine tasks; sense of responsibility; physically able to be on feet a great deal |
| Office Boy or Girl: Page or Messenger | All types of businesses, large and small | Picks up and delivers mail and papers from "in" and "out" boxes on office desks; runs interoffice delivery or message center; mail work in small offices | Physically able to be on feet a great deal; sense of responsibility; get along well with others; follow directions well |
| Office-Machine Operator | Manufacturing and business offices of all types; banks; department stores | Operates various office machines; performs varied clerical duties; some typing required | Ability to work well with others; follow directions easily; neatness; accuracy |
| Receptionist | Industrial and business firms of all kinds | Greets, announces, and directs callers to offices; often does typing or runs switchboard | Pleasant speaking voice; gracious manner; pleasant disposition; ability to remember names and faces |

# RECENT GRADUATES

| Education and Training | Starting Job | Preparation for Advancement | Career Possibilities |
|---|---|---|---|
| H.S.G.; typing; get all possible experience with voice machines | As typist, then trained on job to transcribe from records or tape; likely to be in typing pool | On-job experience increases ability to produce, on which salary increase depends | Transcription supervisor in charge of training operators, assigning and supervising their work; educational director in charge of training |
| H.S.G. usually; knowledge of typing useful | See under Column 3, on opposite page | May be dead-end job; evening courses in whatever business areas are available in each office | Opportunity to move on to job with more responsibility; good place to discover which departments of office appeal |
| H.S.G. usually | See under Column 3, on opposite page | On-job training; openings different in every type of business; may be dead-end job; talk with people to find out what business area to study at night | This is "bottom rung of ladder" but can be steppingstone to any department in office, as work brings contacts with department supervisors, heads, and executives who can advise study and aid promotion |
| H.S.G. with general commercial training; on-job training for various machines | Different routine in each office, as in Column 3, on opposite page | On-job training; evening work in bookkeeping or statistics | Supervisor of department in charge of training operators; an expert in operation of many types of machines |
| H.S.G. | See under Column 3, on opposite page | May be dead-end job unless other definite skills are developed through on-job training or extra night courses | Little chance for advancement unless person has office skills or takes outside courses in machine operation, typing, and stenography |

## BEGINNING-JOB CHART FOR

| Job Title | Where Work Performed | Duties and Responsibilities | Personal Requirements |
|---|---|---|---|
| Stenographer | Industrial and business firms of all kinds | Takes dictation and transcribes; often does general clerical work; often works in typing pool taking dictation from various executives | Neatness; accuracy; good use of English; patience; poise; sense of detail |
| Private Switchboard Operator | All types of businesses; hotels; apartment houses; hospitals | Operates plug or monitor board taking incoming and outgoing calls; may do clerical or receptionist work also; should know typing | Clear diction; pleasing voice; even disposition; keep information to self; discretion |
| Telephone Operator | Telephone companies | Operates local and long-distance switchboards | Clear diction; even disposition; calmness when working under pressure |
| Typist | Business and industrial firms of all kinds | Straight typing and letter forms, tabulating, invoicing; addresses envelopes; rough drafts for letters; finished typing | Sense of responsibility; accuracy; neatness; willingness to work |

## QUESTIONS

1. What is the difference between a career and a job?
2. What qualities should a person have to become an accountant?
3. Can a beginner start as a junior accountant? If not, why not?
4. What is the most important quality a person must have to be a successful manager?
5. What is meant by a "white-collar job"?
6. Is a stenographer entitled to call herself a secretary?
7. What is the difference between a stenographer and a secretary?
8. What do the initials C.P.A. stand for? C.P.S.?
9. Why does a court reporter need to have greater dictation speed than, say, a male secretary working in a business office?
10. In what kind of offices can filing become a career? Why?

## RECENT GRADUATES

| Education and Training | Starting Job | Preparation for Advancement | Career Possibilities |
|---|---|---|---|
| H.S.G., jr. college, or private business school; minimum typing 45 words a minute; minimum dictation 85 words a minute | May start as straight typist until ability is proved | On-job training; extra courses toward secretarial duties, if needed | Logical advance to secretary; skills are entree to fields, as advertising, art, radio, etc., for non-secretarial future |
| H.S.G.; usually trained on job, sometimes by telephone company | See under Column 3, on opposite page | Improve personality and diction; learn other skills if desire to do other work; study to perfect typing | None, unless effort and study are directed to typing, stenography, secretarial work |
| H.S.G. with several weeks on-job training | See under Column 3, on opposite page | On-job training program | On-job training for career as training supervisor, chief operator, personnel assistant |
| H.S.G. with training in typing; minimum 45 words a minute | See under Column 3, on opposite page | Night school for shorthand and secretarial training | Advance to stenographic and secretarial work when qualified |

## ARE THESE STATEMENTS TRUE OR FALSE?

1. The chances of advancement and of a career are as good in Government employment as in private business.
2. There are today more male stenographers than business has openings for.
3. Women are more likely to reach the top in businesses where their feminine know-how gives them an advantage over men.
4. Anyone who has studied bookkeeping in school can call himself an accountant and apply for an accounting job.
5. A beginning stenographer whose dictation speed is good can start as a court reporter if he or she will work very hard.

## TOPICS FOR DISCUSSION

1. The two lines of advancement for an accountant are in private accounting and in public accounting. Discuss these, explaining the difference between the two. Explain what the line of promotion is in each, starting with a beginning office job.
2. Name several kinds of management jobs mentioned in the text. Select one of these, and explain in detail (*a*) what management in this business consists of, (*b*) the duties of the manager, (*c*) the starting point, and (*d*) the steps up to becoming manager. You may get this information from a friend or relative who is now acting as a manager in a business or as a supervisor in a factory.
3. Name several kinds of secretarial jobs, and discuss the responsibilities and duties of each.
4. Discuss why such businesses as railroads, air lines, and oil, construction, and mining companies prefer to employ men in secretarial work.
5. Be prepared to discuss the advantages and disadvantages of Federal civil-service positions as compared with private employment. Do you know anyone holding a Government job? If so, interview this person, and bring a personal story to class for discussion.

## PROJECTS

1. The following words are found in Chapter 2. Look up each word in a dictionary. Write only the meaning of each word as it applies to the use of the word in this chapter. One sentence for each should be sufficient.

   *a.* apprenticeship                 *g.* inventory
   *b.* vocation                       *h.* technique
   *c.* comptroller                    *i.* typical
   *d.* statistical                    *j.* certified (as used in Certified
   *e.* logical                            Public Accountant and Certified
   *f.* management                         Professional Secretary)

2. If you know someone who is a private secretary, ask that person to give you a list of the many things that have to be done in a typical day. Compare this with the list given in this chapter, and write a brief paper commenting on the comparison between the two lists, such as which secretary performed more tasks and the relative importance of the things done. Also, analyze the list to see which duties require the ability to take responsibility.
3. Prepare a 500-word paper discussing the career possibilities that may grow out of stenographic and secretarial work. Young men should write about positions that a male secretary may attain. Young women will do the same for advancement possible for young women stenographers and typists.

# CHAPTER 3

# Jobs for Beginners

To give you a bird's-eye view of where you might start your career, fourteen jobs were outlined briefly on the Beginning-Job Chart for Recent Graduates in Chapter 2. An objective study of fields, and the careers within them, seldom goes so far as to indicate the lowest jobs on the vocational ladder. The time has come when, with your career plan in mind, you are ready to decide what job will offer you the needed start from which to advance. The purpose of this chapter, therefore, is to give you more detailed information about a number of beginning jobs. When you have chosen one or possibly two that you feel qualified to fill, we shall be ready to discuss ways of going after your all-important first job.

There is no need for you to feel nervous because, as yet, you don't know how to go about finding work. The ideas and suggested plans for job getting, which are offered in future chapters, have been tried and proved. By following them, you will be able to overcome most of the disadvantages of being a beginner.

Let me assure you that business feels kindly toward you as a graduate with commercial training. It assumes that you have something to offer, and it is willing to try you out in any opening where experience is not essential. Reasonably enough, however, business would like beginners to be able to state clearly what they can do. Too many young people apply for "anything," leaving it to the busy personnel director to sort out their training and skills and decide where they belong, if anywhere. You will not make this common mistake if you have a more or less definite career plan.

## THREE GATEWAYS TO BUSINESS

There are three main approaches to office work which we will call three gateways—clerical, stenographic, and bookkeeping. Depending on

Which route shall I take?

your training and skills, you will find one of these gates easier to enter than the others, and more attractive to you. If you are headed toward secretarial work, you will doubtless enter through the Stenographic Gateway. Normally, you would not enter through the Bookkeeping Gateway without some knowledge of bookkeeping. Yet the ability to operate several kinds of business machines and to type might be an entree for that gateway. The Clerical Gateway is broad, and it carries a WELCOME sign for those with few skills or none. Suppose that we start there.

### THROUGH THE CLERICAL GATEWAY

The beginning clerical jobs that require little or no commercial training are usually filled by young men and women who may or may not have graduated from high school. These employees receive on-the-job training of a type determined by the nature of the business. When young people with no skills to offer secure these starting jobs, they are hired because they have pleasing personalities plus physical and mental alertness.

Before we embark on our study of clerical occupations, let me explain the way the word "clerical" is used here. Many books call all office positions clerical; this means that they include bookkeeping, stenography, typing, and secretarial positions under the general heading of "clerical work." If we were using the same method of classification, we should have only one gateway. In the United States census, these positions are all grouped together, and a great many other occupations are included.

I shall use the word "clerical" in a narrower sense, as applying to a great many positions that call for general business ability and some training, though not necessarily including a knowledge of bookkeeping and shorthand. Most of these positions are clerkships, some of which will be enlarged on here. Among the many kinds of clerical jobs found in business offices are those of information clerk, billing clerk, cost clerk, invoice clerk, order clerk, adjustment clerk, time clerk, payroll clerk, voucher clerk, posting clerk, and stock clerk.

*Office Boy or Girl: Page or Messenger.* There are beginning jobs as office boy or girl, sometimes called page or messenger. The names mean much the same, but the duties vary according to the nature of the business. The office boy usually works under the direction of the office manager or the manager's secretary, and he receives many of his instructions through the telephone receptionist. In most businesses, the main responsibility of the office boy is the handling of incoming and outgoing mail and office memorandums. While he has a fixed routine for his office duties, he also runs errands throughout the city and is on call for any emergency job.

There is nothing monotonous about his job, but he needs strong arches and comfortable shoes. In small offices, one boy or girl can handle the work, but in large offices, a staff of from ten to fifteen may be needed. On a typical day, the office boy will do everything from filling the executives' water jugs to purchasing $50 worth of stamps. If he is to make good on this job, the office boy must learn to respond cheerfully to all calls for his services. He must be loyal, obedient, dependable, honest, pleasant, and hard-working.

Exciting as this job often is, it can be a dead-ender. Arthur Lake was a bright lad whose first job after he left high school was as a messenger for an architectural firm. He did the usual office-boy chores, but his chief duty was to deliver drawings and pick up blueprints. Arthur was the type of boy who appreciated the professional surroundings. Everyone was friendly—the partners, the draftsmen, and the secretary-receptionist—and he had received a couple of raises in the year or more he had been there. Everything was serene until a hint from his girl friend prompted Arthur to ask about a promotion. He was shocked and surprised when the junior partner told him that without at least two years of technical training he could not qualify for the only step up—junior draftsman. Arthur made his first career plan that night, and gave two weeks' notice the next morning. Only part of the blame for this vocational disaster can be placed on Arthur. As sometimes happens, a busy employer had failed to mention to a satisfactory employee that the job he was in held no future.

The field of accounting offers excellent
opportunities for young people in business.

In contrast to this thoughtless policy, some office managers, when hiring young people in these minor positions, tell them frankly, "This is a dead-end job." Other employers, whose policy is to promote from within, have established promotional procedures that begin with the lowest job. In such firms, the next job up may be to mail, file, or posting clerk.

If you think the position of office boy is not worth considering, there were over 55,000 young people who in 1950 felt it was a good place to start. Over 10,000 of these were girls.

*The Mail Clerk.* Often this is another term for office boy or messenger. This is as good a spot as any in which to develop, or to prove that one has a sense of responsibility. The mail is a very important part of all businesses and one of the most interesting parts. Being responsible for it, in even a small way, is the beginning of a valuable experience. In addition to receiving the incoming mail and collecting and dispatching the outgoing mail, the duties of mail clerk usually include buying and accounting for a large number of stamps and operating a postal meter machine. If the firm is a branch of a large corporation, one of the main responsibilities of the mail clerk is to route interoffice correspondence and memorandums to the proper department heads and sections. At the earliest opportunity, the mail clerk must memorize the names and titles of everyone in the local organization and sometimes those of executives in other branches of the company.

In many offices, the mail clerk is assisted during the early-morning and late-afternoon hours by one or more office boys. When things are less rushed, the mail clerk performs various light clerical duties, such as filing invoices, operating duplicating machines, wrapping packages for express and mailing, and keeping a supply and inventory of office stationery and supplies. Often the responsibility for these last-mentioned chores is shared by the office boy. If the company operates a coffeeroom, he may make the coffee and clean up afterward. When the mail clerk takes the next step up, to file clerk or order clerk, his successor will inherit all his tasks—and possibly the privilege of getting his coffee free.

One of the chief advantages of these very-beginning jobs, apart from the experience, is the opportunity they afford for contact with key executives. The office boy or girl is in and out the private offices of top personnel many times a day. Part of the job of an executive is to be always on the lookout for good workers to promote to better jobs in the organization. And one of the things that makes an executive is his ability to recognize promising material. Since the executive has power to make promotions, his daily and friendly contact with a beginner provides an opportunity for the recognition of good work and often opens channels for advancement.

**The General Clerk.** A commercial course in school should qualify you to start as a general clerk, a position that can be one or two steps above office boy. In fact, the term "general clerk" can mean anything from the most elementary job with the smallest pay check to a real position in which you will need some knowledge of bookkeeping and the ability to use a calculating machine. Many small firms employ one or two general clerks to handle all such tasks as answering the telephone, handling the mail, checking orders, making out bills, and doing routine typing, in addition to filing correspondence, orders, and other office records.

You can see at a glance that to do all these sundry tasks well is no small achievement and that a variety of abilities and quite a few skills are absolutely essential. Shorthand is not necessary. Knowing how to run the simpler office machines will help, although often you can learn them on the job. Typing, some bookkeeping, and a general knowledge of in-

*Remington Rand Inc.*

Filing enters into many phases of secretarial work.


dexing and filing are needed. A good personality is an asset, as always, while a cheerful disposition and the ability to get along with others are prime qualifications.

Although a general clerk is one of the busiest of persons in any organization, his varied activities may or may not lead to advancement. Much depends on whether the business is one in which this type of work is merely routine or very important.

If you take the job of general clerk as a starter, you must watch out that you don't get stranded there. Keep your eyes open, and say to yourself every now and then: "Where do I go from here? What will my next job be?" By keeping mentally alert, you can observe the other positions, the persons who hold them, and the evident requirements. You can pick up information about different occupations in business and start to train after hours for the one that most attracts you. You may wish to prepare yourself for work in the sales, purchasing, or advertising departments. Or you may wish to study advanced bookkeeping and then accounting in order to work up into the financial end of the business. It is not too much to say that your humble clerical start can lead to the top if you really want to go there.

*The File Clerk.* Although in small offices the filing may be done by a general clerk, stenographer, typist, or even office boy, more and more firms are hiring full-time expert file clerks to handle this essential and often complicated work. An encouraging number of beginners are taken on as file clerks because they have had business-school training in the fundamental principles and systems of filing. For students who expect to make filing a career, graduate business schools offer a general course in filing. The classwork consists of development of office filing, rules for indexing and filing, operating the files, alphabetic filing, numeric filing, geographic filing, subject filing, filing supplies, filing equipment, follow-up methods, Kardex job analysis records, Kardex prospect meth-

A receptionist must have the ability to meet
people easily and effectively. The receptionist is
often thought of as the "office ambassador of
good will."

ods, Triple Check Automatic filing, Soundex filing, cross-referencing, Variadex filing system, and decimal filing.

Educated young women will do well to consider the vocational possibilities of filing, for filing is no longer regarded as a job that just anybody can do. The equipment houses have done much to professionalize the work by showing businessmen that filing requires brains. Filing demands other qualities, too, such as imagination, resourcefulness, patience, accuracy, and a strict sense of orderliness and responsibility. Typewriting skill is also essential.

Moreover, if a beginner with qualifications for filing regards the initial position of file clerk as an opportunity to progress toward responsible executive work as a file supervisor, she will make the most of that experience. Don't consider a position in the filing department as merely a place in which to wait until something better in the office opens up. You may be passing up a future position that will pay as well as secretarial work and even better.

**The Office Receptionist.** Often girls who say they want to be receptionists have none of the requirements and are merely building up a picture of a dream job that does not exist. Many of them imagine that all the receptionist has to do is sit at a desk and greet callers in the glamorous fashion of a Hollywood star. The real picture is quite different. Receptionists are frequently required to run a switchboard, a difficult job when one is constantly interrupted to answer inquiries and give directions. Sometimes, but not always, receptionists are required to do typing. The standard qualifications for this kind of work are poise, a pleasing personality, an attractive appearance, and the ability to meet the public with intelligence, courtesy, and tact. Because the personality requirement of this position is so high, firms often have trouble finding satisfactory receptionists. The girl who has what the job demands usually has a good job already, sometimes one with a future.

The young woman who holds this position in the editorial department of a newspaper, an advertising agency, a law office, or other place of business where there are many callers needs a sense of humor plus boundless tact to carry her through. Personal appearance and intelligence count about equally in this position. Since this is a job that calls for meeting the public at close range, it is no place for the shy and retiring. To succeed here, the receptionist must like all kinds of people, meet them on a friendly but impersonal basis, and be able to handle them with discretion and courtesy. She must be ready also to detect the tricks used in efforts to get past her to the inner offices. She is guarding the persons and the time of a number of busy and important people, and if she wastes their time by admitting unwelcome callers she may be re-placed by someone more discerning.

However, although she is the dragon standing guard, she must take care not to display an offending suspicion of every caller, or she may turn away business for her firm. Sometimes, the caller who is reluctant to state his errand is an out-of-town visitor with an important contract to place, whom the firm's executives would surely like to meet. Another such caller, hiding his purpose beneath reluctance, may be a salesman who knows that he is intruding but conceals his real errand under the insistence that his business is "personal," because to reveal it would mean polite dismissal by the receptionist. The competent person in this job develops a technique which after a time unerringly separates the desir-able callers from the unwelcome. A keen memory is a prime asset in this constant sorting process. Without it, a receptionist cannot hope to suc-ceed, even though she has all the other qualifications.

But the tactful, beautifully dressed, and well-groomed young woman in the foyer of many an important corporation will never get beyond the desk she sits behind so decoratively. Her starting salary is almost, if not quite, her final salary. The ambitious girl who starts out as a recep-tionist, perhaps because it is the only job available for the inexperienced and unskilled, should remember that she is in a blind-alley job. By a "blind-alley" or "pocket" job, I mean a position that may look all right on the surface—a good place to start, in fact. But after you are in it, you discover it leads nowhere. No one is ever promoted into it, or it is not likely you would have got it from the outside. And, in most cases, no one is ever promoted out of it.

A truthful personnel director cannot tell a girl there is anything ahead for a receptionist. However, there have been instances where the recep-tion room has been the vestibule to a better job in the same firm. Em-ployers have been known to suggest that able receptionists study short-hand at night in order to take stenographic positions with promotional possibilities. But all employers are not so unselfish, so watch out for that "blind alley."

Up to now, we have assumed that all receptionists are ambitious, but this is far from the truth. Today, many young married women are working solely to help out the family budget. Their ambition is not to further themselves in a planned career but to have a steady income in a pleasant, interesting job. The position of receptionist is tailor-made for them.

*The Doctor's or Dentist's Assistant.* Many of the personal qualifica-tions for a doctor's or a dentist's assistant are the same as described for

A. Devaney, Inc.

Medical assistants and secretaries perform
important and interesting roles in the doctor's
office.

the receptionist. Along with her freshly laundered white uniform, this
professional assistant needs to have tact, poise, courtesy, neatness, and
an interest in people. Above all, she should possess a memory for names
and faces. Jane Rogers, a dental assistant, is a case in point. Jane's mental
filing cabinet is so neatly arranged that, as she opens the door into the
reception room, she can always greet by name the person waiting there.
Furthermore, she usually follows this up with a polite reference to the
patient's family or friends, as, "Mrs. Hills, how is your daughter
Helen?" This would not be remarkable if Jane had talked with Mrs.
Hills a few months earlier, but when the patient has not been in the
office for a year or so, both Mrs. Hills and the dentist are astounded.

There are three areas of work in doctors' and dentists' offices: (1) receptionist and appointment secretary, (2) assistant to the doctor, and (3) bookkeeping, billing, and correspondence. In large offices, there may be one girl for each of these functions, but in a small office, one person may handle them all.

A girl just out of high school can take a job as dentist's or doctor's assistant, and get her training on the job, provided she can find a professional man who is willing to break her in. Usually, they are too busy to take on such an assignment. Let's hope that a beginner who is fortunate enough to get such a start will have taken a commercial course in high school and have some knowledge of typing and bookkeeping. These would be helpful, in fact almost essential. But if, when she has finished high school, our graduate wishes to take special training for this type of work, there are schools giving short courses that would prepare her in from four to six months. The names of such schools vary with the locality, but the title of School for Dental Assistants is used quite generally. Some of these schools also give a course in medical technology for doctors' assistants.

*The Telephone-Receptionist.* In some organizations that do not need a full-time receptionist, the switchboard operator acts in the capacity of telephone-receptionist. If you think this is a desirable beginning job for you, consider first whether or not your stock of patience is virtually limitless and whether your nerves are well under control. For besides needing the skill to handle a switchboard, you will need a sympathetic understanding of human nature. The telephone-receptionist's job is no place for anyone who has been spoiled at home, for a young woman with a quick, sharp temper, or for one with a chip on her shoulder. But if you will enjoy meeting and dealing with strange and different personalities all day long, you may find this job a fascinating entrance to the business world.

The telephone-receptionist's desk is usually at a counter or inside window, so that callers can get to her easily. She must be able to answer their questions, arrange for them to see members of the firm on whom they are calling, or dismiss them tactfully if the occasion requires. In this double job, the firm's switchboard business cannot be neglected for a moment. Yet many telephone-receptionists take time for long conversations with their personal friends about their own private affairs while business stands still. How many business callers have stood in line in outer offices, waiting while the telephone-receptionist argued with mother at home or the boy friend over at his own office!

A man who had an appointment at four o'clock with the president of an important business concern was kept waiting until his appointment was ten minutes overdue, while the receptionist chatted with her girl friend about last night's date. The caller happened to be the efficiency expert who was being engaged to come in and put the business on a paying basis. Naturally, he had no desire to appear late for his appointment with the president. After he was taken on, it can well be imagined that one of the first spots he checked for inefficiency was that switchboard. Perhaps the friendly, gossipy, well-meaning receptionist is still wondering why she lost that job!

The PBX (Private Branch Exchange) Operator. When you examine the occupation of switchboard operator for a business organization, you will realize that this start is not so lowly as it might seem. For much can be learned on any business switchboard. A good voice, tact, discretion, and common sense are major requirements. A girl who exercises these qualities on a private switchboard job, filling in her spare time with typing, will often be advanced to other work in the organization. Some employees like the swift changes and the human element of the switchboard work so well that they prefer to remain there. By attending to their work, they often manage to make real jobs for themselves operating switchboards in hotels, apartment houses, banks, department stores, public utilities, newspaper offices, insurance firms, or law offices. The boards handled by these girls vary in size from the small cordless type, usually operated by someone who has other duties such as typing or acting as receptionist, to boards of twenty, thirty, or even forty or more positions in the larger firms.

In getting started as a PBX operator, you have to find your own job. When you have done this, the telephone company in your city or town will train you before you start work. This training may be in the offices of the telephone company, or it may be in the office where you are going to work. In any event, you will be trained on the type of board you are going to use. In small towns, and cities up to, let's say, 100,000 population, most PBX jobs require another skill. They are combination jobs as telephone-receptionist, or you are given typing to do in your free moments while on the board. In large cities and on heavy boards, as in hotels, you would have no time to type. Also, several girls may be employed on a board that is similar to those used in the telephone companies.

Executives are coming to appreciate more and more what an important part the PBX attendant plays in the successful conduct of their business. They know that the voice that says, "Good morning, Blank and Company," over the telephone stands for the firm itself in the mind of the customer at the other end of the wire. Courtesy, interest, and intelligence can handle incoming calls to the firm's profit; but flippant, rude, or ignorant replies tend to alienate customers forever. As for the switchboard operator whose soothing voice turneth away wrath on the part of a client on an incoming call—she is worth more to her firm than could ever be estimated in mere dollars and cents.

At that, she can be too friendly, even downright chummy. "Okay," "Bye-bye," and "All righty," although spoken pleasantly, will hardly impress the man on the other end of the wire with the dignity and trust-worthiness that the business firm wishes to convey to its clients. Telephone personality, the ability to create a good impression over the wire, requires not only specific character traits but an education in the proper and courteous use of the English language. The person who has these qualifications is extremely valuable to her employer, and in certain instances he pays her a private secretary's salary in recognition of the fact.

Although PBX attendants are employed in widely diversified fields of work, they are closely associated with the telephone operating forces and hold the same ideals of service and loyalty as do telephone company operators. Since 1920, the American Telephone and Telegraph Company has had an annual system of awards in memory of its former president, Theodore N. Vail. The awards are made "for noteworthy public service," which often includes heroism and saving of lives. They have been won many times by PBX operators whose quick and sometimes self-sacrificing attention to duty has been outstanding.

*The Telephone Operator.* Interesting as the work of a PBX operator often is, it does not have as good promotional possibilities as are to be found in working as an operator for a telephone company. I say *a* telephone company because there are over six thousand telephone companies in the United States, in addition to the two nationwide services that have thousands of branch offices. Because one of these telephone offices is probably near you, we suggest that you go in and talk with someone about the starting jobs there. All over our country, the telephone companies are advertising for help in an effort to get more young people as employees. The fact that you have not worked anywhere before does not count against you with the telephone companies. They prefer to take inexperienced girls just out of high school and train them on the job to be local or long-distance operators. The greatest demand is for girls, since seven out of every ten telephone employees is a woman. But there are starting jobs for boys, too, in the technical side of the business.

To be a success as an operator, and advance to the position of supervisor or chief operator, a young woman must have a pleasant voice and the ability to be calm under pressure. The standard of service in telephone companies is high, and operators are required to be courteous under trying conditions, and to be faithful and brave in time of disaster. So

dependent is every community on its communications with the outside
world that in flood, fire, earthquake, or any other emergency the telephone office becomes the center of information, and often the front
line of organized relief. A plucky and foresighted chief operator in Gays
Mills, Wisconsin, was honored by her town at a civic dinner and received the Vail medal for warning residents of an approaching flood
from the Kickapoo River. When Wilma Gander learned one Sunday
morning that the river was flooding its banks fifteen miles upstream, she
set off the town siren, aroused citizens in time for them to flee, called
the Red Cross and the National Guard, and had a lineman install an upstairs line for her. There Mrs. Gander stayed, keeping telephone service
normal, until after the crest of the flood had passed, by which time the
water was five feet deep in the telephone office.

The telephone industry has a definite policy of promotion from
within. You will read in later chapters how important such a policy is
to you as a beginning employee. It means that your good work will be
rewarded by advancement within the organization as fast as you merit
promotion. As an operator, you would be given first consideration for
an advanced assignment, and you could become a supervisor, training
and overseeing the work of others. The next step up would be to assistant chief operator and then to chief operator. In the last job, you
might head an office of from 150 to 200 girls. Of course, to do this you
would have had to learn much about the telephone business and to have
shown outstanding executive ability. But you can see that, if you are
ambitious and anxious to have a career, it would pay you to apply yourself on this job.

Another line of promotion within the telephone companies is to the
position of service representative. Many young women who hold this
title are college graduates, but an efficient operator with only a high
school diploma, who meets the public pleasantly, is often chosen for this
job. A young friend of mine was at a service desk in a city telephone
office while her husband was in Korea. She told me of the strict rules under which she and the other service representatives work. These employees sit at desks in the business office of the company and talk in person
to customers who call to pay bills, ask about the service, or to complain
about it. Regardless of the errand, these visitors must be treated with
unfailing courtesy. According to my friend, a service representative
cannot say to a telephone user who is delinquent, "You will have to pay
this bill by tomorrow, or your service will be cut off." Oh, no. What is
said, ever so politely, is something like this: "Do you think, Mrs. Jones,
that you could possibly pay this bill tomorrow? We would greatly appreciate your arranging to do so. We should prefer not to have to dis-

continue your service, and we know you won't let that happen." If tact
is one of your personal assets, you could qualify for this position, I'm
sure.

## THROUGH THE STENOGRAPHIC GATEWAY

We shall begin our discussion of jobs approached through the Stenographic Gateway by talking of typing positions. You may question
whether typing is an approach to stenography, since a great many persons learn to type who never plan to learn shorthand. But we are not
talking about typing as a skill everybody should have. We are talking
about various kinds of jobs in which typing is a major skill. Any young
person whose typing is good enough to constitute the major part of his
work can study shorthand, if he wishes, on the side, or brush up on
what he may already know of it, and advance into a stenographic position. A typist, in that sense, enters the business scene through the Stenographic Gateway.

*The Typist-Clerk.* Of various kinds of beginning jobs, one of the
most numerous is the position of typist-clerk. For the beginner with
other skills at his or her command, it offers opportunity for advancement. Primarily, this job requires a knowledge of typing and the ability
to perform many of the duties already described for the general clerk.
The distinction between the two jobs is that the typist-clerk is employed as a typist, and other clerical duties are added to that job;
whereas, the general clerk needs a knowledge of typing, though he may
use it very little. The 1950 census does not state how many of the 1½
million secretaries, stenographers, and typists throughout the country
are employed as typists or typist-clerks. But the Government bulletin [1]
referred to earlier, states that in 1957 there were 89,741 clerk-typists
employed by the Government at an average annual salary of $3,358.
Of these, 9,722 worked in Washington, D. C. and the remaining 80,019
were employed in Federal offices throughout the United States. This
number is very nearly twice that of the clerk-stenographers who were
on the Government payroll at the same time. While the figures in private employment may not be in exactly the same proportion, I mention
this to show that there is, very decidedly, a starting point labeled "Typist-Clerk," and that you might very well start there in the kind of business that most attracts you. The clerical work in any such job gives a
beginner an insight into business in general and into his employer's business in particular. Both kinds of learning are necessary if you are to advance. And your typing will improve greatly as you use it day after day.

[1] *Occupations of Federal White-Collar Workers.* Pamphlet 56-1 issued by the
Employment Statistics Office, U. S. Civil Service Commission.

The logical next step is to full-time typist, a job many girls dislike when it requires steady typing, such as form letters, addressing envelopes, or copying from rough drafts. As you will learn in the next chapter, the electric typewriter has done much to overcome the fatigue that may be experienced by the full-time typist.

*Office Organization—the Centralized Office.* Because office organization affects the kinds of typing and stenographic positions that will be available to you, I want to explain the way that offices are organized and how they function. If you have this knowledge clearly in mind, it may influence your choice of a beginning job. There are two kinds of cffices: *centralized* and *decentralized.* All small offices are decentralized, but not all decentralized offices are small.

First, let me tell you what constitutes a centralized office. In this type of organization, the stenographic and typing work for the entire business is centralized in one department in charge of a transcription supervisor. Only the president of the firm and a few of the more important executives have secretaries. When stenographic service is needed by other executives, a request is made to the supervisor, who sends a member of the stenographic force to take the dictation. Minor executives are required to use voice machines, and a corps of machine transcribers works constantly, taking from records, disks, or tape recorders, the dictation of men whom they rarely meet. Often stenographers do this transcribing, but a good typist can be trained to handle it, thus freeing stenographers for direct dictation.

Banks, insurance companies, brokerage houses, telephone companies, laboratories, manufacturers, railway companies, oil companies, and law firms are among the important businesses that have adopted the centralized department. Most law offices do not use voice machines, but instead, the stenographic department, staffed by high-grade legal stenographers, functions for those lawyers in the large firms who do not rate private secretaries of their own.

There are many advantages in having all the correspondence work centralized. While, generally speaking, stenographers prefer to take dictation direct from an executive rather than listen to his "canned" voice, many girls find the centralized work easier because they are responsible to an understanding woman supervisor. Their letters are checked for errors by the supervisor, and corrections are made before the letters are sent to the person who dictated them. This method relieves the voice-machine operator of the responsibility of dealing directly with one or more dictators who may be fussy or hard to please. "Let the supervisor put up with them," say many girls who prefer the centralized method after working under both systems. From the viewpoint of business, considerable saving is effected by centralizing the part of the office force that handles correspondence. However, the saving that used to be estimated at from one-third to one-half the cost of using stenographers and direct dictation has declined greatly. Voice-machine operators used to be paid on a line basis, and a superfast operator sometimes could make as much as $80 a week when secretaries were earning much less. But, now, fast operators are scarce, as is all experienced office help, and the companies that are organized along centralized lines have to pay salaries —and good ones—to transcribers. This means that the cost of running the department has gone up while production has gone down.

To what extent you, as a typist or stenographer, will need to consider whether to work in a centralized or a decentralized office will depend on where you live. In the East, especially in New York City, Philadelphia, or Boston, if you wish to work in a large organization, the chances are great that it will be centralized. But in the Government offices in Washington, D. C., where there used to be a large pool in virtually every department, all have been done away with. In Chicago and St. Louis, there are not so many centralized departments as formerly, partly because girls object to working in them. On the Pacific Coast, some of the largest companies have centralized departments, either stenographic or transcription—and they tell me they have had these pools for twenty-five years. In one large railroad office, there is a small pool in each department.

There is an organization called the Transcription Supervisors' Association of New York, which is made up solely of women supervisors in charge of from ten to a hundred girls in centralized offices in large firms. This club was founded in 1930, with thirteen members. It now has over 170 members. The similar organization in Chicago, formerly called the Office Supervisors' Club, has changed its name to Women Junior Executives, because the number of supervisors was not growing, and the members wished to include other women who were doing executive work. That may give you some idea of trends in office organization.

Perhaps you think you wouldn't like working under the centralized system. Before you decide definitely, consider the advantages. The members of the Transcription Supervisors' Association (a list of whose employers reads like a "Who's Who" of American business) say that *secretaries in their firms are almost invariably promoted from the stenographic departments.* In their opinion—and they ought to know—if you wish eventually to become a private secretary in a big corporation, you must start in a centralized department. Also leading out of centralized stenographic work are such positions as head stenographer, assistant supervisor, supervisor, and office manager. So think twice before you turn down a job that has such promotional possibilities.

A supervisor in a New York City office outlines the advantages to the operator in a centralized department where voice machines predominate, as follows:

1. Uniform standards of performance for all jobs of major importance.
2. An opportunity to become proficient in many skills beyond stenography and typing, since most large offices have up-to-date mechanical equipment of various kinds for manifolding, and the like.
3. The use of manuals that outline a company's methods and business policy.
4. Written instead of oral instructions when work is assigned—thus eliminating unnecessary questions and the danger of misunderstanding.
5. A more normalized day's work. Under supervision, mail for local districts is held for the next day, in order that preference may be given to mail taking longer for delivery.
6. Help on rewrites. Often a stenographer working for an individual has much rewriting to do at the end of the day through no fault of her own. This necessary evil can be disposed of very quickly in a large department with the assistance of several members.

Where a centralized department uses no voice machines, as in many law offices, the chief advantage as a beginning stenographer is that you get a broad experience by taking dictation from a number of executives. If, perhaps, your vocabulary is limited, this sort of work extends it immeasurably. Naturally, when the correspondence of each man deals with a different phase of the business, you are bound, as you work, to build up the background you need for a higher position in the company.

*Office Organization—the Decentralized Office.* Now, let's consider what is meant by a decentralized office. In such an office, you may be alone or be one of a dozen or more employees. Though you will work under the direction of one of the executives or a department head, you will be more or less on your own. Your work may be assigned by the chief himself, by another executive, or by an older employee, or you may have to dig it out for yourself. Here, you will learn a little of this and a little of that in an unorganized fashion. There may be no set standard for the appearance of your work; you may sacrifice neatness to speed, acquire bad typing habits, and get off to a poor start because of lack of supervision and direction.

On the other hand, if you have initiative, are a good self-organizer, and are willing to discipline yourself, you may sometimes find advancement more quickly in this type of organization than in one where the stenographic work is centralized. But it is only fair to warn you that the one- or two-man office is likely to have an end point that is reached almost at the start. Then the only recourse for an ambitious girl is to leave and make another beginning, this time with her eyes open and her mind wary.

Some very large businesses have, so far, refrained from mechanizing or centralizing their offices. The large decentralized office is similar to the small one- or two-employee office in that there is no central planning or supervision of the office work. The chief difference is that in large offices the important executives have private secretaries who are responsible only to them.

In the small office, usually secretaryless, the stenographer performs many other duties besides taking dictation. If she works alone, she does all the odd jobs that are to be done and may even keep the books. In some offices, the only employee apart from the bookkeeper takes dictation from all the executives, runs the switchboard, acts as receptionist and file clerk, and does any typing needed. If you become such a general worker, you will find that everybody in the office expects you to perform secretarial work for him. "The girl" will look up library data. "The girl" will break appointments. "The girl" will do any errands—even to buying theater tickets. Everybody will want his letters out first, regardless of their importance, and there will be no one to take your part and work out a program, unless you can interest the boss in doing it. Some young women thrive on all this responsibility. They love it. But don't make the mistake of thinking there is much advancement in such a position. Experience—yes, but not promotion. For your comfort on such a job, if you are bent on the title of "secretary," this is one stenographic job in which you may appropriate the title to yourself, but skip the "private"!

*The Voice-Machine Operator.* Now that you have been introduced to both types of office organization, let's assume that you have decided to try your hand at a job in a centralized department. You will need to be a rapid typist, so increase your typing speed while you are in school. Also, if possible, add to your vocational equipment with some experience in transcribing from disks, records, or tape recorders before you leave school. This will be another string to your bow when you go job hunting. For there are jobs to be had, if you are good at voice-machine work. For example, in one large New York City insurance office, in addition to forty secretaries, there are ninety-four girls in the correspondence department whose work is chiefly with dictating machines.

Also, employment agencies in many cities report difficulty in finding girls with training or experience in machine transcribing. The fact is that, to date, in spite of new jobs on the horizon, students are more interested in the human than the mechanical aspect of getting out the correspondence. In an effort to diagnose the reluctance of students to learn voice-machine operation, one commercial teacher said: "All the success stories are written about the girl who became a private secretary. There are no success stories written about the young women who operate office machines."

The story writers who will popularize heroines who transcribe for unseen dictators will perform a great service to the oncoming generation of businesswomen. As a matter of fact, the boss has been greatly overrated as a matrimonial prospect, whereas a well-paying job has often been known to provide the means and background for desirable social contacts outside the job. Indeed, it has often set wedding bells jingling.

But, understand that you have to be very good indeed to become a successful voice-machine operator. This is no occupation for the person with a low I.Q. or inadequate preparation in English. As one transcription supervisor said: "The voice-machine operator does not have to worry about the accuracy of her outlines, but she does have to concentrate very carefully on the dictation in order to produce an intelligent result. Some words sound alike. Others are mispronounced or incoherently spoken. And it is only by distinguishing the meaning or by grasping the sense of the dictation that one is able to transcribe accurately. The actual handling of the voice machine is learned quickly, but I feel that the operator should be given at least the same educational background as the stenographer. The operator does not hear the actual dictation, as does the stenographer, and therefore she cannot preview it. Being removed from the dictator, her common sense and her judgment are challenged constantly, and for that reason she needs the foundation of a large vocabulary and a real understanding of words."

*Voice-Machine Training Offered by Employers.* If you cannot get training in transcribing from records before you leave school, and you are interested in doing this work, there are many companies that will train you on the job. Of course, you first have to know how to type. Madeline C. Gorman, a member of the Transcription Supervisors' Association of New York, has outlined for me the training program she conducts for her firm. Before she was put in charge of training, Miss Gorman was supervisor of the transcription department of an important division of the American Cyanamid Company, so she knows what office employees need to be taught. Here is on-the-job training as it is offered to office workers by one progressive company.[2]

Large organizations have found it essential to establish training programs for new employees, together with continuing refresher courses and advanced courses for job incumbents. This necessity has originated, of course, from the shortage of trained personnel, and from the very desirable promotion-from-within policies existing in most sizable companies.

Training programs may be any one of several types—vestibule school, on-the-job training, or work-experience programs carried out with the co-operation of school officials. Our training school for typists and stenographers, which I conduct, is of the vestibule school type, which is particularly well suited to the company's policy of hiring beginners. A typical vestibule school would be conducted on a regular class schedule by an instructor well-versed in the needs, policies, and procedures of the organization. Instruction may be combined with actual work assignments and is geared to the requirements of the particular industry.

The usual office job categories for which training classes are held are: typist, clerk, file clerk, voice-machine operator, and stenographer. The basic skills of typing and stenography are not ordinarily taught. An outline of a representative training course for prospective typists and stenographers and voice-machine operators is given here:

1. Organization and functions of various departments, company policies, benefits, insurance plans, and the like
2. Trade nomenclature and general vocabulary
3. Grammar and rhetoric, including spelling and vocabulary
4. Correct usage
5. Letter writing and setups for company forms
6. Use of equipment—typewriter, duplicating, transcribing
7. Secretarial duties

The availability of a company procedures manual and of visual aids greatly facilitates the work of the instructor.

*From Typist to Stenographer.* In decentralized offices, you will not get such well-planned formal training, but often you will be tried out on the job and given a chance to prove your ability. For instance, small banks and business firms that do not use voice machines may employ typists for form letters and other routine beginning work. In such firms, after a few months of typing, a young woman who has shown

[2] "Training Program for Typists and Stenographers," conducted by Madeline C. Gorman for the Calco Division of the American Cyanamid Company, Bound Brook, New Jersey.

interest in her work and a grasp of what she is doing will be tested through the dictation of a few letters. If her first letters are acceptable, she will gradually be given more dictation. Then, depending on the volume of work, her helpfulness, and her luck, before long she will be spending most of her time on stenography, and someone else will have been hired to help with the typing.

Don't make the mistake of refusing a typing position because you think you will lose shorthand speed through lack of practice. The head of a large business school declares, "This idea that you'll lose your shorthand if you don't use it is all nonsense. It is like swimming, dancing, or riding a bicycle. Once learned, although you may get a bit rusty, it is really yours forever. You may never take a letter in your first job, but if you have mastered shorthand, with a little practice it will come back to you when you need it."

If you fear your shorthand will leave you, you can keep ready for dictation by having someone in your family give you some practice letters each evening, or you can go to night school twice a week. Another way to get good speed practice is to take down radio or television talks and announcements.

*The Position of Stenographer.* You may be saying, "Why so much talk about starting as a typist? I'd like to start as a stenographer." After you have spent months concentrating on learning shorthand, you are quite right in wanting to start there. Often you can begin as a stenographer, but seldom as a secretary. The two jobs are not the same at all. The word "secretary" is used much too loosely. The stenographer has very definite and limited duties, few of them executive, whereas the secretary's work includes everything that could possibly concern the individual from whom she takes dictation. The secretary actually represents the man for whom she works. She plans his day and makes his appointments for him. She coaches him, reminds him, often handles his personal bank account, and is, in fact, his "other self," during his absences from the office. It takes time and experience to grow into a real secretarial position. You need to know a lot about business in general, and about your business firm in particular.

As a stenographer, you would be occupied chiefly with taking dictation and transcribing it. In some concerns, other duties would be added, of course, but in no sense would you have the semiexecutive responsibility that is shouldered by a private secretary. And as a beginner, you are better off not to jump in knee-deep right from the start.

There are several different types of stenographic positions. First of all, let us look at the various classifications under which stenographers may be grouped.

1. The stenographer who takes dictation from one or several specified executives, yet who works independently of other stenographers or office staff. She may be self-directed or under the supervision of a department head or of the boss himself. This procedure is followed in a decentralized office.
2. The stenographer who takes dictation without discrimination from a number of persons in many departments and whose work for these executives is directed by a supervisor in a centralized department.
3. The stenographer-clerk, sometimes called a junior stenographer, whose full time is not taken up with shorthand and transcribing but who also has duties of a clerical nature.
4. The reporting stenographer, who reports meetings. This position is rather rare but a very desirable one. It calls for high speed and carries varied responsibilities, pleasant contacts, and a certain amount of variety. Large corporations often need such special service.

Each of these stenographic positions makes different demands. After making good as a stenographer in the first or second classification, you may become a secretary, depending on your ability and the way you have demonstrated it. The third group offers the most usual beginning job. Certainly, fresh from school, you would hardly start as a reporting stenographer. But later on, if you are good enough to be a reporting stenographer, you might become a public stenographer with offices of your own, serving clients who do not have enough steady work to employ full-time stenographers. Often, a very good living is made in this type of work by women who have offices in hotels or large business buildings, or who are centrally located in business areas. Still another career open to you as a top-speed stenographer is that of court reporter, as was explained in Chapter 2. Since for that you would need a dictation speed of about 200 words a minute, it is better to consider starting as a stenographer and later advancing into a secretarial position.

Let me tell you how one stenographer did just that. Ellen graduated from a high school commercial course and went right to work as a stenographer. When I met her, a tall, handsome girl with a lot of poise, she was twenty years old and secretary to a managing editor in a publishing house. When I exclaimed about her being a secretary while so young, I was told how she got the upgrading. It seems that the editor was new in this company. He had come to New York City from Chicago to tackle a big job. The company was providing him with a secretary, and he had his choice of several. Why did he choose Ellen? He wanted someone who was new with that employer, as he was. If he took as secretary one of the young women who had been there for several years, working for other editors, she might constantly be telling him, "We always do it this way." The editor did not want to be held down to past procedures. He had been hired because he could bring new ideas to the business, and he wanted a secretary who would help him develop those ideas—not hold him to the past. So, over a period of several weeks, he gave rapid dictation to several stenographers in the firm. Ellen proved by test that she could take his dictation at 120 words a minute. She had the personality for the job and won the job—with an excellent chance of advancing with the young editor.

In a large bank that has a well-planned promotional program for its employees, I learned that they cannot keep stenographers working at shorthand. Why? Promotion from machine bookkeeping to positions as tellers looks better to them than going from stenographic jobs to secretaryships. So the bank's stenographers often request a chance to start all over again, learning on the job how to operate the bookkeeping machines with which the bank does much of its work. The vice-president in charge of personnel believes that women make better tellers than men, with the result that women tellers outnumber the men there. This bank prefers women tellers because it has found that they have better manual dexterity and handle the cash more quickly; they move more rapidly at the windows; and they are more attractive to the men customers.

*The Women's Armed Services.* Knowing that, in peacetime, the WAC and the WAVES have difficulty getting all the young women they need to handle their office work, I wrote to both organizations at their Washington, D. C., headquarters. I had heard that stenographers and typists hesitated to enlist because they might be assigned to other types of work and so lose their skills. My question was, "Do typists and stenographers who enlist in your service have any assurance that they will continue in their line of work?"

Space does not permit my giving you in detail the courteous and definite replies I received from officers in both organizations. Neither, it seems, makes any promise, on enlistment, as to assigned duties or promotion. Both organizations give tests to determine the enlistee's aptitudes and skills in an effort to classify her. Based on her score, a girl will be given further schooling and special training as needed. To qualify as a stenographer in the United States Army, a Wac must be able to take dictation at a minimum rate of 90 words a minute and to type at a minimum of 45 words a minute. The same typing speed is required for typists. However, if your career plan takes you well beyond the use of your present skills, it is possible that the courses given in other types of work might be of greater interest to you. Here is what Emily C. Gorman,

Lieut. Colonel, GS, Deputy Director WAC, wrote regarding such training.

When a qualified high school graduate enlists in the WAC today, she may select one of the following 16 Army School courses in which she will be enrolled on completion of WAC basic training: cryptography, dental assistant, dental laboratory, finance procedures, information and education, machine accounting, medical laboratory, medical technician, occupational therapy, personnel administration, personnel management, pharmacy, physical therapy, public information, stenography, X-ray.

### Through the Bookkeeping Gateway

We are now ready to talk about the kind of jobs that young people who are mathematically inclined, and not at all interested in settling down inside the Stenographic Gateway, will want to get into. But, before we leave shorthand entirely, let me tell of a combination job that may attract some of you.

*The Bookkeeper-Stenographer.* Suppose that you are equally prepared to enter business from either the shorthand or the bookkeeping approach. Then you may be interested in one of two possible occupations—that of the bookkeeper-stenographer or of the stenographer-bookkeeper. The work that would occupy more than half your time is indicated by putting it first in the hyphenated title. Usually, this combination job occurs in a small office where there isn't enough bookkeeping or enough stenography to occupy one person's full time. However, in either case, you might have to keep a simple set of books, and you had better not tackle it unless you can do so.

Should you prefer a small office to a large one and like a variety of duties, this combination of work is often a happy one. It has the added advantage of giving you, as a beginner, an opportunity to try out two widely different kinds of office work and to judge which you like better. The young person with a flair for mathematics is likely to be better satisfied in a position where at least part of the work is with figures. If you find yourself taking greater interest in the figuring end, you need have no hesitancy in deciding to go into full-time bookkeeping and to begin spending your evenings in study and planning for this next step forward.

My personal feeling, based on employment experience, is that every commercial student should have some basic training in bookkeeping. When I was placing girls in a New York City employment agency, we had numerous requests for a combination of shorthand, typing, and a little bookkeeping. When I called the placement bureaus of several private business schools I was told, "So few of our students like figures;

they don't study bookkeeping." On the other hand, there were schools that required all students to take a general course in bookkeeping, and from them I could always get a suitable applicant for the frequent combination job.

Naturally, every person has not sufficient flair for figures to do advanced work in this field, and I am recommending it only to the mathematically minded. The latter, when well trained, will find plenty of opportunity to interpret accounts for the management of a business concern and, if he wishes, to go later into public or private accounting work.

*The Assistant Bookkeeper.* You were told in Chapter 2, under accounting as a career, that your starting point would most likely be in the position of assistant bookkeeper. No matter how good your training, it is not likely that as a beginner you could ever start in a full-time job in the bookkeeping field higher than that of assistant bookkeeper. Be glad you can't. The responsibility is much too great for anyone unfamiliar with general business practices. But if you like to work with figures, why not plan to look for a position as an assistant bookkeeper? It is an excellent way to get practical training under an experienced person, for in large offices bookkeepers work under accountants and are delegated to keep various detailed records. The next step up for the assistant bookkeeper is to full-charge bookkeeper, a position of greater responsibility and, of course, a larger pay check.

So, it is easy to see how, if you have a liking for figures and choose the higher brackets of bookkeeping as your goal, you can begin to plan your career with more or less certainty from the day you leave school. By outside study, coupled with your training on the job, you could prepare yourself to assume full responsibility for the books of a partnership or a corporation.

"But what about bookkeeping as a career?" you may well ask. I'm glad to tell you that in spite of the many mechanical inventions that have threatened to put the human bookkeeping machine out of business, the 1940 census showed only a very *small* per cent of decrease in the number of bookkeepers and accountants, as compared with the working force as a whole. Since then, the total number of bookkeepers has increased greatly. Census figures show that, of the total amount of persons shown as bookkeepers, women accounted for 77 per cent of the total. There is no indication as to how much bookkeeping is still done by hand, but as part of his equipment the bookkeeper must know how to use adding and calculating machines, and he should be familiar with the operation of a number of the other business machines. Billing and bookkeeping machines have been perfected to such an extent that they are being adopted by more and more business organizations.

*The Office-Machine Operator.* There has been a marked increase since 1940 in the number of persons employed as office-machine operators. In 1940, the total persons employed in this type of work was 59,738. In 1958, it is estimated that well over 200,000 office machine operators were employed—approximately 80 per cent of them women. It is also interesting to note that the number of male operators has tripled although still greatly outnumbered by the women. Census figures give no breakdown to show what kinds of machines are used by these operators, but they indicate the ever-increasing mechanization of office tasks. A scarcity of available workers, and the advent on the market of greatly improved machines, and a wider variety of them, have combined to bring about more machine record making and bookkeeping. And the need to cut the cost of operating the nonproductive office side of business has helped to popularize office machines with the management.

Of course, not all jobs as machine operator can be filled by beginners. But if you have acquired a knowledge of the simpler machines while in school, it may give you an entree to this kind of office work. Many school and other placement bureaus report that they are not able to fill all the requests they receive for skilled calculating-machine operators. This includes beginners as well as experienced workers. Because of the scarcity of competent operators, this field of business skills is considered in many localities to be one of the best for beginners. And with the increase of mechanical figuring methods in business, it seems likely that this field will become more and more important as time goes on.

Generally speaking, positions calling for skill in the operation of calculating machines fall into two groups that we shall designate as junior and senior. Junior positions require skilled operators who spend part of their time typing, filing, working on the books, and sometimes even taking dictation. The senior positions require the full time of operators who are highly skilled on all rotary- and key-driven calculating machines. In addition to business openings, both the United States and the state civil services offer well-paid positions to those who can pass the examinations for either junior or senior calculating-machine operators.

Why not put in some time learning these machines before you leave school? If you like arithmetic and are familiar with all the fundamental processes of it, and if you can write numerals rapidly and legibly, knowing how to operate a calculating machine might be the opening door to a good junior job. I must warn you, however, that good eyesight and the physical ability to work at high speed over long periods of time are

*Monroe Calculating Machine Company*

Skilled operators of computing machines are in
demand by banks and large business offices.

as essential as your special skill. You have heard it said, no doubt, that
the machine is an extension of personality. Well, these machines that add,
subtract, multiply, divide, and then some, certainly extend your personality in a way that is thrilling to some persons and utterly nerve-racking
to others.

By learning enough about operating a calculating machine in school
to hold a junior position, you can easily determine whether you like the
work well enough to take additional evening courses in advanced machine calculation. This is the road to a senior position at considerable advance in salary. And it's worth thinking about, right now, in connection
with that plan you are making for your business life.

What has been said about the calculating machine is equally true of
other business machines, for instance, those that do bookkeeping and
billing mechanically. A New York City placement director has said:
"We find a definite need for the right kind of persons who can operate
a Comptometer, a billing machine, or a tabulating machine. I wish the
schools would divert those students who are not particularly adapted to
stenography into the field of office appliances."

If you have a liking for this type of work, you would do well to get specific training along these lines. Many office-machine manufacturers maintain schools where they teach the operating of their machines to young people who have graduated from business courses. Since they are in constant touch with the business firms that have bought or leased their machines, these companies are often able to place promising applicants whom they have trained. This is a tip you can look into, provided you are strongly attracted to machine methods of figuring. New machines are coming on the market all the time. You, as a prospective office worker, will need to keep informed, whether you use these contrivances or not. So keep your eyes open, read the business magazines, and be ever alert for inventions that may tend to revolutionize the work you are now preparing to do.

No one took the electric typewriter very seriously when it first came on the market. But when several manufacturers went after this business seriously, and even got their typewriters into the schools, the time-and-energy-saving value of electric typewriters put them into quite general office use.

**The Statistical Clerk.** Statistical work, much of it in Government offices, has opened up a new and very attractive field for young men and women with mathematical ability. The United States Government classifies its statistical workers as statistical clerks and statisticians. The former includes junior statistical, assistant, senior, principal, and head statistical clerks. Apart from Government, business in general is employing more and more statistical workers. Banks, insurance companies, business research organizations, publishers of periodicals, and many industries are now hiring employees for this type of work.

Although the statistical clerk need not be a college graduate, a thorough grounding in mathematics and statistics on the college level is necessary. Some knowledge of economics is also helpful. These subjects can be mastered by evening attendance at a university, if a person's stick-to-itiveness equals his ambition. It goes without saying that the statistical clerk must know how to operate certain business machines.

In a business in an Eastern city, where compilations are made of the statistics kept by other businesses, I came across two interesting trainee jobs that were available to high school graduates. A statistician for this firm told me she had placed an order with a high school in New Jersey for two girls who would be graduating from the college-preparatory course in June. The only requirement was that they had done well in their high school mathematics. They need not know how to type. They did not even need to know how to run a calculating machine. They would be taught on the job. The duties of these lucky young women would be the copying of statistical reports from, say, insurance companies, and comparing them. The work would include some adding, multiplying, and division. The statistician who was hiring these recent graduates told me she expected them to take college courses at night and added that they could get a degree if they would stay with it long enough. She cited the case of a young woman she had hired similarly several years before, who now has junior standing in college (through night classes) and is getting $80 a week from her daytime job as a research assistant Class I.

In the placement office of a Chicago university, I looked over a sheaf of job orders they had received—and could not fill. One of them was for a statistical clerk who also knew shorthand. Don't ask me why that combination. It merely shows that the combinations in a job can be strange bedfellows. It also suggests that with the constant increase of records there will be more and more positions opening up for statistical clerks and statisticians.

### BEGINNING JOBS IN GOVERNMENT

In the preceding chapter, you were given a brief sketch of the career possibilities growing out of United States Government employment. In Chapter 5, you will be told how to apply for permission to take a civil-service examination leading to employment by the Government. Here, I wish to tell you of a few of the many beginning office jobs available in Washington, D. C., and throughout the United States, wherever Federal employees work.

When in Washington, the expression you hear most often in connection with white-collar workers is, "He's a 3," or "She took the 4 examination, but didn't pass." This numbering of everyone means that employees are graded as to rank, work, and salary from Grade 1 through Grade 8. Since all Government employees are familiar with this system, they take a short cut and quickly explain the status of their friends and acquaintances by saying they are a 2 or a 6, or some other grade number.

Beginners who wanted to work for the Federal Government used to take the Grade 1 examination, which was strictly clerical. Now, the Grade 1 examination is seldom given, since the Grade 2 includes clerical work with typing, pays more, and has seemed to offer more inducements to beginners. The Federal Government has been, and is, actively in the labor market, seeking to attract young people to qualify under civil service for work in its many departments. The salary inducement is one of its strongest selling points.

Four out of every five white-collar jobs with the Government are outside the Washington, D. C., area, which includes offices in nearby Maryland and Virginia. So, if you would like to work for the Government and start at a salary that is likely to be a bit better than you would get if starting in private employment, why not look up the dates of examinations, and see if you can qualify to take one or more of them? *Under no circumstances, pay money to attend a so-called civil-service school that claims it will prepare you to take a civil-service examination.* The Civil Service Commission warns that fraudulent claims have been made by schools, stating that they had advance tips as to when certain examinations would be given and what questions would be asked. The Commission says that none of these schools are connected with the Government, that their claims are false, and that you do not need to go to any special school to prepare for a civil-service examination.

As in any private business, there is work for stenographers, typists, and clerks in all departments of the Government. Depending on the difficulty of the work, there will often be several "grades" for one kind of skill, such as typing or shorthand. To illustrate, the largest single occupational group of white-collar employees in Government service is that of clerk-typist. Of the 89,741 clerk-typists on the Federal payroll on February 28, 1957, less than 23 per cent were Grades 1 and 2, while over 74 per cent were grades 3 and 4. On that same date, over one-third of the Government white-collar workers were in Grades 1 through 4, with more than 53 per cent of all typists and stenographers in Grade 3. In case you are curious about salaries, the booklet from which I am quoting, *Occupations of Federal White-Collar Workers*, referred to earlier, gives the average annual salary of these workers as $4,208. This figure is according to a new and higher schedule which went into effect on January 1, 1958. Of course, the higher salaries of the top grades bring up the average. The starting salary for a Grade 3 is $3,495 a year, and allowing for nine raises, the final step is to $4,350 annually.

You may wonder why I have detailed the Government salary scale and have not done so for employment in private business. The reason is simple. Government salaries are uniform, according to grade. They are printed for anyone to read and are not subject to the many changing conditions that occur in other businesses. Salaries for white-collar or office workers in private industry are governed to a great extent by supply and demand, and for that same reason will be about the same throughout a given area. But in another city or town, possibly in the same state, different local conditions will cause a different salary scale to prevail. Sometimes, higher living costs in one part of the country will bring about a rise in salaries in that section. You can learn what salaries are being paid in the city or town where you live by reading the classified advertisements in your daily or Sunday newspaper. And your post office will be glad to give you printed matter showing what you will be paid in case you are interested in working for the Federal Government.

You may be interested to know that in 1960 there were 500,000 Federal Government employees working for the Post Office Department. This includes city and rural mail carriers and all those working behind the scenes in post offices throughout the country as well as in the 15 regional offices and in Washington, D. C. I suggest that young men inquire about examinations for work in the Post Office Department. For instance, the position of continuous substitute clerk which start at $2 an hour, exists in every part of the United States. There are some post office jobs for women, though not so many. A young friend of mine, who grew tired of working in a city, went to a small resort town intending to vacation there with relatives for a while but never dreaming she would find work there. When she saw an examination for postal clerk (local) advertised, she took it and passed. Within a few weeks, she had a permanent job in the local post office, one of three employees, doing all kinds of work and very happy. She says she will never return to office work in the city.

## QUESTIONS

1. Is it true that no one wants to employ beginners? Explain.
2. What are the three gateways through which a beginner may enter business?
3. Which gateway looks most attractive to you? Why?
4. Does a telephone-receptionist need to know typing? Shorthand?
5. What is the difference between a PBX operator and a telephone-receptionist? Is the position of voice-machine operator the same as that of PBX operator?
6. If you were offered, as your first job, a position as office boy or messenger, would you take it? Give your reasons.
7. Can a girl who is a poor typist do well as a voice-machine operator?
8. If you can't find a beginning job as a secretary, should you turn down everything else and keep on looking for secretarial work?
9. Does secretarial training fit one only for actual secretarial work?
10. What type of information does the secretary need to have about business which she cannot be expected to acquire in school?
11. What besides the skillful running of the machine is necessary if one is to succeed as a calculating-machine operator?
12. If you were unable to secure a position in the kind of work you think now you prefer in private business, would you investigate civil service? Why?

13. If you were a typist and were told you were to be trained for promotion into the position of voice-machine operator, would you be pleased? Would you quit? Why?
14. What is the title of a person in charge of a centralized department?
15. In what part of the United States is the centralized system used most at present?
16. Can you think of several reasons why this is so?
17. Do all centralized departments use voice machines as well as stenographers and secretaries?
18. Are all decentralized offices small offices? Explain.
19. Do you think that filing can be stimulating work, or that it seldom goes beyond the putting away of papers in drawers?
20. How many different kinds of stenographic positions can you name? How do their duties differ?
21. Which would attract you most? Why?
22. In which do you think a beginner would be most likely to secure employment?
23. If a school advertises that it is a civil-service school and can teach you how to pass a civil-service examination, would you believe this and pay to be taught?

## TOPICS FOR DISCUSSION

1. Discuss the two major types of office organization—the decentralized and the centralized.
2. What are the advantages of working in a decentralized office? The disadvantages?
3. State what you consider the advantages of starting out in a centralized stenographic department. The disadvantages.
4. If you aspire to become a private secretary to an executive in a large corporation in an Eastern city, which of these types of organization will you probably need to work up in?
5. Based on what you know of the kind of work done in a large office (not necessarily centralized) as compared with that in a small office, which do you think would give you the more valuable experience?
6. What are some of the advantages of starting as a general clerk?
7. Could one be a successful general clerk without some knowledge of (a) arithmetic, (b) bookkeeping, (c) typing, (d) shorthand, (e) filing. Discuss the list of skills in the order of their importance to a general clerk.
8. What are some of the expressions a PBX operator would not be permitted to use if she were running the switchboard in an average business office? Discuss your own experiences in this line.
9. State the advantages of a position as receptionist. The disadvantages

How does the position differ when the receptionist also answers the telephone?

10. Name some of the personal qualifications of a good file clerk.

11. What qualities are needed for becoming a successful PBX operator?

12. The telephone company endeavors to inspire its own employees and the PBX operators whom it trains for private switchboards with a high sense of devotion to duty and responsibility. They point proudly to girls who have valiantly stuck to their posts though in danger even of death.

When an explosion occurred at the Cleveland Clinic, causing a major disaster, Gladys Gibson could have escaped through a window at the side of her switchboard. But she stuck to her post in order that she might save other lives. She was found dead at her switchboard. In a fire at the Hotel Plaza in Jersey City, Helen Sullivan, PBX operator for the hotel, stayed at her switchboard calling for help and warning guests until finally her dress caught fire. Helen died as a result of burns, a few weeks later. Both these girls were awarded the Vail medal for bravery, posthumously.

Of course, there are many other true stories such as these where PBX operators warned guests of fire and flood and lived to enjoy their honors and awards. But they took the same risks as Gladys Gibson and Helen Sullivan. Do you feel that any job has the right to ask such a high type of service? Do you feel that employees are justified in giving their lives in the line of duty?

13. Although you wish to start as a stenographer, would you accept a beginning position as typist if that were offered to you first? State your reasons.

14. If the first position available to you looked like a dead-end job, would you take it? If not, why not? If you would, discuss why you think taking this job would not necessarily keep you from realizing your career plan. Explain what a "pocket" or "dead-end" job is.

15. The terms "apprenticeship" and "vestibule job" are being used more and more regarding office positions. What do they mean?

## PROJECTS

1. Select one of the positions, other than that of typist, outlined in this chapter, and write a paper of not more than 500 words about it. Do outside reading on this position; and, if possible, talk with one or two persons who now hold such jobs or who have held them. Discuss the personal qualifications necessary for success in this job and the promotional possibilities ahead for those who make good.

2. You are the telephone-receptionist in an industrial firm where there are ten top executives and many minor ones. One morning, when you are very busy, a man calls in person and demands to see Mr. Hayes, the manager of the company. Your duty is to keep out the unwanted and

yet to offend no one. The conversation at your desk goes something like this:

YOU: Mr. Hayes is busy. Who shall I say is calling?
VISITOR: My name doesn't matter. But my business does. It is important.
YOU: What company do you represent? I shall have to tell Mr. Hayes.
VISITOR: (*Becoming angry*) That doesn't matter, young lady. Take my word for it, Mr. Hayes will be glad to see me. How long will I have to wait?
YOU: I'm sorry, but Mr. Hayes does not see anyone unless he knows who they are and what they wish to see him about.
VISITOR: (*Losing control of temper*) Just tell him my business is personal, then. And for your benefit, when I do see Mr. Hayes I shall suggest that he have a more polite person out here unless he wants to lose business.

You have no way of telling whether this caller is a prospect who wishes to place an order with the company, a gate crasher who wishes to sell Mr. Hayes something, or a man looking for a job. You will be reprimanded if you let business get away from the firm and also if you admit someone who will waste Mr. Hayes's time. What would you do?

Think out the different possible steps you could take, and then write what you would say further to the visitor. If you decide to telephone Mr. Hayes about the matter in the caller's presence, what do you think you would say?

3. Prepare a 500-word paper discussing the career possibilities growing out of a beginning position as typist.
4. Get all the information you can about employment in the Post Office Department—the positions for which beginners can qualify, the salaries paid, and the opportunities for advancement. Organize this material, and be prepared to give the class full information. Be sure to include rural-mail-carrier jobs in your presentation.

# CHAPTER 4

# What Business Wants in Skills and Abilities

Up to now, you have had only hints as to what will be expected of you when you start to work on your beginning job. You will be able to put your best foot forward with more confidence if you know what business requires of you. Before you present yourself to any business firm as an applicant for work, you should size up your qualifications in relation to the employer's needs. So this chapter is a preview of business standards by which you can measure your fitness.

We shall not be able to cover all types of businesses. Even in the same line of work, no two organizations are exactly alike in their practices and management. But we can study a composite picture of office requirements. What I shall tell you is based on informal statements made by employers in many parts of the United States in reply to my direct questions as to what they expect of employees.

It may seem as you read this chapter that too much emphasis is placed on the skills and abilities needed by stenographers. "Why bother about a knowledge of words if I am going to be a bookkeeper?" you may ask. But I assume that you wish to be a well-rounded young business person, capable of being promoted from one type of office position to another as your capacities develop. Please note that, while this chapter speaks definitely of requirements in skills, it also deals with *abilities*. You may not be learning to write shorthand, but you use words in one form or other every waking minute.

Even though you are a general clerk, a file clerk, or an assistant bookkeeper, you will do better work if you have a sound background in spelling, grammar, and business research methods and know how to organize your time and your work. In fact, the required abilities, besides the skills outlined in this chapter, constitute for the young business person today a type of culture as basic as reading and writing were in an earlier time. Certainly you do not wish to appear illiterate when you go to work. And you will not if you are already familiar with what business requires of office employees. Nothing helps so much to put you at ease and on a comparable basis with experienced office associates as knowing, without being told, certain things that are expected of you.

### DICTATION, TYPING, AND TRANSCRIPTION REQUIREMENTS

The ability to type is becoming a must for everyone—almost as important as knowing how to write. In some schools, the children are taught typewriting, starting in the fourth grade. Because a check with the children has shown that there are typewriters in more than half of their homes, they are encouraged to practice at home. You may not have started typing so young, but I hope that by now you already have some knowledge of typing. You may not be interested in or qualified for a typing job, but you'll find that the ability to type is a valuable tool in whatever kind of work you do.

Although a great deal has been said and written about the desirability of rapid typing, experience has shown that for office requirements the typist needs much more than the ability to copy at high speed. As a typist doing general office work, you must have all-round typing competence, for you will be called on to type all sorts of miscellaneous material. Such proficiency means that you must be accurate and work at an even, steady pace that you can maintain at a speed adequate to the work in hand. Fifty words a minute is a good pace for beginners. As you gain experience, your typing speed will increase, and you will be doing the 70 to 80, or more, words of the seasoned typist.

If you find yourself in a routine typing job, here are some of the typical pieces of work you will be called on to turn out:

1. Filling in letters and forms
2. Typing on cards
3. Copying from rough draft
4. Tabulating
5. Invoicing
6. Addressing envelopes
7. Copying form letters

In virtually every one of these routine typing tasks you must be able to follow instructions carefully, be able to think ahead and understand what you are doing, and be capable of turning out well-arranged, neat, and acceptable work. You will need to know how to spell and to understand the principles of simple arithmetic, which underlie many of the forms you will be required to type.

Another duty you may encounter occasionally is taking dictation directly on the typewriter. When this happens, you must be able to arrange the letter correctly on the page as you go along. Also you will have to know how to make an attractive setup for reports and other papers that may be assigned to you.

*The Electric Typewriter.* The electric typewriter has come into more general use within the past few years, as more companies are manufacturing these machines and introducing them into the schools. Now students in high schools and in private business schools are being taught to use the electric typewriter, and more and more business firms are installing them.

The transcription supervisor in charge of a pool in the home office of one of the country's leading typewriter companies told me that production in her department had risen about 15 per cent since electric typewriters were installed. Naturally, I asked whether the electrically operated carriage shift produced this increase and was told it had not, except incidentally perhaps. "The whole operation is so much easier," said the supervisor. "The operators 'play' the machine with a light touch that does not tire them. Consequently, the three-o'clock lag no longer occurs to slow down the typists and bring down the day's production. Better still, our girls no longer dread typing and don't mind doing it all day, day after day."

*Typing Tests for Specific Jobs.* Instead of requiring the same typing speed from all those who do stenographic or typing work, some business firms have analyzed their jobs, so that they know just what speed is needed in each. After they have learned this by testing their present employees, the personnel department, when asked to hire a typist for a particular job, knows what speed is needed and tests applicants accordingly. This is an economical use of skills, for a typist who can do 60 words a minute or better is not wasted in a job where 45 words is sufficient.

An international engineering company on the Pacific Coast has chosen a large percentage of its 180 office workers in this manner. To illustrate: For the girls who are to type labels, 45 to 50 words a minute is satisfactory. But if a typist is to cut stencils, do Multilith work, or straight typing, she must be able to do 55 words a minute. Figure-typing tests are given for those who are to work as statistical typists in the purchasing department, but here, accuracy is more important than speed, and some knowledge of tabulating is necessary. Job analysis has shown this firm that stenographers in the purchasing department can do the work if their dictation speed is 90 words a minute, while stenographers who take dictation from the engineers must have a *minimum* dictation speed of 100 words a minute.

In some kinds of business, figure typing is all-important. When I took over the hiring of office help for a California shipyard during World War II, there were one thousand office jobs, most of them scattered throughout the yard. When I started, all typists and stenographers were required to type 70 words a minute by test. My first step was to call on all the department heads and find out just what they needed in skills, and I learned that in many departments they didn't need word typists. The head of engineering, the man who ran the warehouse, and executives in many other departments dealing with figures said, "Get us figure typists. These girls you send us, who can type 70 words a minute, often can't type figures at all."

They were right. Many a good stenographer had never typed figures except on the date line of a letter. My job was to set up figure-typing tests, and get the kind of typists those departments needed. After much experimenting, we settled for straight tabulating tests. From then on, all typists and stenographers were given both word- and figure-typing tests, and the papers showing the work and grading in the tests were sent to the department head along with the applicant. Needless to say, the departments that needed statistical typists now got them, and the chief problem of their office work was solved.

**How Important Is Speed?** The questions most frequently asked stenographic applicants have to do with speed: "What is your dictation speed? your transcription speed? your typing speed?" These questions do not mean that business is concerned primarily with speed. They serve merely as a measuring stick. Speed without accuracy would be as undesirable as accuracy without speed. But since speed is a generally accepted yardstick, let us discuss the requirements of business in regard to it.

Office managers often speak about the desirability of "excess capacity over the minimum requirement." This is a technical way of describing the extra store of speed and endurance that helps the beginner to make good on his first job and goes on helping him thereafter. Any beginner with a dictation speed of 110 words a minute has this excess capacity. Anything less than 100 words a minute is a bid for trouble. To illustrate: When you, as a stenographer, have a reserve of from 10 to 20 words a minute, you can keep up with almost any dictator. If he gets a sudden burst of speed, you will be right there thinking with him. Because of your precious reserve, you won't become flustered.

Picture the opposite! Suppose you start on your first job with a dictation speed of from 80 to 100 words a minute. You are hopeful you can "get by" with that. You suspect that the dictator has slowed down somewhat the first few times you take his letters, and you are sure of it on the third day. For when everything is going along smoothly, suddenly he springs a new word on you. You hesitate and immediately you are no longer with him. He continues and seems to hit an even faster pace when he gets on a subject he knows well. Need I dwell on your predicament? Unless good luck causes a break in the dictation, you have lost the train of thought, are several jumps behind him, and are no longer taking dictation intelligently.

Unless the telephone rings, or some other interruption occurs and gives you a chance to catch up, you will have to ask the dictator to slow down or to repeat a sentence or two. If this happens only once or twice, it will be overlooked. But if the basis of your trouble is your inability to take dictation at the required speed with sufficient reserve, the consequences can be serious. In case you find yourself unable to go along with the dictator, don't wait to be demoted to a typing job or to be asked to go to night school to get your speed up. Beat the office manager to it by enrolling in a night school at once. Of course, a much better way is to be sure you have a safe reserve before you leave school. This will give you confidence and do much to rout the stage fright from which many beginners suffer when they first go to work.

*Research Shows Dictation Speed Uneven.* One reason for the desirability of above-average speed is that businessmen are irregular in their dictation tempo. How irregular was not established until a college professor who teaches business subjects in a collegiate school of commerce made a study of the actual dictation of 72 different businessmen in 37 firms.[1] The businesses were located in cities and in medium-sized towns in a generous coverage of Midwestern and Eastern states; they included banks, hotels, utilities, manufacturers, insurance companies, school offices, retail and wholesale firms, construction companies, and some Government offices. The men who dictated were managers of businesses, sales executives, administrators, personnel directors, and public-relations counselors. In other words, the sampling was spread over a wide territory and a representative range of businesses.

The purpose of Dr. Green's study was to find out exactly how dictation is given in business offices, so that the schools can more nearly prepare beginning stenographers for the conditions they will meet when employed. The method used in conducting the study was explained to me by Dr. Green in his office in Chicago where I saw some of the transcripts of recordings. This was no wire-tapping expedition. Arrangements were made with a number of employers for recording in the

---

[1] H. H. Green, B.Ed., M.A., Ph.D., *The Nature of Business Dictation.* Abstract of a Doctor's Dissertation, University of Pittsburgh Bulletin, Volume 48, Number 10. June 5, 1952.

companies' offices everyday dictation given by their executives to their stenographers. Unseen microphones were set up, but everyone knew that the dictation was being recorded by a SoundScriber recording machine. The stenographers were told that their bosses were to be the guinea pigs, so they need not be nervous.

The dictation ranged in length from a 2-minute letter to one that took 20½ minutes. Because this was run-of-the-mill dictation, there were the usual interruptions, such as phone calls, and requests following the interruption that the stenographer read back from her notes. The gross dictation included everything that was said during the dictation period, such as instructions to the stenographer and the spelling of names or unusual words. The number of words dictated by each executive was counted and tabulated. Then the words that would not appear in the letter were eliminated. The result was the *net* dictation—a total of 720 minutes.

In summarizing the results of his valuable study, Dr. Green says, "Businessmen dictate at many rates of speed which, seemingly, are dependent on rate of thinking and on ability to phrase thoughts. Each dictator has, generally, three areas of dictation speed."

As I understand it, these areas are as follows:

1. The *slow* speed—the period when dictators are thinking what to say. This ranges, for all dictators, from 0 to 40 gross words a minute
2. The *middle* speed—the person's usual way of talking—ranges for
   a. the *slowest* dictators, from 40 to 50 gross words a minute
   b. the *average* dictators, from 50 to 80 gross words a minute
   c. the *most rapid* dictators, from 100 to 130 gross words a minute
3. The *spurt*—the speed-up which occurs when the dictator deals with familiar subject matter—ranges for
   a. the *slowest* dictators, from 60 to 90 gross words a minute
   b. the *average* dictators, from 70 to 120 gross words a minute
   c. the *most rapid* dictators, from 100 to 150 gross words a minute

Based on these findings, Dr. Green concluded that no dictator has any pattern of speed. The slowest will speed up when he has an idea and wants to get rid of it. The fastest will slow down or even stop while he thinks something out. According to this authority, there is no constant rate of speed in a given letter or even in a single sentence. Since the stenographic student is preparing to take dictation under general conditions, she needs to be ready for any and all kinds of dictators. To quote Dr. Green again: "There is no substitute for speed in taking dictation easily and fluently. A stenographer experiences no difficulties in slowing down but is handicapped by continued pressures to keep up with the dictator." Therefore Dr. Green recommends to the schools that: "A minimum, tentative standard of not less than 100 words a minute be established for instructional purposes. The stenographer who can write shorthand at 100 words a minute has sufficient skill to be competent in approximately one-half of the stenographic jobs."

*Transcription Speed Essential.* Transcription speed varies with the individual. Actually, a stenographer's salary depends on her transcription speed. What good is it to take shorthand notes rapidly if you transcribe so slowly that the initial gain is lost? Then, too, it is the dictator who actually determines how fast his letters are taken down even by the most experienced stenographer. He may dictate slowly, or he may waste your time by looking up material and answering telephone calls while you wait at his desk, pencil in hand. So your chance to make up for delays and interruptions over which you have no control comes when you are alone with your notes and a good typewriter.

*The Dictator's Vocabulary.* One of the things that will affect your dictation speed is the vocabulary used by the businessmen for whom you work. In many businesses, the dictation is confined to words that seldom average over 1.2 to 1.4 syllables to each word. Such words are among the one to two thousand commonest in the English language. You might take 120 words a minute with ease in this type of dictation, but find yourself slowed down to 80 words by a dictator whose vocabulary consisted of a great number of unusual or many-syllabled words. Generally speaking, university offices, publishing houses, advertising agencies, and authors hold the record for using the more difficult words. If the dictator also has a personal mannerism of speaking rapidly, you might easily find your excess-ability reserve running low. A stenographer with a limited vocabulary would have no difficulty in taking dictation in a wholesale house or even in a bank, where the dictation is largely routine. But let this same person change to a position where she is given highly original letters containing lengthy words and she will find she has more than her shorthand to worry about.

Virginia Wilson, a beginning stenographer, had worked for a few months in the general office of a small magazine when one day she was asked to take dictation from the editor in the absence of his secretary. Before she entered business, Virginia had graduated from the college-preparatory course in high school, and she knew her Latin, but philosophy had not yet entered her young life or her vocabulary. When the editor glibly dictated a sentence containing the words "categorical imperative," Virginia's eyes popped, but her fingers flew over the paper without hesitation. She used her head and her ear and sped to the office dictionary before transcribing her notes.

*What Is a Day's Work?* The number of letters you will be required to turn out each day depends on the kind of business, the type of office organization, and the correspondence load. There is, you will find, a generally accepted standard for a day's work. And you may get quite a shock when you first come up against it. If your job is to take dictation from several men, you are almost certain to be given letters from nine o'clock until noon. This means that you must transcribe all afternoon. The grind will be unlike anything you have previously experienced. And there will be no begging off! Letters dictated in the morning must be got out that day. They should be on the dictator's desk by four o'clock. This allows time for necessary changes to be made without stenographic overtime. And, mind you, the changes are those made by the dictator, revisions of thought or policy, *never* at this point the redoing of careless work on your part!

Changes due to your inability to read your notes or to incorrect spelling, paragraphing, or punctuation must be taken care of long before the four o'clock deadline. These, along with typographical errors, are inexcusable in the finished transcript. Executives often ask for changes in their letters because, on reading the transcription, they feel that the words they dictated first do not best convey the idea, or because further information that has come in during the day necessitates changing the content of the letter. This may even mean that several letters must be entirely retyped through no fault of yours.

In centralized offices, where most of the work consists of transcribing from disks, tape recordings, or the new telephone dictation system, a girl was formerly paid on a piece basis—that is, according to the number of lines of transcription she turned out in a day. Competent operators in many of these departments averaged around a thousand lines a day, while a star operator could turn out fourteen hundred $5\frac{1}{2}$-inch lines of elite type in a seven-hour day. A recent check with a number of supervisors in these departments, in large Eastern firms, indicates that they no longer pay on this basis. Daily records of individual output are still kept, but they no longer have operators who can reach the daily average output mentioned above. As one of the supervisors expressed it, "Salaries for voice-machine operators are now based on past experience and present-day production." How long this combination of higher salaries and lower production will continue is anybody's guess. Several supervisors told me they did not consider it permanent.

*Organize Yourself.* Because of the possibility of last-minute legitimate alterations in letters, one of the first things you will have to learn on a job is to organize yourself. You must make the very best use of your time throughout the day. Otherwise, you will be forced to leave unfinished business on your desk and will be guilty of that crime of crimes, holding untranscribed letters overnight in your notebook. And the fact of such letters being delayed in reaching their destination is not the only consideration! Worse still, they are likely to go stale on you, so that you are put in the uncomfortable position of asking the executive to help you read back your notes. And does that annoy him!

He will be cross because the letters did not go out promptly on the day he dictated them. He will have forgotten the wording and perhaps the content. And he will be provoked that he must stop in the midst of a busy day to help a subordinate whose chief duty is to ease his day. He may even be irritated enough to report you for inefficiency. A complaint of this sort means trouble, and a series of them can lead to your dismissal.

If you find yourself taking more dictation than you can reasonably be expected to transcribe before four o'clock, you should report to the office manager or whoever is in charge of the correspondence. But be certain that the fault is not yours! You will be fortunate if you work under an understanding supervisor who gauges the time it will take you as a beginner to adjust yourself, and who sees to it that the work is laid out with fairness to both the executives and the girls under her. One such woman discovered that the stenographers in her department were working overtime on letters which did not need to go out at once. She sent a memorandum to the executives saying: "Unless a letter is marked 'rush,' the transcription department will hereafter have out-of-town mail on your desk at 4 p.m. and local mail for you at 9 a.m. the following day. This will ease the load in our department and will not seriously delay the receipt of your correspondence." However, this is a ruling that only a department head could make.

Suppose you are the only employee in an office, with a million things to do, and your boss has dictated more letters than you can possibly get out that day. What to do! In my opinion, your best move is to ask your employer frankly which letters he considers most important and which can be held over. Then, if you are well organized, you will put less important work aside and transcribe these letters at once. The next morning you will start early on the less important letters and have them on your employer's desk before the day's rush begins.

**Brush Up to Keep Up.** It is quite possible that on your first job you will have little dictation to take. Of course, your speed suffers when this happens. And it is most essential for you to keep growing in skill in order that you will be ready for the next step up when it comes. In a small Eastern city, eighty office employees went back to school at night to brush up on their dictation. When they left school, they had all taken dictation at 110 to 130. In their brush-up class, the teacher started them at 100 words dictation speed. This, she thought, would be a good average for the group. But few were successful at that rate, and a final test showed that 60 words was the best the class as a whole could do. So, let me suggest that you do not let much time elapse after you have taken your first job before you begin to check up on your skills, and if you find you are slipping in any of them, do something about it. Probably the best thing to do is to go back to school one or two nights a week. If that is impossible, try taking down radio or television talks and announcements. This is considered excellent practice. If you can take this rapid-fire dictation successfully, you are good!

### Small but Essential Skills

But dictation and typing are not the beginning and end of skills needed on the job. Accuracy and neatness are of great importance, though business cannot follow the rule of "*no erasures*" so prevalent in business schools. To pull out a half-filled sheet from the typewriter and begin all over again when an error has been made is too costly in time and stationery. So, whether or not your school teaches skill in making erasures, learn to do it neatly. Learn, too, to crowd inserted letters into place, when necessary, and to space out letters when words have been deleted. Naturally, such corrections have to be made very well indeed. Strikeovers, smudgy corrections, or typographical errors are never acceptable. Don't think they will be overlooked by the dictator, for they won't be. The rule, "Positively no strikeovers," must never be broken.

Another skill in which you should train yourself is the ability to make as many as six clear carbons. Unless your touch is strong and even, the fifth and sixth carbons are rarely legible. This is especially important, for business as a whole has found it economical to use a good grade of carbon paper, and if your carbons are not clear, the blame will fall on you.

Still another not unreasonable requirement of business is that those responsible for getting out the correspondence know how to set up a letter properly. In spite of the attention paid to letter forms in all business schools, there is a shocking indifference to the subject among transcribers. You will be expected to know something about the most approved forms of setting up business letters. However, the beginner should be very careful to note the forms already in use by the employing firm and to follow them. It is a frequent complaint among businessmen that new stenographers are careless about following the rules of form already established.

Business executives would be pleased if, as a new employee, you take enough time and interest to count words and arrange margins. Such a simple precaution, regardless of the length of a letter, would result in its being properly centered on a page. "I thought from my notes that the letter was longer than it turned out to be" is a pretty thin excuse. A little experience will enable you to judge quite accurately the length of a letter in relation to your notes. So, see to it that your touch is even and sufficiently heavy to assure good carbons, that your margins are balanced and your spacing is accurate. These are details of major importance that will help you win approval from the start.

Every office employee who uses a typewriter should know how to take care of one. You can turn out the best work only if your machine is in first-class condition, and though some offices subscribe to a regular cleaning and repair service, the added care you give your typewriter will show in your work.

The duties of a typist, stenographer, or general clerk often include making stencils. In many offices, you would be expected to make a setup from rough copy directly to the stencil. From stencil cutting to operating a mimeograph machine is but a step. If you can list this skill among your assets you will be that much more valuable as an employee. As I have said before, business is more interested in employees who can do several things than it is in specialists. Many a girl holds her job when an office staff is cut because, in addition to being able to type and tabulate on a wide-carriage machine, she can run a duplicating machine and cut a clear stencil.

### The Importance of English

The English language is the head, tail, and backbone of the correspondence division of business. To emphasize this fact, the dean of a collegiate school of business administration insists that shorthand and typewriting are not commercial subjects but should be classed as English subjects.

You are fortunate if you have had the advantage of college courses in English composition and literature. Such a background helps to make the paths of beginners wide and straight. I know a girl who graduated from a state university with a degree in English. She taught a year and then decided she might be better suited to a business career. She took a business course and, owing to her educational background, was able to start as a secretary at a time when this seldom happened. From then on, she had her choice of positions at the highest salaries paid for secretarial work in the city in which she lived—all owing to her knowledge of English.

However, not everyone has such an advantage, nor in many very good positions is so much English necessary. For instance, a beginner's job with a wholesale grocery company would not require a knowledge of words out of the ordinary, as most of the correspondence would be strictly related to the grocery business. Neither would the college graduate who makes a stenographic job a springboard into social-service work need advanced English. The rudiments, if not more, of economics, sociology, and psychology would be far more useful. But the ambitious young person will recognize that in general a thorough knowledge of English will be a tool that can lift him or her out of the crowd. The question is how to get such knowledge after leaving school.

The principal of one business school suggests to his pupils that they make a practice of reading the editorials in the local newspapers. This type of reading is a mine of forceful ideas well expressed. You may encounter many words that are new to you. Always look up their meaning, learn to spell them, and practice using them in conversation. I think it was the late Arthur Brisbane who made the statement that, if a young man would read *The New York Times* from the front to the back every day for two years and would look up all the references with which he was unfamiliar, he would by that time have become a thoroughly educated person. Of course, there are many other ways of stimulating one's interest in words and expression. The main thing is to realize the importance of it.

## Good Spelling Necessary to Success

Twenty years ago, it was considered a sign of illiteracy to misspell a single word in a letter or composition. Now the pendulum has swung so far in the opposite direction that a good speller is rare. Some young people even laugh off their inability to spell with, "Oh, you don't need to know how to spell any more." If stenographers could hear, as I do, the complaints of employers all over the United States about the spelling mistakes of their stenographers, young people would get to work on this branch of English or choose another occupation. True, many employers cannot spell, but this does not mean that they will permit their letters to go out full of misspelled words. Employers are dismayed at the nonchalance of the average stenographic bad speller when her mistakes are called to her attention. Remember that part of your responsibility as a stenographer is the technical correctness of your transcriptions. Correct spelling is just as important to the perfection of your work as is your mechanical skill with a typewriter.

In centralized offices, all letters are checked by the supervisor to detect and correct any misspelling or poor grammar. But an able supervisor will not long be patient with a girl who cannot spell. Because the supervisor is there to save money, she cannot approve of the costliness of many erasures and retyping of letters.

In decentralized offices, correct spelling is even more important. In this type of office organization, there is no go-between to detect the offending words. Unless a beginner working in a small office, more or less without supervision, realizes her responsibility for perfection in spelling, her place may shortly be filled by someone who can be depended on for accuracy.

Jane Holmes had remained a poor speller, though she had seven years' business experience to her credit. She lost one position because of two small words she misspelled, which finally wore out the patience of two long-suffering executives. One of them dictated a statement for the newspapers in which he said, "I do not claim to be a prophet." When he read his speech in print, after Jane had typed it and handed it to the reporters, he was astounded to see he made no claim to being a "profit." The other executive dictated, "We will not ask you to perjure your souls." The finished letter on his desk assured the recipient that his firm was not asked to perjure their "soles." When the office staff heard that Jane had gone to work for a chain of shoe-repair shops, the acid comment was, "Good. Now she can perjure soles, and not be fired for doing it."

Mary Smith, a stenographer with a college degree, was amused that her employers were so old-fashioned as to fly into a rage when she repeatedly spelled "too" with one "o." When Mary lost her job, she went to work in the stationery section of a department store. Mary was clever at learning the stock; she studied about paper after hours, and she took courses in salesmanship. Her ambition was to become an assistant buyer and then a buyer, and she had the qualifications. But after Mary had ruined several orders of expensive wedding invitations by misspelling the bride's name, the department head decided her initiative was overshadowed by her incompetence. This was the end to Mary's hopes. Before long she was transferred to another department, where spelling was not so important. Mary felt sad about the change, for her heart was in handling fine papers. Yet she still thinks it is foolish to make such a fuss about spelling!

**Correct Spelling Can Be Learned.** Poor spellers often contend they're "born that way." "I simply can't learn to spell. Some people are born spellers, and some aren't," they say, as though that ended it. What a feeble excuse for mental laziness! The common-sense answer is that if you can learn to spell some words you can learn to spell others. And if you want to succeed in stenographic work, you have to be a good speller So, if your spelling is weak, get busy and strengthen it.

One business executive with whom I discussed the matter of learning to spell had this suggestion to offer: "Poor spellers should make a list of words they don't know, and study them. Each time a word is misspelled, or they come across a word they don't know and have to look it up, they should write it down and memorize the correct spelling. That is the only way to be entirely sure of that word in the future." But this sounds rather like locking the stable door after the horse is stolen.

Fortunately, there are helpful books that give lists of ordinary words often misspelled. And better yet, there are books that give the rules for learning to spell difficult words before making embarrassing mistakes. One [2] of the best of these is Woolley's *College Handbook of Composition*. Woolley not only gives methods of correcting spelling faults but analyzes why some persons can't seem to spell. He doesn't believe the ability to spell is a gift withheld by evil fairies at birth but calls attention to defective vision and incorrect hearing as some of the reasons for having difficulty with words. Among other things he, too, recommends keeping a list of words you misspell, and doing something about it.

More than any other group, the private schools have been appalled by the inability of the students to spell. They cannot risk their reputations by sending graduates into the business world until their spelling is as accurate as their shorthand and typing. Consequently, business schools have to teach spelling along with shorthand, typewriting, and office practice.

**Don't Use Dictionary As a Crutch.** Poor spellers give another excuse. "Oh, I can always use the dictionary," they say glibly and with self-satisfaction. To believe that you can use the dictionary as a daily crutch for your spelling is wishful thinking! A standard dictionary is essential equipment in the modern office, but its use should be for defining and spelling *unusual* words. These are not the words that show up the careless or poor speller. You will have no time in a busy day to stop and look up words you should know how to spell. Nor should you expect an employer to pay you while you repair the gaps in your education.

Let's take a look at those everyday words that poor spellers don't know, and don't know they don't know. The poor speller rarely looks them up; or if he does, he doesn't remember from one time to the next how they should be spelled. So words are transcribed with *ei* instead of *ie*, or vice versa; *c* is used for *s* or *k*; or *ance* takes the place of *ence*, and *ent* for *ant*, to mention only a few. As for *affect* for *effect*, or the other way around, the disturbing effect produced by the misuse of these two words in all the offices in the United States on any one day is enough to

[2] Another useful text is Hagar and Hutchinson's *Words—Their Spelling, Pronunciation, Definition, Application*, Fourth Edition.

affect the sanity of those countless executives who know how to spell.

But before we consign the dictionary to its many legitimate uses in an office, let me tell you a secret. There's a catch to using the dictionary. Only *if you know how to spell* will it be of much use to you! You have to know how to alphabetize before the dictionary will yield its treasures. How much of that sort of elementary training do you think you can get on office time?

**Misspelled Words on Application Blanks.** Although many applicants never know it, the everyday words they misspell on application blanks ruin their chances of being hired. Here are a few I have copied from applications handed to me by hopeful applicants.

| | |
|---|---|
| "filling" for filing | "inthing" for anything |
| "booking" for bookkeeping | "tempory" for temporary |
| "personal" for personnel | "stastical" for statistical |
| "septerated" for separated | "navery" for navy |
| "typest" for typist | |

You may say those are just careless mistakes. Perhaps so, but much too careless for a personnel director to overlook. Anyone that careless would certainly not be an exact and painstaking worker. And what would you say about the person who wanted "any execative work," or the college graduate who stated he had a "Batchalor" of Science degree? What I said to them was, "We have nothing open in your line."

A friend who hires office boys as well as clerks, typists, and stenographers wrote me from New York about a fifteen-year-old high school student she hired as a part-time office boy on a work permit. "On his application he gave the date of his birth as 'May 21, 1938.' But when he started on the job, he presented his Work Certificate showing he was born on January 21. Knowing he had had to present a birth certificate to get the work permit, I asked him why he had written May on the application blank. Much embarrassed, he said he put May on the application because he couldn't spell January! That's not all he can't spell," my friend added. "He can't spell anything."

**A National Spelling Bee.** Because of the seriousness of the spelling— or misspelling—among young people today, some wide-awake newspapers organized an annual nationwide spelling contest. Spelling bees are held on city and, finally, on state levels. Then after a process of "spelling down," each state sends its winning contestant to compete with the top spellers from other states. There are several prizes for the final winner, one of which is a trip to the White House to meet the President in person. When the ninth-grade girl who won a recent national contest met President Eisenhower, he confided to her that he had always had trouble spelling "syzygy." Perhaps one needs to know how to spell this astronomical word to become President, but employers will settle for anyone who can spell "too" and a dozen or more commonly used words they can't avoid dictating.

## A Good Vocabulary Is an Asset

If the tests made several years ago by the Human Engineering Laboratory of Stevens Institute of Technology at Hoboken, New Jersey, tell the truth, there's a definite relationship between the size of a person's vocabulary and his success in the world. Almost invariably, these tests showed that the most successful men had the largest vocabularies. As the less and less successful were measured, their vocabularies were found to be proportionately limited.

With this in mind, I suggest vocabulary building as a hobby that everyone, from the newest beginning typist to the head of the firm, can pursue to his pleasure and advantage and to the betterment of both correspondence and dispositions. A curiosity about words, as well as a love for them that leads one spontaneously to the dictionary, stimulates the imagination and will eventually rout that poverty of language that is such a handicap in business.

It is said that to read an ordinary newspaper a vocabulary of 5,000 to 14,000 words is needed. Yet in normal conversation, we use only one-fourth to one-half of the words we recognize in print. Various estimates of the number of different words used in the average telephone call or business letter range from 700 to 2,000. In *The Command of Words*,[3] S. Stephenson Smith states that these estimates are far too low and concludes that anyone with a high school education or its equivalent probably has a reading vocabulary of 9,000 to 14,000 words. With this encouraging assurance, Mr. Smith shows how a reading vocabulary can be expanded and how words recognized in print can be added to one's daily speech.

I believe that some such systematic program of self-improvement in both spoken and written English would prove one of the best means that a beginner could employ to rise from the novice class to that of the experienced young business person. It would probably do more to lift a discouraged stenographer out of a rut and into secretarial work than any other equal investment of time and money.

"But why should I improve my vocabulary?" asks Frances Jones, who works for an executive whose dictation never rises above the second thousand commonest words. Frances should ask herself whether she ex-

[3] *The Command of Words*. New York: Thomas Y. Crowell Company, Revised, 1949.

Even the most experienced office worker relies
on the dictionary—rather than on memory—for
spelling, word division, and shades of meaning.

pects always to work for the same person. The truth is that when a
man's vocabulary is so limited his frequent mispronunciation and misuse
of words place a very great responsibility on the stenographer.

*Nonexistent Words.* In former editions of this book, I referred to the
word "irregardless," so commonly used by dictators, as a word that *did
not exist.* Recently, not expecting to find it, I looked up the word in
Webster's *New Word Dictionary of the American Language,* but there
it was! The boss has made the dictionary! He will not know, or care,
that the definition says it is "a substandard or humorous redundancy"
for the word "regardless." In spite of the dictionary, my recommendation is the same as formerly—substitute the word the dictator meant to
use. I remember one occasion, during my advertising agency days, when
one of our stenographers came to me almost in tears. "Mrs. MacGibbon,
what shall I do?" she pleaded. "Mr. Brush is in a rage because I told him
I can't find any such words as 'diffugalty' in the dictionary." I laughed

and told her to write it "difficulty," and he would think her a very bright girl. You can see what had happened. The junior executive had so often playfully talked about a "diffugalty" that he thought at the moment there really was such a hybrid word.

Sometimes, mistakes in dictating are the result of careless pronunciation. There will be a transposition of syllables, such as "renumeration" for "remuneration." Or a syllable will be omitted, as "incidently" for "incidentally," or added, as "athaletic" for "athletic." These are corrections every transcriber is expected to make. She must train herself to hear such errors and know how to correct them, if she is to be really useful to a slovenly dictator.

"Schedual" for "schedule" is an error one hears often on the air and in conversations. Watch out for that one—as it will reach the office sooner or later. I have never known a dictator to write to his Senator or Congressman at "Washing, D. C.," but a teacher once told me of several of her former students who reported that they were working in "Washing, D. C." And a college graduate who worked for me always referred to the nation's capital thus, until I called the mistake to his attention. These were cases, I am sure, of a poor ear for words, but a secretary or stenographer cannot afford to have such a poorly trained ear, though she will often work for an employer who seems to have two of them.

If a knowledge of English will smooth your way when dealing with less educated employers, you will find a good general background of English indispensable when you work for a highly educated executive. And how welcome you will be to such a man! To be interrupted in the flow of dictation with "I didn't catch that word, please spell it" is doubly exasperating when the dictator realizes that the trouble is not due to faulty hearing or mumbled dictation but to actual word ignorance. The words that startle stenographers by their unfamiliar sounds are often no more unusual than "intrigue," "caucus," "inveterate," "irrelevant," or "flagrant."

*Technical Vocabularies.* Many businesses, especially technical ones, require special vocabularies, and they understand that a beginner must be trained until the unfamiliar words become part of her business equipment. The office manager of a large electrical manufacturing firm told me, "Our particular work is very technical; we have a vocabulary and a terminology all our own. However, we do not expect a beginner to come in, either from high school or college, and know 'lumens per watt' and other such phrases we use all day long. But we do expect her to have such a good background that she will not look aghast when she hears dictated reasonably common words that are part of the everyday conversation of our executives."

The legal profession has an extensive vocabulary that can be learned only by working in a law office or going to night school for a course in legal stenography. There is such a demand for trained legal stenographers that such evening courses are offered in the larger cities. This gives experienced stenographers who are employed an opportunity to prepare for these better paying positions. Legal terminology is largely derived from Latin. Fortunately, it is becoming more and more the custom in law offices to use the English pronunciation for Latin words and phrases. This is a big help to the stenographer who has not studied Latin.

The stock in trade of the medical stenographer is her knowledge of scientific, and especially medical, terms. The college graduate with a B.S. often finds her vocation in such a position, or as a chemical secretary, after she masters shorthand.

## NOT ALL EXECUTIVES ARE GRAMMARIANS

You may be surprised to learn that part of your job as a good stenographer is to correct the grammatical errors of your boss. But you must do it tactfully. One of the best ways to undermine yourself would be to say: "Mr. Brown, you dictated, 'What will we do now?' That's wrong. It ought to be, 'What shall we do now?' If you don't mind, I'll change it." Nine times out of ten, the Mr. Browns of the business world are too busy or too uninformed to notice when such changes have been made. So why mention them? Once in a while, you come up against executives who are sensitive about their lack of education and perversely defend their errors. "I don't care what the rule is, I want it to sound the way people talk," they will say. All you can do under such circumstances is to transcribe the dictation exactly as it is given you despite the error in grammar.

Susan Dean found this out in time to save a brand-new job. She had a degree in English and was overjoyed when the president of a manufacturing company employed her with the instruction that she was to make the correspondence of the executives more nearly grammatical. After Susan had straightened out their faulty construction and removed the split infinitives, the dictators did not recognize their own statements. They complained so loudly that Susan hastened to retype their letters as dictated, mistakes and all. Though the president of the company was a family friend, Susan wisely said nothing to him about the incident. Except for correcting an occasional "you was" or a mistake such as "talk it over with Mr. Day and I," she followed her intuition. Better to type "Yours of the ultimate instant received and contents noted" than suddenly to join the ranks of the unemployed! Not every executive wishes to be corrected, and not all of them realize the value of good grammatical construction.

It isn't likely that on a beginning job you will be given the full responsibility for sending out correct letters. But when you become a full-fledged secretary, you may be employed in an office where dictators are completely dependent on their amanuenses. Under such circumstances, executives often dictate hurriedly, without regard for form. "You fix it up," they will tell you confidently. Your responsibility then is heavy indeed. You must know the parts of speech and their proper usage, as well as all about nouns and their antecedents, and the rules governing their agreement. Sentence structure, case, mode, and tense become matters of importance in your life. Sometimes, you will have to consult a good grammar to trail a fine point—such as the use of the subjunctive—until you find the answer. You must be so familiar with the rules governing punctuation, paragraphing, hyphenation, capitalization, abbreviation, and syllabication that you know just what to do with a notebook full of straight dictation.

Actually work of this sort is editing and calls for editorial skill. You will find much sound help and advice in several of the handbooks for secretaries now on the market. And even though you are a beginner doing general typing, it is not too soon for you to get one of these excellent guides and study it. Such reaching for the stars will prepare you for advancement.

### THE GOOD SECRETARY COMPOSES LETTERS

Be assured that a flair for English composition is one sure route from stenographic to secretarial work. As one executive expressed it, "A businessman has to spend so much time directing the work of others, he is often pinched for time to give to his own work." He went on to say that the greatest aid he had found was a secretary who could answer half of his letters without his dictating them. Describing his perfect secretary he added, "I can say to her 'Tell him no,' and she will write a polite but definite note settling the matter. In contrast to this, I've had stenographers, who, given such an order, would write, 'Dear Sir: He says no. Very truly yours.' Of course, such girls will never become secretaries."

If you go to work for a not-too-large business firm, you may find a great deal of food for your ambition. For instance, if you are capable, you will soon learn to take routine correspondence off the hands of the busy executive for whom you work. Katherine Hall started as stenographer to the sales manager of a fair-sized manufacturing firm. She soon learned from his dictation the sort of letters he customarily wrote to the salesmen. Her next step was to study the salesmen's territories. She watched for her chance, and when it came, she was ready to say to her boss: "Here are letters from four of the salesmen wanting to know when the new catalogue will be ready; and two of them in nearby states wish to come in over the week end. I know about the catalogues, and if you'll settle the week-end plans, I can write the salesmen without taking your time for dictation." Soon her boss gratefully transferred all such correspondence to her. Katherine knew how to write clear and tactful letters to which the sales manager was glad to sign his name. And what a hound she was for watching detail!

In some businesses, a number of correspondents are employed who compose letters without dictation. In one manufacturing plant I know, the general manager handles all his work in this way. He keeps six able secretaries busy. Each one is in charge of a division of the correspondence, such as advertising, purchasing, brokers, and so on. The sales territory is divided among several of them. The manager discusses with each in turn what he wishes to have written, and then the secretary prepares the letters and brings them to him for his approval and signature.

### You Must Know Information Sources

In many firms, you will be expected to know not only English but a dozen other things. As a stenographer, you will be looked on as a source of miscellaneous information. For instance, if an executive asks, "Do they measure distance in miles or kilometers in El Salvador?" and you don't know, you should say, "I don't know, but I'll find out." And find out you must, within a few minutes or at most a few hours. The question would not have been asked if it were not important. Similarly, if an executive wishes to quote something in a letter and is not sure either of the exact wording or of the source, you will have to take whatever clue is given and look it up.

To do this creditably, you can see that your skills and abilities should range far beyond the limits of mechanical facility. Part of your training should be to know what you will need and where to locate it. In some offices, you will find a good reference library at hand. But it is just as well to build your own. Dictionaries, grammars, and handbooks are virtually part of your stock in trade, and a good investment. When it becomes the custom in an office for other stenographers to say, "Grace, may I borrow your grammar to look up something?" it is evident Grace is establishing herself both as a source of information and as an authority. She is putting herself another step ahead on the way to promotion. More often than employees realize, someone higher up discovers the person in the ranks who is depended on for general information by other members of the office staff. I heard of one smart girl who was paid

$20 a month more than the other stenographers because her employers felt she improved everybody's work.

And apart from the books on your desk, there are many other sources of reference that you will do well to learn how to use. The office of your local chamber of commerce is one of them. It will provide local data by telephone, or it will be glad to furnish pamphlets on request. You might call in person and find out what is available there.

The information desk in any city library can answer an astonishing number of seemingly unanswerable questions and can refer you to books that will answer many more. And knowing how to use a library to look up references is a great help. The Civil Service Commission, the United States Department of Commerce, and the Department of Labor are invaluable sources of statistical material and are most accommodating. A request to the Superintendent of Documents at Washington, D. C., or the United States Government Printing Office in Washington, will bring you a list of the pamphlets published by the Government. In their fields, the Department of Agriculture and the Office of Education, now in the newly formed Department of Health, Education, and Welfare, have assembled much useful information, which they are glad to give on request. Naturally, you will not fill your desk with unnecessary material of this sort, but you should know where to get the information you are likely to need in any position you take.

## Business Wants Legible Handwriting

You may think that, because your training provides you with the skill to use machines of one sort or another, you will have little need for writing by hand when working in an office. That is a mistaken idea that has defeated many a hopeful young business aspirant. There will be many times when you will have to "take pen in hand" if only to make notations and to write figures. Legible handwriting will help avoid errors.

To discover how necessary handwriting is today, a survey was made in a representative group of Eastern firms employing several thousand clerks. The employing firms were asked to state their views on the importance of handwriting (1) in selecting employees, and (2) in performing the job. Without exception, the business organizations stated that they preferred to have applicants fill out their application blanks in longhand. The assumption was that employment managers consider legibility and neatness of handwriting important when they are filling jobs where a certain amount of writing is required. Five companies reported that they sometimes rejected applicants at once because of poor handwriting, while the majority of the other firms admitted that, all other qualifications being equal, poor penmanship would tend to eliminate certain applicants in the final selection if penmanship were a requirement of the position. Among the 5,000 clerical workers employed by these firms, it was reported that over 50 per cent were doing some work that called for legible handwriting.

Bookkeeping and accounting headed the list of jobs in which handwriting was important because of the necessity for easily read figures. As one organization explained, you can guess at a word, but a figure must be read exactly the same by everyone. General clerical jobs were listed next in importance, followed by such other jobs as payroll, order, inventory, and schedule clerks, sales correspondents, telephone operators, and secretaries. "Legibility" was the word most often used in stating business demands in handwriting.

A state employment office had to interview one hundred applicants before it found ten persons who could write the small neat hand that an architectural client needed for drafting work. This same office told me it had frequent calls for persons to take inventory and here, too, had difficulty in finding individuals who could write neatly and legibly.

*Print Handwriting.* In recent years, a new type of handwriting, which is actually printing, has been taught in the schools in some parts of the country. Young people who have had the benefit of this training find it very helpful to them in filling out application forms. And does the clear, simple printing make a hit! The personnel director in a large department store in the South showed me the blanks filled out by the last hundred or more applicants. About a dozen of them were neatly printed. The remainder were quite illegible. "Perhaps I've overlooked some fine material," she said to me. "But I couldn't be bothered trying to decipher these messy-looking and unreadable applications. So I hired the people whose records I could read—those who used print handwriting." Of course, it isn't always as simple as this. But there is little doubt that print handwriting is especially important in stores, restaurants, and other places where employees have to make out sales checks.

### BOOKKEEPING REQUIREMENTS

So far, we have dealt chiefly with what business requires of employees engaged in the correspondence part of office work, where words are the medium. But there is that other equally important part, the recording or bookkeeping, where figures take the place of words. Here, perhaps fortunately, one's vocabulary is limited to the nine Arabic numerals and their zero, whose various combinations tell so many stories of profit and loss . . . and which for brevity put fiction to shame.

In this field, business requires all-round bookkeeping efficiency; that is to say, a knowledge of the principles of accounting and the ability to apply them in solving bookkeeping problems, the ability to interpret bookkeeping records and to record accurately all transactions of every kind according to the system in use. Business assumes, often wrongly, that while the student is acquiring this proficiency he is also gaining sufficient understanding of business itself to enable him to grasp the meaning of the different transactions. The student learns business theory in school, but only by experience in business can he acquire a real insight into the whys and wherefores.

As a beginner, in a small business where the work is not highly specialized, you may possibly be given an opportunity to keep the books and prepare profit-and-loss statements and balance sheets. However, if you know only the theory of keeping books and understand little of why books are kept and what the terms mean, you can easily make mistakes that may cost you your job. Sometimes, these mistakes could have been avoided by the simple application of common sense and reasoning, but in most cases you will need frequent conferences with executives as you go along.

*Figures Should Have Meaning.* To get students to think of bookkeeping transactions as life situations instead of merely rules to be followed, an instructor in a collegiate school of business asked a class to open a hypothetical shop and keep its books for a month. Two girls chose a hosiery shop in a town they knew well. They found out what rent they would have to pay, what their advertising would cost, and learned from a hosiery manufacturer that the markup should be 39 per cent. When their neatly typed final report was handed to the instructor, it showed that on an imaginary purchase of $3,000 worth of hosiery they had made a net profit of $2,100, in spite of the fact that they had paid out $1,100 for expenses and still had $2,000 of their original purchase in stock.

"You're money-makers, all right," laughed the instructor. He showed them that to make such a colossal profit they would have to sell stockings for several times the cost price, instead of at a markup of only 39 per cent. Yet neither of the girls was aware of the absurdity of their conclusions. The whole transaction was just so many figures to them, not life savings, worry, work, and hope deferred, as it would have been in real life.

Here's another instance of failure to realize what figures mean. The educational director of a nationally known office-machine company told me he once served with a group set up to test girls for cost accounting work. Several standard tests were tried to determine the girls' aptitude for figure work, but the committee finally discovered that all they needed was a simple arithmetic test: Multiply $\frac{1}{2} \times \frac{1}{2}$, or $.5 \times .5$

Only one out of ten applicants could do this fifth-grade problem. I believe that, regardless of how much or how little instruction these girls may have had in fractions and decimals, they could have solved it by common sense alone, as: One-half of one-half of an apple is one-fourth (or one-quarter) of an apple.

*Mathematics and Science Courses Help.* Time was, when shorthand and typing, plus the ability to spell and to do simple filing prepared the beginner for office work. Now, due to present technological trends, many high school graduates entering business need additional training. An interviewer in a state employment bureau, whose work takes her into high schools with vocational counseling, says that two or three years of high school mathematics and two years of science are desirable. If you doubt this, look over the advertisements for "Men Wanted" in any metropolitan newspaper and observe the demand for electronics engineers and physicists. A beginner going to work for one of these present-day executives should have some idea of what the business is all about.

REQUIREMENTS OF CLERICAL WORKERS

This chapter is scarcely complete without some mention of what management looks for in clerical workers. Because there are so many different kinds of clerical positions, generalizations as to knowledge requirements are impossible. However, whether your clerical work is simple or highly complex, you can be sure you will be able to use virtually everything you learned in school, with the possible exception of shorthand. You will need to be good at arithmetic, spelling, handwriting, and typing. Filing is also required in many clerical positions.

But apart from the skills fundamental to positions that are largely clerical, personal qualifications are equally fundamental, especially in routine jobs. Accuracy is absolutely essential. Common sense is a big help. To perform dull tasks, often in endless repetition, requires infinite patience. Monotony of work is so boring to some types of persons that they lose all interest in what they are doing, fall into a habit of daydreaming, and soon make mistakes in their work. For this reason, the temperamental who dislike doing the same thing twice in the same way are not well suited to clerical jobs. Among those who are most successful in these tasks are the individuals who take pride in turning out quality work and those who feel satisfaction in seeing their output run into quantity. Many clerical positions are best filled by men and women who like to see finished work piling up. But the need for accuracy puts on the brake with a warning, "Don't try to gain speed at the cost of quality!" It's the steady, patient worker who fits best into these jobs. Don't head toward clerical work unless you are sure that you have these qualifications in abundance.

## NATIONAL BUSINESS ENTRANCE TESTS

You may know about the National Business Entrance Tests. If not, inquire about them because the Certificate of Proficiency (or the Certificate of Superior Proficiency) awarded students who pass one or more of these tests is often the passport into a beginning office job. The National Business Entrance Testing Program, a cooperative project of business educators, school administrators, and office and personnel managers, is making a significant contribution to the growth and educational development of nearly 200,000 examinees in hundreds of school and businesses throughout the United States and neighboring countries.

The idea for this testing program originated with the late Professor Frederick G. Nichols who was on the faculty of the Graduate School of Education, Harvard University. Professor Nichols felt that both business and the schools would be aided if a series of tests simulating office duties could be developed and used to test the vocational ability of students entering office occupations. It was thought that students with proficiency in any of the major office skills who were also certified to possess a satisfactory background in business fundamentals and general information would be readily acceptable to business. The first tests were given in 1937 under the name of the National Clerical Ability Tests. Following World War II, the program was taken over as a nonprofit service project under the sponsorship of the United Business Education Association and the National Office Management Association. In 1947, the new series of tests were released under the title National Business Entrance Tests. The tests are currently administered under the direction of the Joint Committee on Tests, United Business Education Association. The tests are revised periodically to keep them in line with current office occupations skills.

The National Business Entrance Tests are given in April, May, and June in an ever-increasing number of testing centers. If five or more persons request that the tests be given in their locality and apply through their school to the Joint Committee on Tests,[4] arrangements will be made to establish a Testing Center at a place convenient for

[4] Address inquiries to Joint Committee on Tests, United Business Education Association (Dept. of N.E.A.), 1201 Sixteenth Street, N.W., Washington 6, D. C.

them. In order that you may know the wide scope of each test, here is a statement of the tests now given, with information as to what each test covers. A student taking any one of the skill tests is required also to take the Business Fundamentals and General Information Test.

1. *Stenographic Tests.* The work of a stenographer assumes the ability to take ordinary dictation for a reasonable length of time and transcribe the notes promptly and acceptably. Thus, these tests require the taking of dictation for extended periods of time. Only mailable letters are acceptable.

2. *Typewriting Tests.* Only infrequently is a typist required to type from straight copy. The tests in typewriting follow the more common office jobs, such as filling in forms, copying forms, setting up statistics, addressing envelopes, typing from rough drafts, and the like. Following directions is important in these tests.

3. *Machine Calculation Tests.* The calculating-machine operator must be able to handle a variety of computations rapidly and accurately as well as to maintain a satisfactory, sustained pace. Hence, the test is made up of samplings of computational work common to many offices. Only correct answers are acceptable.

4. *Bookkeeping Tests.* It is difficult to test the work of a bookkeeper in a short time. It is, therefore, necessary to sample common bookkeeping operations and knowledge. The tests include the application of recording techniques, the preparation of statements, the locating and correcting of inaccuracies, and so on.

5. *General Office Clerical Tests (Including Filing).* These tests measure facility in the skills of checking and classification, ability to interpret and produce business forms common to this field of work, and a knowledge of and speed in the finding and filing of business material.

6. *Business Fundamentals and General Information Tests.* These tests cover school-taught items, such as the mechanics of English, spelling, business vocabulary, and the like, and nonschool-taught knowledge that is absorbed from the radio, television, newspaper, and common customs.

The sponsors of this testing program insist that these are not aptitude tests but tests of vocational ability. Their definition of "vocational ability" is "the ability to handle successfully all the various classes of work associated with a specific type of job." To employers they say, "Any examinee passing these tests with a rating high enough to warrant certification by the Joint Committee has demonstrated potential ability to handle these specific types of work in an office, and is of productive value *immediately following employment, without additional training in the elementals associated with the job.*"

If you are interested in taking these tests, inquire whether they are given in your community, and if so, where and when. If they are not being given, your school will co-operate with you to ask that they be given in or near your school next spring. I can wish nothing better for you than that you become the proud owner of a Certificate of Superior Proficiency.

## QUESTIONS

1. What besides speed is required of a good typist?
2. What is meant by "excess capacity over the minimum requirement" in shorthand?
3. How important is transcription speed in holding one's job?
4. Is what constitutes a day's work different in various kinds of businesses? If so, why?
5. Do you think a typist should work to increase her speed after she gets a job? Should a stenographer do the same? If so, how would she go about it? Does the same thing apply to a bookkeeper?
6. In going to work for a company whose letter forms are unlike those taught in your school classes, would you call the attention of the office manager or the supervisor to the forms with which you are familiar?
7. Does the fact that a stenographer is overworked and lacks time to estimate how many lines her notes will occupy when transcribed constitute an alibi for poorly set-up letters?
8. Do you believe that a person is or is not a "born speller"? Is it a waste of time for a poor speller to try to improve?
   Would inability to spell be a handicap to a voice-machine operator? a file clerk? a PBX operator? a general clerk? a bookkeeper?
9. If you had difficulty with the spelling of certain words, to what extent could you make use of the dictionary to help hold your job?
10. Who needs a good vocabularly more, the stenographer who works for an educated man, or the one who takes dictation from a man of limited education?
11. Is it a safe practice to correct a dictator's English? If you do, should you
    a. Tell him what you have done?
    b. Let him discover it for himself?
    c. Take a chance on his not noticing the changes?
12. To advance into secretarial work, is it essential that a stenographer be able to compose letters with or without a word of instruction?
13. In what positions is legible handwriting considered important? What advantage can you see in print handwriting?
14. Why is it important that bookkeeping transactions be understood rather than merely be recorded as entries made according to certain rules?
15. Is a bookkeeper's ability judged by the time it takes him to do his work? If not, why not?
16. Why does a file clerk require a knowledge of alphabetizing? Why a good memory?

## TOPICS FOR DISCUSSION

1. What are the advantages, if any, of knowing before you go to work what business will require of you in skills and abilities?
2. Discuss why speed is not the only important thing in taking dictation and in typing and transcribing. If you are accurate but slow, are you competent to hold a position as a stenographer? What, according to Dr. Green's study, is the minimum dictation speed sufficient in approximately one-half of the stenographic jobs?
3. Whose responsibility is it to see that a letter is properly arranged on the letter sheet?
4. What kinds of positions seem to require an interest in and a knowledge of words, grammar, and spelling? Give your reasons. Is this knowledge wasted if you are engaged in clerical work, or are working with figures?
5. If you were never very good in English and felt that your study of it to date had not equipped you to meet the demands for stenographic success stated in this text, would you decide to

   a. Look more seriously at the other gateways to business?
   b. Enter on a more strenuous program of study to improve your English background?
   c. Laugh it off and take a chance?

6. A marine insurance company complained that Mary Boyle, a clerk, lacked ordinary common sense. The instance cited was this: In figuring the insurance on a ship valued at $20,000,000, Mary arrived at the cost of the policy as $1,000,000 and made out the papers accordingly. Mary was sure her figuring was correct and could not understand how her chief saw at once that she was wrong, and said, "Take that back, and make it right." The rate was 0.005 per cent, or 50 cents per $100. What was wrong?

   Discuss whether Mary's employer was making an unfair demand on her comprehension.

7. If you should find that you have taken more dictation than you can possibly transcribe before the hour when the letters must be ready for signature, will you

   a. Decide which are the most important letters and transcribe only those?
   b. Tell the dictator the situation and ask him which letters *must* go out that day?
   c. Say nothing and transcribe the letters in the order in which they were dictated, letting the balance remain in your book overnight?

8. In case you decide on the last-mentioned solution, what will you say if your employer notices that not all the letters he dictated have come to his desk to be signed?

## PROJECTS

1. Check with someone you know who is doing stenographic work in an office, and find out what is considered a day's work in her organization. Ask the number of letters (and their length) that your friend normally turns out; also, what other duties she performs, and the approximate amount of time devoted to each type of work. Prepare a brief report.
2. Make a list of ten words that you habitually misspell. State one or more ways in which you can correct this erroneous practice so that you will be sure of spelling them correctly in the future.
3. A college senior wrote the following letter to a vocational counselor who had spoken on the campus:

> The girls all enjoyed your lecture a lot and say they feel it has effected their whole life. Your advice was certainly practical. We wish we had more like it, for we are not as keen about the advice our parents give us. Probably it is alright, too, but they treat us like children, which don't help us develope. We are looking foreward to having you with us again next year.

   Check the misspelled words. Are they excusable? Are there any grammatical errors in the letter? If so, cite them.

   Rewrite the letter so that it contains no errors in spelling or grammar.
4. If you were Miss White, in the text, and were asked to find out how distance is measured in El Salvador, how would you go about it? Get the information for class, and be prepared to report how and where you found it.
5. Choose one of the following businesses, and state how you would build up sources of information if you went to work in a stenographic position there, with the prospect of working into a secretaryship.

   a. Manufacturing chemist, specializing in cosmetics
   b. Travel bureau, specializing in foreign tours
   c. Trust department of a bank

   Without going into too much detail, indicate the kinds of books or periodicals to which you would need access and where you would find them; also, other channels of information that might prove useful.
6. In addition to a knowledge of bookkeeping, state five traits or aptitudes a person who wishes to remain in bookkeeping should have. Be prepared to discuss these in class.
7. Write a 500-word paper on the National Business Entrance Tests, explaining what they are and when and where they are given; also name the sponsoring organization. Following this, add your own comment on the value of these tests and the Certificate of Proficiency, or Superior Proficiency, to a beginner who plans to enter business.

# CHAPTER 5

# Sources of Jobs

Now that you know something about possible positions open to you and what you will be expected to do as an employee, what about getting a job? Well, that is a job in itself. But like every other thing worth doing, there is a right way to go about it. First, you need to know *where* to look for work. Then, *how* to look. Let's begin by finding out where the sources of jobs are.

Some graduates are lucky in finding work almost immediately after they leave school. I say *lucky,* but often this is not true. You may jump at the first job offered, when it might be wiser to take a bit more time to look around, learn more about what jobs are available, and try for the most suitable ones. For it is possible that a first job, carefully selected, may be one in which you might stay on, and advance. But a first job, snapped up with little thought, may turn out to be something for which you are not well suited or properly prepared—yet you may spend weeks, months, or even years before you realize it. To prevent that from happening, this chapter will provide you with information as to *where,* *when,* and *what* jobs are to be had. Then you will know better how to go about lining up that all-important first job. In other words, we want to help your luck.

Speaking of luck, Carl F. Wente, formerly president of the Bank of America, in a talk before a group of San Francisco high school students, said: "Luck is not something that happens to you. It is something you make. In fairy tales, the hero, when grown, sets out to make his fortune. You can't wait until you are grown. You have to begin in early life."

Before you leave school is a good time to lay your plans. What will be your first step? Obviously, you can't get a job without being interviewed by people who have positions to fill. What you will need is appointments for interviews with these people. There are several ways to secure such appointments, ways in which other persons with the right contacts can help you. But you must help them help you. You are not yet the hero or heroine of the piece, but you have a definite part to play. Here are the first things you can do:

1. Register and work closely with your school placement bureau.
2. Consult family, friends, and acquaintances for possible leads.
3. Visit employment agencies.
4. Read the want ads.

*When* shall you start? Right now. *Where* shall you start? Right where you are. The first two items on the above list are things you can begin at once. The last two should be left until you have graduated and are ready to apply for a job. We shall discuss all four points in detail, but confidentially, if you really work at the first two, you may get a good job without needing to visit an employment agency or answer a want ad. Even though your graduation may be months off, it is not too soon to ask the advice and help of your school placement bureau. If you have been consulting with your teachers and the placement office while making your tentative career plan, they know something about the type of work you hope to get. Tell them you plan to co-operate with them, and ask how you can do so.

## WORK CLOSELY WITH YOUR SCHOOL PLACEMENT BUREAU

Perhaps you have not realized how important the placement office of your school is, and how much it can help you. Today, most four-year colleges, junior colleges, private business schools, and vocational high schools maintain employment bureaus for the sole purpose of placing their graduates in jobs. Naturally, the number of calls these offices receive from employers depends on the state of the labor market. When times are not too good and plenty of experienced office workers are available, the schools and colleges do not always get enough orders to place all their graduates in jobs. Then they have to choose the students they think will make the best employees, and they send several to be interviewed for every position. Under these conditions, they can only hope, "May the best man win."

But when times are good, with business booming and needing many new workers, those employers who would normally prefer to hire experienced persons are forced to take beginners. Then the schools and colleges get more orders, or listings, than they can fill. Beginners really have a chance to show their newly acquired skills and abilities. The truth is that school employment bureaus are in a better position to place their graduates than are other types of employment agencies. Because the schools know their students well, they can make a better selection of applicants for a position than can an interviewer in an employment agency who has barely met the graduate.

So if your school has such a bureau, co-operate with it. Go in and talk with the placement officer a few weeks before you graduate. Go now. It's none too soon. Find out what kinds of jobs are listed in the school office, what salaries are paid, and what positions you can reasonably expect to be available. Ask for advice and help. Go out on every interview the bureau can arrange for you. If one of these interviews leads to a job, take it, for it is likely to be your best bet. Remember, no one will be quite so interested in placing you as the school from which you are graduated.

And do your part. Don't say to yourself: "Oh, I'm in no hurry. My school will get me a job. I'll just stay at home and wait until they do." It's surprising how many students take this attitude. Of course, if they don't care how long they wait, their schools doubtless will get them jobs. But that may take several weeks, or even months, since the number of jobs listed with the schools depends on the needs of business. Remember that the students who co-operate most closely with their schools usually go to work first. When a school placement officer knows that a graduate is leaving no stone unturned on his own account, it is only natural that the officer will applaud this attitude by doing his best for such an up-and-coming young person.

When a school does not have enough job orders for all its graduates, the principal or the placement director will often suggest that you go to a commercial employment agency. Some schools multigraph a list of names and addresses of employment agencies in the locality. Your school will not charge a fee for getting you a job, and neither will your state employment service, but private agencies will. In case you wish to open up more possible channels of employment than your school provides, other types of employment agencies are discussed later in this chapter.

### CONSULT FAMILY, FRIENDS, AND ACQUAINTANCES

You will be surprised to find how many worth-while leads are close at hand, in your own home, among friends, and acquaintances. I don't mean they have jobs to hand out to you immediately. But unless you have been so rash as to go to a strange community to seek a position, there are sure to be persons in your immediate circle who, because they go to business daily, can offer you invaluable advice and assistance.

Apparently, this group close at hand is one of the best possible sources of jobs, if a survey made of high school graduates in a California city of 350,000 is even fairly typical. A year after the graduates of this city's eight high schools had gone to work, the city's vocational schools checked these former students by post card, asking them through what sources they had got their first permanent jobs. By far the largest single source was "Tips from friends, relatives, and acquaintances," which accounted for 47 per cent of the jobs. The remaining 53 per cent was divided between employment agencies, both school and private, unaided personal efforts, and miscellaneous sources. Since this may indicate a gold mine in your own back yard, why not do some digging there?

Here is another study, this one from the employers' point of view, for they want to know how best to recruit office workers. The personnel practices of 324 companies were checked, and a tabulation made as to how 1,594 employees for office jobs were secured. Here it is:

| SOURCE OF EMPLOYMENT | NUMBER OF EMPLOYEES |
|---|---|
| Direct application to personnel office | 273 |
| Employee recommendation | 256 |
| Advertising (want ads) | 232 |
| Private employment agencies | 195 |
| State employment service | 194 |
| High school placement offices | 156 |
| University and college placement offices | 146 |
| Private business school placement offices | 142 |

You see that "employee recommendation" was a close second here—and this is another term for friends and relatives.

Start considering your relatives and friends and making a list of them and their business connections. Begin with the family, and then add the names of old friends, especially older people who may be in positions of prominence or may be employers in their own right. Putting such information in concrete form will open your eyes to many possibilities you might otherwise overlook. Next on the list, put your acquaintances, schoolmates who are employed, friends of friends who may be able to help you, and possibly neighbors. List everyone who constitutes even a remote link with business, and note the position and the name and address of the firm with which the person is connected. You cannot tell which of them may prove important, so list them all!

*There Is a Right Kind of Pull.* Self-reliant young people often object to using *pull* or seeking out their relatives and friends in getting work. There is no disgrace in using pull in its best sense. By "pull" I do not mean forcing anyone through family or social connections to give you a job you don't deserve. I do mean following up and consulting all your friends, relatives, and acquaintances whose interest and recommendation may help you to meet people who can employ you. If you are the kind of person who is backward and retiring in social contacts, friendly assistance can smooth the way and help you present your qualifications more forcefully. Another point to consider is that many vacancies never reach the schools, employment agencies, or the want-ad columns. They are filled within the organization by friends of those already employed, as in the employer survey just quoted. You might as well be one of them.

I suggested that you make a list of your relatives and friends, with their addresses as well as the names of the firms where they are employed. Add any specific information they give you about jobs or persons to see in those firms at a later date. This is something you can do while you are still in school, and it will be practical homework that should pay off later. But unless you are businesslike and systematic about keeping these records for yourself, there is not much use in your asking for the information. You can't possibly remember it all, and you would be embarrassed to have to ask later, "What was the name of that man in the steel company—the one you told me about last month?"

Obviously, you will not be in a position to call on these leads until you have been graduated, for you don't apply for a job until you are ready to take one. Put this material in a 3-×-5-inch card file, or keep it in a notebook, until you are ready to use it. Allow a reasonable time, say, ten days to two weeks after you have finished school, and if by that time you have not got work with the aid of your school office, get out your list, and get busy on it. Now you want appointments for interviews. "Calling cold"—that is, without an appointment in advance—is difficult, even for experienced interviewees, and I don't advise your doing it unless it is absolutely necessary. Your reason for collecting names is to avoid this. (The procedure for "calling cold" is explained in Chapter 8. If you do not get work in one of the other ways suggested, you can use the method outlined there.)

*Make Appointments for Interviews.* Use your judgment in deciding on the best approach to each person on your list. If possible, you should see these individuals in person; but when unavoidable, you may use the telephone, and under special circumstances, which will be explained in a later chapter, you may write to them. You are seeking information from them—asking a favor—so it is important to consider their convenience. Under no circumstances should you call anyone who has an ordinary business position to the office telephone for such a personal reason as giving you job information. This applies to relatives as well as friends, for business makes no distinction in asking that personal phone calls to employees be limited to emergencies. If the person can be reached at home after hours, call then, and ask for suggestions about positions likely to be available in his firm or elsewhere.

If any of your relatives or intimate family friends own their own businesses or are in important executive positions, it is not incorrect for you to telephone them at their offices, but it may be ill-advised. Interrupted at a busy moment, they may dismiss the matter without giving your problem the thought they would have given it at a more suitable time. So it is better, in calling them, simply to ask for an appointment.

For instance, you might phone Mr. Brown, a family friend whom you always call Uncle George, and say: "This is Mary Wells, Uncle George. I have just finished school and am starting to look for work. Would you be good enough to take time some day soon to give me a little advice?" If he says he has no jobs, you might hasten to assure him that you are only seeking his advice because he has had business experience and is in a better position than you to know where there may be openings. Since most people enjoy giving advice, such an appeal should either bring suggestions right away, or at least gain for you the desired appointment and consideration of your problem.

An interested friend, who knows you and your background and potentialities, can do more for you by a mere word than a stranger, such as an employment agent. And appealed to with courtesy and dignity, the average person is almost invariably helpful and kind.

Let us suppose that Mr. Brown (Uncle George) has agreed to see you and give you the advice you asked for. He might say, "Well, Mary, I can't realize you are grown up and ready to go to work. Sorry we haven't a thing here now. What can you do?" When you have told him, he may say, "I have an idea. I know John Williams over at the Central Bank. One of my best friends. Go see him, and tell him I sent you. They take on beginners, I know." Mr. Brown may even be interested enough to call up his friend and make an appointment for you. Or he may give you a letter of introduction to Mr. Williams. In fact, your Uncle George may get so interested in giving you advice that he will provide a whole list of leads that you can follow up. And one of them may send you to the job that is waiting for you. The circles from a casual stone tossed into the pond of possibilities may grow very wide indeed.

Perhaps, instead of offering definite suggestions and actual names, Mr. Brown may dispense advice and plenty of it. Then it is wise to listen politely and *really* listen, for in this way you may get valuable tips that can come only from someone who is in the thick of business. Mr. Brown may say he understands that a certain insurance company is expanding; although he knows no one there, it might be well for you to go and see them. He may end the conversation by saying, "Sorry I couldn't be more helpful, but I'll bear you in mind." Here is where your manners help you. Thank him sincerely, and keep the door open for a return visit by saying, "If I haven't found work, may I call you in a week or so to remind you of that promise?"

*Leads Provide Prospects.* Friends who may have been working only a few months themselves can be a gold mine of suggestions and information. Ask if you can have a "Dutch" lunch with them, and meet them promptly wherever they lunch, at whatever time they say. (Remember, they probably have to watch the clock.) They can give you the names of employment agencies they found useful, or they may even know of jobs. When you don't need a job, you often know of several that are available. Ask these young friends or acquaintances for advice, and you'll get it. Take their advice, for they have been through the business of job seeking recently themselves.

When any of these sources of information provides what appear to be live job prospects, follow them up in your most efficient manner, and try to secure an interview with the person in charge of employment. (The way to do this is explained in the next chapter.)

Your own list of people you know may or may not prove productive in locating a job, but usually this is one of the best possible sources of tips. One young man I recall, John Graham, carefully listed all the family friends and relatives and called on everybody they sent him to, only to decide it was all "the bunk," as he put it. "They just stall by sending me from one person to another," he complained. "I'm sick and tired of the run-around." So he concentrated on employment agencies.

Then out of a clear sky a distant relative, whom he had never met, heard through John's grandmother that he was looking for a job. Instantly, the relative took an interest and asked John to come and see him. The result of that interview was that John went out with three letters of introduction to men this employer knew and who he felt might be able to employ John. At the first place he called, they were looking for the very skill he had to sell, that of making store displays for the holidays, and he was asked to report for work after lunch. John has changed his mind and now says that the personal recommendation and the letter of introduction are "swell" ways to get a job.

### REGISTER AT EMPLOYMENT AGENCIES

As stated earlier, your chances of securing a job through your school or through contacts made via the friendship and acquaintance route are so good that you may never have to call on an employment agency. But you should have information about them, just in case.

In large cities, experienced workers who, for one reason or another, are seeking work usually find the employment agency the best source of jobs. But beginners cannot depend too much on this means of securing employment, since all agencies do not handle jobs for the inexperienced. When they do, they usually have a special department by some such name as the junior division, since in placement terms beginners are known as juniors.

The best way to find out which employment agencies are interested in placing beginners is to ask them. And the quickest way to do this is to make a list of commercial employment agencies from the classified section of the telephone directory, noting only those that specialize in office positions. Some of the agencies will not answer questions from applicants over the telephone, but enough of them will supply information on this point to give you a few places to begin making calls.

*Your State Employment Service.* There are several kinds of employment agencies other than your school placement bureau, which you as a prospective worker should know about. First on your list should be your state employment service, provided there is an office in your city. Throughout the United States, there is a free employment-agency service, in both large and small cities, set up under Federal and state laws. You will find one under the name of your state, as "Wisconsin State Employment Service," "Connecticut State Employment Service," and so on. In many localities, these are the only employment offices available and so are doubly important for you to know. Not only do these state employment offices function without charging a fee for placing applicants in jobs, but they have special departments and, in some cases, even special headquarters for junior placement. Where junior departments are maintained, there are vocational counselors as well as interviewers, since these state offices believe that recent high school and even college graduates, with or without specific training in skills, often need counseling when looking for their first jobs.

But there is another reason why you should call early on your state employment service. These offices handle the United States social security registration, and before you can hold a job, you will have to obtain your individual number. This is an entirely separate transaction from registering for employment. So remember that you have two errands—both important—at the state employment office in your city. Some schools advise their students to obtain their social security numbers before they are graduated. You might ask your teachers what they recommend. In case there is no state employment service in your locality, your school will be able to tell you how to secure your social security card and number. And when you get your card, always carry it with you.

*Private or Commercial Agencies.* Next in importance are those employment agencies known as private or "commercial" agencies that pay their expenses out of the fees they charge applicants for securing positions for them. The services of such agencies are usually free to employers. But in some cities, at times when it is difficult to get enough employees, the employer, and not the applicant, is willing to pay the fee. This was a fact at one time in New York, Chicago, and St. Louis, when in San Francisco and other cities, the fee still was paid by the applicant.

There are many high-grade commercial agencies operating in cities throughout the United States. Visit some of them, provided they accept registration from beginners. Because their reputation and their success depend on the kind of employees they send out, these agencies are usually careful to deal only with applicants and employers who are responsible. Such agencies can often put applicants in touch with employers whom they would not be able to reach themselves.

A reliable employment agency saves employers much time by selecting, from many applicants listed with it, a few whom it thinks best qualified to fill each existing vacancy. After they have worked together for years, an interviewer in an agency knows, almost as well as a firm's personnel director, what type of applicant has a fair chance of being accepted by certain employers. Knowing an employer's whims and preferences and wishing to retain his business, the head of a commercial agency is careful to send only those who merit recommendation.

But sometimes mistakes occur. A New York employment-agency executive tells of sending a stenographer to one of its best clients, only to receive an irate telephone call from the employer. "What do you mean, sending us a girl with green shoes?" he demanded. The employment interviewer apologized, explaining that above the desk she had seen only the applicant's neat black and green costume. The too-extreme footwear had escaped her eagle eye.

When you call on a commercial employment agency, if you are asked to register you may know that the interviewer thinks you can be placed. Most agencies of this type will not waste words or application cards on anyone whom they consider unemployable. When you register, it is customary to sign a contract agreeing to pay a certain percentage of your first month's salary, if and when a position has been secured for you through the agency. These percentages vary in different localities and range from 10 to 35 per cent of the first month's salary. In some states, the fee charged is regulated by law, and the owners of the agency are licensed by the state. As with any written agreement, you should

read carefully the contract you sign with an agency, so that you understand what you will be obligated to pay if they place you.

This is a legitimate system of employment-agency operation. But
you should beware, however, if you are ever asked to pay for registering, or if an advance fee is demanded to put you on a "preferred" list.
Such procedure is not the accepted one. When you deal with a first-class
agency, you pay nothing until the job is obtained and you have received
your first salary check. Usually, the fee is payable in several install-
ments, if this is more convenient to the payee.

You can easily secure from employed friends the names of agencies
they have found reliable. When you have found an agency through
your own efforts, check it through your school or indirectly through
business firms. Most businesses secure employees through commercial
agencies, and any of them would be willing to give you the names of the
select few that have been supplying them with help over a period of
years.

*Other Types of Agencies.* Non-fee-charging agencies are maintained
by the Y.W.C.A., Y.M.C.A., Hebrew and Catholic young people's organizations, and some of the fraternal orders and welfare agencies. Although many satisfactory positions have been secured through the kind
offices of these groups, sometimes they do not have as good listings of
positions as are to be found in the commercial agencies or the state employment offices. However, if you have any connection with such an
organization, which handles placement and is interested in assisting beginners, by all means get your name on its list of applicants as soon
as possible. You never can tell from what source that job of yours will
materialize.

*Technique in Visiting Agencies.* To get the best results from any
type of employment agency, you must keep in close touch with it. This
means calling frequently at an agency that has registered you, if you are
encouraged to do so. Otherwise, your registration card is likely to be
closed out because, not having heard from you, they assume you have
secured employment. This is especially true with all the state employment services which, because they handle so many registrations, can deal
only with live material.

All agency calls should be made in the morning, since it is then they
usually receive listings by phone from employers who are short of
workers. Some agencies like to have placeable applicants sit in the waiting rooms for an hour or so every morning on the chance that positions
for which they are fitted will be telephoned in. Ask advice on this point
from any interviewer who seems interested in placing you. Different offices have different preferences and procedures in this matter. The main

thing for you to keep in mind is that no matter how desirable an applicant you seem to the agency, you may be forgotten in favor of someone who is on the spot at the moment. Only when there is no qualified person on hand does the agency telephone registrants.

You cannot possibly be in more than one agency at once, and yet you may wish to be registered with several. Consequently, you will not only have to spread your mornings, but you will need to arrange some way to receive telephone calls. Your mother can be of service to you in this. She can take calls and either say where you are or promise to get a message to you promptly. By telephoning home at stated intervals, you can catch important emergency calls. If you are living in a club or boarding-house, it is important that you arrange for intelligent telephone service. Otherwise, you may miss a call that might be the "go" signal for the very job you are looking for.

Be sure that the telephone number where messages for you can be received is recorded accurately at the agency, and keep any changes up to date. If an agency takes sufficient interest to telephone you about a position, you're lucky. But if they don't get the number or, getting it, find that you are out of town or have moved, your luck is against you. A notation is made on your registration card, and you are taken out of the active file. This means that you will never hear from them again. They are too busy with the applicants they can reach to have time to indulge in detective work to find you.

## READ THE HELP-WANTED ADVERTISEMENTS

This section will be helpful to you only if you live or seek work in a city whose newspapers carry classified advertisements, "Help Wanted—Men," "Help Wanted—Women." In large cities and some smaller ones, employers use such advertisements to get in touch with applicants. In many cities, employment agencies also use these columns to advertise positions they are trying to fill. If your newspapers carry such listings, I suggest that, while you are following up personal leads and registering at employment offices, you also keep an eye on the help-wanted columns. In fact, I urge you to acquire the habit of reading the want ads while you are in school. It is an excellent way to become familiar with the type of positions available. It will also give you an idea of what salaries are being paid and what qualifications are most frequently demanded. The help-wanted columns of the classified advertising in your Sunday newspaper, in particular, may be considered a barometer of employment conditions in your community. When times are good, there are many advertisements of firms seeking help. In bad times, most of the advertisements are inserted by persons seeking jobs.

The want-ad section of the daily newspaper is one of the most popular sources of information about job openings.

A. Devaney, Inc.

***When Agencies Use Help-Wanted Advertisements.*** When the employment agencies advertise positions that have been listed with them, the agency's name and address are given and not those of the employer. If you are interested in the position advertised, you should call at the agency at once and try to convince an interviewer that you are someone she can recommend for the job. If you succeed, you, and sometimes one or two other applicants, will be sent for interviews at hours arranged by the agency. When jobs are scarce and applicants abundant, the private agencies do a sorting job and send, or "refer," two or three persons for each job order. At such times, when they can choose from many selections, some employers insist on seeing more. But when the situation is reversed and the agencies are short of placeable applicants, an employer is lucky if an agency can send him one acceptable secretary, stenographer, typist, or bookkeeper.

While in New York City to get material to pass on to you, I was in a small but select employment agency. The phone rang, and the interviewer to whom I was talking began to apologize to an employer because she had not been able to send him a secretary. She tried to encourage him by saying she would keep on looking but that good secretaries were scarce. A nice-looking girl who had been filling out an application at a nearby desk brought it to my interviewer friend. Immediately, the young lady was given a card of introduction to an employer. The interviewer then called the man to whom she had just been talking. "I'm sending you a secretary," she said. "She types 45 words a minute, can take dictation at 80 words a minute, and can run an Underwood Elliott Fisher billing machine. You can get her for $245 a month."

The employer was evidently delighted, but I was amazed. The interviewer handed me the girl's application, which showed five years' experience as a billing-machine operator and one year as a typist. "She didn't like the billing machine and wants to change," the interviewer told me.

"You don't mean to say you can send out as a secretary a girl with no better skills or work experience than that," I commented.

"Oh, she won't be a secretary for a while yet," said the interviewer, well pleased at making the placement. "They will put her in their stenographic pool for two months so she can get her speed up. She'd be due for a raise then, anyway, so she will become a secretary then." This is how easy it is for anyone with experience to get a good job when office help is scarce.

*Replying to Box Numbers.* When an employer advertises direct, he usually gives a box number, which means that you will have to apply by letter to that number, stating your qualifications. Read each advertisement carefully, and do not apply unless you have the skills and other qualifications specified in the advertisement. Should your letter interest the employer or personnel director, you will receive a reply asking you to call for an interview. Young people have told me they answer all the advertisements and never get a reply. This is proof that they are wasting their time, stationery, and postage answering advertisements for which they are not qualified. You can congratulate yourself when you do get an answer to your letter. It shows not only that you were selective in your choice of advertisements, but that your letter was outstanding. It indicates, too, that you know how to write a good letter of application —an important part of your job-seeking equipment.

When a help-wanted advertisement does not specify that experience is necessary and the job seems something a beginner could do, it is a good thing to follow through on it. You may get nothing out of it but experience, but anything that helps you learn work-seeking procedures is of value to you.

*Picture This Scene.* Occasionally, in advertising a position, an employer will give his street address. He seldom does more than once, for when there are many applicants (as often happens in large cities), he wishes he had given a box number. Don't let a situation like this scare you away. It will be valuable experience for you to have a good look at your competition and a lesson in how not to act! The employer sometimes tries to fill the position without interviewing everyone, and often he can. The applicants may be interviewed in the order of their arrival. But when a firm has a great many applicants, as may happen if the job is a good one and such jobs are scarce, an employee of the company may be asked to select the most likely-looking ones. If your appearance is promising, you may be asked to stay for an interview. Many a young person has finally reached the employer because he or she knew enough to sit quietly in a waiting room and to refrain from chewing gum or slouching.

In all these sources of jobs, we have been talking about positions in private business. But there is another important source of work in which you may be interested, where most of the jobs are under civil service. Let's start with Government jobs.

## THE UNITED STATES GOVERNMENT AS EMPLOYER

Do you know that the United States Government is the largest employer in our country? Largest in number of civilian employees, and largest in breadth of employment, since its jobs are all over the world. However, in starting out, you are not likely to seek overseas employment, so we shall confine ourselves to the Government work available for young men and women in Washington, D. C., and in your own city or state.

At one time, working for the Government usually meant going to Washington, where most of the jobs were. But because of decentralization of Government activities, this is no longer true. Today, the headquarters offices of most Federal agencies are in Washington, D. C., and what are called the "field establishments" of the agencies are located throughout the various states and territories. The great majority of Federal civilian employees work in these field establishments, which consist of navy yards, arsenals, quartermaster depots, post offices, veterans' hospitals, and agricultural research centers.

The number of Federal employees is constantly changing. Before World War II, they numbered about 1,000,000. During wartime, a peak of 3,700,000 was reached. After the war, the number decreased to around 2,000,000, but when hostilities broke out in Korea, the number rose again. Today, there are approximately 2,500,000 civilians on the Federal payroll. But less than one-tenth of these work in Washington. California, with 260,848 Federal workers, tops all the other states and actually has more Government employees than there are in the Washington metropolitan area. You may be interested to know that, according to census reports, one out of every four Government employees is a woman.

Now that the United States Government has jobs all over the country, its policy is to recruit new employees for work near their homes. To accomplish this, Government representatives go in person to the high schools and private business schools, as well as to the colleges, offering good jobs to seniors on graduation.

*Many Kinds of Federal Jobs.* "What kinds of jobs?" you may ask. The answer is, "All kinds." The idea that all Government employees are clerks is not true. In fact, they work in as great a variety of jobs as do employees in private industry.

I have before me a booklet entitled *Working for the U.S.A.*, issued by the United States Government. It tells how to apply for a civil-service job and what the Government expects of Federal workers. This booklet lists one hundred examination titles, since you have to pass a civil-service examination for most Government jobs. Many of the positions on this list—such as engineer, librarian, nurse, horticulturist, social worker, and meteorologist—require specialized college training. But there are many jobs—such as telephone operator, typist, office-machine operator, stenographer, storekeeper, and rural mail carrier—that would not require a college education. Just as in civilian life, a vocational college education fits you for a higher starting job.

Apprentice training programs are conducted in many Government establishments, such as shipyards, air stations, and arsenals, which employ large numbers of men in mechanical trades. Young men with mechanical aptitudes can earn a salary while learning a trade, and at the end of the four-year course become journeymen in their chosen trades.

*How to Apply for a Government Job.* Your local post office is your first and nearest source of information about civil-service examinations. In most post offices, except those in the 15 cities where civil service regional offices are located, there is one employee, called a Civil Service Information Representative, who can give you complete information. He has application forms and notices of local, regional, and nationwide examinations for which applications are currently being accepted. If he does not have the particular information you are seeking, he will tell you where to write for it. And he can tell you where an examination is to be held, as well as the final date when your application for permission to take the examination will be accepted. Notices of forthcoming examinations are often displayed in local post offices. From these you may get information without having to ask the representative referred to above.

Everything you will be told in the next chapter about filling out an application form is true when you apply for permission to take a Government examination. The announcement will list the general requirements for the examination, and you should read these carefully. There are age limits for some examinations; almost all require American citizenship; some require a stated amount of experience in a certain line; and sometimes the positions are in Washington, while you may be interested only in local employment. If you cannot meet all the requirements stated in an announcement, you should not apply, for you will not be accepted.

The first application form you fill out—that in which you apply for permission to take a certain examination—will be short, but it must be filled out neatly and truthfully. After you send this in, you will be notified as to whether or not you are accepted to take the examination. If you are accepted, you will be sent a two-page or four-page application, on which your future may depend. If possible, type your statements on this longer form; otherwise, print carefully, and answer *all* the questions. For many Government positions, the examinations are not written tests. Instead, you are graded by the civil-service examiners on the training and experience shown on your detailed application. Also, be sure to spell every word correctly, and *do not abbreviate*. Fill out all the required forms before you report for an examination; otherwise you may not be admitted to the examination room.

Let's suppose you are accepted to take a written examination. You go to the designated place at the appointed time, take the test, and pass it. Your name is then placed on a list of "eligibles." The higher your rating in the examination, the higher will be your place on the list. Appointments are made from the top of the list, with the appointing officer allowed to choose from the first three names that top the list. The lengthy application form you filled out, along with your name, goes to the appointing officer in the department where a vacancy is to be filled. You may then be called for a personal interview. If you were careless, and your application is full of blots and erasures, not to mention misspelled words, you run the risk of not being chosen. Each person on a given list is entitled to be considered three times, but if he has not been chosen after the third interview, in the discretion of the hiring officer he may be eliminated from the list.

*Advantages of Working for the United States Government.* Your Uncle Sam is a good boss. If you go to work for him, your starting salary will probably be somewhat higher than it would be for the same work in private employment. Raises are automatic, and you have the opportunity to take promotional examinations so as to advance in both your work and your pay. Civil service does not protect incompetence, however, and you can be fired for inefficiency or unbecoming conduct, as you would be by a non-Government employer. Your work week is five 8-hour days, with 13 days vacation, called "annual leave" your first year. After 15 years you would receive 26 days vacation. You are given 15 days sick leave annually, cumulative indefinitely.

## STATE, COUNTY, AND MUNICIPAL JOBS

In addition to Federal jobs, there are opportunities for employment in your state, county, and city governments. In most areas, these are now under civil service or the merit system. The state department of employment in your city or town is your best source of information as to when and where examinations will be held. Sometimes, these examinations are given in the offices of the state department of employment by its personnel. Also, your school should be able to tell you what positions in state, county, or municipal offices your training would fit you for, and when examinations will be given.

## QUESTIONS

1. Do you know whether your school maintains a placement bureau? If not, find out.
2. If it does, what is the advantage to you of working closely with this bureau?
3. Why should relatives, friends, and acquaintances be advised of your job-getting activities?
4. Should you use pull when you start looking for work?
5. Is it considered right to telephone to business people you know at their offices to ask whether they can tell you of any job openings?
6. What other placement or employment agencies besides those operated by schools are recommended as supplementary means of obtaining interviews? Which charge fees for securing positions for applicants? Which perform this service free of charge?
7. Why does your text suggest that you call first on your state employment service?
8. Do all employment agencies place beginners? What is the term used in agencies to designate beginners?
9. Is it necessary to call at an employment agency more than once? Should an agency be expected to get you a job after the first interview?
10. Do employment agencies send out on interviews everyone who applies to them? If not, why not? On what basis do they make their selections?
11. What is the value to you of beginning to read the help-wanted columns in your daily paper before you leave school, since you are not yet ready to answer advertisements?
12. Why do so many persons who answer help-wanted advertisements get no replies?

13. What are some of the advantages of working for the United States Government?
14. Are most of the Federal jobs in Washington D. C.? Explain.

## TOPICS FOR DISCUSSION

1. Is it a good idea to do nothing yourself and wait for your school to find you a job? If you do so, does it show that you have great confidence in your school placement bureau or that you lack self-confidence?
2. Why should your first step be to secure interviews? With whom do you desire interviews? Who can get them for you, or must you arrange for them yourself?
3. Comment on what is wrong with the approach, "You don't need a stenographer, do you?"
4. Discuss various ways of making contacts with business people whose advice would be helpful to you.
5. Explain the difference between the right and the wrong kinds of pull.

## ARE THE FOLLOWING STATEMENTS TRUE OR FALSE?

1. Your school will get you a job. They always have more jobs than they can fill.
2. Friends and relatives are good sources of jobs, especially if they are employed in business.
3. Pull is a bad thing and should never be used in getting a job.
4. You should answer all the help-wanted advertisements, whether you've had experience or not. The more you answer, the better chance you have of getting a job.
5. Your post office is notified when examinations are to be held for Government positions.

## PROJECTS

This chapter contains a plan for lining up interviews and suggests that some of the steps can be taken before you leave school. Because anything you can do in this direction now will save time and labor later, the first five exercises and the last should be undertaken by all the class as an actual project in self-help.

1. Make a list of your relatives, friends, and acquaintances who might be helpful in supplying leads that would help you locate actual job prospects.
2. Go to the state employment-service offices in your city, and get your social security number. Then you will have it ready when you go to work. Report to the class anything you learn when on this errand.

3. Make a list of local employment agencies, dividing them into the fee-charging and the non-fee-charging. Take your original list from the telephone directory. Then ask employed friends or acquaintances or business people who employ office workers for information about these agencies. Find out, and note the following facts about each.

   a. Whether the agency places beginners
   b. What fee, if any, is charged
   c. What types of positions the agency specializes in
   d. Whether it has a desirable employer clientele
   e. Whether it has a high-class employee clientele
   f. What its standing is in the community

   Based on this information, revise your list, rating the agencies as A, B, and C, for your future guidance.

4. Read the help-wanted advertisements in last Sunday's newspaper, and bring to class one or two that you feel you would be qualified to answer as soon as you have been graduated. Be prepared to give reasons for this belief.

5. Read the help-wanted advertisements in last Sunday's newspaper, and report to class the salaries offered for all the following positions that may be advertised that day.

   a. Stenographer
   b. Secretary
   c. Typist
   d. Bookkeeper
   e. File clerk
   f. Voice-machine operator
   g. Clerical worker (list type of work)
   h. PBX operator

   If there are differences in the salaries offered for the same type of position, examine the requirements carefully, and see whether you can find the reasons.

6. Present a written report to class on what civil-service examinations for junior office positions will be given next in your locality. Your information should include the stated requirements for taking the examinations; where the examinations will be given and when; whether the examination is for a Federal, state, county, or municipal civil-service position; the duties of each position, as announced; and the salary. Check and report on whether these positions are better paid than the same in private business in your vicinity. (Do not report on positions that call for experience.)

7. The following sample questions are taken from circulars issued by the United States Government Printing Office, which give applicants for civil-service examinations an idea of the type and difficulty of the questions that will be used in the written examinations. See what you can do with them.

COMPUTATIONS: Work each problem, and compare your answer with suggested answers *A, B, C,* and *D.*

7a. Add:  Answers
963  *A.* 1,516
257  *B.* 1,526
216  *C.* 1,636
   *D.* 1,726
   *E.* None of these

7b. Divide:  *A.* 160.2
27√4379.4  *B.* 160.22
   *C.* 1,620.2
   *D.* 1,622
   *E.* None of these

7c. From a shipment of supplies, an inspector accepts 32 boxes and rejects 8 boxes. What percentage of the boxes of supplies is accepted?
*A.* 20  *D.* 80
*B.* 25  *E.* None of these
*C.* 75

VERBAL ABILITIES: Each sample question has suggested answers lettered *A, B, C, D, E.* Decide which one is the best answer to the question.

7d. *Feasible* means most nearly
   *A.* capable  *D.* beneficial
   *B.* practicable  *E.* reliable
   *C.* helpful

7e. *Encounter* means most nearly
   *A.* meet  *D.* weaken
   *B.* recall  *E.* retreat
   *C.* overcome

8. Select the sentence that is preferable with respect to grammar and usage such as would be suitable in a formal letter or report.

*A.* They do not ordinarily present these kind of reports in detail like this.

*B.* Reports like this is not generally given in such great detail.

*C.* A report of this kind is not hardly ever given in such detail as this one.

*D.* This report is more detailed than what such reports ordinarily are.

*E.* A report of this kind is not ordinarily presented in such detail as this one.

CHAPTER 6

# Preparing for the Interview

Now you have looked over the fields, surveyed the many possible starting points, and, we hope, made a career plan. With your career plan in mind, and with some idea of how to secure an entree to the job you want, let's get ready for your big moment—the interview. For between you and that long-anticipated job, there's an interview—perhaps several of them—before you will be on an employer's payroll. Your first interviews are likely to come through your school placement bureau, so you must be ready for them from the day you are graduated. By that time, you must know how to handle your part in the interview, and how to make a good impression on an interested employer. Indeed, knowing how to do this is just as important as being capable of filling the job. There's no need to dread the interview. This preliminary to business—like the various functions of business—can be studied and mastered. Let's get to work.

Statistics reveal that the average person goes through a season of looking for work only seven times in his entire life. At each of these periods, ability in obtaining interviews and in conducting yourself well during even the most difficult one is very important. For a brief space of time, this is the most vital thing in your life, so you must be good at it. The test of how good you are is how quickly you are accepted by an actual employer who will pay you for your time and services.

THE TECHNIQUE OF BEING INTERVIEWED

In your case, the art of applying for a job need not remain the mystery it is to many uninformed beginners. You can learn a great deal about interviewing technique before you leave school. At least you can learn enough of the theory behind it to handle yourself adequately in your first interviews. Knowledge of what to do and say will help you get rid of nervousness and fear, and putting the technique learned in

140

school into actual practice will increase your experience and education in this important branch of knowledge. As your schedule of applications, appointments, and interviews progresses, your poise and assurance will increase steadily. Soon you will be able to meet new people with ease and learn to estimate the most effective approach to each new type of executive.

But again, you must *plan!* It is just as important to figure in advance what you are going to say in an employment interview as it is to arrange the appointment. Sometimes, luck will smooth the way for you, but you cannot always count on luck. You will find that common sense is more consistently productive of satisfactory results, so don't take chances. There is no substitute for well-thought-out plans to get you a job or an advancement in life. Going into an interview and saying anything that comes spontaneously into your head will not get the results that you want.

*You Are Selling Your Services.* Approach the problem of selling your services as a skilled salesman would go about selling his product. A good salesman learns everything there is to know about the article he is selling. No firm would send him out until he did. Those young men who go from door to door, asking permission to demonstrate a vacuum cleaner, for example, have spent at least a week in the manufacturer's salesrooms learning all about the product and how to sell it. They have rehearsed their sales talk under the direction of experts, and they have tried it out on their relatives and friends before they are permitted to talk to actual prospects. Without all this careful preparation, they could not be expected to present the merits of the cleaner or to answer questions intelligently.

When you set out to sell your services through interviews with prospective employers, you, too, must know what you have to offer. Obviously, what you are selling is your ability to use certain skills learned in school and needed in business offices. Your appearance and your personality will speak for (or against) you from the beginning of the conversation. If these factors are favorable, they will go far in convincing the employer that you are the kind of person he would like to employ. But, important as such things are, you cannot depend entirely on appearance and personality. Usually, without definite skills to offer, you would not be taking part in this interview.

*Be Ready with the Answers.* Every worth-while interview is divided into two parts. First come the questions such as, "What can you do?" These deal largely with the skills you have learned. When jobs are scarce, untrained applicants, even with college degrees, do not last long in an interview unless somewhere along the line they have picked up something that will be useful in business. If they are not willing to start as errand boys or messengers, they are soon dismissed because they cannot offer technical proficiency. But when there are more jobs than young men and women to fill them, employers often hire applicants with no skills to offer and set up training programs.

However, those beginners with something to offer don't always make the most of this advantage. Many applicants lack the ability to answer specific questions about specific skills. Also, vagueness or nonchalance characterizes the replies of more than half the experienced workers who visit employment agencies looking for work. The words "rapid" or "fair" will be written after the questions on application blanks that say: "What is your dictation speed?" "What is your transcription speed?" "How rapidly can you type?" I have sometimes tried to get more definite information by asking, "How is your typing?" only to have the applicant reply, "Oh, it's all right." Another frequent answer is: "I haven't taken a test lately, but don't worry. I've always held good jobs, so I'd have to be O.K." Such self-satisfaction often belies the fact. A test right then in dictation has often shown that only one out of three stenographers with one to six years' experience can transcribe a mailable letter. Beginners, fresh from school tests, have an advantage here. They know definitely what their dictation, transcription, and typing speeds are, and this sometimes gets them a job when an experienced worker has flunked a test given in an interview.

Although you must expect and be prepared to answer these and similar questions about speed, don't get the idea that speed is the only thing business requires. Accuracy and general clerical competency are equally important today. Such skills cannot be clocked or estimated easily by questions and answers. Your general efficiency will be judged by indirect means.

### THE KINDS OF QUESTIONS TO EXPECT

Suppose you are applying for a combination position as stenographer-bookkeeper in a small business. You will be questioned about your shorthand ability and about your knowledge of keeping books. In preparing yourself for such an interview, think over what you will say to show that you know the principles of accounting and can apply them to solving ordinary bookkeeping problems. Try to gain and keep in mind the point of view of the employer. Let us visualize the scene. You have stated what you can do with shorthand. Then—

INTERVIEWER: Have you ever kept books?

YOU: I haven't kept books for a business firm, but I am sure I can do the work because I learned in school how to keep a simple set of books. I understand records and can record all kinds of transactions according to whatever system your firm uses.

INTERVIEWER: Can you operate an adding machine?

YOU: Yes (or No).

INTERVIEWER: What kind of calculating machines have you used? Which of the four Comptometer operations can you do?

Answer truthfully. There is no use bluffing when it comes to figures. Why not offer to show what you can do by taking a practical test?

In any interview, you should be prepared also to answer a general question about your skills, such as, "What position are you qualified to fill?" Or you may meet in your rounds a personnel director who has several positions to fill and who is sounding you out. This is no time to say, "I want to be a secretary or nothing." (It's likely to be nothing, if you are as choosy as that!) State first the thing you want most to do and think you can do best, but you are not likely to go above stenography in seeking your first position. You may be allowed to call yourself a secretary in a beginning job, but you will probably find that you are merely assisting a real secretary. Don't refuse such a job. It's a wonderful way to learn what a full-fledged secretary's duties are.

Here is how the interview for such a job might run:

EMPLOYER: What can you do?

YOU: I can take dictation, do bookkeeping, typing, general clerical work, and filing.

EMPLOYER: Ever operate a switchboard?

YOU: Oh yes, I forgot that.

If you know how to operate any kind of office machine, by all means say so. Don't wait for a busy businessman to drag the information out of you piecemeal. But don't go into details, either. It is enough for you to enumerate your skills. Only the untrained say, "I'm willing to do *any-thing*." That is a confession they know how to do nothing. The only statement worse than this is the frequently heard, "I can do *everything*."

Anticipating such questions and planning your answers is simple, for here you are dealing with tangible things. You either know how to keep a set of books, or you don't. You either know how to run a mimeographing machine, or you don't. The employer wants to know how skilled you are on the technical side, and you should be able to tell him. But he will want to know other things about you and will ask other questions for which you also need to be prepared. When you have answered all the questions about what you can do, the first and most definite part of the interview is over.

When giving a series of talks on job getting to the seniors of a private business school, I ended a lecture with the statement, "Next week I shall tell you what kind of questions you will be asked." Immediately, an eager young woman rushed up to me and said: "I can't wait until next week. I've an appointment with an insurance company tomorrow. Just what questions will they ask me?"

One would have to be clairvoyant to know exactly what questions will be asked beyond those related to your skills. But I am passing on to you interviewing knowledge gained through ten years as an employer in my own advertising agency; experience in a New York employment agency; the hiring of thousands of office workers for a Pacific Coast shipyard during World War II, and, since then, seven years as an interviewer for the California Department of Employment. This practical information I give you should help you anticipate the trend of the questioning. If you are ready for as many questions as you can foresee, you will be sufficiently poised and self-confident to answer the rest as they are presented.

### DON'T BE EMBARRASSED BY PERSONAL QUESTIONS

Applicants who have passed through the technical interrogation part of an interview with flying colors sometimes become confused and embarrassed when more personal questions are asked. If you will remember that whoever interviews you is not trying to be unduly personal, but is merely trying to estimate what sort of person you are, you will not resent the questioning. Here are some of the things most likely to be asked, to which you should be able to reply briefly and truthfully:

1. What do you do in your leisure time?
2. What were your extracurricular activities in high school? in college?
3. What subjects did you like best in school? least?
4. What business experience have you had?
5. What makes you think you can fill this position?
6. Do you live at home or board?
7. Have you lost much time in the past year because of ill health?
8. Why do you think you want to work for us?
9. If you have worked before, why did you leave your last position?

*What Kind of Person Are You?* The first question should not be construed by young women applicants as an attempt on the part of a male interviewer to make a date. The first and the second questions are intended to get you to talk naturally about your outside interests so that the employer can size you up. He may want to know something about your home and family background, which your diction will help him to determine. Knowing what you like to do will give him an idea of your personality and intelligence. If he asks this first question, he hopes you will tell him your hobbies, whether you are interested in athletics actively or as a spectator, whether you like to read or go to the movies, work in the garden, or collect stamps.

You will impress the interviewer more favorably if you show him that you are a human being than if you try to pose as a person who never reads anything lighter than Shakespeare and who wouldn't be so frivolous as to adore dancing. Such a line would suggest that you were staging an act and give rise to a doubt of the truth of some of your claims about your business skills. Answer the questions honestly and in an interesting manner, but be brief and to the point. To launch into a discussion of your favorite movie star, tell the plot of the picture you saw last night, or talk about where you and your boy friend (or girl friend) go dancing would hardly be suitable to the occasion or win approval of your good taste and business sense.

One personnel director I know was interested when a stenographic applicant said that her hobby was collecting photographs of rooms. Queried about this unusual turn of the collecting craze, the girl explained that she had scrapbooks into which she put her own snapshots of interiors and clippings of the type of rooms she liked to study. The personnel director did not care whether this interest indicated a frustrated talent for interior decorating or perhaps a domestic urge. She merely applauded the girl's interest in an original hobby and used it as a means of getting acquainted with her.

The questions, "What subjects did you like best in school?" and "What subjects did you like least?" are obvious in purpose. You met them in Chapter 1 and know that they are mildly disguised attempts to get a general picture of your aptitudes. Business feels that applicants who admit they dislike mathematics, for example, would be unfit for positions dealing with figures, whereas those who like English, spelling, and languages would probably make good stenographers and might be promising secretarial material. Although the average employer does not go very far into the matter of aptitudes, an interviewer realizes that you would not be likely to succeed if your daily work dealt with a subject you disliked.

*Personal Questions Are Not Impertinent.* When persons who are interviewing you ask, "Do you live at home or board?" will you assume they are being unduly inquisitive about your personal affairs? You may think it is none of their business, but they feel differently, and for good reason. This question usually grows out of unfortunate experiences that companies have had with young people who were on their own, away from home for the first time. Freed from home supervision, they may have gone out too much at night, had insufficient sleep and nourishment, and have been unable to maintain their efficiency at work. In the best type of office, the management likes to know that their younger employees have some sort of supervision as to hours and living conditions, because employers recognize the business asset of health.

When my sixteen-year-old niece was living with me and looking for her first position in the business world, I was delighted when she reported that a certain firm had asked her whether she lived at home. It was in her favor, in their eyes, that she made her home with a relative, since it relieved her employer of feeling any moral responsibility for a pretty country girl, alone in a strange city.

**Look and Act Healthy.** If for any reason you look pale or ill, you will probably be asked if you have had any serious illness recently. Your conscience will have to guide your reply. There is no use in taking a hard job if you are physically unequal to it. On the other hand, if you have been ill but are definitely recovered, you are justified in claiming health. If you are naturally pale or underweight but are really in excellent health, you may explain this briefly, or simply say you are always well. Employers have had so much trouble with people who either were not well or claimed illness as an excuse for frequent absence or lateness that they are cautious about hiring applicants who appear to fall into this classification. And they are just as wary of the overweight individual as the thin one. If, by firm muscles and good color, you show that you spend your week ends out of doors and take other precautions to preserve health, it's all in your favor.

### THAT DREADED QUESTION OF EXPERIENCE

The question, "What experience have you had?" can take the heart out of a confident beginner and bring on a case of jitters. Actually, this question is not so difficult to answer as you might suppose. When you are sent on an interview by your school, it is always to a firm that is willing to take beginners; hence, the employer knows you cannot have had much, if any, experience. The question may be purely routine, or he may want to know whether you have worked while going to school. This is another instance where bluffing is useless, for if you say you have held a paying position, you will have to give details that can be easily verified. And firms do check references.

A brand-new graduate from a business school once consulted me about arranging with a relative to say she had worked a year in his office. "You'd only make your situation worse," I told her. "You couldn't hide your inexperience, and your employer would soon wonder how you could be so dumb if you'd held a job that long."

There are different kinds of experience. You may have had more than you realize. If you have done any kind of store, office, or camp work during your vacations, by all means mention it. If you have worked after school or on Saturdays at anything for which you were paid, that, too, is good for your record. And if you have worked in the business office of your school, mention this as experience. Any of these will be helpful to you. Also, be sure to list these experiences when you fill out application forms.

*State Your Experience Constructively.* But if you have had no working experience of any sort, you will have to say so. This can be done negatively, or constructively. Here you are, with a job dangling before your eyes, and that disturbing question has come up to damage your chances. Will you say hesitantly, with a droop in your voice: "I'm sorry, but I haven't worked before. If experience is required, I guess I'm out." (And you are!) Or will you say confidently something like this: "I've just finished business school, Mr. Brown (mentioning the name of the school and the course you took), and I'm out to get my first experience now. While I can't say I've been paid for working *yet*, I don't feel totally inexperienced because we studied bookkeeping (or whatever subject is under discussion) in school, much as we would have to use it in a business position. I feel I can do the work to your satisfaction, Mr. Brown, partly because I've just come through a stiff course in accounting (or stenography), and also because I'm not afraid of hard work. I'd like to learn to do the job the way you want it done, and I naturally expect to begin at the bottom and work up." This last sentence is music to his ears.

Probably, you wouldn't have the time or the nerve to make such a long speech. There would be interruptions from the employer and some give and take. But if you will handle that disturbing question of experience in some such constructive way, you won't find it an insurmountable barrier. What you have done is to minimize your lack of experience and bring out certain advantages possessed by a beginner. Also, you have stated something about yourself that employers like to hear: your willingness to learn how the firm wants its work done and your desire to work up from the bottom. This is a refreshing contrast to overconfident beginners whose manner suggests that they expect to start near the top and take over the management of the firm within six months.

*Speak Frankly Without Boasting.* The question, "What makes you think you can fill this position?" should be answered after a moment's thought. You have no experience in a similar job to back you up, so you must rely on your recent training, your interest in the work itself, and your determination to make good. Speak frankly and positively without boasting. More than one personnel director has told me that there is an indefinable something about certain applicants that offers conviction that this boy or that girl will take hold and prove very helpful. Try to give that impression. In all sincerity, you could say: "I don't know for certain. But I believe I am well prepared for a beginning job like this. If you employ me, I'll do my best to make good." Don't say, "Oh, I just *know* I could do it!" Unknowingly, you may have picked a job beyond your depth, and such empty phrases will count against you doubly if you fail.

### QUESTIONS THAT REQUIRE THOUGHTFUL ANSWERS

The question, "What makes you think you want to work for us?" can be a difficult one for beginners, unless you are applying for a job in a business that especially interests you or about which you have informed yourself. You must think about this question a little before each interview. It is a subtle one. The employer is usually trying to find out if you think you have something special to offer him. If your reason for seeking that particular position is based on the fact, and nothing else, that there is a beginner's job open, keep that to yourself, and consider a reason that betrays less self-interest. If you have picked that firm for some reason related to the firm, such as their reputation, be careful not to appear so flattering as to cause your sincerity to be doubted. If you think you have something to contribute to the business within your sphere of experience, say so. But this rarely happens on beginning jobs. You must thoughtfully consider your own answer to this question. It may be the very question that will draw from you the words that will win the job. But mere glib patter will not impress. So watch your step here.

Applicants who have worked before may find "Why did you leave your last position?" as hard to answer as beginners find the question, "Have you ever worked?" If you have not worked, you will be spared this one. If you did have a small job for a short time, be truthful about what happened. The prospective employer can easily check up on what you say, if he is really interested. It is no longer considered a disgrace to lose a job.

In not-too-good times, many beginners have lost their jobs before they were able to gain much experience because, when firms cut down or merge with other companies, the newest employees are usually the first to be dismissed. Businessmen are acquainted with such situations and will understand if you state the case frankly. However, if you stammer and stumble, grow red in the face, and mumble something unintelligible, you are likely to give the impression that you failed outright, when such may not be the case.

***Don't Flit from Job to Job.*** There is a type of semibeginner about whom employers are not enthusiastic. This is the young man or woman who flits from one job to another, giving them all up voluntarily. True, if you have quit one job, or even two, you can admit it and perhaps not be discredited, for you may have had excellent reasons for leaving. But if you have left four or five jobs in a row, after working only a few weeks or months in each, your record will soon count against you. In spite of your explanations, the employer may fear you are one of those restless persons who lose interest as soon as the novelty wears off. And you may be! Or you may not have to work, and so you take a vacation whenever business conflicts with your personal life or plans. Or you may have an interfering family. Or you may be unable to take correction and discipline, so get another job hoping to escape them. An application card showing a great many positions held and deserted is likely to condemn you in the eyes of prospective employers. It is well to bear this in mind when you are bored with a job or think you can go out and get something better.

Good jobs are never so plentiful that they can be cast aside blithely, and any good employment manager will be inclined to think you lacking in common sense if you are in and out of jobs too frequently. When you have a good reason for changing, or have apparently bettered yourself, that is something in your favor.

***Keep Your Dignity.*** Let us presume that you have worked for a short time and have left a job voluntarily or because your resignation was requested. What are you going to say in self-justification when asked about it? Very little, if you are wise. Think this out before you go to your interviews, and you will be able to speak about the experience without bitterness or pessimism. You would be amazed at the tales told prospective employers regarding former employers. All may be true, but by the time the details are given, they sound like the complaints of a bad-tempered child. They even sound like the justifications of a gossip or a "ne'er-do-well-enough." An employer will hesitate to take you into his firm if you run down the last place you worked. Tell your story briefly, honestly, and with dignity, and be content to "damn with faint praise."

If you are a young man with little experience, the person who interviews you is likely to ask, "What do you want to be doing five years from now?" Even though this is a beginning job for which you are applying, and perhaps not related to your career plan other than as a first step in business, be prepared to answer this question. It is asked as a gauge of your ambition and the amount of effort and intelligent application you will give to the job if you get it. Don't attempt to impress the employer with wild dreams and schemes. Be practical and simple. Make your answer show him you are not a drifter, rather that you are anxious to get started toward your goal. The lack of a plan evidenced by so many beginners is regretted by personnel directors. They will be more interested in you if they see you are working toward a certain goal.

## WHEN YOU ARE ASKED TO DO THE TALKING

You are not ready for one type of interview until you realize that someone may say at the very beginning of it, "Tell me something about yourself." Obviously, this is not a question, but rather an invitation for you to take the floor and tell your story. This is your big chance to present yourself in the most favorable light you can. How you meet it will show whether or not you are just another applicant or an outstanding individual. Make the most of it.

In another chapter, you will be told how to make a neatly typed résumé of your schooling, special training, the skills in which you are qualified, and the positions you have filled. This Personal Data Sheet will be of great use to you in all your interviews. In reply to a request to talk about yourself it will prove invaluable. Before you go into any interview, study it as the basis of a concise running statement that will highlight your advantages and minimize your lacks. Make your speech short. Remember the employer is busy. He doesn't want you to become chatty, talk too much, and stay too long. His only interest in giving you the chance to talk is to ascertain whether you might prove a valuable employee. Also, this method of interviewing you, he feels, will give him a slant on your personality that questions might not reveal. Therefore, stick to the point. Conversationally, and not too rapidly, say something like this:

"You can tell from my accent, Mr. Brown, that I was born in the South. I was graduated from a private school in Baltimore, where I took the equivalent of a four-year academic high school course. My family moved north, so I attended the Williams Business School here. After graduation, I worked for six months as stenographer and typist in the Day and Night Bank. Mr. Burke, head of the savings department, can tell you about my work. Day and Night merged with Home Savings in February. They brought the older employees from the Home Savings, and as I was a new employee, I was one of those let go. I'm a rapid typist, and can take dictation at 120 words a minute. I feel that I could be of value to your organization because I am familiar with savings-bank work. However, I have not had so much experience but what it would be easy for me to learn your ways of doing things. I get along well with people, which I think is important." Be yourself while you speak in this fashion, and you are sure to make a favorable impression.

No one interviewer is likely to ask you all the questions I've suggested in this chapter, nor will the questions be phrased as I have phrased them. But by the time you find work you may have answered all these and more, and will have gained some measure of ease and poise thereby. Applicants experience two kinds of nervousness, both induced by fear. They are nervous for fear they won't say the right thing, and they are nervous for fear they won't get the job. Knowing some of the answers before the interview will eliminate the first fear and pave the way to eliminating the second. With these major fears out of the way, you can be yourself during the interview.

## REHEARSING PREVENTS STAGE FRIGHT

Now that you have an idea of the kind of questions that you are likely to be asked during the coming interviews, plan your answers, and rehearse them. And I mean *rehearse*. The greatest actor would be rigid with fright if he had to face an opening night without sufficient rehearsal. And you are going to present yourself on a new stage, so you will need preparation, too. Of course, I am not suggesting that you prepare stock answers, memorize them, and rattle them off like a parrot. But I do want you to think over your ideas, make a few notes, and try yourself out, so that your choice of words will be selective and your performance smooth when you are actually in the interview. One of your parents or a friend will doubtless be willing to play the part of employer in such a preview. If not, stand in front of a mirror, and ask the questions of yourself, watching how you look when replying. Even with a one-man rehearsal, you'll learn a great deal about yourself and how you impress others and about what to do in an interview.

*Listen to Your Voice.* Surprisingly, one of the things a beginner needs most is to become accustomed to the sound of his own voice. Rehearsing the interview helps you to get used to what seems the positive booming of your voice in an otherwise quiet room. When practicing what you will say, also listen to your voice, and adjust the volume so that you are neither whispering nor yelling. If you have a tendency to speak too rapidly, be sure to curb this both in rehearsal and during the interview. Avoid speaking in a stilted manner or in a monotone. Be natural. Use a conversational tone and manner. "Canned" speeches are seldom effective.

While you are practicing for your interviews, be sure to watch your inflection, as well as the tone and pitch of your voice. It is astonishing what a difference the emphasis of one word can make in your reply to certain questions. Many beginners ruin their chances of securing work because their tone of voice is negative. When asked whether they could handle a certain type of work, the timid souls reply doubtfully, "I *think* I could." The interviewer at once becomes dubious, too. The same question can be answered with the same words and still create an entirely different effect. "I think I *could*," said confidently, with some emphasis on *think* and still more on *could*, will often land a job as surely as the wrong emphasis will put you out of the running.

*Watch Your Carriage.* Your carriage in an interview is vastly important. Fortunately, entering a room is something you can rehearse. I am told that at R. H. Macy and Company in New York City, the applicants for positions, male and female alike, must walk across a long approach to the desk of the employment manager. The applicant who is awkward or eccentric in walk or bearing is given no further consideration.

This is scarcely the place to pause for a lesson in posture, and for your sake I am hoping you have already learned how to walk, stand, and sit. If not, a few simple rules may help you. One of the best aids to erect and correct carriage is to learn to walk with a book on your head. This is an exercise invariably mastered by all stage people and models. You can easily practice this stunt in the privacy of your bedroom until you have learned to walk easily and gracefully without tipping the book off. Someone has said you should "stand, sit, and lie *tall*." In other words, stretch yourself so that your back is straight and your shoulders easy, not thrown back.

When you walk, keep your toes turned slightly in, rather than out. The knees should be free, not rigid. Then walk from your hips. Above all, don't slouch, or stick out your stomach. Buttocks and stomach should be held in. All this may come naturally to young women, who are interested in making the most of their appearance. But young men, too, must consider carriage. Those who have had Boy Scout or military training have been taught how to carry themselves. Those who have had no other training can use the rules just given. And don't, above all things, slouch into an office with your head pushed forward, your shoulders drooping, and your hands in your pockets.

Practice walking into a room and standing quietly and at ease until you are asked to sit down. Then sit down, and do not cross your knees. This informal position is too unbusinesslike for your errand. Keep both feet quietly on the floor and near each other. Practice sitting still. Let your hands fall naturally and comfortably in your lap. Girls will have a pocketbook with them, boys possibly may have a brief case. Do not lay either of these on the employer's desk. Try not to have anything else with you. To be laden with packages suggests concern for other matters than the present interview. Sit well back in your chair, erect but relaxed, ready for questioning. You might try this routine before a full-length mirror in the clothes you plan to wear job hunting. Such a preview will probably disclose considerable necessary work with your posture before you are satisfied!

## QUESTIONS YOU MAY ASK THE INTERVIEWER

Some interviewers, when they have finished questioning you, will say, "Is there anything you would like to ask about the position?" Usually, they will not do this unless they are seriously considering you. Here is your opportunity to ask some of the things you would like to know, if this is to be your job. One of these questions, unless it has already been made entirely clear, is, "What are the duties in this position?" You know the chief part of the work is stenographic, let us say, but there will be many things to do besides taking shorthand notes and transcribing them. You would have a better picture of the job if you knew how many men would dictate to you and whether you would need to know how to transcribe from a disk, wire, or tape recorder. You will have some questions to ask, undoubtedly, but don't ask foolish ones about something you ought to realize through using your imagination or common sense.

Often, this is the time to bring up the question of salary, if it has not already been discussed. If you have been sent by an agency, you probably know what salary is to be paid, but sometimes the matter of compensation is left open. This means that what is paid will depend on the ability and experience of the person engaged. If the employer or his representative has encouraged you to feel you will be considered for the position, and it is not clear to you what the salary is, you had better ask. The time for any discussion of price for services or merchandise is at the end of the conversation. If you began an interview by asking, "What does this job pay?" you would be labeled as being interested only in the pay check and not in what you could do to make yourself useful. That would be very poor strategy. But toward the close of the interview, if necessary, it is all right to ask, "What does this position pay?"

Your school will have advised you, or your study of help-wanted advertisements will have given you an idea of the current salary scale in your locality for different office positions. You should be familiar with this for several reasons. If you are asked what you will work for, you should not state a salary that is either more or less than is customarily paid. Should you be offered less than you know this work is ordinarily worth, you can quite properly say, "I thought typists were getting

$\_\_\_\_ a week." If the offer is an effort to take advantage of your inexperience, this will at least show that you are informed on business practices, and the interviewer will respect you. I don't have to tell you what to do if the salary offered is more than is customary. Take it!

There are interviewers who will not give you a chance to ask questions. When they have finished questioning you, the interview is over. In 90 per cent of your interviews, you had better accept this point of view and not try to take the lead into your own hands. But in the other 10 per cent of these cases, and in any instance where the interviewer appears friendly and unhurried, it is legitimate for you to say, "May I ask something?" Have your question ready, and state it as concisely as possible. Be sure it is an intelligent one, not overweighted with self-interest. Such questions as "How much vacation would I get—with pay?" or "Would I have to work after hours?" or "Has the man I'd work for a good disposition?" are better left unasked. These are all things you will find out soon enough once you are on the job—and if you don't get the job, you won't have to worry about them. The questions you can take with you to an interview, all tied up in neat phrases, must be concerned with what would be expected of you on this particular job. Often, they will be answered early in the discussion, so that you need not ask them. .

You were advised earlier to make your own inquiries about any firm with which you have an appointment for an interview. This is recommended so that you will know the kind of business it is, the size of the company, the approximate number of employees, and the products or services of the company. Such information will come in handy if you are given an opportunity to ask a few questions. But unless you are reasonably sure of getting the position, you have no right to prolong the interview by asking questions about the firm. To ask, "Would I work here or at your 38th Street branch?" would be rather premature when you don't know whether they are going to put you to work at all.

Now that you know most of the questions and the answers to them, you are *almost* ready for your first interview. A little rehearsing and away you'll go. But before you make your first appointment, let's be sure you know how to make the most of your appearance.

## YOUR APPEARANCE CAN MAKE OR BREAK YOU

Essential as all your preparation is, it won't mean a thing unless your appearance wins the interviewer's approval at a glance. Believe it or not, *appearance counts 75 per cent in every employment interview.*

So let's talk it over from head to toe before you have any interviews. For I want you to write "dress and grooming" at the top of your list of

The smart applicant makes a last-minute checkup
before meeting the interviewer.

things you must rehearse. And that goes for both young men and young
women.

When I say *rehearse* dressing correctly for a job, I mean not just a
casual once-over of possible clothes you might wear, but actually putting them on and sitting and standing in them. It is being done in several
modern commercial schools that I know of, and probably in many
more. The Merritt Business School, a postgraduate school operated by
the public school system of Oakland, California, insists that its seniors
wear business clothes one day a week during the last few months before
graduation. "Our students often say they don't feel at ease in formal
business clothes. All right then, they'd better wear them more often, so
they won't feel strange when they go after jobs," the principal of the
school told me. Talk about up to date! This principal now writes me,
"We have placed a 3-dimensional mirror in our front hall, with a re-
minder to students to 'Look Your Best.'" If your school doesn't give
you this personal coaching on appearance, you'll have to do it for yourself. And you can.

Employment agencies—school, state, and private—are most interested
in the beginner who looks prepared to meet the business world. The
same is true of employers. No busy businessman has time to dig for the
character, capability, and skills that may be hiding under an untidy ex-

terior. You may have been a straight A student, and you may have a beautiful character, but when you present yourself to be interviewed, neither is immediately apparent. The interviewer sees first one of two things: either a person whose trim appearance is pleasing, or one whose inappropriate costume and poor grooming offend good business taste.

*Skills, of Course—But Appearance, Too!* When jobs are plentiful and employers are harassed with much work and little help, they can't be as choosy as when jobs are scarce. Then they can, and do, interview a number of applicants for every opening, and nine times out of ten, they employ the person who makes the best appearance. The value employers place on appearance is never more evident than when they telephone their orders to the employment agencies. Invariably, they state all the personal requirements first, starting with appearance, before they say a word about ability. Typical requests are: "Send me an attractive-looking stenographer, not over twenty-five. Accuracy is more important than speed in this job." Or, "Have you a young man about twenty-three whose appearance is outstanding? He must know something about bookkeeping. A good disposition is important. We'll start him as a general clerk, and he can go on up into executive work, provided he has what it takes." Employers rather naïvely assume they are getting proficiency in all the necessary skills, along with honesty, industry, and adaptability. What they fuss about is that the product be attractively or neatly packaged.

## WHAT IS MEANT BY "A GOOD APPEARANCE"

High as these requirements are, they are not unattainable. It has been estimated that 90 per cent of those seeking jobs can meet appearance standards, if they will only try. When employers stress "looks," they do not mean that they will employ only beautiful young women and handsome men. Far from it. Often a plain person who is neatly groomed and appropriately dressed will win out over a competitor who, however stunning, has had the bad taste to dress conspicuously or who didn't bother to look clean. Very often, too, an *interesting* person, dressed both suitably for business and becomingly as to type, will outdistance all other applicants.

Be reassured that virtually everything an employer hopes for in appearance is within your power to achieve. There are plenty of guideposts along the way. One of these is a Personality Chart [1] for girls. It is put out by the women who are department executives in the largest business offices in New York City, the members of the Transcription

---

[1] Reproduced by permission of the Transcription Supervisors' Association of New York City. Printed in full in a booklet, *From Books to Business.*

Supervisors' Association. These women were asked by commercial high schools and private business schools to summarize what they wanted girls to wear when applying for jobs. A complete Personality Chart was their answer; and, first in importance, they placed appearance, as will be seen in that portion of the chart reproduced here.

PERSONALITY CHART FOR THE YOUNG BUSINESSWOMAN

A. *Wearing Apparel*

| | |
|---|---|
| 1. Coat or suit | 1. Of conservative cut and color |
| 2. Dress | 2. Of conservative cut and color. Modish but not extreme as to length of skirt and sleeve and as to depth of neckline. Even as to hemline |
| 3. Accessories | 3. Immaculate. Free from rip or tear. Feminine |
| 4. Hat | 4. Smart and becoming but not rakish or bizarre |
| 5. Shoes | 5. Clean. Conservative. No runover heels |
| 6. Jewelry | 6. Appropriate to the costume. Unobtrusive |
| 7. Restraining garments | 7. Girdle, brassière, etc., when necessary |

B. *Personal Grooming*

| | |
|---|---|
| 1. Hair | 1. Clean, vital, neat, suitably coifed for daytime wear. Natural color |
| 2. Skin | 2. Clean and clear |
| 3. Brows | 3. Following the natural lines |
| 4. Teeth | 4. Free from stains |
| 5. Nails | 5. Well tended. Free from nicotine or other stain. Only light shades of polish permissible |
| 6. Make-up | 6. Not too much. Suited to daytime wear and to one's natural coloring |

And the requirements for young men are no less definite. Let no one imagine that meticulous regard for dress and grooming is not important in business today. From his first appointment for a job-hunting interview until the last day of his business career, the young man is also judged by his appearance. Here are ten points the employer considers important:

CORRECT APPEARANCE FOR THE YOUNG BUSINESSMAN

1. Suit
   1. Conservative in cut. Navy, brown, or gray. Spotless, well pressed, and well brushed. Sport coats and slacks are permissible if conservative in cut and color. Sweaters and loud sport shirts are not appropriate. Pocket handkerchief optional

2. Hat
   2. Optional. Never a cap. If hat is worn, hold in hand while being interviewed.

3. Linen
   3. Immaculate. No frayed collars and cuffs. A clean handkerchief always

4. Tie
   4. In harmony with his suit. Half or full Windsor knot, if collar style indicates this. No fads such as string bow tie or exaggerated collar styles

5. Socks
   5. In harmony with his suit. No loud patterns or fancy argyles

6. Shoes
   6. Oxfords, brown or cordovan

7. Face
   7. Well shaved

8. Teeth
   8. Free from stains

9. Hair
   9. Frequently shampooed. No dandruff

10. Hands and nails
    10. Clean. No nicotine stains

## THE IMPORTANCE OF GOOD GROOMING

You will notice that good grooming follows closely on dress in both lists of requirements. How could it be otherwise? The most correct business clothes, if soiled, unpressed, and worn by an individual obviously in need of a bath, would be of little use in landing a job. Likewise, an immaculately groomed person if dressed in an extreme style would not make a good impression. A combination of appropriate dress and careful grooming is what the employer expects—in fact, demands.

Good grooming is a matter of habit. The young woman whose hair needs washing and the lad with dirty fingernails never suspect that their negligence may be the cause of fruitless interviews. Being habitually careless in grooming, they are equally casual on that momentous occasion. They might as well say in so many words, "I didn't bother to get fixed up. This isn't a party." It is truly no party, but it is a parting of the ways—yours and the interviewer's—then and there! I have had employers and personnel directors say to me, "If Miss Blank didn't think enough of this interview to wash and iron her blouse, she isn't the sort of person we want." Sometimes, they are not so specific and merely say, "I can't see her fitting in here," or "That boy wouldn't be neat in his work."

I recall an episode in my employment agency days when I was forced to tell a roomful of young women I could not interview any more that day. We had advertised for receptionists. As I looked over the applicants, I said, "None of you could be sent out on this job on account of your hair." Only one out of the thirty returned the next day. "I took your tip and had my hair set," she greeted me with. For her ready acceptance of such a hurried criticism, I gave her a card of introduction. She had what a job hunter needs—the ability to profit by criticism. Need I add that she was hired? A permanent wave has got a job for many a woman. Hair grooming is just as important to the young man—a lad's "flat-top" haircut never makes a hit with an interviewer.

*Employers' Pet Peeves.* The employer is a most conservative fellow. Whatever the new thing is, he's against it, even if his wife and daughter are wearing it. When this book was first published, it was red nail polish that was his pet peeve. Employers clear across the country told me they had fired able stenographers who ignored hints, suggestions, and requests to "leave the stuff off." But time and feminine persistence, at home and in the office, have worn the poor man down. He still does not like red or purple nails pounding on his typewriters, but he keeps his opinion to himself. Help may be too scarce for him to risk losing it for anything as small as fingernails. Bearing the boss's prejudice in mind, the wise job seeker will wear light polish for an interview or remember to keep her gloves on. Also, she won't overwhelm the interviewer with her favorite, or any, perfume. If she gets the job, she may later learn the employer's current peeve—red toenails and bare legs. But no one with common sense would go to an interview showing either, nor would she try this beach fashion in the office after she goes to work.

*A Little Make-up Goes a Long Way.* And now we come to make-up; another matter on which employers have very definite ideas. Be both artful and artistic in laying on the paint. The rule is simple and the results lovely: Use just enough to look naturally healthy and well groomed, and no more. If you have a naturally high color, be content with a light film of powder and a dash of lipstick. Nervousness caused by talking face to face with an executive who might possibly become your employer may make your color flare up. It would be a pity to spoil the effect with a purple flush of rouge, plus your own color. If, however, you need rouge, by all means use it. But be sure it blends with your own coloring. If necessary, seek expert advice on just what shades of powder, rouge, and lipstick are best for you. Then be sparing in using them. A little eyebrow pencil is all right, if you need it. Remember, many employers think they object to all make-up, just on principle. If you are clever in putting it on, they'll never suspect you!

*What Your Best Friend Won't Tell You.* That daily bath—stepped up to the two-a-day from June to September—also needs to be supplemented by the frequent use of a deodorant. More about this in our chapter on dress and grooming to keep the job. Here I want merely to say that "No B.O. please," is as frequent an order to an employment agency as is the usual. "Send me a stenographer." Men and women alike seem to have a blind spot about themselves when it comes to the matter of perspiration. They always think it's the other fellow who offends. Employers, nurses, and personnel directors find employees so dense about taking a hint that rarely is the situation solved short of dismissal. Hence, my earnest tip, "Be sure you are careful on this point while you are job hunting—and afterward." When you are looking for work, you are under nervous strain. And nervousness is likely to cause excessive perspiration. Hence, an even greater need than usual to safeguard yourself by using a deodorant. If you have once perspired in a blouse, dress, coat, or suit, be sure to send it to the cleaner, or it will offset your other precautions.

In the matter of using deodorants, men assume a smug air, as much as to say, "Wonder why women offend? We never do." Oh, don't they! It is quite as necessary for men to use deodorants as for women. Well-groomed men are very careful on this score, for they know that perspiration odor is a handicap to success.

*Feminine Appropriateness.* To return to dress requirements for young women, the one word that sums up everything desired in an interview is "appropriateness." Many highly capable girls must have got jobs through lucky accidents, for their clothes certainly bear no relation whatsoever to job getting or job holding. When out of work, they may even buy something special for job hunting, not realizing they'd much better have worn something they already had, such as a trim tailored suit, which happens to be tops for suitability.

Here's a case in point. One day, in my employment-agency work, I received a call for an experienced stenographer for the New York City office of a nationwide group of department stores. Anne Harvey was listed in our files as an able and responsible worker whom we had placed in several positions, with good results. So I phoned Anne to come in and talk with me. She came, wearing a bright-red coat over a bright-green dress, topped off with a Spanish hat tied under her chin with a black velvet band. What to do? She would never get a job in that bizarre costume!

I suggested to Anne that she hide the strap under her hat, making it just a large black hat with a high crown. Since the office she was going to was in our building, I suggested that she leave the red coat with us. Her green dress, with her black hat, gloves, and bag, had a certain unity that would at least get by. "Employers are likely to judge applicants by their appearance," I told her. "It's better not to wear too-bright colors on an interview." Anne indignantly answered that she had bought her coat and dress especially for job hunting, and she thought I was very fussy indeed. So the red coat went. She didn't get the job, and I was criticized for selecting her. "You ought to know that appearance is very important in our business," the personnel director snapped at me. And that was the last time Anne was sent out from our office.

But the wrong clothes are not always bright in color. Sometimes, they are very wrong in type, more suited to a cocktail party or an afternoon tea than to the business scene. Here's what happened to Mary Smith, a college graduate, who was interviewed by officials in a bank that planned to open a children's savings department. This was in a fairly small community and the bank required a young woman who would call at rural homes and explain the idea. When they heard of Mary's education, they were sure she was just the girl they wanted. She had an advanced degree in child psychology and several years' banking experience. But the official needed only one look at Mary. "Sorry to disappoint you," he said. "The position is filled."

Mary realized from his manner, and because she had been virtually assured of the job, that the position was not filled. Something had gone wrong. What, she did not know. A friend asked someone in the bank and passed the story along to me. For that all-important interview, Mary had worn a close-fitting black print afternoon gown, with a veiled toque, long glittering earrings, and elaborate accessories. The executive had to consider the opinions of the mothers, teachers, and children Mary would be meeting in her work; and he quickly decided that a more suitably dressed young woman, even with fewer qualifications, would be better for the job.

*Young Men Err in Different Ways.* A young man may go to an interview dressed in Ivy League style, with which the accessories will, of course, be conservative. He may wear Argyle socks, provided they are not in loud colors. His necktie should not be a shocker. Young men forget that the interviewer, especially if he is the big boss, may be a generation or two removed and that he thinks college or sports attire worn to business betrays a frivolous attitude toward life and work. Business is not looking for playboys. Golf enthusiasts and fishing experts are listed among the executives, and no more need apply.

An employment-agency owner in Minneapolis once told me that he believed a man's appearance counted 90 per cent in getting a job. "There's no use in my sending out a man to see an employer," he said, "unless he is immaculately groomed and tastefully dressed. If he can't impress me, the chances are he won't impress the employer. We get our fee—as opposed to the 'no-fee' agencies—because we are selective. Consequently, we eliminate all those who don't qualify in appearance."

Similarly, a young man employed by the New York State Employment Service, in the Rochester office, showed me a list he had prepared for distribution among the men who applied to him. It occupied a letter-sized sheet and listed everything from a fresh shave to pressed trousers. As in the ten-point table given earlier in this chapter, it warned those just out of school not to go looking for work wearing khakis, a sport shirt, or a sweater. Furthermore, it warned applicants that a businessman would not overlook a slovenly appearance, whereas he would often be willing to overlook youth and inexperience when he was favorably impressed by appearance.

Such details as gay-colored shirts, loud socks, and a rakish hat with a feather in the band are immediately spied by the eagle eye of business. Doubtless, if one were applying for a job as a night-club entertainer, or aspired to be a movie actor, he might wear clothes in the latest fad.

### PLAN A JOB-HUNTING OUTFIT EARLY

Six months before getting through school is not too early for young people to begin planning job-hunting wardrobes. If you are getting a complete new outfit for graduation, be smart and select a suit you can use for job hunting. Don't be tempted by an extreme model that "all the fellas are wearing." Anticipate your needs, and gradually assemble an appropriate costume. With such foresight, you will need to add very little when you are ready to start out on your first interview.

To be a smart-looking young man, you must wear a businesslike suit. So, see to it that you own one in navy, brown, or gray. If you must buy one, look at it as an employer would, and make a fairly mature choice. Forget those extra slacks you want or the new coat to go with the slacks you have. Both are all right in their place, but they won't help you when you are job hunting. From now on, you must plan *first* for the clothes you will wear to *get* a job, and then to *hold* it.

As you purchase shirts and ties, select them to harmonize with the suit. Avoid the extreme sport shoes that tempt you, in favor of brown Oxfords. It will be fun to get this outfit together. Perhaps your only purchase just before the momentous interview might be an initialed handkerchief to fold neatly in your breast pocket. As soon as you get a job you'll have to begin planning what to wear to work.

A woman interviewer who hires beginners of both sexes for a large railroad company has this to say about the way the young men dress. "Often, they look very neat and are well dressed when they apply. But you should see how they dress for work! I've learned to tell them, when I hire them, just how we want them to look when they report for work. Usually, a boy just out of high school has one good suit, and he wants to save it. All right, he can wear slacks to work, but sweat shirts and Hawaiian shirts are not acceptable. If he is going to work in the warehouse, I tell him he can wear khakis there, but they must be clean. Here is one bit of advice I give them, and does it work! 'When you go into your department, observe how the men dress. Pick out one of the younger men, and make him your ideal.' " Smart woman, and smart boys to take her words to heart.

Young women, in looking ahead toward their interviewing days will do well to concentrate on the simple tailored suit. A navy, black, or brown suit, or a tweed mixture, with a small hat and pumps are correct. But no spiked or high French heels. No sandals or ballet slippers, please. A tailored blouse is best with a suit, white, if you prefer—provided it always is immaculately white. A scarf in a harmonious color or in pleasing contrast will complete your costume. Be sure your gloves, preferably in a dark shade, are clean and whole. And *wear* them—do *not* carry them. Depending on what is the fashion, you can combine two colors in your costume or stick to one, as you choose. But whatever you do, keep it quiet-looking and businesslike.

Should you think you don't look well in a suit, the alternative is a dress of simple style worn under a coat. Again you are safest in black, navy, or brown. A mixed-tweed sports coat over a solid-color dress in a shade to harmonize with the tweed is a good choice. Both dress and coat should be simple in line—never fussy or elaborate. The best-dressed women, whether they spend a fortune or only a limited amount, always wear the simplest possible clothes. Remember, you may be asked to take your coat off during an interview. The employer may be interested to see how you would look in the office. White or light-colored cuffs, collar, or scarf, as well as gloves, must be spotless. The same rule of harmonizing or contrasting hat, shoes, gloves, and purse applies as well to dresses and coats as to suits.

"What if I go job hunting in the late spring and summer?" you ask. Well, then you're lucky, I think. For a very plain, dark sheer fabric, a cotton, or a modest print and a little jacket that goes with it will be cool, comfortable, and attractive looking. You might even make a hit by wearing a simple white hat, if you are willing to clean it daily. White washable gloves—two or three pairs a day tucked in your bag—would help, too. It's that dainty look that registers. But you'll have to watch your make-up in summer job-hunting days. Powder has a way of disappearing when the day is hot and humid, and a shiny nose is no help.

## Why All the Fuss?

You may think, as you come to the end of this chapter, that business is an old "fuss-budget." I admit that business is fussy, but I think it has a right to be so. It does not demand quiet dress and perfect grooming just to be cranky. The businessman knows that the appearance of his employees contributes to the character of his business. Consider how the young people working in an office can create an atmosphere of dignity and stability if they are neatly attired and working quietly at their desks, or moving quietly and conversing in low, pleasant tones when necessary. Looking at such a scene, if you were calling as a customer or client, you would have confidence in that firm. But if all the young people wore loud clothes, if they called back and forth to each other, and if they were all chewing gum, you would quickly feel there was something wrong with a business conducted like that. "Too free and easy. Not conservative enough. Wonder if the executives are as flashy. Guess this is no place to put my money," might very well be your mental checkup on the scene. Since most businesses are conservative, they prefer employees who express this quality. Naturally, they view prospective employees with an eye to how they will fit into the picture.

Employers are right in having high standards of appearance. You can't go wrong in heeding them. But apart from what business requires, such standards for yourself will be a great help to you. You will find that your poise is increased when dress and grooming have been thoughtfully considered. The whole story can be summed up in a few words: When you have been careful in getting yourself ready for an interview, you can then forget how you look. When you know that you are just about 100 per cent right, your self-confidence will reach a new high. You need only to concentrate on what you have to say, secure in your knowledge that, if appearance counts 75 per cent, you've passed that test already. If you are equally sure of your business skills, you're all set to make a perfect score—and of course you will!

## QUESTIONS

The following questions, actually asked applicants, will give you additional preparation for employment interviews. Study them, and answer them thoughtfully. Be prepared to discuss them.

1. Are you living at home? If so, how many are in your family?
2. What is your father's occupation, also your brothers' and sisters'?
3. Do you contribute toward keeping the home?
4. If you live away from home, do you send money home?
5. Are you engaged? Do you intend to marry soon? If you are a girl, do you intend to work after your marriage?
6. What are your interests outside the office?
7. How much time do you give to reading, and what do you like to read?
8. Are you interested in music, and are you talented in it?
9. Where do you go for amusement and recreation?
10. How many nights during a week are you out after ten-thirty?
11. Have you traveled to any extent, and where? If not, would you like to? Where?
12. Do you like people? Do you think people like you?
13. Do you learn quickly? Have you a good memory?
14. Are you able to take instructions and follow them accurately?
15. How well do you take constructive criticism?
16. When you have completed one piece of work, will you hunt more work to do?
17. Do you think for yourself or follow the majority?
18. Can you admit your mistakes with good grace?
19. Have you a sense of humor?
20. If your work brings you in contact with people whom you consider inferior, either mentally or socially, what will be your attitude?
21. Do you want to be outstanding in your work, or just get by?
22. What salary do you want? What salary do you think you are worth?
23. How soon will you want a raise? How much of your salary will you save?
24. What salary did you make on your last job? Why are you willing to take less? (or) Why are you asking for more?
25. Will your former employer give you a good reference?
26. What kind of person was your former employer?
27. If your future employer does not conduct his business in the same way

as your former employer, and you think his methods are wrong, what will you do?

28. Do you think that you prefer a woman or a man boss? Why?

29. What would you do if you found that a department head was not fair in dealing with the employees?

30. If you were the president's secretary, would you help fold and mail the general correspondence of the entire office, if not busy with your own duties?

31. Would you talk about your employer or the company outside the office, even at home?

32. What would you do if your employer asked you to get for him some information on a fellow employee?

33. Would you repeat office gossip?

34. If you had not been told to do so, would you open your employer's mail and arrange it for him, or would you wait until he arrives at the office?

35. In high school were you in the upper third of your class?

36. Do you like figures?

37. Why do you want a job?

38. What magazines do you read regularly?

39. Give the names of a few books you have read recently (not in school).

40. Have you had a physical examination recently?

41. What serious illnesses have you had?

42. Are you willing to be examined now by our male physician at the company's expense, and regularly once a year while in our employ?

## TOPICS FOR DISCUSSION

Because it is important for their future happiness that young men and women know something of the cost, style, and quality of each other's clothes, no separation on a basis of sex has been made in the topics for discussion or the exercises in this chapter.

1. Your textbook is conservative in saying, "Appearance counts 75 per cent in every employment interview." Many personnel directors place it at 90 per cent. Why is appearance so important when you are looking for work? Discuss whether you can afford to be indifferent to your dress and grooming when you prepare to go job hunting.

2. Why should you rehearse correct dressing for business in advance of an interview? Why isn't it enough just to get suitable clothes together and put them on when you start out to look for work?

3. Explain what is meant by "a good appearance." To have an attractive appearance, is it necessary that a young woman be pretty or that a young man be handsome?

4. See whether you can tell what was wrong with the appearance of these two applicants:

*a.* When she went to be interviewed, Nora Burns dressed most carefully. She wore an Oxford-gray tailor-made suit, an immaculate white blouse, a becoming black sports hat, and suitable walking shoes. Nora carried her black gloves so that her long red fingernails would show, as she thought they added life to her somewhat somber outfit. Nora's lipstick matched her nail polish, and she wore a lot of it. In the sense of cleanliness, Nora's grooming was perfect, but the odor of her expensive perfume was very noticeable.

Nora's appearance lost her the job, but no one thought it worth while to explain this. Do you see why she did? What changes would be necessary for Nora to meet the requirements?

*b.* Joseph McKay was called a "snappy dresser." He thought a lot about surface appearance and confidently wore his newest sport clothes when he went out to apply for a job. These consisted of a bright-blue sweater, gray slacks, and a brown coat. Joe combed his hair carefully, but did not wear a hat. In fact, he did not own one. Joe shined his shoes for the interview, but failed to wash his hands and clean his nails. When he needed a handkerchief during the interview, Joe pulled from his pocket one that was both gaily colored and soiled.

What should Joe have worn? Where was his grooming all right, and where was it at fault? When should Joe have considered businesslike job-getting clothes and assembled them?

5. What do you understand the word "appropriate" to mean in relation to correct business dress? Also the word "businesslike"? Taking navy blue, brown, or black as a basic color, describe what you would select for job hunting, if you could buy whatever you like. Do expensive clothes necessarily make a better impression on an interviewer than inexpensive ones? If not, why not?

6. Why are employment agencies as particular as employers about the appearance of applicants who call on them? Would you be as careful of your appearance when calling on an employment agency as on an employer to whom you were sent?

Do you think an employment-agency interviewer has any right to tell an applicant that he or she is not dressed or groomed correctly for an interview, and to suggest changes? If an agent talked with you about your unsatisfactory appearance, would you resent it or be grateful for the interest?

7. Will the knowledge that you are appropriately dressed and well groomed help you to walk, sit, and speak with more ease in an interview? What does the word "poise" mean in this connection?

8. Discuss the actual value of make-up to a young woman preparing for an interview. What should cosmetics, rightly used, do for a young woman applying for a position? Just how much make-up should she use on this important occasion?

## PROJECTS

1. Based on the explanation in this chapter of what is correct to wear when looking for work—

    a. Make an inventory of your present wardrobe and assemble those clothes that will be suitable for job hunting.
    b. Plan and list in detail what you will need to complete a suitable, businesslike costume.
    c. Find out by window shopping what these additions will cost, keeping the cost well within your means.
    d. Write a description of your job-seeking outfit, discussing the suitability of its type, color scheme, accessories, and the like.
    e. Work out a schedule for adding the necessary items between now and your graduation, so as to have the right things to wear, with a minimum of financial outlay.

2. Here is a sample interview. Study it carefully, and see what is wrong with the applicant's method of approach, her attitude, her remarks, and so on.

    Ann Markham made an excellent impression on the placement bureau of her school, because she was among the top students in her class and she knew how to dress. Also, Ann had good family and social background, and the school felt she would handle herself well in an interview. Consequently, when the Holt Manufacturing Company asked for a promising beginner, the placement director gave Ann the first chance at the job.

    Looking her most businesslike best, Ann called at the offices of the company. She had been told to telephone in advance for an appointment, but Ann decided that would not be necessary, because she had met Mr. Holt socially and that ought to get her in and get the job for her, too.

    We meet Ann at the reception desk.

    ANN: I'd like to talk with Mr. Holt, if he's in.
    RECEPTIONIST: (*Looking Ann over*) Which Mr. Holt? And who shall I say is calling?
    ANN: Why, Mr. . . . Mr. I'm not sure. I didn't know there was more than one. The young Mr. Holt, I mean. You can tell him it is Miss Markham to see about that secretarial position.
    RECEPTIONIST: Oh, you want to see Mr. Armstrong, our personnel director. Who sent you?
    ANN: The Blank School. They felt I was just the girl for the position, and I'm sure I am, too.
    RECEPTIONIST: I'll see whether Mr. Armstrong can see you. He has several appointments, and there are some other applicants ahead of you.

ANN: (*Becoming flustered*) Well, I don't get that. I understood he expected our school to send him somebody very, very good, and I am the Blank School's first choice. Please tell him I'm here.

The receptionist tells Ann to sit down, and an hour later a somewhat subdued Ann is sent in to see Mr. Armstrong.
The interview has progressed very well, up to the point where Mr. Armstrong asks Ann what her outside interests are.

ANN: (*Feeling very sure of herself*) Oh, dancing . . . I just love to dance! And I sing, of course. Maybe you read about my last recital, in the *Tribune*. I suppose I'd call music my hobby, really, but I hope to be able to go into it professionally someday.

ARMSTRONG: Then business isn't your first love, Miss Markham?

ANN: Well, no, not exactly. I went to business school so I could work and get money for my singing and dancing lessons. But my school will tell you I am very good at shorthand, and, of course, I'd just love to be a secretary, too.

ARMSTRONG: We don't start beginners as secretaries, but after working here a year or so, several girls from your school have become secretaries.

ANN: Oh, yes. I know Mary Meighan has gone right up with you people. She's one of my very best friends.

ARMSTRONG: Yes? And Helen Dobson is another. Do you know her?

ANN: No, she was several years ahead of my class. (*Looking up excitedly*) Wasn't that Harry Holt who went through the hall just then?

ARMSTRONG: Yes. Do you know him? He's understudying his father.

ANN: No, really? I don't know Mr. Holt well, but I've danced with him at the country club.

ARMSTRONG: If you know Harry, you must know Joe Wilcox.

ANN: (*Thinking she is getting along famously*) Do I? And his fiancée, Hazel Cross! I went to boarding school with Hazel.

ARMSTRONG: (*Rising*) It's been very pleasant talking with you, Miss Markham. I'll tell Harry you were in.

ANN: (*Rising also, and realizing she has used all the time allotted to her*) Thank you. Yes, do remember me to Mr. Holt. And thank you so much for the interview. I'm sure it would be wonderful to work here. Good afternoon.

Rewrite this interview from the time Ann arrived at the offices of the Holt Manufacturing Company. Using no more words, show how she could have utilized the time to better advantage.
What did Ann say that would have been better left unsaid?
Even though the interview got out of hand, how could Ann have brought it back to a discussion of the position for which she was applying and to her fitness for it?

# TEST YOUR KNOWLEDGE

*For Young Women.* Select the answer that you consider best for each of the following:

1. When looking for work, you should preferably wear a dress and coat that are (*a*) plaid, (*b*) dark red, (*c*) navy blue, (*d*) tan, (*e*) Kelly green.
2. Your hair should be worn in (*a*) elaborate curls, (*b*) neat and close to your head, (*c*) long and fuzzy.
3. Your fingernails should be (*a*) without any polish, (*b*) extremely long, (*c*) deep red, (*d*) normal length, with a light shade of polish.
4. The correct shoes to wear to business are (*a*) open-toed, backless slippers, (*b*) wedge-heeled novelty shoes, (*c*) pumps with medium-height heel, (*d*) flat-heeled sports shoes.
5. When you go to an employment interview, your hat should be (*a*) large and floppy, (*b*) trim and tailored, (*c*) extreme and amusing, (*d*) left at home.

*For Young Men.* What is wrong with these statements?

1. When you go to an interview, wear the shirt that was clean yesterday. It is good enough.
2. You might feel stiff in a suit if you are not used to wearing one, so just go informally, in your sport clothes.
3. It is "sissy" to be particular about the cleanliness of your hands, nails, and neck. Nobody notices them.
4. If you can't afford to have your suit pressed, never mind. Certainly no one should expect you to do it yourself.
5. Brighten up a dark suit with a red tie and loud socks and shirt. That will show you know how to dress.
6. Businessmen like the collegiate type, so it is a good plan to imitate the latest college fad, such as no necktie or hat, when you call on conservative executives.

CHAPTER 7

# Writing Letters of Application

"Is it better to apply for a position personally or by letter?" This question turns up frequently in my mail. There is only one answer. A personal interview is always more desirable than a letter of application. But there are times and circumstances when a letter may be the means of obtaining an interview. It is a waste of time to apply for a position by letter unless you can follow it up with a personal call. For no matter how excellent your letter, no employer is going to hire you unseen.

Many young business-school graduates and even some experienced office people imagine that letters of application alone can get them jobs. I've known young people just out of school to send out job-seeking letters in all directions, confidently expecting offers of positions to result. One young woman I talked to in New York City had been out of business school several months and was still unemployed. "What have you done?" I asked. "I've written letters—dozens of them—to lots of the big firms," she answered.

One or two companies had replied in routine fashion, saying they had nothing just then, but to "come in sometime." The rest of them had not bothered to answer. Since large business organizations receive hundreds of such communications each month, only an exceptional letter of application will attract attention. The proper way to approach such firms is in person, through their personnel departments, whose sole business is the sorting and selecting of employable people.

## WHEN TO APPLY BY LETTER

Don't waste your time and your stationery on ill-considered letters of application. Well-planned letters of application should be written as a step toward interviews. The head of a Chicago business school told me to what good advantage some of his graduates used letters leading to interviews.

"Once," he said, "when jobs were scarce and not coming into our placement bureau, I offered to pay the postage for any student who wished to start a letter campaign. Some graduates sent out a few letters, hit or miss, and when nothing happened grew discouraged and quit. But one young woman wrote fifty letters to a carefully selected list. In reply, she received seven or eight telephone calls and, following interviews, had three jobs offered her. Another girl, who wanted to work in a travel bureau, concentrated on writing to companies in that field. Having traveled extensively, she had a great deal to offer besides her knowledge of shorthand and typing. Her well-written letters and her travel experience led to interviews and a good job for her."

These cases are excellent examples of the intelligent use of letters as a possible introduction to prospective employers. Very different from aimless canvassing by mail!

But before you start an extensive letter-writing campaign instead of personal appearances, answer these questions:

Are you seeking refuge behind your typewriter because you are too timid to appear personally to ask for a job?

Do you really want a job?

Are you merely making a show of activity because your parents insist on it?

Here are four occasions when applying for a position by letter is recommended:

1. In reply to help-wanted advertisements
2. To firms you hear have vacancies you could fill
3. To firms in a field for which you are especially qualified
4. To business people who know you or your family

In every case, your letter should ask for a personal interview. Keep this in mind. It will help you to write letters that keep to the point.

Later, we shall discuss the writing of good letters of application, and I shall give you a few sample letters to study. For the moment, let us assume you know how to write an acceptable letter of this sort and that you need only a few hints as to the specific points to cover in each of the classifications just mentioned.

*In Reply to Help-Wanted Advertisements.* In Chapter 5, the matter of answering help-wanted advertisements was discussed from the point of view of applying in person when an address was given. Now we will assume that the advertisement gives only a box number and requires a letter of application. Remember that the firm advertising will receive a number of replies, which will be sorted first on the basis of appearance and second on content. You will be called for an interview only if your letter ranks among the top 5 to 10 per cent. Therefore, it must be good.

Perhaps the most important point to keep in mind when answering an advertisement by letter is to cover all the requirements mentioned. Here is a typical help-wanted advertisement.

> STENOGRAPHER—22 to 26 years—
> casualty insurance experience preferred.
> In answer give education, experience,
> and salary desired. Y 120—Daily News.

A certain kind of experience is suggested, but not specified as essential. However, an experienced stenographer is definitely wanted; therefore, if you have had no experience, it would be a mistake to answer this advertisement. One reason that many young people never receive replies to their letters is that they apply for positions for which they are not qualified. In this advertisement, three other items are listed: age, education, and salary expected. In replying, you must not fail to give information on all three of these points besides stating your experience.

In composing letters in response to help-wanted advertisements, be sure always to write out the word "advertisement." Never use the abbreviation "ad." (To write "add" would further convict you of being an ignoramus, there being no such abbreviation.) If you are answering an advertisement in which only a box number is given, you should put this number in your letter in the same position where you would ordinarily place the firm name, as

Box No. X-191
Toledo *Examiner*
Toledo 2, Ohio

In the opening sentence, your letter should formally apply for the position advertised. You might begin it in one of the following ways:

In reply to your advertisement in the *Sunday Telegram*, I am submitting my qualifications for your consideration.

I should like to apply for the position of stenographer that you advertised in today's *Tribune*.

This is my application for the position of junior bookkeeper that you advertised in the *Chronicle* of March 19.

The remainder of the letter would follow the general rules which will be covered later in this chapter.

**To Firms You Hear Have Vacancies You Could Fill.** In talking with friends already in business, you may hear of vacancies that are about to occur or already existing. If you want a particular job, write a letter at once. Try to find out the name of the person who will select the new employee, and address your letter to the firm, marked for his attention. If you have not been told confidentially about the opening, mention the source of your information. Here are opening sentences for such a letter:

Miss Jones, of your credit department, tells me that you have asked her to secure the names of available typists for a possible vacancy. I wish to be considered for the position.

I have been told you expect to add several clerks to your filing department. If my information is correct, I should like to be considered an applicant. I am an experienced file clerk.

Mr. Albert Edwards, personnel manager of Brown-Jones & Company, has told me you wish to secure the names of several applicants for the position of bookkeeper-stenographer. After you have looked over my qualifications, listed on the enclosed personal data sheet, I hope you will grant me an interview.

**To Firms in a Field for Which You Are Especially Qualified.** Perhaps you have something special to offer, like the Chicago girl whose traveling experience fitted her for a position in a travel bureau. If so, a letter can be a great help in bringing your qualifications to the attention of an employer in your special field. Possibly your family owns a store, and during vacations you have sold behind the counter or learned to buy certain lines of merchandise. Or you may have a flair for fashion. You have a right to assume these experiences and interests might make you valuable in the office of a department store or in a buying exchange. Or, if you are a stenographer who has studied nursing, you would be especially well fitted for work in a doctor's office.

The introductory sentence of your letter should call attention to any such experience in your equipment for business. Since I cannot know what your special experience may have been, I shall have to leave the composition of the opening of this letter to you.

**To Business People Who Know You or Your Family.** Refer again to Chapter 5 and our discussion of the value of friends and acquaintances as a possible means of securing interviews.

Letters sent to business people who know you or your family can be more personal in tone than those in the previous classifications. Even if you have not personally met those to whom you are writing, the assumption is that, since they know your family or who you are, they will take some interest in you as an individual. For instance, graduates of a private business school in St. Louis have been most successful in securing positions in their smaller home communities by writing to bankers, lawyers, and other prominent citizens who knew their parents and, in some instances, the writers of the letters. Writing home from a large city proved sufficiently intriguing to produce interviews for the applicants.

In using this type of list, write directly to the individual, not to his firm, giving his business title and addressing him as follows:

Mr. George Evans, President
Central Bank
244 Parkside Row
Rochester 10, New York

Dear Mr. Evans:

Your introductory paragraph should be friendly and rather informal. Here are two suggestions:

You may not remember me, but I am the daughter of David Hamilton, and my father has often spoken of you to me. Father may have told you that following two years at college, I came to New York for a thorough business course in the Blank Business School. I shall graduate in another month and hope to go home to work. May I call on you someday soon to discuss the possibility of a position in your bank either as a typist or a stenographer?

My cousin, James Elwood, says he has spoken to you about me as a possible employee in the business office of your organization. I shall greatly appreciate an appointment to call on you and discuss this matter in person. I need not tell you that I should consider myself most fortunate to work for your company, and especially under your supervision.

## WHAT CONSTITUTES A GOOD LETTER OF APPLICATION

I am continually surprised at the lack of knowledge among applicants of what constitutes a good letter of application. Though self-expression, especially on paper, is more difficult for some persons than for others, it ought to be possible to state one's case in simple declarative sentences when applying for a position. But, alas, the average letter received by business organizations from would-be employees proves this is not so.

I have several hundred letters given to me by business friends from their application files. They are written on all sorts of paper, often on daintily tinted social stationery, occasionally penciled on ruled paper torn from a school tablet. Even when standard-sized business paper has been used, the applicant has often written on both sides. Many letters have no margins. At least 50 per cent of the handwritten letters

Letters of application, usually, should be
typewritten. This young lady is making sure
that she has all names and titles correct—a *must*
in application letters.

are illegible. Among such poor applications, a letter that is neat and
well arranged is bound to win a reading, and perhaps the job.

It should not be necessary to tell business students that letters of
application, like all business letters, should be written on plain white
paper, regulation size (8½ by 11 inches). The excuse, "I saw the ad
in the newspaper, and the only stationery in the house was notepaper,"
is never acceptable. Anyone who is job hunting should have the proper
businesslike equipment at hand and be ready to write a letter at a moment's notice. If you do not wish to invest in heavy white bond paper
by the box, the nearest dime store will provide the few necessary sheets
and envelopes in the proper size.

*Your Letter Is a Sample of Your Work.* There is some difference of
opinion as to whether letters of application should be written by hand
or on a typewriter. As was explained in an earlier chapter, legible handwriting is an asset in many office positions, especially those connected
with bookkeeping. Perhaps this is why some authorities say the application should be handwritten. I concede that a person applying for an

accounting or a bookkeeping position should use pen and ink for the letter itself, but suggest that the accompanying Personal Data Sheet be typed. In my opinion, applicants who wish to be employed as typists, stenographers, or dictating-machine operators should by all means use a typewriter whenever possible.

After all, in what other line of work does a job seeker have such an opportunity to present a sample of his work? For a letter of application tells a great deal more about your ability as a typist than any mere statement of your qualifications and experience. It shows your knowledge of letter forms and your ability to compose, and gives a demonstration of your typing. And none of this is lost on the person who reads your letter. Of course, if you do not have access to a machine that does good work, all you can do is to write neatly and legibly by hand.

### Follow the Rules in Setting Up Your Letter

It is to be supposed that senior commercial students know how to set up a business letter. But since so many letters of application show either carelessness or ignorance of the fundamental rules, I shall restate the basic principles of a business letter.

Consider the margins a white frame for your letter. Top and bottom margins should be fairly equal; the two side margins should be about the same width. Your address should appear at the upper right as follows:

42 Melvin Road
Boston 17, Massachusetts
January 12, 19—

Note that the date follows immediately below. Putting your address and the date together is more businesslike than to have your address follow your name at the end of the letter. An address at the top takes the place of a letterhead, such as is used by all business firms, giving the firm name and address.

*Inside Address.* At the left margin, write the *exact* name of the person or firm you are addressing. I mention this because so many typists are careless about the spelling of names and about using correct initials.

If you are writing to an individual who knows you, as in classification three, you may address the letter to him, and follow his name with his title, thus:

Mr. George Glastonbury, Vice-President
Crowell & Brown Company
1221 Broadway
Louisville, Kentucky

But unless there is a personal reason why you should write to an individual member of a business firm, it is better form to address your letter to the company itself, marking it for the attention of the person you wish to reach. This is true of all types of business letters, because you have no way of knowing whether the person to whom you write may be out of the city or may even have left the organization. To illustrate, if your letter is addressed as follows, it will go to Mr. Hilton, if he is in town and is still personnel director. Otherwise, it will be opened and routed to the person acting for him or to his successor.

Crowell & Brown Company
1221 Broadway
Louisville, Kentucky
Attention Mr. Fred Hilton, Personnel Director

This letter would carry the salutation, "Gentlemen," whereas if you wrote direct to the officer of the company, as previously indicated, the salutation should be either "Dear Mr. Glastonbury" or "Dear Sir."

Note that no periods follow the date line, name, or address in headings to letters.

*The Closing.* Authorities differ as to the correct closing for letters of application. Some feel that only "Yours truly," "Very truly yours," or "Yours very truly" are permissible. Other very good schools teach their students that "Sincerely yours" and even "Very sincerely yours" are not only allowable but the best form. I suggest that you follow the advice of your own school in this matter. However, "Cordially yours" is definitely too intimate, and "Respectfully yours" too servile, to be used. Whatever closing you use, only the first word should begin with a capital, and the phrase should end with a comma, thus:

Yours truly,

In all correspondence, it is important that the closing conform with the spirit of the letter. An application letter sent to someone you know would end more cordially than one addressed to a stranger.

*Typed Name Not a Signature.* There seems to be a misunderstanding among some business students as to the correct use of a typed name at the close of a letter. The custom of typing the correspondent's name below his actual signature has become general because so many executives sign their letters illegibly. The typed name, however, is not a signature; it only serves to clarify the handwritten name. Yet, because they have seen printed signatures in books and have been told to type the dictator's name at the end of the letter, many young business graduates send out their own business letters with only their typewritten names at the end. This practice makes a poor impression on businessmen, and they would not care to trust their correspondence to employees who are so little aware of the correct procedure in letter writing. Do not type your name *at all* at the end of your letter. This is an executive privilege.

An error often made by young women is to sign their names with "Miss" or "Mrs." as a prefix, without placing parentheses around it. The reason for placing such a prefix before your name is to make known your state of life, which is sometimes important to the employing firm. When you use the title in application letters, you should always place it in parentheses, as (Miss) Mary Brown. When writing their names, both young men and women should write out the first name in full; initials are not enough.

## WHAT TO AVOID IN YOUR LETTER OF APPLICATION

Before giving the most approved three forms of application, let us analyze some of the errors in actual letters. Many writers have difficulty in outlining their personal histories without overworking the personal pronoun "I." The writers may not be unduly conceited or self-centered, but that is the effect their letters create. A skeletonized version of one such letter runs like this:

I saw your ad in the *Post* today. Please consider . . .
I graduated from Warren Harding High School—business course. While in school . . .
I have worked for the General Electric Company for approximately two . . .
I am 20 years old, weigh 150 pounds . . .
I can be ready to come down to your office . . .

In endeavoring to avoid the ever-present "I," some applicants fall into the equally bad error of dispensing with the personal pronoun entirely. This, of course, produces a sentence without a subject. Consider the following examples:

Am happy to have seen your advertisement.
Was educated in the Walton High School and Case Business School.
Employed for six months as stenographer.
Graduate of Hope Secretarial School and have had experience in various kinds of office work.
Am 20 years old, unmarried, and can give the best of references.
Can offer excellent references.
Trust an interview can be arranged.

Other applicants inconveniently refer to themselves as "the writer" or "the applicant," where a judicious use of the first person singular would be less stilted.

*Too Much Self-praise.* A common practice among writers of application letters is to comment favorably on their own qualifications in an apparent effort to sell themselves to the reader. Here are a few examples from actual letters:

My education, qualifications, and references should satisfy the requirements.

I am 21 years old, an honor graduate of the secretarial course of the Blank High School; am attractive and have an even disposition.

I have been doing secretarial work for the past six years and am considered quite a conscientious worker.

I am considered a neat and not bad-looking person.

Kindly give consideration to this application of a sincere, mathematically minded American fellow, aged 24, possessing both business experience and a college education.

With modesty I would say I am a personable young woman, have initiative, expert stenographer, typist, bookkeeper, capable of taking charge of an office. . . .

Faithful, conscientious—just the man for you, I'm sure.

*Watch Your Grammar and Spelling.* As you undoubtedly notice, the self-praise is not the only thing wrong with some of these statements. Poor phrasing and incorrect sentence structure characterize some of these and many other letters of application. Here are a few examples:

My education consists of high school and a business college of which I am a graduate.

Due to the present economical conditions, I am one of those who must seek new connections.

Am now employed, and although I am thankful for same, would like to do better.

Errors in spelling in letters of application certainly do nothing to smooth the path toward employment. Here are a few examples taken at random from my collection:

Yours truely,

Let me know if you are interrested.

You know doubt come in contact with a great many applicants.

I adapt myself to my job and am also cortious.

No doubt your just swamped with applications.

I should be greatful if you. . . .

Neither they nor I faired any the worst for the contact.

The renumeration I receive means something to me.

*Don't Set Your Own Time for the Interview.* Although it is important not to lose sight of the fact that you are primarily seeking an interview, you should not dictate how, where, or when the interview might take place, or attempt to force one. The following quotations show how applicants can do themselves more harm than good by such urgency.

I would be grateful if an interview could be granted me within the next few days as I have to go out of town on Friday.

Hoping to have the pleasure of hearing from you Saturday, as I shall be at home all day.

Please let me hear from you right away, as I have other prospects.

*Always Spell Out Proper Names.* Although I am certain that no teacher of business subjects advises students to abbreviate in correspondence the names of cities, colleges, or schools, apparently many graduates take such short cuts. Letters on my desk refer to "Mnpls.," "Brdgpt.," "L.A.," and "Frisco." One is from "J.C.N.J.," which I finally deciphered as Jersey City, New Jersey. A businessman is not likely to be impressed with a letter containing such abuse of proper names, nor will it mean anything to him that an applicant spent two years at "U. of P." or is a graduate of "Tech." These are marks of provincialism and should never appear in any correspondence. And such errors occur even in well-staffed offices. I once borrowed for dictation the private secretary to the president of a department store at which I was a guest speaker. I was amazed to find "N.Y." used in the body of my transcribed letters, not to mention "L.A." and "S.F." When I remonstrated, the young secretary assured me that her chief made no objection to these abbreviations. A busy man sometimes grows lax about checking such details. But let it never be forgotten that one reason he hires a secretary rather than a stenographer is to relieve him of the burden of watching the details of correct correspondence and other office procedure.

*Avoid Alibis, Self-interest, and Whining.* In a later chapter, you will be told that employers take strict account of an employee's attitude. This is equally true in dealing with potential employees by correspondence. When an applicant apologizes in his letter, the employer suspects that the writer is an "alibier." Here are some typical excuses taken from letters of application:

Please do not judge my typing ability by this letter, as the machine is an old one. I assure you a modern machine would produce good work.

Excuse the pencil, please. My pen has gone dry.

Some applicants consider first what they will get out of the job, rather than what they can do for the employer.

> I am visiting in New York and most eager to locate here for personal reasons.
> I find school teaching very nerve-racking, and it would be so lovely to work surrounded by your beautiful merchandise.

Another group of applicants approaches jobs by attempting to be ingratiating. From my files I quote:

> Your ad reads as though it were written just for me.
> Your advertisement in this morning's *Times* seems a finger of Fate.

But the worst mistake of all is the complaint about the conditions the applicant faces. Here is a sample of what I mean:

> Of course I realize my speed is not what it should be, but how can I gain speed when the call is for girls who have already had experience and are fast?

And this is surely from a whiner:

> How can a girl have experience if businessmen don't want to give a girl a chance?

Can't you hear employers and personnel directors say, "So what?" to these selfish, fawning, and disgruntled whiners? Can you imagine any of them ever gaining an interview, much less a job?

### LETTERS THAT WIN INTERVIEWS

Mastering the art of writing good letters of application is something you can and should do before you leave business school. Either then, or during your early job-seeking days, spend all the time it takes—several days if necessary—constructing an excellent letter. In some interviews, you may be asked to sit down right then and write a letter of application, stating why you think the firm should employ you. If you take this chapter to heart, such a request need not put you in a panic.

When you have constructed a good letter, you can make it the basis of all your written applications. You will need only to vary the opening sentence to fit the situation. Getting yourself organized on paper will give you self-confidence and will be of great help on those occasions when you need a letter to gain an interview. Such a letter can be used with the Personal Data Sheet, as will be explained shortly. In case you think the importance of neatness, correct form, and good appearance in letters of application has been overemphasized, read what an office manager in Chicago has to say. "Recently, I urgently needed an experienced stenographer and ran a newspaper advertisement stating the

*Keystone View Co. of New York, Inc.*

Although application letters do not often land jobs outright, they can be the means of a successful entree into the personnel office.

necessary job qualifications. Most of the replies fell into two groups—those written illegibly by hand, and those so poorly constructed and so badly typed that the writers immediately disqualified themselves. There was only one good application in the lot: one letter that brought its writer an interview and got me a good stenographer."

### Personal Data Sheet or Résumé

These days a young man or woman seeking a job doesn't merely write a letter asking for an interview. He does that, and more. Whether the applicant has had experience or has none to offer, the method of applying by mail is practically the same. Business has come to expect that the person looking for work will take the trouble to assemble all the needed information about himself—education, skills, personal qualifications (age, health, and the like), experience if any, and references—in a form easily grasped by an interviewer. These summaries are known by various names, with Personal Data Sheet and Résumé the most accepted titles. There are three methods of presenting these, any of which is correct. The point to remember is that the material must be assembled in advance of job hunting, and put in such shape that it is ready for use in connection with the letter of application.

As an aid in the organization of such a Personal Data Sheet, here is the type of form generally approved.

## PERSONAL DATA

NAME

ADDRESS

TELEPHONE

POSITION APPLIED FOR:

State the type of job you are applying for, or use the phrase, "a beginning job that will lead to . . ."

EXPERIENCE:

List any positions held, and give job titles, with duties performed.

PART-TIME OR SUMMER WORK:

List here any work of the type indicated above, as this is considered working experience.

SKILLS:

List any abilities you have, such as bookkeeping, typing, shorthand, business machines operated, and filing. Mention speeds, if you wish. Sometimes this section is headed "Job Qualifications."

EDUCATION:

Name schools and colleges attended, and give graduation dates. List major subjects and those that interested you most. Include any night courses taken.

OUTSIDE INTERESTS AND HOBBIES:

A recent graduate may include academic honors, school offices, and the like, if they are pertinent. Mention of clubs, hobbies, and other outside interests will help to give the interviewer an all-round picture of you.

PERSONAL QUALIFICATIONS:

Age—             Height—
Health—          Marital status—
Weight—

REFERENCES:

List at least three persons who know you well enough to recommend you, not including relatives. It is best to have both business and character references. Be sure to ask permission before using anyone's name as a reference.

When you have worked out your own résumé after the example shown here, type, or have typed, a number of copies for use in your job-seeking campaign. Carbons are acceptable, if neat and clean, but if the interviewer cannot read a sixth carbon, your cause won't be advanced. Two, or at the most three, clear carbons can be used for this purpose. Try to condense your data so as to use only one page. Make your remarks brief. If you wish, you may simplify the form.

Here are the principal ways to use your Personal Data Sheet:

1. As an enclosure, accompanying a short letter
2. As the basis for a longer letter (as shown later)
3. As the main body of a letter, with opening and closing paragraphs added

Carry several copies of your Personal Data Sheet with you when looking for work. Often you can leave one with an interviewer to whom you have not already given a copy. Also, when filling out an application form, you can save much time by consulting your Personal Data Sheet for dates and other information.

## A LETTER PLUS A PERSONAL DATA SHEET

The letters reproduced here will show the difference in construction of these three forms of application. Any of these methods of presenting your qualifications is correct. However, there is a growing preference among business firms for the separate data sheet, because it enables an interviewer to get the important facts at a glance. Also, it is convenient for filing. From your point of view, its advantage is that it enables you to write a very short letter of application. Once you have assembled your data concretely, your letter writing will be easy. The following letter illustrates the method of using a two-paragraph letter, with the Personal Data Sheet enclosed. Note the use of a simplified form.

593 Sycamore Street
Tulsa 15, Oklahoma
June 5, 19—

Tulsa Oil Company
73 Broadway
Tulsa 1, Oklahoma

Attention: Mr. Oscar Hills, Personnel Director

Gentlemen:

Within the next week I shall graduate from the Tulsa High School and shall be looking for employment. While I have majored in the college-preparatory course, I have taken my electives in commercial subjects. This seemed to me the best way to get a good general educational background along with the needed skills of shorthand and typewriting. As a result, I am qualified to start as a stenographer or typist.

On the enclosed Personal Data Sheet you will find a résumé of my educational and personal qualifications as well as other information that should be helpful to you in considering my application. My plan is to call at your office on the first business day following graduation, and I hope that you will then grant me the courtesy of an interview.

Very truly yours,

Elizabeth Allen

### PERSONAL DATA of
### ELIZABETH ALLEN
593 Sycamore Street
Tulsa 15, Oklahoma
SE 4-3220

EDUCATION:

Four years at Tulsa High School; took College Preparatory Course; Major: English; Minor: Commercial Subjects

QUALIFICATIONS:

Typing—45 words a minute
Shorthand—80 to 90 words a minute
Filing
Adding machine

EXPERIENCE:

Counselor at Y.W.C.A. camp last summer, supervising thirty girls for period of six weeks
    Part-time job in school office, three afternoons a week during senior year; duties: typing and filing

PERSONAL:

Age—18
Single—live at home with parents
Height—5 feet 4 inches
Weight—111 pounds
Complexion—medium brunette
Health—excellent

HOBBIES:

Tennis and badminton; photography and record collecting

REFERENCES (by permission):

Mr. Kenneth Brown, Credit Manager
Morton Howell Company
247 North Scott Street, Tulsa 3, Oklahoma
FR 2-9546

Dr. Charles H. Harwell
836 Adams Avenue, Oklahoma City 6, Oklahoma

Mr. James Downey, Principal
Tulsa High School
1406 Landon Avenue, Tulsa 10, Oklahoma

## WHEN THE PERSONAL DATA ARE IN THE LETTER

In the next letter, you will observe that the necessary information about the applicant is embodied in the letter.

> 1541 Derby Street
> Berkeley 17, California
> January 14, 19—

Box 75321
Berkeley *Gazette*
Berkeley 3, California

Gentlemen:

In answer to your advertisement in the Berkeley *Gazette*, I am submitting my application for the position of bookkeeper-stenographer that you have open.

I am twenty-four years old; an American, born in Illinois; single; height, 6 feet; weight, 165 pounds; health, good.

I was graduated from Lincoln High School, Chicago, in June, 19—. After two years at the University of California, I spent a year preparing for business at the Calaveras Secretarial School, San Francisco.

As to experience—my first position was as a typist-clerk with the Traymore Oil Company, of California. After six months, I was promoted to a stenographic position, while retaining a few clerical duties. I left this company after a year to take a better-paying position as stenographer-clerk with the Morgan Securities Company in their Oakland office.

For the past two years, I have been in the Army, where my work was clerical in the Quartermaster Corps. I have kept up my shorthand, so that I feel I could step at once into the position you advertise.

Permission has been given me to refer you to Mr. Henry Parker, office manager of the Traymore Company, and to Mr. Frederick H. Belknap, secretary and treasurer of the Morgan Securities Company. Both can tell you about the quality of my work and about me personally.

If my application interests you, I shall be available for an interview at your convenience. My residence telephone number is BErkeley 4592, where a message may be left, setting a time for me to call on you.

> Very truly yours,
> (Signature) George Hanson

A Combined Letter and Data Sheet

Here is a method of combining the letter and the Personal Data Sheet.

752 Bond Street
Bridgeport 4, Connecticut
February 1, 19—

John B. Mackintosh, Inc.
700 Bell Road
Hartford 2, Connecticut
Attention Mr. R. B. Bell, Office Manager

Gentlemen:

Through my present employer, Mr. David Hughes of the Bridgeport Metal Company, I have learned that you are looking for an experienced stenographer who can assume responsibility. Mr. Hughes knows that I wish to move to Hartford because my family now resides there.

Briefly, here is my history.

EDUCATION:

Graduate Polytechnic High School, New York City, June, 1950
Graduate New York Junior College, 1952

EXPERIENCE:

Present position, secretary-stenographer, Bridgeport Metal Company (1954)
Stenographer, Bailey and Hatch Company, Bridgeport, Connecticut, nine months (1953-1954)
Typist, Hope Insurance Company, New York City, one year (1952-1953)

PERSONAL:

Age—23
Height—5 feet 3 inches
Weight—115 pounds
Health—excellent

RECOMMENDATIONS (by permission):

Miss Mary Dale, Office Manager
Hope Insurance Company, New York City

Mr. Paul Murphy, Personnel Director
Bailey and Hatch Company
Bridgeport, Connecticut

Mr. David Hughes, Vice-President
Bridgeport Metal Company
Bridgeport, Connecticut

May I have an opportunity to talk with you at your convenience? Mr. Hughes has said I may go to Hartford to see you, if you will set a time.

Yours truly,

(Signature) Jane Small

## You May Need a Portfolio

In applying for certain kinds of work, you will need to present proof of your talent and ability. These jobs are chiefly in the creative fields—commercial art, industrial design, photography, and writing. When you seek employment in any of these areas, you should carry with you a portfolio showing samples of your work. The person who interviews you wants to see what you can do, and a portfolio is your opportunity to impress him. To prepare your portfolio for presentation, organize your samples so that they appear in order, using whatever arrangement you decide on. For example, a portfolio for a writer could include sections showing articles, advertisements, stories, poems, and fashion copy, while a portfolio for an artist might show groupings of lettering, layouts, sketches, cartoons, and original artwork. You should arrange your material in the portfolio so that emphasis is placed on the type of work you hope to do for a particular employer. If any of your work has appeared in print, by all means include clippings. Remember that, important as a portfolio is, it does not take the place of your Résumé or Personal Data Sheet, but supplements it. Be sure to include a copy of this personal record whenever you present your portfolio.

Although your experience to date may not qualify you as a commercial artist, a portfolio showing your art work will strengthen your application for a job in an allied field, such as interior decorating, drafting, or window and interior department-store display. Anyone interviewing you for employment in one of these occupations will regard your portfolio as proof that you have a good background for this vocation.

### Closing Your Letter of Application

Either in your letter or on your Personal Data Sheet, you should give both business and character references. If you are applying for your first position and have had no experience, your references, of necessity, will be character references only. Do not neglect including them. Before writing letters of application, you should ask permission to use as references the names of friends of established position in your community, school officials or businessmen who know you, giving their full names, addresses, and titles. Whenever possible, list their business telephones. Do not include names of relatives.

*Character References.* Here are some suggestions for sentences introducing references, when these are given in the letter itself.

I refer you by permission to . . .
I have permission to refer you to . . .

Mr. G. E. Williams, Principal of Blank School, has given me permission to refer you to him for information regarding my personal skills.

Mr. Albert Haynes, manager of the book department of Blank Department Store, has known me for ten years. He will be willing to give you any personal information you may wish to have concerning me.

*Request for an Interview.* Your letter should close with a definite request for an interview and give the telephone where you may be reached. Such a request could be phrased like this:

May I have a personal interview at your convenience? My telephone number is . . .

I can be reached by telephone at MArket 4427. I shall appreciate an opportunity for a personal interview.

May I call at your office for an interview? If you wish to telephone me, I can be reached at . . .

Each letter should end with a positive sentence, as in the above illustrations. Always avoid such obsolete expressions as "Looking forward to an early reply," "Hoping I may hear from you, I am," "Thanking you in anticipation of a reply."

*When to Enclose a Photograph—and What Kind.* When an advertisement requests a photograph, you should always enclose one, of course; otherwise, it is better not to distribute pictures of yourself. However, be sure that any photograph you use in such a way is small and looks businesslike, which means that a broad grin or evening clothes would not be in good business taste. Also, be sure that it does you justice. You might be able to get some prints of any photograph that was taken for your school paper, if you are only a year or so beyond graduation. Enclose it with your Personal Data Sheet only to your best prospects.

## FOLLOW-UP LETTERS

In a preceding chapter, letters were mentioned along with calls in person and by telephone as a means of following up your leads. I cannot think of any circumstances where a letter of application would be followed immediately by a second letter. You cannot expect a businessman to enter into correspondence with you. If he is willing to grant you an interview, fine. If he is not, you cannot secure an interview by flooding him with letters. You will only make a pest of yourself.

But after you have been interviewed by an employer or his representative, you may occasionally have a good reason to write and remind the interviewer of your existence. Perhaps the interviewer asked for some information you did not have with you, such as would be contained in a Personal Data Sheet. Under such circumstances, a brief follow-up letter would be in order. To thank the interviewer for his courtesy would be a graceful way to begin such a letter. Here is a good example of a follow-up letter that fits such a situation.

560 North Williams
Milwaukee 7, Wisconsin
January 14, 19—

Mr. Paul Brown
Humboldt Building
Milwaukee 3, Wisconsin

Dear Mr. Brown:

Thank you so much for the courteous interview you gave me this afternoon.

I am confident that I can do competent, accurate stenographic work and meet the high standard that your work requires.

A Personal Data Sheet is enclosed. It will set before you in compact form my qualifications and experience, and also give you an opportunity to judge my work.

May I look forward to your favorable decision?

Sincerely yours,

(Signature) Margaret A. Jones

Enc.

I do not suggest following *every* interview with a thank-you note as some authorities do. However, when you have been so fortunate as to be interviewed by someone who has jobs to give and who seems really interested in you, by all means follow this up with a brief and courteous letter of thanks. Such a gesture will show your appreciation of the time the interviewer spent with you and will serve also to recall you to his attention. If the interviewer already has a copy of your Personal Data Sheet, you could use the letter given above and omit the paragraph that refers to the enclosure.

Having sent your thank-you note, consider the correspondence closed, as far as you are concerned. If your prospect wishes to hear further from you, he will let you know. The only possible thing you can do now about this particular job, except perhaps for one telephone call to show your interest, is to wait. Better begin on other prospects right away, for these matters are never settled until you hear those happy words, "Please report for work Monday morning."

## QUESTIONS

1. Should a letter of application attempt to get a job or an interview?
2. If you apply to a great many firms by letter and get no answers, should you conclude that job seeking is useless?
3. What is the difference between aimless canvassing by mail and writing to a carefully selected list of business firms in a field for which you are qualified?
4. What kind of help-wanted advertisements can be answered only by letter?
5. Why do you need to study an advertisement very carefully before composing your letter of application?
6. Does the form in which a letter of application is set up have anything to do with the attention it receives?
7. When should a letter of application be written by hand? When on the typewriter?
8. Why do you think all three approved letter forms given in this chapter recommend that applicants state their age, height, weight, and health?
9. Does a name typed at the end of a letter constitute a signature?
10. Should you write a thank-you letter to an interviewer who did not offer you any encouragement or suggest your calling again?

## TOPICS FOR DISCUSSION

1. Discuss the place that letters of application have in the procedure of job hunting. Can letters be counted on actually to get jobs?
2. When is it desirable to use a letter? Discuss the three situations in which the text recommends writing letters of application.
3. Many letters of application are written because of—

   a. Dread of personal interviews
   b. Belief that letters produce jobs
   c. Desire to please parents

   Explain why none of these is a legitimate reason for applying by letter.
4. Name four things you should bear in mind when writing a letter in reply to a help-wanted advertisement.
5. In writing a letter to a firm that you hear has a vacancy you could fill, should you state the source of your information? What if you were given this tip confidentially?
6. A well-trained beginner is applying for a stenographic position. She wishes to use her letter as a sample of her work. What skills and abilities can her letter demonstrate?
7. Should you praise yourself in your application letters, in the belief that unless you tell how good you are no one will know it? Or can you

depend on your letter's speaking for you through its appearance and content?

8. Discuss the distinguishing features of the three approved types of letters recommended in the text. Which form do you like best? Why would you adopt it for your applications?

# PROJECTS

1. *a.* Assemble a Personal Data Sheet. Give accurate information and details about your education, personal qualifications, experience, and the like. Use the Personal Data Sheet given in this chapter as a guide.

   *b.* Write a letter to accompany this information. Address your letter as though it were to be sent to someone who knows you or knows who you are.

2. Select an advertisement from among those reproduced here, and make an application for the position described. Use any of the three types of letters described in this chapter. In writing your letter, confine yourself to your actual experience, or assume that you have the experience required.

---

### FEMALE HELP WANTED

CLERK-TYPIST—General clerical experience in typing, posting, etc. Employe benefits. 5-day week. Apply Division & Essex Sts., Trenton, N. J.

---

### CLERKS
Inventory Control

Some bookkeeping experience helpful. Knowledge of adding machines, good legible handwriting. Northeast Phila. location. Willing to work 8-hr. day, 5 days a week on inventory figures. Salary $75 to $80 per week depending on experience & qualifications. Vacation, paid holidays & insurance benefits. Cafeteria on premises. Reply in own handwriting giving age, experience & phone number to

P. O. BOX 423
PHILADELPHIA, PA.

---

TYPIST, order clerk for growing mail-order company. 5-day week. Air cond. office, $275 per month. Call Miss Davis, VI-1780, or apply in person. 550 Coulter St.

---

### FEMALE HELP WANTED

### FILE CLERKS
### STENOGRAPHERS
### TYPISTS
BEGINNERS OR EXPERIENCED

Increase after 3 months for beginners. Advancement. Liberal benefits plan, 5-day week.

### REX LIFE INSURANCE CO.
### ROCKEFELLER PLAZA, N. Y.

---

SWITCHBD OPER—RELIEF (Plug)

Exp. preferred. Will consider good beginner. Typing and general office work. 5 days. Many employe benefits.

### NEW-DAY RADIO CORP.
105 MAIN ST., BKLYN.

---

### STENOGRAPHER-SECRETARY
Downtown law office, young, personable, some switchboard (will teach). 9:30-6, 5 days, 3 weeks vacation. $100. Box MA 2572, Herald Tribune.

---

## FEMALE HELP WANTED

### STENO-CLERK

35-HOUR WEEK

Little dictation, small office routine, attention details essential; start $75; some exp. Monitor board; neat alert girl; permanent; P.O. Box F 425, Chicago.

### RECEPTIONIST

Typing, will train switchboard; small, attractive downtown insurance office; benefits, advancement; H S grad; to $250 month start. Apply 16th floor.

BOND LIFE INSURANCE CO.

845 Broadway

### BOOKKEEPER

Once-in-a-lifetime opportunity for bookkeeper and Girl Friday in modern, small, growing factory in Summit, N J; 1-gal office, congenial surroundings; permanent; salary plus bonus. Box 2-523 Times.

### STENOGRAPHER

Bright Beginner Considered

Small 3-girl office, 5 days, congenial surroundings, vacation with pay, hospitalization. 92 Park Place. YU 3-2429.

### DICTAPHONE OPERATOR

General office work, small sales office and showroom. Downtown Manhattan. 5-day week. Box 8-2310, Daily News.

### FILE CLERK, $60

For small sales dept of mfg concern. Good oppty for recent grad or beginner; typing helpful! Liberal benefits including vacation in current year. Write full details. Box 745 Times.

SECTY, DR'S OFFICE . . . . . . . . . $100

Some medical exp. Knowl steno. Good typist. Smith Agcy, 180 Bway. Rm 503.

## FEMALE HELP WANTED

### BOOKKEEPER

General office work in construction field or kindred. Bronx or Westchester resident. Box RR41 Times.

### STATISTICAL TYPISTS

Large corporation Radio City requires statistical typists with some experience. 5-day, 35-hour week. Electromatic machines. Pleasant surroundings, including Muzak. Air-conditioned offices. Salary dependent on ability and experience.

Box OR 9245, World Telegram

## MALE HELP WANTED

### OFFICE BOY

Bright beginner, act as messenger and make self generally useful in exceptionally attractive midtown office; congenial surroundings, good opportunity, 5-day week.

P.O. Box 92, Cleveland

### YOUNG MAN

To keep books, do typing and handle correspondence. Excellent opportunity. Box W 1260 Tribune.

### SECRETARY

Opportunity for one interested in advertising or publishing. Small firm. To 25. Write age, experience, education. Box RR99 Times.

### SECRETARY-STENOGRAPHER

for president of downtown banking institution. Must have neat appearance and a minimum of two years active experience as efficient secretary-stenographer. Liberal salary, paid vacations, holidays, other benefits. Air-conditioned offices convenient to all transportation. Write age, complete business background, and salary desired. Box R1033 Times.

MALE HELP WANTED

ACCOUNTING CLERK
Unusual opportunity with leading engineering firm for capable person, with some experience, college training preferred. New air-conditioned offices. Grand Central area. Liberal benefits, 5 days, 35 hours. Write Brown & Smith, 23 W. 43rd St.

YOUNG MAN
TAKE CHARGE OF MAIL ROOM
Position with large established automobile manufacturer. Must be young, aggressive, desire advancement. Typing essential. Good salary, excellent opportunity. Write full details. Box 432 Inquirer.

YOUNG MAN, TRAINEE
Excellent oppty to learn business, know bookkeeping, typing, 5D, 9-5, $65-$75 start. HART AGCY, 19 Fulton St, NYC

MALE HELP WANTED

YOUNG MAN
HS grad. knowledge of micrometer and blueprint reading. Interesting job with future. Call. 9-5, HY 7-3245 or write P.O. Box 732, Oakland.

ACCNTG or Cost Clerk: (Rahway, NJ) Excellent opening for young chap in mfg. company (near station) who is good at figures with knowl. of bkpg. St. $4,000. Manning Agcy, 55 Church.

ACCOUNTANTS
For CPA Firm
Permanent openings for beginners and experienced accountants in commercial field or stock brokerage and taxes. Splendid opportunity for increasing knowledge income taxes. P.O. Box 721, New York City.

3. There are mistakes in all the following quotations from letters of application. Rewrite them correctly, and be prepared to give orally your reasons for the changes.

I would very much like to apply for the position in the lawyer's office of which you mentioned in your add in this morning's *News*.

I read your adv. in the evening *Examiner* of May 26, and I am writing to you for more details about the position you have to offer.

In reference to your ad, the writer has a High-Prep and Business School experience.

Was employed for three years in the Merchandising Dept. of the AT&T in NJ and NY.

Can offer excellent references and ask for a personal interview.

While I have not had the two years legal experience your ad requires, it occurred to me you might have some other jobs which I could be fitted for, so I am answering anyway.

I am a twenty-one years old, personable, well-groomed and a high-school graduate.

This is the work I can do: file clerk and a little typing.

Am a young lady twenty-three yrs. of age. American and refined. Have had sevrl yrs. experience & am a good worker. Have good references. Will close in hopes of some good news from you.

Thank you for giving my application your special attention.

                                                    Yours respectfully
                                                    Mrs Ann Martin (typed)

Thanking you for your attention, I am

                                                    Yours truly

Please let me know by return mail if this application is excepted.

If you care for references I will be glad to furnish you with names and addresses of people who will tell you I'm O.K.

4. This chapter contains many erroneous sentences from actual letters of application. Examine these, and be prepared to state the errors. Rewrite correctly.

CHAPTER 8

# The Interview

When I was lecturing in a Seattle theater on "How to Get and Keep a Job," I was asked this question: "How can I give the impression of being a self-confident person?" My reply was, "*Be* a self-confident person." Feeling sure of yourself is an inner condition, a state of mind. It is not something that you can assume. But it *is* something that you can cultivate.

If you have thoughtfully put into practice the suggestions in the preceding chapters, you have been doing just that—cultivating self-confidence and poise as you advanced from point to point in your job-getting preparations. Now you are ready for that long-anticipated moment when you will actually look into the eyes of an employer or someone who represents that important person.

Your first interview may be something you have got through your own efforts, or it may be handed to you in the form of a letter or a card of introduction. At any rate, after such thorough preparation as you have undergone, your first interview should not be a dreaded or dreadful experience. Actually, you should have begun to look forward to this first interview, regarding it as an opportunity to prove your skills and ability. This is your chance to test out the ideas offered here. In fact, these ideas should no longer be just something read in a book; you should have made them your own, in a way that will help you in selling yourself as an alert young business person.

INTERVIEWS ARRANGED BY SCHOOL

In a previous chapter, you were told that your school placement office would probably send you on your first interview, around graduation time. You may or may not emerge from that interview wearing a broad smile that means "Hired." This is not nearly so important as that you have the experience of a school-sponsored interview early in your job-seeking campaign. Why? Because in no other type of interview will the cards be so stacked in your favor.

Throughout the school year, business firms that are not able to get enough experienced workers get in touch with colleges, junior colleges, high schools, and private business schools, asking for additional help as soon as students are graduated. And here is where *you* come in. You complete the triangle—school, employer, and applicant.

You can go to such an interview with confidence. The employer is willing to take a beginner, or he would not have called the school. He knows something about your school and expects it to send him someone good. He can, and probably will, ask the school placement officer these questions about you:

1. What kind of person are you?
2. What was the quality of your schoolwork?
3. Do you get along well with others?
4. Do your teachers think you will make a satisfactory employee?

Here's hoping your school records are such that an interested employer will get a good report on you. Because you won't want to let your school down, you'll wear to the interview a carefully selected, correct job-seeking outfit. Also, you'll give the right answers to all the questions. You will be a credit to yourself and to your school. Flushed with the success of your first interview, you will have an increased store of self-confidence to carry over into future interviews.

The procedure in any interview arranged by your school will be much like that described shortly, where an employment agency gives you a card of introduction to an employer. There will be an application form to fill out and opening and closing conversations as outlined in Chapter 6. It is possible that the employer to whom your school sends you may be a bit more cordial than if you were sent by an agency. But, between you and me, the chief difference in the school-arranged interview will be in *your* attitude toward the situation; it may seem like an extension of your school life, so you will feel at home in it. Consequently, you will be less self-conscious, and you should make an excellent impression on the person who interviews you.

AGENCY INTERVIEWS

If you have already called on commercial employment agencies, as suggested earlier, you may have had one or two experiences in that type of interview. But there are a few things I have to tell you about the employment-agency interview, before we discuss that face-to-face talk with a potential boss. In many ways, it is just as important to make a favorable impression on an interviewer in an employment agency as on the person who interviews you directly for a job in a place of business. For the agency interviewer determines whether you will be sent out on job interviews, and on that decision may depend whether you actually get opportunities for employment through this source. Everything we have said about the importance of your appearance in an office interview applies equally to those conversations you have in employment agencies. How you look, what you say, and how you act will determine whether or not the agency has confidence in you and your ability, and whether or not it feels you are an employable person whom it can place.

Although you may not realize it, your every action is being watched when you visit an employment agency. Remember that, though you pay the agency to help you, it cannot afford to try to place you unless you will do it credit. Even free employment agencies have to be selective in their choice of applicants for various positions. Although the applicant is not their source of income, they still have to create confidence in their selections or lose their employer clientele.

Once, when I was to interview young women for a stenographic position for one of our agency's fussiest clients, the agency manager went into the reception room to look over the girls waiting there. He returned to tell me, "Don't send that sloppy-looking girl with the long tangled hair and no stockings or hat. Bill Jones (the employer) would never take her." Because so many girls who apply at agencies are so careless of their appearance, a San Francisco employment agency is, according to a newspaper columnist, "branching into the charm-school field." I quote: "R—— H——, who runs the Tower Employment Agency, got so discouraged over the personal appearance of some of the candidates for secretarial jobs who showed up in his office that he installed a prop room on the premises. Those who need help can borrow hats, gloves, and veils, or make use of cosmetics, brushes, and even an ironing board before facing prospective employers."

At one time, I kept a tweed coat to lend our applicants when necessary and had in my desk a supply of hairpins to give to applicants with the advice, "Please go into the dressing room, and pin up that long bob. Then you will look neater and be more employable." So bear in mind that in an agency you are being sized up as to appearance and also as to whether you have the ability and common sense to act in a businesslike manner. I was told that in a New York State Employment Office many applicants who came to the recent college graduates department had trouble deciding at what counter they should line up to register. Signs reading A–F, G–K, L–S, T–Z were in the room, but some graduates had difficulty deciding where they belonged. None of this was lost on the interviewers, who doubted whether these young people knew the alphabet, could find a telephone number, use a dictionary, or hold down a simple filing job!

## AGENCY APPLICATION FORMS

You are likely to make the acquaintance of application forms in your early calls on employment agencies. So an application form is reproduced here, which is fairly typical of those you will be asked to fill out in agencies. It will pay you to study this form carefully and to rehearse in your own mind what answers you would make to these fundamental questions. Do not take the attitude of many beginners, and even experienced persons, who say in effect: "This is all a lot of nonsense. I can't be bothered filling out all this." Employment-agency executives are unanimous in saying: "Fill out every line. Answer every question. If you have nothing to say in answer to a particular question, draw a line through the space to show you have at least given it consideration." These questions would not be asked if the information desired were not important to the agency.

| Last name (Print) Barnes | First Name Muriel | Mr. Mrs. Miss ✓ | Social Security No. 354-26-4784 Work Preferred Secretarial, in an importing and exporting concern | Today's Date August 10, 19– | |
|---|---|---|---|---|---|
| Address 310 River Road | | | Languages Spanish, French, German | Salary desired $75 | |
| City Salem, N.J. Zone – | Will you pay for Telegram? Yes | | How did you learn of us A neighbor | Minimum Salary $65 | |
| Home phone Main 7-8020 | Nearest phone — | | Location preferred New York City | No. years exp. 2 | |
| Bus. phone Ba. 5-6000 | Will you accept temporary work? No | | Personal reference Rev. John Stone Carlton | Single ✓ Married Divorced | |
| Age 24 | Birth Date June 2, 19– | | Address St. Paul's Rectory, Salem, N.J. | No. children — | |
| Height 5 feet 2 inches Weight 120 lbs. | Live at Home Yes Board — | Date | Special training European travel | Draft status — | |
| Education High School | No. Years 4 | grad. June 19– | College Wellesley Year 4 Degree B.A. | Major English | |

|  |  |  |  |  |  |
|---|---|---|---|---|---|
| (Check (X) if experienced in following) | | | | | |
| ( ) Secretary | ( ) Bookkeeper | ( ) Sales | ( ) Underwood Bkg. | ( ) Adding Machine | ( ) Monroe Cal. |
| ( x ) Stenographer | ( x ) File Clerk | ( x ) Switchbd. (plug) | ( ) Nat'l Cash Reg. | ( ) Elliot Fisher Billing | ( x ) Teletype |
| ( ) Typist ( ) Stencil | ( ) Proofreader | ( x ) Switchbd. (mon.) | ( ) Underwood Billing | ( ) Elliot Fisher Bkg. | ( ) Addressograph |
| ( ) Cashier | ( ) Statistician | ( ) Edi or Dictaphone | ( ) Varitype Machine | ( ) Remington Wahl | ( x ) Mimeograph |
| ( ) Ledger Clerk | ( ) | ( ) Fanfold | ( ) Moon Hopkins | ( ) Burroughs Billing | ( x ) Ditto Machine |
| ( ) Stock Clerk ( ) Sales | ( ) | ( ) Comptometer | ( ) | ( ) Burroughs Bkg. | ( ) Multigraph |

| Name of firm | Present or last position Capitol Products Co. | Next to last | Next to that |
|---|---|---|---|
| Address? | 501 Market St. Newark N.J. | | |
| Their business? | General Merchandise | | |
| To whom may we refer? | T.B. Cox Manager | | |
| Your work there? | Secretarial | | |
| How long employed? Give Dates | July 1, 19– to August 1, 19– | | |
| Salary | $60 a week | | |
| Why did you leave? | To use languages | | |

A typical agency form filled in.

The personnel director of a New Jersey insurance company employing 400 girls complains that applicants often put on the application form only the street name and number as their address and omit the city and state. In a large suburban district, this is equivalent to no address. New Jersey isn't the only place where this omission occurs.

On the reverse side of the application form given to you by a private employment agency, there is usually a printed statement naming the fee for placing you in a job. Be sure to read this carefully so there will be no misunderstanding. When you sign your name on the application, you agree to pay for placement, as was explained in an earlier chapter. In case this is not clear to you, before you sign this agreement to pay, ask the person interviewing you to explain *what, how,* and *when* you are to pay the agency's commission if they get you a job.

In speaking to the interviewer, you may make a favorable impression but, since she interviews many persons a day, she is not likely to remember just what you told her. The record you leave in the office will be the means of getting you a call from the agency, if it has a position you can fill. It is up to you to be sure this record really represents you and that it gives definite information.

On the line that asks your preference as to work, you should write the kind of position you feel qualified to fill. Here, the answer, "Anything," will not help the agency. If you do not know what minimum salary you could expect for the type of work you want, ask for information on this point. But wait until you have completed the record as far as you are able and are ready to hand it in. Constantly running to the interviewer to ask for aid and information will make you appear helpless.

*Ready Data about Yourself.* If you list yourself with several employment agencies, you could spend many hours laboriously working over application forms such as the one shown. The better way, both for you and for the impression you make, is to save time by having these data with you, neatly typed. Your Personal Data Sheet, as described in the preceding chapter, should contain your personal, school, and work history to date. Copy from it when filling out an application form, as this will save your time and the need of recalling names and dates. After you have carefully answered all the questions, add any other facts that may be helpful to the agency in placing you. For instance, if you speak both Italian and English, record it. If you have traveled, say so. Such advantages might take you into a better job than the average beginner could hope to get. Knowing more than one language, travel, and other cultural assets can be valuable in business as well as in the social world.

*Spelling and Handwriting.* When you are filling out an application form in an agency or in a business firm, be sure to watch your spelling and handwriting. This is a time when an error or slovenliness will count badly against you. A young woman who operates a free school for one of the business-machine manufacturers says that many applicants, born in a community with such a name as Poughkeepsie or Wequetonsing, usually erase and rewrite the name several times because they are unsure of the spelling. You may have moved away from the picturesquely named town of your birth, but spelling its name correctly will be important to you from time to time as long as you live. And your handwriting should be legible. This is important not only for those who have to read your record but, as was said earlier, because many positions require good handwriting.

Unless a form states definitely that it is to be filled out in your own handwriting, it is a good idea to print your answers to the questions. You are usually requested to print your name at the top, and to sign your name elsewhere, so that your signature is on record.

On many application forms, above the lines where you are to list your experience, you will find the instruction: List Your Last Employer, and Work Backward. Cases are cited in employment-agency circles of applicants who took this command literally. A woman is said to have asked an interviewer, "How do I write drill-press operator backward?" The prize story is of a man who completed an entire application form, spelling every word backward. The interviewer who assured me that she saw this application says it looked like a foreign language; and, of course, no one could read it.

*Your Correct Signature.* When you print and sign your name on an application form, be sure to write your correct name and not a nickname, such as "Babe." Even a diminutive—Dick, Kate, or Molly—of a dignified name, such as Richard, Katherine, or Mary is not in order. Your family and your friends may call you Dick or Molly; but neither of these would be a legal name and should never be used in print, on a visiting card, or as a signature on letters, applications, or other business papers.

To go through life using a childish nickname as a signature is not in good taste. Neither is the incorrect spelling of an otherwise familiar name. I once noticed that the application form of a girl whom I was interviewing for a beginning file job gave her first name as "Dorthy." I questioned what I thought was a careless mistake. "No," she replied, "that's my name. I was named for my Aunt Dorothy, but my father was excited when he signed the papers in the hospital and wrote 'Dorthy.' So, I've been 'Dorthy' ever since." I didn't hire her because I figured, if she didn't have the common sense to use her correct name, she wasn't bright enough to learn filing.

Decide now, before you leave school, how you intend to sign your name. You will need to adopt your correct signature—preferably your first name in full with your middle initial—and stick to it. Practice writing your signature so that it can be read. If you do this, when you are an executive, your secretary won't have to type your name beneath it so your correspondents will know who is writing to them.

*Meticulous Accuracy.* I cannot say too firmly, "Be very exact and careful in filling out all application forms." Your exactness, or the lack of it, may be all that stands between you and success or failure. I was once looking for a young woman who had held a minor bookkeeping job and would be able to make out orders for an import concern. Our files had not produced many likely candidates, and I was hoping that the morning callers might provide potential material. My assistant brought Mary Graves to my desk. "I think this is the person you are looking for," she said hopefully.

I asked Mary what her experience had been and told her to fill out an application card. Fifteen minutes later, Mary and her card were ready for my inspection. I had only to glance at the application to know that she would not do. "It will not be possible for us to recommend you for the office position I had in mind," I told her, "because of the way you have filled out the line stating what salary you received in previous positions." Mary said, "But that's what I got." "You must have been paid more than that. Don't you see anything wrong with the way you have written these figures?" No, she did not. This made the matter even a little worse, for here is the way she had written the information:

| | Last position | Second position | First position |
|---|---|---|---|
| Salary received | $ .60 | $ .50 | $ .40 |

Since Mary apparently did not know where to place the decimal point, she would hardly be helpful at figures in an import office or any other place.

*Introduction to an Employer.* Let us assume that you have learned all there is to know about being interviewed in an employment agency and that you have made so favorable an impression on one agency that it has given you a "referral" card introducing you to a prospective employer. Here is the way such a card will look:

UP-AND-COMING EMPLOYMENT AGENCY

450 Market Street

TO: Mr. David Gray, Personnel Director

FIRM: Acme Metal Products Co.

ADDRESS: 189 South Street

INTRODUCING: George Beale

FOR POSITION AS: Assistant Bookkeeper

HOUR OF APPOINTMENT: 2 p.m., March 4

SALARY: $75 week    REFERRED BY: Margaret Jones

Usually, the hour of your appointment is arranged by the agency and noted on your card, but occasionally you will be told to telephone the employer and find out what time he can see you. In any event, you will have been given the name of the individual who is to consider you. If it is up to you to telephone him, organize yourself so as to make a favorable impression in your part of the phone conversation. Get the company, and ask for the person whose name you have, or that person's secretary. An important point to remember is that often you will do better to ask for an executive's secretary and transact your business with the secretary than to be mysterious and insist on talking directly with the head of the company. If you speak to the secretary, say something like this: "I am George Beale, and I am being sent by the Up-and-Coming Employment Agency to talk with Mr. Gray about the position of assistant bookkeeper. Can you find out what time it will be convenient for Mr. Gray to see me?" This type of approach will bring immediate results. An efficient secretary will either check then with Mr. Gray or promise to do so later and give you the information if you will call her.

Sometimes, an interview is lost because an individual lacks tact in trying to make the appointment. A woman employer whose business is that of manuscript typist (work conducted from her apartment) told me of an incident in which an employment agency had recommended Hazel Doane highly. Hazel had had two years of college, was a rapid typist, and sounded like just the person this employer was looking for. However, Hazel telephoned about nine o'clock in the morning and prefaced her remarks by saying, "Did I get you up?" The employer, not liking this approach, replied, "No. Why?" "Oh, your voice sounded like it," came the pert retort over the wire. Although this remark was followed by a polite enough request for an interview, it is not surprising that the employer felt that any girl who would become so personal and so tactless would not be a desirable employee. Consequently, she refused the interview.

With a card of introduction from an agency stating the time of your appointment, you are justified in arriving, say, ten minutes ahead of the hour set. It is better to be a few minutes early than to run the risk of being late. Nor is there any point in letting someone else get in ahead of you or in making a wrong impression by tardiness. Your first contact with the organization will be the telephone-receptionist, who usually sits at an outer desk. Do not try to get past her or to avoid a little direct questioning there. In fact, it is a much better policy to attempt to make a friend of this young woman on your first appearance at her place of business. She can do a great deal to help you, and conversely, she often has the power to ruin your chances. Instead of being closemouthed and saying merely "I want to see Mr. Gray," it is better to say, "I have a card from the Up-and-Coming Employment Agency to be presented to Mr. Gray at two o'clock. Will you please tell him I am here, and let me know when he is free?" Then seat yourself on the bench or chair provided for callers. Unless you can sit quietly without twitching or fiddling, it is well to have a newspaper or magazine to occupy you. But avoid a scandal sheet or a motion-picture publication. You never know who is making a mental note of your literary taste at this particular moment. And, whatever you do, *don't chew gum!*

*Waiting to Good Advantage.* Even though you appear to be reading, it is a good idea to keep your ears open, because often you can pick up information that will prove valuable to you later. At any rate, you can gain an idea of what kind of people already work there by watching those within your line of vision or those who are passing you as they go from office to office. Sometimes, you can learn what sort of firm it is by the manners of the telephone-receptionist. If she is quiet and polite in handling calls and callers, it is probable that the business is a conservative one and that it wants only top-notch employees. But if the operator is abrupt, rude, or flippant and seems to carry on endless personal chats of her own as she plugs business calls in and out and receives callers, the chances are that the heads of the firm have not a very high standard for their employees. If they had, they would never tolerate this presentation of their company to the public.

Keep your eye on your watch as well as on the switchboard-receptionist. If your appointment is for two o'clock and you are not called by two or three minutes past the hour, step up to the receptionist's desk and remind her you are waiting. If she is not busy, this may be a good time to exchange a word or two with her and try to win her favor. You can begin by asking whether Mr. Gray is still tied up or whether you can see him now, since it is time for your appointment. If you smile when you speak to her, you will gain her co-operation more easily. She will then either send you to Mr. Gray or tell you he is likely to be busy for some time. You might politely suggest that you don't wish to bother her further and will wait for her to call you. Whereupon you return to your seat.

Often, it is necessary to please three or more persons in an organization before you are hired. And sometimes the first person you must impress favorably is the telephone-receptionist. Some young men in applying for work think that to exchange wisecracks with the receptionist gets them in, and perhaps it does in some cases. Only their good judgment can tell them whether that is the method to use. But such tactics will not help a young woman applicant. All she can do is to be pleasant and friendly—but not too much so—and hope for the best.

### THE LONG-ANTICIPATED EMPLOYMENT INTERVIEW

For the purpose of instructing you in the interview itself, let us assume that you are past the operator and have been admitted to the personnel director. Should you speak first, or wait for him to recognize your presence and say something? If he does not look up from his work or is speaking to another person, of course, you will have to wait. Beyond that, it makes no difference. Perhaps the best way is for you to mention your name, "I am George Beale (or Mary Smith)." Or you say, "The Up-and-Coming Employment Agency sent me," and present your agency card. In some instances, the interview will begin then and there. In others, you will be told to step into the outer office and fill out an application form. It will do you no good to argue that you'd rather tell the interviewer what he or she wishes to know. Actually, it is to your advantage to have in the company records a detailed account of your education, qualifications, and experience, if any. In some businesses, the application blank is a pre-employment test, and this may be your only chance to take a test in this office. If you fill it out poorly, an interview may not be granted you, for by your carelessness you will have eliminated yourself. So, realize that it is necessary for the records of the firm, and begin to fill out the form, which will be similar to the one reproduced here. Do it as quickly as possible, allowing for accuracy and neatness. And be sure to sign your name!

Many office jokes originate in the answers that applicants make to the printed questions on application forms. There's the one about the girl who, on the line for date, wrote "Yes." In answer to Birth Record, "I was born . . . ," many persons write the name of the hospital instead of the city where they were born. One application handed to me by a hopeful lad said he was born "upstairs at Grandpa's." Don't help the jokesmiths with your replies.

Your references will be especially important on this application form, so have them with you. Be ready to list the names, addresses, and telephone numbers of five persons, not relatives, who are willing to recommend you for character, work, or both. These should be persons who know you well and whose position in life is stable. Be sure you have first asked and obtained permission to use them as references. If you are a stranger in town, you will have to list names of persons to whom the firm can write. When you have finished filling out the form, return to the personnel director and hand it to him.

*Watch Your Business Manners.* Your business manners will never be more important than at the beginning of an interview. You positively must not offer to shake hands. Only when the personnel director makes the first move will you shake hands, and that will seldom occur. Stand quietly, and wait until you are asked to be seated. In most places, you will be offered a seat, but if you are not, you should stand throughout the conversation. When you are seated, keep your hat, purse, brief case, and your hands off the interviewer's desk, and your eyes, too. This sounds like superfluous advice, but you have no idea how often it is needed. A young teacher friend of mine was looking for a new position after he had taught ten years. He suddenly discovered he had laid his hat on the superintendent's important papers. He had carefully put his brief case on the floor, but the hat was laid on the nearest and, in this case, the worst place. He was much embarrassed when the superintendent reached for his papers. "And," as my friend said, "being forced to start the interview with an apology didn't help any!"

*Be Quiet, Self-contained.* When you are seated, you should not cross your knees or swing a foot. No matter how nervous or frightened you are, you should not try to cover up by forced gaiety or giggling, if you are a young woman, or by boasting, if you are a young man. The know-it-all attitude does nothing for you. Neither does it help your cause to tell a lot of unimportant, meaningless things. To say you are out of breath from hurrying or that you have just got lost in the subway is superfluous. The less you say that is unrelated to the interview, the better impression you will make, and the easier the ordeal will be for you. Silence has a great power to help you gather courage and poise when they seem to have deserted you. So be as quiet as you can, inwardly and outwardly, and reply briefly, pleasantly, and truthfully to the questions put to you.

In your experience of being interviewed, you may observe that many executives, department heads, or owners of firms are not quite so much at ease as are personnel directors. This is quite natural, since the personnel director is a professional interviewer and other interviewers in the firm are not. For those of you who are nervous about interviews and find yourselves frightened when you are actually in one, just remember that not all the strain is on your side. Actually, it is not an especially pleasant task to ask personal and semipersonal questions of other people. Even the professional interviewer finds it distasteful at times.

*Tests Will Be Simple.* One thing that causes the applicant to be nervous is the fear of being asked to take tests. The truth is that business does not use tests extensively. You will not meet so many tests in business interviews as you have been accustomed to in school or college.

---

(Do Not Write In This Box)
INTERVIEWED BY_____

DATE EMPLOYED_____
DEPARTMENT_____
POSITION_____
SALARY_____

PERSONNEL RELATIONS DEPARTMENT

**EMPLOYMENT APPLICATION**

DATE OF APPLICATION *May 6, 19--*

SALARY DESIRED *$55*

POSITION APPLIED FOR *Editorial Secretary* _First Choice_    *Stenographer* _Second Choice_

Please answer each question fully. All information will be considered confidential.

FULL NAME (Printed)   *Barbara*   _First_   *Jean* _Middle_   *Simmons* _Last_   MALE ☐   FEMALE ☒   AGE *21*

PRESENT ADDRESS   *1318 Elm Street,* _Street_   *Linden,* _City_   *New Jersey* _State_   PHONE NO. *Jr 3-4201*

DATE OF BIRTH *June 18, 19--*   ARE YOU A CITIZEN OF THE U.S.A.   YES ☒ NO ☐   FATHER'S OCCUPATION *Printer*

IF YOU HAVE SERVED IN THE U.S. ARMED SERVICES PLEASE ANSWER
BRANCH *--*   FROM *--*   TO *--*   RANK *--*
DESCRIBE ANY DUTIES PERFORMED THAT MIGHT APPLY TO CIVILIAN OCCUPATIONS

Check Your Status:
SINGLE ✓   SEPARATED ___
MARRIED ___   WIDOW ___
DIVORCED ___   WIDOWER ___

HOME OWNER ___
LIVING AT HOME ✓
BOARD ___
RENT ___

NUMBER OF DEPENDENTS *0* (DO NOT COUNT YOURSELF)

SOCIAL SECURITY NO. *355-24-4896*

STATE OF HEALTH   EXC. ☒   GOOD ☐   POOR ☐   WEIGHT *116*   HEIGHT *5'4"*   TIME LOST THROUGH ILLNESS IN LAST THREE YEARS *4 days*   NATURE OF ILLNESS *Colds*

WHO REFERRED YOU TO US?_____ PLEASE GIVE PARTICULARS____

SPECIAL INTERESTS OUT-SIDE OF BUSINESS ARE:
1. *Photography*
2. *Church activities*
3. *Reading*

HOURS PER WEEK DEVOTED TO INTERESTS:
1. *4*
2. *3*
3. *5*

PARENT OR OTHER PERSON TO BE NOTIFIED IN CASE OF ILLNESS OR EMERGENCY:   NAME *Dwight E. Simmons* PHONE NO. *Jr 3-4201*   ADDRESS *1318 Elm Street, Linden, New Jersey*

**EDUCATION**

| GRADE | NAME OF SCHOOL | LOCATION | MAJOR | COURSES TAKEN | No. Years Attended | Did You Graduate? | Year Graduated |
|---|---|---|---|---|---|---|---|
| ELEMENTARY | *Jackson School* | *Linden, N.J.* | X X X X X | | *8* | *Yes* | *19--* |
| PREPARATORY OR HIGH | *Linden High School* | " " | X X X X X | *Commercial* | *4* | *Yes* | *19--* |
| COLLEGE | *New Jersey College for Women* | *New Brunswick, N.J.* | | *English* | *2* | *no* | |
| OTHERS | | | | | | | |
| BUSINESS OR VOCATIONAL | *Brockton Business School* | *Elizabeth, N.J.* | | *Secretarial* | *1* | *Yes* | *19--* |
| PRESENT | | | | | | | |

5078                                                                        (over)

---

A company application blank filled in (*face*).

And for your comfort let me add that the tests given will be simple. Business tests are more likely to be performance or aptitude tests than intelligence tests. You will often be given a letter to test your dictation, transcription, and typing ability. But this is only fair, and you will, of course, acquit yourself creditably.

One employment manager I know, who gives typing tests to applicants, assures me she allows for nervousness and timidity. She says she

**EMPLOYMENT RECORD**
(Beginning with Last)

| FORMER EMPLOYERS | YOUR POSITION AND DUTIES | DATES | SALARY RECEIVED | SUPERVISOR'S NAME | REASON FOR LEAVING |
|---|---|---|---|---|---|
| NAME Anderson Motors ADDRESS Linden, New Jersey | Secretary – general clerical work and payroll | FROM June, 19-- TO Present | START $47.50 FINAL $50.00 | John Anderson Manager. Owner TITLE | Desire better job |
| NAME Beekman Dept. Store ADDRESS Linden, New Jersey | Salesclerk | Summers 1952 and 1953 | START $38.00 FINAL $40.00 | Gene Durwood TITLE Asst. Manager | Attending School |
| NAME ADDRESS | | FROM TO | START FINAL | TITLE | |
| NAME ADDRESS | | FROM TO | START FINAL | TITLE | |
| NAME ADDRESS | | FROM TO | START FINAL | TITLE | |

**PERSONAL REFERENCES**
(Not Relatives or Former Employers)

| NAME | ADDRESS | OCCUPATION | YEARS ACQUAINTED |
|---|---|---|---|
| Peter K. Rahway | 1814 South Main Street | Engineer | 6 |
| Mrs. Andre Shelby | 243 Franklin Avenue | YWCA Director | 13 |

**KNOWLEDGE SUMMARY**

OFFICE

PLEASE GIVE SPECIFIC INFORMATION CONCERNING YOUR WORKING KNOWLEDGE OF:

CLERICAL One year – all types of clerical work in a one-girl office

BOOKKEEPING OR ACCOUNTING Three years' study in high school

TYPING YES ☑ NO ☐ SPEED: 60 w.p.m. SHORTHAND YES ☑ NO ☐ SPEED: 120 w.p.m.

OFFICE MACHINES Adding and billing

PUBLISHING

EDITORIAL High School correspondent for Linden Gazette

BUSINESS

SELLING

ILLUSTRATION

GENERAL

Other

(Do Not Fill In Space Below)

I certify that answers given in this application are correct. As a condition of employment I agree to undergo a physical examination by a physician designated by the Company.

SIGNED Barbara Jean Simmons

A company application blank filled in (reverse).

does not expect to secure in this test the speed actually needed on the job. Employers and office managers who test applicants are more likely to evaluate the conduct of the individual during the test than to place too much importance on the result itself. While the person giving the test may appear to be busy at an adjoining desk, he is usually watching to see how you go about your assignment. If you are businesslike in assembling stationery and applying yourself to your work, you will

The applicant who is well-groomed and poised
displays confidence in herself—and usually makes
a favorable impression at the interview.

create a good impression. But if you get flustered and start a letter a
dozen times only to fill the wastebasket with spoiled stationery, you may
find yourself rejected.

An employment agent in New York City told me that she tries to
suggest ways by which, during an interview dictation test, the girls can
take a minute or so to relieve the strain and renew their effort. You've
all seen a football team do the same thing during a grueling game. One
of her suggestions to a number of applicants she was sending out on
interviews was to relieve nervous strain by coughing. She said to me,
"These young women can take tests perfectly well in my office, but
they get jittery when a man is dictating to them and they know so
much is at stake." But one day a client to whom she had sent several
of these applicants called her to say, "Those girls you sent me seem to
be all right, but haven't you someone who isn't about to die of tuberculosis?"

My niece, when applying to an insurance company for her first posi-

*Ewing Galloway*

You should expect to take a simple skill test,
particularly if you are applying for a stenographic
job. Be prepared—bring your notebook and pen
with you.

tion, was given some problems in arithmetic. Fortunately, she was good
at mathematics and had no difficulty with the test. She got the job and
found that the major part of her work was clerical, involving the figuring of simple problems.

*Tests for Character and Personality.* Sometimes, instead of being
given a performance test, you are unknowingly being tested for certain
character traits which business considers important. One employer I
know tests a candidate's ability to mind his own business. Let me quote
what he wrote to me about his testing method: "I have an ironclad rule
that anyone applying to me for a job waits for me a minute while I
leave him or her alone in my office. After a full minute, I return and
see whether anything on my desk has been moved or whether any effort
has been made to read a 'property' paper with an intriguing title, which
I keep for this exact purpose. I learned to do that in a rather costly way
about a year ago."

Sometimes, as a sort of test you will be asked to talk with a second member of the organization. Usually, this means you have succeeded in pleasing the original interviewer. However, he would like his partner or another member of the firm to pass on you before he offers you the job. Probably, the second person will not go into as detailed an interview as the first one has, but you should be ready to review your whole story. If you find that the second person does not intend to ask you questions, you may start the interview yourself, saying something like this, "As I have just told Mr. Brown, I am a high school graduate with a year's additional business training." From there, you can go on to a short review of what you told Mr. Brown. After you have finished, you will probably be asked a few questions that you will answer courteously and briefly. I call this duplicate interview a test because its purpose is largely to find out more about your personality and ability. The first interviewer usually only wants his own judgment backed up or to assure himself that you will be as acceptable to other members of the organization as you are to him. This is especially true in a small firm where a limited staff works closely together.

**Show an Alert Mind.** You have heard it said and truly that "ideas get the job." Your objective in each interview should be to show that you are a person with ideas (if you really are). This does not mean that you will try to get your first job by going to a firm and telling how it can make more money. Such a procedure would be resented. Also, in all probability, your idea would not be helpful, since you could not possibly know enough about the business yet to make a sound suggestion about marketing, advertising, or general policy.

But even though you are a beginner, you can still take ideas with you to the interview, and one of them may win the job for you. Suppose you are going to be interviewed by a firm that you find on investigation makes an advertised product called Sunshine soap. If you have a day or even a few hours before the interview, buy a cake of the soap, and try it. In addition to testing the product yourself, shop for it in some department store or perhaps a drugstore. Find out from the salespeople how well it sells in comparison with other toilet soaps at the same price. You can check up and see whether it is also sold in grocery stores or in the dime stores and, if so, in what size cakes and at what prices. Perhaps in your rounds you will hear someone ask for the soap at a counter, or when you ask for it, a salesman will tell you they don't carry it, and why. You may not be able to use any of this information, but your research will serve you as a backlog during the interview.

It is always possible that if you have some ideas about the product or service of the firm that is interviewing you, there will be an opportunity for you to show that you have a mind and have been using it in connection with the anticipated interview. For instance, you may know of a new way in which Sunshine soap is being used. At the close of the interview, you might have a chance to say, truthfully, "I've always been interested in Sunshine soap. At home we like it especially as a shampoo —cut up and dissolved in boiling water. Mother says nothing makes our hair so clean or brings out so many highlights." Any idea like that, suggesting a new use for a product or showing that you see the sales side, will help you to appear more than just a maker of pothooks and a pounder of typewriter keys—a person with helpful hands and an alert mind.

*Questions You Do Not Ask.* In a previous chapter, you were told that in an employment interview you should not ask questions about the salary you would receive, unless you were sure of being hired, in which case the interviewer would bring up the subject. I must warn you, however, about another type of salary question that is being asked often these days. Sometimes, it is preceded by the question, "What salary would I get in this job?" When that has been answered, the applicant asks, "How soon would I get more?" And finally, "How much more?" These questions cannot be answered offhand, because how rapidly you advance and become more valuable to your employer depends to a great extent on you. The point I am making is that they should not be asked. There is no surer way to kill your chances of getting a job than by showing only an interest in what you will get out of it.

*When It's Time to Go—Go!* Many applicants talk themselves into a job, then stay and talk themselves out of it. There is an art in knowing when to leave, and when to leave well enough alone. You should listen carefully and sense when the interview is over. This is not hard to do. If the person to whom you are talking seems to run out of questions or begins to pick up papers from his desk, it is evident that the interview is over, or that you may even have stayed a minute too long. If he looks at his watch, you should rise, because it is certain that he wants you to go. When an applicant will not leave, even after the air has become thick with hints, the situation grows embarrassing for the interviewer, and he may usher out the offender—perhaps none too politely.

A friend of mine needed a typist to get out the annual report of our club. As my friend had only her living room in which to receive them, the applicants who were waiting were present during the interviews ahead of them. This is always unfortunate, and in this case it was especially so because none of them had the good taste to leave after her interview was over. Out of the five or six young women we talked to, only one left of her own accord. When we were eliminating them one by one, they still wanted to tell more about themselves. We had to say each time, "You have told us all that is necessary and if we decide on you we will let you know." In several instances, this was not sufficient, and one of us had to rise, thank the young woman for coming, and say, "Good-by. You will hear from us if we want you." How can an employer feel that an applicant will be a worth-while addition to his office force if he or she lacks judgment in such an important thing as knowing when to go? There will be many times on the job when a graceful exit is essential to the situation.

So when you feel the interview is over, end the conversation quickly but pleasantly. Go at once. You have already had your share of a busy person's time. Rise and thank your interviewer, say "Good-by," and leave. If the position has not been offered to you, you can perhaps find out whether you are being favorably considered by asking a question just before you say good-by. "May I expect to hear from you when you have made your decision?" is a good exit line. Or you might say, "Would it be agreeable to you if I telephone you in a few days to see what you have decided?" These are little tricks which a good salesman uses to "keep the door open," as he says. As you leave, do not attempt to shake hands unless the other person extends his hand. The situation is scarcely less formal than when you arrived, fifteen minutes earlier. You may feel that because you have told your life story you are now well acquainted, but such is not the case. To the interviewer, you are merely part of the day's work and to be too familiar at this stage will not better your cause. The chances are he will see no reason to shake hands with you. So just say "Good-by," and walk out of the room quickly and quietly.

If the interviewer closes your talk with him, he will probably say: "We are interviewing several persons for this position and will not decide until we have talked with others. I have your name and address here and will let you know." If you have been sent on the interview by an agency, the employer will communicate with you through them. In that case, you can thank him and add that you will keep in touch with the employment agency. You should, of course, always report to an agency on the result of an interview that they have arranged for you.

CALLING WITHOUT AN INTRODUCTION

We have assumed that the interview we have been discussing was arranged through an employment agency, or it might have been through a friend or relative. You might even have made the appointment yourself through hearing of a vacancy and telephoning to the proper person.

But there is another kind of interview that is far more difficult. Everything I have said about interviews in employment agencies and with employers or their representatives will apply equally to this type of interview. But it has pitfalls of its own for which you must be prepared. Have you ever heard the expression "calling cold"? That is what you are about to do. It means calling without a letter or card to introduce you (get you in), and perhaps not much information about how you will be received if you do get in.

Even this type of interview can be planned, as you will soon see. Suppose you have heard that a certain firm is hiring recent high school graduates and training them to operate business machines. You want to look into this, and you should. Obviously, the first information you need is the name of the person who does the hiring. Perhaps your informer can tell you whom you should see. If not, the direct way is to telephone the company and ask their switchboard operator. If she tells you to go to their employment or personnel office, there is no need for you to know the interviewer's name, as you do not ask for anyone in particular. The next most important thing is for you to get what information you can about the company. This is especially important when you are "calling cold," for knowing something about the company warms up the situation considerably.

There are various ways to get information about a business firm, such as talking with friends who work there, reading the company's advertising, or calling at their offices and asking for advertising literature.

The hiring of competent employees has become such an important part of business that firms requiring a lot of help usually have employment offices that are open all day, every day, sometimes even Saturday. Such offices are usually in the charge of an employment manager or a personnel director who may have several assistants. If the company on which you plan to call "cold" has such a specialized department, you may call any time during business hours, and one day is as good as another. There may be no job available at that time for which you qualify, but you will be courteously received and given information about the possibility of future employment. Employment managers are always on the lookout for desirable employees, and they keep files of better-class applicants so as to have good material to draw on when necessary. Even if there are no vacancies, you may be asked to fill out an application form, and it will be to your interest to do so.

Should you be calling "cold" on a smaller firm where the head of the business or one of his associates or executives does the hiring, it will not be so easy to get an interview. You will be asking to see a busy person who does interviewing in addition to other work, and unless he is in immediate need of additional help, he will not welcome the interruption of your call. Better not try to see such an employer on Monday morning or on Friday afternoon, as on Monday he will be busy getting the week started, and on Friday he will be catching up on work before leaving for the week end. Other days, calling between eleven o'clock and noon, or between three and four in the afternoon, is best.

*Receptionists and Secretaries Can Be Helpful.* When you have the name of the executive who interviews applicants for his company, present yourself at the receptionist's desk or to the telephone-receptionist. Say you would like to see Mr. Holt, and when you are asked what your business is, say that you wish to speak to him about employment. There is no use in being evasive or trying to put over your call as "personal." That method of getting into an executive's office does not work. When you mention employment, the receptionist may say to you, "We're not taking on anyone just now." And then what do you do?

The best approach to an executive is through his secretary. She is the buffer between her boss and the many people who would take his time needlessly, so she sees all those who call on him without appointments. So ask for Mr. Holt's secretary instead of for Mr. Holt. Often, a secretary can and will consult her chief or look at his appointment book and set a time for you to call on him. Failing this, she may say, "I'll see what I can do for you. Call me up tomorrow." You have no idea what a help such an accommodating secretary can be to you, if you make a good impression on her.

If it has been impossible for you to find out who is in charge of the employment interviewing in a firm you wish to contact, all you can do is call and hope you can get the needed information at the front desk. Do not tell your story to the janitor or the first person you meet in the hall. Many an applicant has been brushed off by someone who has nothing to do with issuing jobs, when if he had reached the right person he might have had a satisfactory interview. Go straight to the receptionist, and ask her to tell you who handles employment. Such a direct question calls for a direct reply, and usually you will get it. Suppose she says that Mr. Smith takes care of employment. Your next question is, "May I see Mr. Smith?" Should that be impossible, you can ask for Mr. Smith's secretary, and proceed as on the call when you asked for Mr. Holt's secretary. The important thing is not to be sidetracked to someone who has nothing to do with hiring.

*Introduce Yourself.* Because you may not be asked to fill out an application form, you will probably have to start an interview directly with an employer by introducing yourself. Since you do not know what positions are open, you can then ask if there are any vacancies in typing, a combination of bookkeeping and stenography, or whatever it is you want to do.

By all means, be very businesslike. This is especially important in an interview that you have secured by your own initiative. Your only excuse for being received is that you have certain skills and abilities that this business might be able to use. To begin talking about the weather or to make conversation would be in poor taste and would make you appear to be without poise or judgment. Come straight to the point and, as quickly as possible, interest the interviewer in what you can do. Of course, now, as in any interview, you will not linger a second beyond the right moment for leaving.

## GETTING THE JOB

A good salesman tries to get his prospect to sign on the dotted line. In other words, he tries to make a sale. You, too, must try to make a sale in every interview. This does *not* mean you should use high-pressure methods. It means that you should present yourself as favorably as possible—your manners, your appearance, and your abilities. Your expression should be bright, alert, and interested. You should speak distinctly, but not too loudly. Looking glum and mumbling out of sheer awkwardness and fright, as you have seen some of your schoolmates recite in class, never got a job for anyone!

If you should be so fortunate as to win a job in your first interview with a business firm, you will, of course, ask when they want you to come to work. If you are not told to whom you are to report for work and at what time, you should ask. However, these happy details need little preparation—they are not easily overlooked or forgotten!

*Recognize Unprofitable Interviews.* There are times when certain facts are given during an interview that convince you the job is not for you. In such a case, there is no need to keep answering questions about yourself and your ability and taking up further time of the person who is interviewing you. However, you must be careful not to refuse a job that has not been offered to you. It is difficult to tell you exactly what to say under such circumstances. You will have to be guided by the situation as it develops and meet it as gracefully as you can. If you feel a position requires more experience than you have had or skills that are not your best, you might honestly say so. If you are being interviewed by a personnel director who has other positions to fill, this need not necessarily injure your future chances with this organization. He may offer you another job then or later.

*Don't Think Out Loud.* One fatal error in applying for a job is to mention its disadvantages during the interview. One girl talked herself out of a job by saying, "This would be a long way for me to come every day. You see I live quite far out. The fare would be so much I don't think it would pay me to take the job. Still, I suppose if nothing better turns up, I could try it and see how it works out."

The distance and the carfare involved are probably legitimate reasons for questioning the desirability of the position. But keep such things to yourself. After you have secured the job, you can ignore such difficulties or overcome them, as you see fit. Such objections, given voice to, make an astute employer feel that you will never really be contented in the job, and he is likely to agree that this is no position for you.

If you take a position that is not what you had in mind, as many have had to do when jobs were scarce, don't belittle the job. Such remarks as "If nothing better comes up" or "I'll try it for a while" might even lose the job for you. Companies, large and small, want employees who are interested in their jobs and who will stay a reasonable length of time. They cannot afford to be a training ground for transient youth.

*Recognize a Polite Turndown.* Do not take too seriously the words, "We'll put your application on file and let you know when we have something." This is usually a way of getting rid of you. If you wait for some firms to call you back, you will wait a long time—probably forever. Another way of saying they don't want you is, "Sorry, the job is filled." Even when you know the job is still open, because your school or an agency sent you, don't argue the point. Better get to a mirror fast, and see what is wrong with your appearance. Also ask yourself whether you used a deodorant that morning. Your carelessness in either of these will quickly fill that job—with someone else.

*Experienced Employees Can Mishandle an Interview.* There is some excuse for beginners who fail to get jobs because of their blunders in an interview. Experienced applicants should be able to conduct themselves better. An editor in a sizable publishing house told me why he turned down an applicant who had all the qualifications for a position requiring publicity experience. Mabel Wells presented a Personal Data Sheet showing four years' experience writing publicity for top firms— and then killed her chances of getting the job. How? By boasting. She wanted that job because of the high salary and the prestige that went with it. So she told the editor at great length how very good she was. He told *her* he'd let her know. He told *me* that her experience was perfect for the job, but that he didn't hire her because from her conversation and manner he could see that she'd try to boss everybody. He wasn't looking for a supervisor for the department.

## What About Follow-ups?

When jobs are plentiful, you may not need to follow up on any of your calls. In those cases where you were sent on an interview by your school or an employment agency, you can check back with them to see whether your application is under consideration and whether there is anything more that you can do. Usually there isn't.

But if, on your own, you discovered a prospect, secured an interview, and want very much to work for that employer, follow it up. An application is said to get very cold by the end of a week. If you feel sure that the interviewer will remember you favorably, you may telephone him. This will remind him of the interview and perhaps lead to information as to whether the job you applied for is still open or whether there is another position you might fill. Under such circumstances, it may be desirable to make another call. On a second call, do not sit down unless you are asked to do so. After all, you covered the ground quite fully on your first call, and you are here only to keep that ground well plowed. All you need do is to remind the employer or personnel director that you are still interested in anything that may develop there.

Brevity is your cue in any follow-up calls. Whether you telephone, write, or call in person, your purpose is merely to see that you are not forgotten. New applicants may be calling daily, and you may be lost sight of unless you keep your memory green. So do all the follow-up work you wish, short of becoming a nuisance. You alone can tell when you have made a good impression, perhaps even made a friend, and where you are likely to be considered as promising material.

## There Are Many Kinds of Interviewers

A chapter on interviewing would not be complete without a look at some of the personalities you will meet while you are job seeking. Your success is as dependent on the person to whom you talk as on your own efforts. There are co-operative, friendly interviewers who will help to bring out the very best there is in you. These you will leave feeling you are really quite a person yourself!

Then there are cold, formal individuals who are apparently too busy to take time to find out what sort of person you are. These will make you miserable, if you let them. Although you may have been sent to one of them with the certain knowledge that there is a position available, this chilly person may appear to regard your call as an intrusion. He may even appear so indifferent that at the end of the interview you feel you have made a poor impression. When you meet this type, you will have to be as patient and courteous as you can. Timidity in others usually delights him, but if you can muster at least the appearance of unfrightened composure, you may have won his approval.

Another type is the occasional man who says nothing, scowls at you, and forces you to do all the talking. Even experienced employees are put to rout by such an interviewer. Out of sheer embarrassment, the impulse is to talk, say anything, just to avoid the appalling silence with which he fills the room. One young man met such a personnel director in a large radio corporation where he was seeking work as a page or messenger. After stating his errand, the young man waited courteously. Nothing happened. "Mr. Hazlitt told me I could use him as a reference," the boy added hopefully. Still silence. "I haven't known Mr. Hazlitt long," he plunged on. "In fact, I only met him yesterday when I knew I was going to see you. Mr. Hazlitt said that he had done you a great many favors, and it was about time you did one for him." This bright remark did evoke a hollow laugh, but the poor lad was so chagrined at his own tactless stupidity that he made a hasty exit, never to return. This was probably what the personnel director intended!

It is the opinion of some interviewers that the applicant should be made to do most of the talking. This is called the "silent interview." I heard the theory explained by the personnel director of an important public-utility company of New York State, and he was loud in its praise. It seems that supervisors in the company are trained to interview applicants for their departments. At first, in these interviews, they were embarrassed to sit silently, thus forcing the interviewee to take the lead in the conversation. However, the speaker explained, before long the supervisors found that they could direct the interviews so there were fewer gaps. The idea is not to embarrass the applicant or cause him to feel ill at ease, but rather to see whether he will not talk more freely than when he merely answers questions. The interviewer makes notes throughout the conversation and guides the interview to the extent that when the applicant gets off the track he is brought gently back to the subject—*himself*, and what he has to offer.

Evidently, this kind of interviewing has also reached the educational field, for a young teacher was confronted with the technique when interviewed by a board of trustees for a position as teacher of industrial arts. No one in the group did him the favor of saying who was the chairman, so the applicant did not know to whom he should primarily address his remarks. "They just sat there," he told me. "They didn't question me, or say a word. I don't know what I'd have done if I had not had my portfolio to pass around and explain. When all of them had looked at my drawings and photographs, without saying anything,

I thanked them for the courtesy (?) of the interview and departed. But was I burned up! I didn't hear anything from them about the position, and I didn't care, for what would a fellow do, working for such a bunch of knotheads!" This young man had a couple of college degrees, had taught a year or so, and had plenty of poise. If such an interview confused and outraged him, what would it do to a beginner? While I disagree heartily with this method of interviewing, I am telling you about it in case you should someday find yourself in the middle of such a silence. All you can do in that kind of situation is "grin and bear it." When you are satisfied that you have done all you can, make a courteous and graceful exit, leaving the results to fate.

## Regarding Letters of Recommendation

Before we leave this chapter, I must answer a question that those of you who have worked are thinking, "How valuable are letters of recommendation in landing a job?" Not so valuable as applicants think.

Employers and personnel directors know all too well that almost any employer, when cornered, will say something good about even a dismissed employee, so they are inclined to discount those high-sounding letters that you copied so carefully. If you have had enough experience to obtain letters of recommendation, carry them with you, but don't depend on them too much. Above all, don't think they will save the day for you. An applicant who expects an employer to take time to read a number of letters is not well prepared for his interview.

The important thing is to deserve a recommendation. You don't really need a letter. Ask your former employer's permission to use his name as a reference, and then merely list it on the application form, giving his telephone number. You may be sure a prospective employer, if interested, will telephone him. Among employers, it is generally understood that over the telephone one comes nearer getting the truth about an ex-employee than in a formal letter of recommendation. Most persons will hesitate to write that a former stenographer was un-co-operative, for example, but on the telephone this can be discussed more frankly.

## Analyze Your Calls and Improve Your Technique

All interviews are valuable experience. When there are more jobs than applicants to fill them and you find a job almost immediately, you fail to get a workout that teaches you as no book can. On the contrary, if work is not too plentiful when you start job hunting and you have a number of interviews before you are hired, you can be thankful for the experience. Analyze your calls, and review your mistakes as well as your successes. Ask yourself, "Why did I reply as I did to the question about my preference for bookkeeping work? Did I say the right thing? Would it have been better if I had handled it differently?" Did you feel awkward in a certain interview? Go back to your rehearsing, and see if you cannot do better now. If a brand-new question was asked and you did not do credit to yourself in answering it, work up a better answer, and be ready with it the next time.

We all learn by our disappointments and mistakes, so do not be discouraged, no matter how poorly you feel you have managed your first few interviews. You can perfect your technique only by practice. As you review your experiences, you will learn to improve your answers and your general conduct during interviews. You will learn to distinguish your poor approaches and discard them. You will recognize your improvements and use them more skillfully. Then, one day, your perfected interview will win you a job!

## QUESTIONS

1. If there are questions on an application form that you do not understand, will you

   a. Take time to study them more carefully?
   b. Interrupt an interviewer, and ask that they be explained?
   c. Omit answering those questions?

2. Why is it necessary to have their permission before you give as references the names of older people who know you?
3. What is wrong with giving relatives as references, since they know you better than anyone else does?
4. Name the advantage, if any, of carrying with you to any interview a typed Personal Data Sheet. If you have worked, should you have your employment data in your mind or typed for prompt reference?
5. Would you feel more at ease in an interview if you gave a memorized speech about yourself? Would you make a better or a worse impression?
6. Why is it as important to make a good exit from an interview as to make a good entrance?
7. Is the approach, "I should like to file an application," a good way to introduce yourself when you call without an appointment or without knowing who handles employment?
8. If you are a smoker and during the interview the person with whom you are talking offers you a cigarette, would you

   a. Refuse, without explanation?
   b. Say, "Thank you. I don't smoke during business hours"?
   c. Accept the cigarette and smoke with the interviewer?

9. In case you are a gum chewer, would you have gum in your mouth when you go to be interviewed?
10. Should you sit down or take off your coat if the interviewer has not asked you to do so?
11. Why is it important that you understand and follow the printed instructions when filling out an application form?

## CRITICIZE THESE STATEMENTS

1. It makes no difference whether you arrive on time for an interviewing appointment, provided you explain politely why you were late.
2. If you think the interviewer is not going to consider you favorably, you should remain and keep talking until you convince him he should give you the job.
3. When you ask for an important person and cannot see him, refuse to see his secretary.
4. Argue with a receptionist if she tries to find out what your business is.
5. Don't bother to be businesslike. It is more important to be charming in an interview and interest the person in yourself rather than in your skills and ability.
6. While being interviewed, if details about the job reveal that it is nothing you would like, you should rise and say, "I'm not interested in the position."

## TOPICS FOR DISCUSSION

1. When you have filled out an application form in an employment agency and they send you to be interviewed by a business firm, why should you be asked to fill out another form?
2. A personnel director says she often gives typing and stenographic tests to applicants merely to see how they act under strain. Explain why the ability to stand strain is important in certain types of office work.
3. Discuss why you are told, "Don't boast or have a know-it-all attitude during an interview." What is wrong with being funny, chummy, cocky, or coy?
4. On entering an interviewer's presence, is it better to say "I am Miss Smith" or "I am Jane Smith"? If the latter is in better form, does the same rule apply when the applicant is Robert Smith?
5. Since it is the custom for men to shake hands when they are introduced, why should not Robert Smith, when calling on a male interviewer, offer to shake hands?
6. Why are personnel directors unanimous in saying, "Don't take anyone else with you when you go job hunting"?
7. If you were kept waiting too long for an interview when you had an appointment, would you—

    *a.* Complain aloud about being made to wait?
    *b.* Say nothing, and wait?
    *c.* Get huffy and walk out, saying your time is valuable, too?
    *d.* Keep after the telephone-receptionist to see whether she can't get you in?

8. If, as you enter an interviewer's private office, he is busy on the telephone, should you

    *a.* Enter and sit down?
    *b.* Withdraw and wait outside until you are called?
    *c.* Stay, listen to the conversation, and start the interview by commenting on what was said?
    *d.* Interrupt, and force him to notice you?

9. Should you feel encouraged when an interviewer says, "We'll call you when something comes up"? Should you be equally encouraged when he says, "We'll place your application on file"? Under either circumstance, should you cease opening up other leads and wait at home to hear from these employers?

10. If you think an interviewer is not asking questions that help you to explain your skills and ability, is it a good plan to take the interview into your own hands and give him a sales talk?

11. If an interviewer, in turning you down, takes the time to explain why you are unsuited for the position, would you appreciate this interest, or would you resent it?

12. If an interviewer asks you how many times you are out until midnight during the week, and you are actually out late every night, will you

    *a.* Lie, and say you always go to bed early?
    *b.* Tell the truth, because it is none of his business?
    *c.* Try to evade giving a direct answer?

13. The following have aptly been called the "seven points of departure":

| | |
|---|---|
| *a.* Stand up | *e.* Open the door |
| *b.* Hold out your hand | *f.* Walk out |
| *c.* Say good-by | *g.* Walk away |
| *d.* Go to the door | |

    Do all of these apply to an exit from an employment interview? If not, which would you omit, and why?

## PROJECTS

1. Get an application form from a local employer or from your state employment-service office. Fill it out, following instructions carefully. Bring it to class, being prepared to explain why you answered the questions as you did.

2. Look up the following words in a dictionary, and write the meaning of each word. Be able to give the meaning of any one of these words if called on in class to do so.

| meticulous | chagrined | transient | expediency |
|---|---|---|---|
| terminate | mishandle | essential | evaluate |
| superfluous | conversely | potential | |

3. Assume that you have been interviewed by an employer who finally says: "All right. I think I know all I need to about your qualifications." What is your next move? Write in the proper sequence what you will say and do from then on until you are outside the door.

4. The following have been listed as the obstacles that probably do most to prevent graduates from securing positions:

    *a.* Poor appearance        *c.* Lack of a plan

    *b.* Fear                    *d.* Lack of experience

    Write a 1,000-word paper stating how you would overcome each of these in presenting yourself in an interview.

5. You have been told by an employment agency to call up the Acme Plating Company and make an appointment to be interviewed by Mr. James Purvis, the office manager. The position open is a stenographic one. Write what you would say in the telephone conversation, first with the PBX operator, then with Mr. Purvis's secretary, and finally with Mr. Purvis.

6. Write your name in several ways, to decide the correct business signature to use from now on. Bring these to class marked 1, 2, and 3 in the order of preference, and be ready to give the reasons for your first choice.

7. Analyze a recent interview you have had. Write the points on which you would check yourself as having said or done the *right* or the *wrong* thing. What benefit will you derive from carefully reviewing each interview?

# CHAPTER 9

# Making Good on the Job

Congratulations! You conducted yourself well in an interview; you looked the part of a businesslike beginner; you offered one or more wanted skills; and you were *hired*. Now that you have a good job, you feel that you are well on your way to a business career. And you are, provided, of course, that your goal is to *make good* on the job.

A personnel director of a large organization tells me that her greatest problem with beginners is to have them realize that they must make good on the job after they get it. Often, they have the idea that work will be play—though how or where such an idea originates no one knows. The truth is that winning the job is merely a warming-up exercise; after getting the job, the race is really on. Rightly or wrongly, a great deal of service is expected in a business office, even from the greenest recruit. That C average, which is a passing grade in high school and college, is not acceptable in business. Even B plus is not considered good. So try for an A or at least an A minus.

You had something to offer your employer, or you would not have been told that the job was yours. If you have definite skills, chiefly shorthand and typewriting and/or the ability to run a business machine, you will be put to work using them at once. But, if you had acquired no particular skills, you were undoubtedly hired because you were thought to be good material for training. In either case, you will receive considerable training on company time. Since you will be paid while you are learning, you must from the first day absorb the instructions given you and put them into practice as quickly as possible. Bear in mind that the dictionary is the only place where Success comes before Work.

### THE OFFICE ATTITUDE TOWARD THE WILLING BEGINNER

Let's suppose it is your first day at the office. No matter how well you are prepared for what will happen, this is likely to be a trying day.

Office employees who have worked for years agree that the first month on any new job is, to say the least, difficult.

In an article, "Be Kind to Beginners," [1] Blanche S. Eckles, a personnel director, tells how she handles beginners.

To those obtaining employment, the first year out of school is likely to be one of adjustment to office routines, procedures and people. . . . No research is required to spotlight the fact that the beginner goes to her first job with enthusiasm, determination and high hope for the future. A large percentage of personnel managers and employers hire office workers with no experience. . . . There are some who admittedly feel that the average beginner works so hard to make a good impression that she has little time in which to do a full day's work. Still others feel that the new worker lacks initiative and is at times confused or overwhelmed by multiple instructions. But a far greater number welcome the beginner, since she can be molded more easily into the pace and pattern set by a particular office. Employers frankly admit that the beginner's sincere desire to do a good job is an admirable trait, and one that is highly admired.

Then, right out of the kind of office we have been talking about, Miss Eckles states what she thinks the new employee has a right to expect. Evidently, this personnel director has only girls working for her, as she uses the pronoun "she" throughout, but undoubtedly any young men going to work in her office would get the same consideration. Here is the list:

The new employee needs to know who is to give her instructions.

She is entitled to be told the letter setup used and the manner for answering the phone and taking messages.

She should be told the necessity of recognizing the names and faces of office visitors.

Her lunch hour should be definitely set.

She should be instructed in the system of filing.

She should understand that she may be given fill-in work if her regular duties do not take full time.

In conclusion, Miss Eckles says that in the training of and working with office personnel she uses what she terms, "The 3-H Success Plan: Help with the *Hand*, the *Head*, and the *Heart*."

The best I can wish you on your first job is that it will be in such an office. Unfortunately, there are not too many of them. And just in case you do not have the luck to start in an office that is well organized for helping beginners, let's return to that first, momentous day we were discussing earlier.

[1] *Personnel Journal*, October, 1952.

A. Devaney, Inc.

On your first job there will be much to learn. Be
a good listener.

## LISTEN AND LEARN AS YOU GO

You will have been told, at the time you were hired, to report to a
certain person at a certain hour for assignment to your duties. If you
listen carefully during these first instructions, you will get a better start.
Do not be afraid to ask questions. It is so much better to be sure you
understand your work thoroughly at this stage that you can well afford
to be a human question mark. Many beginners fear they will appear
ignorant, and so they nod and say "Yes," when actually they don't
understand all that is being told to them. Don't make that mistake. Don't
trust to luck and hope you can glean enough information as the day
goes on to get the hang of things.

Listen very carefully. It is a good idea to make notes, not only of
what you are to do but of the names of the persons from whom you
are to take work or further instructions. At the end of the day, go back
to the person who first instructed you, and ask further necessary questions. No one will object to your doing this. In fact, they will admire

you for your persistence in trying to clear up anything you fail to understand.

When you are introduced to the men and women in your department, make it a point to get their names correctly. To be able to say from the start "Yes, Mr. Dinkelspiel" or "Thank you, Mr. Deute" is a simple courtesy that makes quite a hit. One way of getting these names right is to repeat them immediately after you have heard them for the first time. In your case, this probably would be when you acknowledge the introduction. At your first opportunity, write each name with the title of the person after it. Then memorize your list so you can use the names correctly when occasion permits.

### THE IMPORTANCE OF OBSERVING OFFICE AND LUNCH HOURS

The office manager or someone else will assign your lunch hour, and although they may not say so, you will be expected to observe it exactly. Apart from being an important office rule, returning promptly from lunch is the courteous thing to do so as not to delay someone else who is waiting to go when you return. You'll be very unpopular if you infringe on the next person's precious lunch hour! If you have not been told the office hours, this is the time to ask. Don't watch other employees to see when they stop work and get ready to leave. They may not be working on the same schedule as you are, or they may be slacking.

When you were hired, you were probably told whether your work week would be forty hours or less. A five-day week of eight hours a day has become quite general for office work, though many firms work an even shorter day, with hours from 8:30 to 5, or 9 to 5. The days worked are usually Monday through Friday, but sometimes when there's a rush of new work or a backlog to get rid of, you will be asked to work a few hours Saturday morning. This is considered overtime, and you will be paid for it, usually at time and a half.

Twice-a-day rest periods, while not so commonly accepted as the five-day week, are taking the spotlight. In soda fountains or drugstores in the downtown district of any city, you will see chattering, hatless customers pouring in and out at midmorning and midafternoon. They are taking what has come to be known as the "coffee break." There is a legal basis for part of this. Some states, like California, require employers to allow women employees a "ten-minute rest period in each four hours of work or fraction thereof." So as not to discriminate, many fair-minded employers in such states allow male employees the same privilege, and the gift of time is more likely to be fifteen minutes. In states having no such law, office opinion has accomplished much the same result. However, there are companies that do not have formal rest periods because the work allows for intermittent pauses.

A New York City company estimated that in one year its employees took 1,800 work-hours a day to go out for coffee. Tea-wagon service was the answer. At certain intervals, a tea wagon is wheeled through the offices by a catering service, and any employee who wishes may have coffee, milk, or pastry at his own expense in a ten-minute break.

It will be important for you to know the office regulations regarding rest periods in your company. The person who gives your first instructions will probably tell you whether there is a general rest period for everyone, whether you take a break at your own discretion, or whether food is served on the premises during relief periods, at lunchtime, or not at all. It is much better for you to get this information from your supervisor than from other employees, but don't put it high on your list of questions to ask. You certainly don't wish to appear more interested in not working than in working. You may be told that you are not permitted to leave the building during your break. Many firms have had to make such a ruling because employees took advantage of the situation, went too far away, and overstayed their rest period.

*Be Punctual.* Regardless of how early the opening hour of the office may be, you must leave home at an hour that will give you ample time to be at your desk at the time the office opens. For instance, if the office opens at 8:30, you are expected to be at your desk, ready to start work at that time. It does not mean that girls can rush into the outer office on the stroke of 8:30 and spend the next ten minutes or longer in the dressing room fixing their faces or arranging their hair, using office time to make themselves presentable. Also, nothing puts an employee so much in the wrong as perpetually making excuses for tardiness. Office managers were not born yesterday, and they have heard that one about the bus or the streetcar breaking down, or the flat tire your car developed overnight.

### WHEN ABSENCE IS NECESSARY

Next to having employees arrive late for work, the office manager's worst problem is their not coming in at all. In the business dictionary, this is called "absenteeism," and the various threats and rewards used to cut it down are the best evidence that it is truly a business problem. Here and now, resolve that, once having agreed to take a job, you will be there every day to perform the work assigned you. Sickness, your own or that of a member of your immediate family, is practically the only valid reason for being absent. If some morning you are really ill and unable to work, the accepted practice is to phone your supervisor during the first half hour of the working day. This gives the department head time to reorganize the day's work and arrange for someone else to take over your duties. You can readily understand how difficult it would be to get out the normal day's work if several persons were unexpectedly absent on the same day.

Most businesses prefer that you stay home for a day or so when you have a cold, as experience shows that, when a sniffling employee continues working, the infection is often spread, with more absences resulting. But don't ever pull that selfish trick of phoning in that you are ill when you want to go downtown to a sale or to see a friend off on a trip. It will serve you right if you are caught on one of these excursions when you are thought to be ill, or if the company's visiting nurse is sent to call on you, and she arrives just as you are taking off.

## Good Business Manners

If ever good business manners help, it is on the first bewildering day on the new job. You know everyone is sizing you up, and you would like to appear to good advantage. Now is the time to watch your conduct. Naturally, you will be very courteous to the person who outlines your duties, and when you meet executives for whom you are to work you will be respectful. If you are introduced to any of the employees on your own level, your cue is to be polite and agreeable, but not too friendly. At the start, it is important not to get chummy before you have had time to learn more about the office routine and to decide with whom you wish to make friends. It is very easy to get in with wrong associates, so it is a good policy to be equally pleasant and impersonal with everyone. But more about that in a later chapter. Right now you have enough to do to learn the job without taking on problems of human relationships.

Bear in mind that you may have been hired to replace someone who is about to be discharged. Keep aloof, and give no one a chance to pour complaints or office politics into your ears. For the moment, see nothing and know nothing but your own job.

Your first day of work behind you, things will begin to shape up, and presently you will be thoroughly at home. If you are quiet and collected and sure that you are equal to whatever the situation demands, the period of adjustment may be very short indeed. So organize your work and your attitude toward it, and make good.

## The Daily Pressure of Work

Sometimes, beginners cannot stand the pressure of normal office work. Even if they have had reasonably long periods of dictation, at

least as long as the school schedule permits, they will have to get used
to much longer periods in an office when their entire time is devoted to
taking dictation and transcribing it. Those who are so fortunate as
to start as stenographers sometimes find the work more than they can
handle. So, having the skills, be sure you have or are acquiring the necessary stamina. Among those who are discharged for lack of skills may
be many who merely lack the ability to use their skills strenuously
enough to satisfy their employers.

In my employment-agency work, I more than once put girls into jobs
that I warned them would be very strenuous. Although without exception they laughed at this prospect, I learned later that several of them
quit because they could not keep up with the terrific pace demanded
of them. How well you adjust to the grind in some high-geared offices
depends largely on how badly you need the job. If you go to work
merely because all your friends are doing so, it is not likely you will
see it through when you find yourself in the confusion of rush work,
endless detail, and frazzled nerves.

*Adjust Yourself to Routine.* Some young people who have looked
forward eagerly to entering the business world are disappointed. Office
routine, the monotony of repetitive tasks, deflates their enthusiasm. I
know one boy who quit after being promoted from mail clerk to order
clerk. He said he wasn't interested in taking orders over the phone all
day long for "Two dozen No. 572." Contrast this lad's restlessness with
the stick-to-itiveness of a young man who, on graduating from college,
went to work packing coffee for one of the big distributors. He worked
in lowly and sometimes menial jobs for three or four years. At times
he was very discouraged. Had his father given him an expensive education that he might know how to sort can sizes? But he kept plugging,
and after hours he studied coffee from A to Z, and Spanish, too. Finally,
he got a promotion, and then one day, before he had been out of college
five years, he found himself a full-fledged coffee buyer for an important broker in Central America. He had not despised the day of small
things.

*Keep Alert and Be Businesslike.* It is very easy to go slack on routine
jobs. You must watch out that the monotony of endless detail does not
dull your attention. Cultivate alertness all you can. This should include
an eagerness to learn. If you show a sincere desire to absorb everything
you should know about your job, it will make up in a measure for your
inexperience. Never mind if your job is on the lowest rung of the
ladder. Without that rung, the ladder would be weaker. Your first effort
should be to achieve businesslike habits of carefulness, neatness, and
accuracy in handling detail. Be most painstaking and exact. So few

people are. Therefore, you will stand out in the crowd. Have a system in going about your work. Be sure your desk contains everything you need and everything in its place. If you have occasion to use names, dates, and figures in your work, be as concerned with accuracy as a newspaper reporter. You would do well to attack your duties as though you were in the employ of the New York editor who fired any reporter who misspelled a name *once only!*

When I was writing a newspaper column on "Manners in Business," I once checked to see how often correspondents spelled my name incorrectly. It may surprise you to know it was wrong more often than it was right. Yet my correspondents were persons who had the newspaper containing my printed name before them. Moreover, most of them were business girls asking for business information! One reason supervisors are necessary in large offices is that the great majority of workers are guilty of this sort of slipshod performance. Individual workers could be paid more if it were not necessary to pay a supervisor to check and double check.

## DON'T OVERESTIMATE YOUR SERVICES

From now on, as you anticipate your office debut, you will be thinking more and more about the world of business that lies ahead. In picturing this, you need to understand two fundamental points, often overlooked even by those who have worked a long time. They are (1) why you are employed, and (2) what you are worth to your employer.

*Why Are You Employed?* The sole purpose of employing office help is to *get out the work,* and the number of employees in any office depends on how many persons are needed to do the necessary paper work. While I learned this when I had my own advertising business, it was brought even more forcibly to my attention during World War II, when I was responsible for keeping a thousand office jobs in a California shipyard filled. In explaining my duties, the personnel director who hired me said: "For every ton of ship we build, there is a ton of paper work." There was, indeed!

The management of a business either estimates or learns by trial and error how much help is needed to handle the company's correspondence, telephone service, reports, and record making, which includes the filing, bookkeeping, and accounting. On the basis of this estimate and the current salary scale, a budget is set up to cover the cost of operating the firm's offices. The tough job assigned the office manager is to employ enough good workers to get out the work and yet keep well within the budget.

Since office occupations are classed as service, this means that office workers are nonproductive—they do not, through their activities, bring in any money. The entire cost of running the offices of a company—salaries, furnishings, equipment such as typewriters and all business machines, and supplies—comes out of the profit made by other workers. If the business is manufacturing, the factory workers produce the goods to sell. (High union wages are justified because skilled, semiskilled, and unskilled labor is production.) The orders taken by the salesmen in any business bring in the money that keeps the company going.

Incidentally, I have heard stenographers say, "I wish the salesmen would keep out of our department. Who do they think they are—coming in late in the day and wanting to dictate letters to their customers?" Who do they think they are? Only the fellows who bring in the money to pay your salary. Better give them a little service. That's what you were hired to do.

**What Are You Worth to Your Employer?** You are worth nothing to your employer when you are hired. During your first weeks, you are a loss because of the time someone has to spend training you or, at best, giving you instructions. You become valuable as soon as you start turning out a volume of good-quality work. As your output improves in both quality and quantity, and as you are able to take more responsibility, your worth to your employer increases. By that time, he has quite an investment in you, and he hopes you'll stay on the job so the investment will pay out. If you do, one day you will be worth to your employer the salary he is paying you. Raises will come as you are able to carry more of your share of the work load.

Young people going to work for the first time often overestimate their value to their employers. This is a natural mistake, because they do not understand the function of the office in a business organization, as outlined above. They think of the salary they receive in terms of their own needs or wants—a board bill paid, new clothes, or a down payment on a used car. A common misconception among employees is that they are being paid for their time, and that by being on the premises for the required number of hours they have fulfilled their part of the bargain. Only when they learn to measure their worth *in terms of their ability to produce for their employer* and tackle their work in an earnest effort to turn out more and better work will they reach what might be called business maturity.

### HIGH STANDARDS IN TOP BUSINESSES

For the sake of your future, as well as your present, I hope your first job will be with a firm whose executives are educated men and women, and where the work standard is high. You will need to be mentally alert to keep up in such an organization, and you will frequently be-come discouraged. But in the end you will be glad of the discipline such a job provides. Working in the correspondence end of a high-grade business, much of your value to your employer will depend on your ability to handle that chief tool—the English language. Too many Americans, students and adults alike, are blind and deaf to the beauty of their language and indifferent in their use of it. If you doubt this, note the poverty of expression among the thousands of persons whose answer to every question, request, or order is "OK." Competing with "OK" for the lowest rank is the reply I once heard a very pretty girl make over and over for a full five minutes—"I'll say!"

In case you start as a stenographer, here are some of the major uses you will make of English. For your information, after each I am placing the criticism made by supervisors of stenographers and transcribers in large offices.

1. *Understand the meaning* of the words dictated to you, in order to transcribe correctly. (The criticism: Girls write sentences the way they sound, whether it makes sense or not.)

2. *Know how to spell* the words dictated to you so that they will appear correctly in your transcription. (The criticism: More rewrites are caused by incorrect spelling than by anything else.)

3. *Know sentence structure* so you can put in punctuation correctly if the dictator has not dictated paragraphs, periods, and commas. (The criti-cism: Many young people do not know what constitutes a complete sentence. Especially when transcribing from a machine, the operator sometimes goes right on, with no punctuation until she comes to "Very truly yours.")

### TRAITS THAT WIN CONFIDENCE

Having told you what basic English you will need, let's see what character traits will help most in your business career. Stick-to-itiveness may be a habit instead of a trait—but by whatever name it is called, do acquire it early. In business, you can't shift a half-finished piece of work onto someone else to finish. It is your obligation to stay with whatever you start until you have brought it to a successful conclusion.

*Ability to Think for Yourself.* The ability to think for yourself is a highly desirable trait. You will learn to draw a fine line between fol-lowing instructions implicitly and using your head. Some people have a way of knowing just what is wanted; they manifest a native good judgment. Others, though faithful and conscientious, lack this almost intuitive sense and so do not always hit on the right solution. No matter how little initiative you are able to use on a beginning job, within the limits of the job itself you should carry on as independently as possible. An employer wants to feel that, when he turns over a job to someone, he can forget it and know it will be done and done correctly.

Such confidence is won through a series of trials. Here is the way one employer tests his subordinates. "When office employees ask foolish questions about things they ought to know or should be able to find out, I have little faith in their ability," he explained. "For a stenographer to ask, 'What shall I do about this?' when it is something she should know or decide shows lack of initiative. But when a girl brings that same problem to me and says, 'This seems to be wrong. I suggest that we handle it this way. Do you approve?' I know she has done some thinking about the matter. After a few such proofs of an employee's ability to see things through, I have confidence to let her go ahead on other similar problems."

*Adaptability.* Adaptability is a trait that business expects without question. The rule is that employees must make the adjustment. So many workers, beginners and experienced persons alike, seem to expect the job to adjust itself to their pleasure, health, hours, and whims. A postmaster in charge of eight hundred clerical employees complained that the incoming workers often expect everything to be changed to suit their ideas. Those who are used to having windows up object to air conditioning. Others who have to stand to sort mail say that their arches cannot take the strain, and they must work sitting down. "Do tell young people going to work that *they* must do the adjusting," this postmaster urged me.

Antagonizing an employer never helped anyone to make good. I've known beginners who insisted that the way they were taught to do things in school was the only correct way, and who made quite an issue of following the established methods of their employers. The truth was that they were in no position to know whether or not the systems or methods they were suggesting would apply. But it is not only beginners who are guilty on this score. No worse pest exists in the business world than the new employee with plenty of experience who wants to install the methods used in the last place he or she worked. "But they were so much better," these tactless persons plead. Until newcomers have won their spurs and made themselves and their ideas respected, they haven't a chance of inaugurating any new ways of doing things, no matter how good. At this point, their cue is to take orders and wait. If they make good, their time will come. When it does, they can tactfully suggest changes, and they will probably be listened to on the strength of their own performance.

*Willingness to Work.* Willingness to work is a trait watched by executives—a trait that will certainly help you make good. Oftentimes, being willing to do a little more than is expected of you will make up for lack of experience and awkwardness in other things. And sometimes doing simple tasks that may seem beneath your job, but that add to executives' comfort and peace of mind, make those higher-ups sing your praise. To illustrate this point: One of the best secretaries I ever knew was a young woman who, in addition to a college education and good secretarial training, was very domestic. She could not stand household disorder. Although she was not only secretary to the president of the company, but office manager in charge of six girls, at certain times of the year when she was not very busy, she saw to it that the offices had a thorough housecleaning. This sometimes meant she did it herself, since the janitor seldom could be inspired to do any extra scrubbing of desks and files. Her domesticity was a delight to her chief, and it never occurred to anyone in the organization to scorn her for doing menial tasks. In fact, she was rather looked up to for her love of cleanliness. When she married and the office gave her a good-by party, someone presented her with a brush and a verse which started, "She came into our consciousness scrubbing."

But not everyone is big enough to do whatever comes to hand. A Chicago employment-agency head told me about Ethel Marsh, whom she had placed in a good stenographic job. One day Ethel phoned her for advice. "They want me to clean out the safe. What would you do?" she demanded.

"Clean out the safe," said the employment agent curtly and hung up. The belief that one is employed to do only certain types of work is false. Not only is this a day of combination jobs, but when business has bought your time it expects you to do whatever needs to be done during business hours. That shortsighted stenographer should have reflected that probably she would not be asked to clean out the safe more than once in several years.

WATCH FOR THESE

Discretion is highly prized in business. And gossip—its exact opposite—is a vicious habit. Worse yet, office gossip can be a most contagious disease. One or two older employees who have acquired the habit of gossiping about everything and everybody in a business can infect an entire organization. But sometimes beginners fall into careless habits of talking too much and in the wrong places through thoughtlessness. Just remember that *all* information acquired on the job is confidential. However small a cog in the wheel you may be, you will do well to copy the standard of the lawyer, the doctor, and the priest—who regard confidences as a trust.

*Keep a Close Mouth.* In New York City, I was told the story of Sue Wing who had a job as secretary to a motion-picture executive. Sue was very proud of her job and talked about it all the time. She even talked at lunch in a Broadway restaurant with her friend Ann, who worked for a rival company. The price Sue's boss was offering for a new Broadway production was exciting tearoom chatter, and both girls felt very important to be discussing Big Business. But Ann took back to her office the news she had picked up. When his rival snatched the play from under his nose, Sue's boss angrily roared, "There's a leak in this office." And Sue, forgetful of her too trusting chat with her friend Ann, was hurt because suspicion was fastened on her. Though the leak was never fully traced, Sue was given less and less confidential work, and her altered position in the office finally made her so unhappy she left. A character trait kept Sue from making good.

A close mouth is as important within the office as on the outside. When gossip comes your way on your new job, smile if you have to listen, but be sure you contribute nothing to it. And keep still after the chatter is over. Never pass along anything you hear, no matter what the temptation. Often, the gossip is the oldest employee, who worked hard in the beginnings of the business and is now virtually pensioned in a light job. Instead of being grateful, this individual resents demotion and compensates by trying to poison the minds of newcomers. According to him or her, the organization is slipping. Sometimes, the newcomer is impressed by this attitude and length of service and feels he must not antagonize such a talebearer. In a later chapter, we shall explain more fully how to handle such situations.

*Your Chief's Affairs Are Confidential.* Don't make the mistake of thinking it is allowable to discuss with other employees the things your immediate chief has discussed with or dictated to you. Take the case of Betty Mead who told the outer office the full particulars of everything her boss said or wrote. One day, when he had gone to the bank to see whether he could borrow money to meet some of his personal obligations, Betty told the office that tale, too. Finally, an older employee decided the staff had had all they wanted of that sort of disloyalty, and Betty was reported and immediately dismissed. When she demanded to know who had tattled on her, Betty got little sympathy from her fellow workers.

*Discretion at the Switchboard.* One of the most confidential positions in any firm is that of the switchboard operator. She knows the personal and business affairs of all the executives. If she lacks discretion, she can make trouble for everyone—including herself. Angry wives of executives who plead nightwork, the touch for $100 "quick" from the boss's spendthrift son, as well as the business of the firm and its clients—all are well known to her.

It is bad enough when a PBX operator broadcasts what she listens in on, but when she doesn't get the story straight, the results can be tragic. Such a case occurred in the branch office of an Eastern distributor. Elsie Sloane, who operated the switchboard in the branch, made a practice of listening in when her boss, the local manager, talked with his boss at the company's headquarters. Most of the time, their conversation was all about sales, and it was boring to Elsie because it gave her no tidbits to pass out to the office force. But one day, she came in on the end of their talk and was certain she heard the Big Boss say "Sales have dropped off so badly, I'm afraid you'll have to get rid of some of your office people." That was news. Bad news. Elsie could hardly wait to tell her friends among the stenographers and the typists that they'd better begin looking for other jobs.

The manager was too busy to notice that a number of the office workers took a day off, but when they began to give him the customary two weeks' notice before leaving, he started asking questions. Everybody was reticent, but finally a bookkeeper said that he hated to leave, but had a family and couldn't risk being out of work. The manager was incensed at the spreading of what he called "an unfounded rumor." No one ever found out exactly what Elsie overheard, but the manager insisted there had been no thought of cutting the force. Everybody felt relieved, and a little ashamed, when the manager called a meeting and said, "If such a move is ever planned, I'll tell you and give you plenty of time to find other jobs."

*Learn to Be Tactful.* That other go-between of business—the receptionist—must have an extra amount of tact to call on. Here courtesy in small ways is most important. When, as a receptionist, you greet a caller with a pleasant, "Good morning, Mr. Jones, I'll tell Mr. Wood you are here," you have done well by your firm and yourself. There are few people who are not flattered at being called spontaneously by their names. An unusual reversal of this general trait is illustrated by the case of Miriam Jones, who presided at the combined switchboard and reception desk of a firm whose clients called often. One man had the name of Stinklebotham and did not like it. Miriam had been warned never to address him by name if she could help it and at least not to do so in a voice that could be heard by other callers. But Miriam couldn't be bothered remembering instructions, faces, or names. She felt that, with such a double job, all that could be expected of her was to ask callers their names pleasantly. Unfortunately for her, Mr. Stinklebotham complained to Miriam's employers that he thought it was about time the girl on the reception desk knew him well enough not to have to ask his name. And Miriam lost her job to a more tactful employee.

**Don't Be Grouchy.** There is an old saying, "Honey catches more flies than vinegar." It goes without saying that an agreeable person is more likely to make good than is the grouch, the fuss-budget, or the "sourpuss." If employers had their way, they would always be surrounded by cheerful people. For two years, I had traveling with me as secretary a girl whose expression and manner were unfailingly cheery. I asked her once how she managed it. It seems that her dramatics teacher had told her that Ina Claire attributed much of her stage success to the fact that she kept the corners of her mouth turned up. So my secretary had worked at it and, in spite of enough family troubles to turn her mouth corners way down, had achieved a smiling serenity. Her popularity with everyone we encountered in traveling 50,000 miles was proof that the system was good.

**OBEY OFFICE RULES AND FOLLOW OFFICE POLICIES**

In speaking of your first day in business, I mentioned the importance of punctuality and of co-operation regarding lunch hours. These are only two of the office rules and policies that you must observe. Each business has many more, and it is well to keep your eyes and ears open to find out what they are.

**Personal Telephone Calls.** In most offices, the rule is, "No personal telephone calls at the office unless for emergencies." Sickness, accident, or death in your home circle are almost the only occasions that justify your being called to the telephone unless you have an office of your own. Even then, unless you are an executive, a minimum of telephone calls is the rule. Beginners often rebel at this regulation, because up to the moment of employment their social life has come first. Now it must take second place. Tell your friends to call you at home in the evening. They will if you insist on it. You have no right to waste office time with personal telephone conversations. They not only take time, but they also take your mind off your work. Instead of thinking that you will appear popular in the eyes of your fellow workers to receive many telephone calls during office hours, realize that by so doing you are laying your private life open to everybody. This is quite as unwise as having others annoyed by your chattering phone conversations. After all, the office phone is there for office business.

It is equally undesirable for you to place personal calls from the office. Not only does this, too, interrupt your work, but every call you make costs your firm several cents. Multiply the number of employees by five cents and see what one call a day by everyone in a large office would do to the company's telephone bill. Do you wonder at such a rule?

If, in spite of all your best efforts, you occasionally receive a personal telephone call at the office, handle it with judgment. Especially if there is someone in the room, cut it short. Say as soon as you can, "I'm busy now. Call me this evening," or "I'll call you at noon." It will save you the embarrassment of carrying on a telephone conversation in the presence of someone else, and it will also give a tip to the person who calls you that such interruptions of your work are unwelcome.

**Smoking and Gum Chewing.** Virtually every business has a definite policy regarding smoking. Either the employees are allowed to smoke on the job or they are not. Sometimes, the ruling applies alike to men and women; sometimes, the men are allowed to smoke at their desks and the women are not. In some organizations, women employees are not permitted to smoke even in the dressing room. This is not usually because of any prudish objections, but because the stenographic force has abused the privilege and taken too much time out for their midmorning and midafternoon cigarettes.

In one sizable office where I was an executive, everyone was allowed to smoke at his desk, and about half of some forty-five men and women did so. Several young women executives, chain smokers, were so deft at lighting up and dousing ashes that they never appeared to lose time from their work. Then one day, Joan Ward, a new employee, was sent in, through civil service, to supervise all the clerks. Joan had a higher grade than any of the girls already there, so no one could argue her right to the job, but she was certain to be unpopular. However, it was not Joan's method of supervising that caused her unpopularity, but her manner of smoking. Joan was tall and thin, and her king-size cigarette was extended by a lengthy cigarette holder. When smoking, Joan leaned back in her chair, crooked a long arm plus cigarette plus holder, gazed contemplatively at the ceiling and puffed away until she had finished that cigarette. In an hour or so, she repeated the performance. Not only was this unfair to the office force, but office visitors were critical. Eventually, the Big Boss had to ask her to cut either the dramatics or the smoking.

If you are a smoker, by all means find out what is permissible before you light up. You can observe what the others do and follow their example. But be cautious, for it is possible that some employees are ignoring the unspoken wishes of the management and smoking when they are not supposed to. You can't afford to take any chances. As soon as possible, find out the rule, and if it is "no smoking," observe it, regardless of your own opinions and your habits. Furthermore, it's not good policy to complain about office rules and regulations.

To date, I haven't heard of any organization having a definite rule against gum chewing, but the practice is frowned on in all high-grade offices. The chewing of gum is offensive to most people, especially to the executive ear and eye. Regardless of your own opinion or your habits away from your job, remember that to executives and to the public, gum chewing is not good behavior in business hours. Persistence in this habit, if those you work for feel strongly on the subject, can lose you your job. I've never heard of its helping anyone to make good in business or to win promotion.

YOUR FIRST PAY CHECK

After what seems an age to you, the day arrives when you get your first pay check. You knew what your salary was to be, but when you look at the check, you see it is for a smaller amount—an uneven amount. You wonder why this is, unless someone has already told you that your take-home pay would be less than your salary. Attached to your check will be a check stub showing that certain deductions have been made, and there will be words or initials telling what the deductions were for, and listing the amount of each. One of these will show a deduction for your Federal income tax. You will recall that when you were hired you filled out a paper about dependents, so you suppose this has something to do with that. And it has. Another deduction will probably be marked F.I.C.A. (Federal Insurance Contribution Act), which means that a percentage of your gross income was deducted for social security payments after age sixty-five. This money goes to the United States Social Security Department office in Baltimore, Maryland, along with an equal amount paid by your employer. An account has been set up for you there under your name and social security number, and you will be credited with this payment. Right now you are not interested in anything that may happen to you when you are sixty-five, but your Government and your employer are helping you to save now so that you will have an assured income then.

In most states, these will be the only deductions. In California and New York and possibly in Rhode Island and New Jersey, since they have a disability insurance program, there are payroll deductions for disability insurance. In Alabama and New Jersey, very small deductions are made for unemployment insurance. More states may add either of these programs to their tax plan, but you will be advised at the time. If you do not understand the deductions made from that first pay check, go to your office manager or the head bookkeeper, who will be glad to explain them to you.

## QUESTIONS TO HELP YOU ANALYZE YOUR WORK

Do not waste too much time in your early working months hoping for promotion. You must make good on the job you have before you can be in line for anything better. In an article in *The Saturday Evening Post*, Loire Brophy, a well-known employment counselor in New York, gives business aspirants some sound advice. Among other things, she suggests a frequent self-catechism on the job. She lists questions you should put to yourself on the topics we have been discussing in this chapter.

Am I looking for extra duties, or am I content to do only the work at hand?
Am I big enough to do little jobs?
Am I willing to help the other fellow out?

Scrupulous honesty in answering these questions, Mrs. Brophy feels, will put you in a position to know whether or not you are making good.

Another question you should ask yourself is, "What is my job for?" I once heard of a young woman who, when asked what the typing she did was used for, replied: "I don't know. My work goes to Mary at the next desk." Employees like this are scarcely more than human stencils. No matter how humble your first position is, you should try to see it from the perspective of the entire business. So be alert and ask yourself:

What relation has my work to that of others around me?
What other jobs are just like mine?
What is the next job ahead?
Could I fill it?

## DO A GOOD JOB—THEN THINK OF ADVANCEMENT

A possible opportunity for promotion within your present grasp is to learn as soon as you can, without jeopardizing your own work, how to do the job just ahead. Sometimes, a sudden illness, a marriage, a death, or other emergency will cause a vacancy at that desk. Then the management asks, "What other employee knows how to do this work?" If you have been willing to help out occasionally at that desk in a rush period or have observed and questioned the person working there, you may be the one who will step into a better job.

But for six months or a little longer, let these be your objectives: be as useful as possible, and get valuable experience just where you are.

As Elihu Root, Jr., advised in a commencement address to seniors at Cooper Union: "Hitch your wagon to the job in hand. Doing that job absolutely as well as you can is what brings competence and character and recognition and also, if you will permit me, happiness." By proving your ability in the job you have, no matter how small, you are paving the way for bigger and better successes.

And having proved yourself in this first job, you should be considering your next move. During these six months, you have had plenty of opportunity to think and plan, to size up your vocational assets in the light of the job you are doing. Is the work you will be happiest in, and do best, to be found in the organization you are already working for? If it is, fine! Go after it. If you must confess that you don't want to go ahead in this kind of work, determine to make a change as soon as possible. But go slowly, and lay your plans carefully. You are going to stay in the second job for some time, we hope. So do not take it on as casually as perhaps you did your first one. That plan for your business life, which we discussed in the first chapter, should be brought out and dusted off. Then ask yourself:

> How does my business plan look now that I have had actual experience?
> Have my ideas changed?
> Do I like working in the type of business I am in?
> What other possibilities have opened up in the light of experience?

Look at your work and your future from all angles before you rush on to the next thing. Be sure you are ready for that next step up. A young friend who was beginning in a wholesale house said to me: "I am sick of having people talk to me about the bottom of the ladder, and how I must take slow steps up. Bottom rung? Today, I am actually sweeping out the floor under the bottom rung."

*Staying Power.* The other side is represented by what the personnel director of a department store told me the same day: "I like to employ college graduates, and I do. But often I wish that I could get them to realize they must first accept the regimentation of business, that they must be patient while they learn, as we are patient with them. Then more of them would go far. But as it is, too many of them after six months expect to be put in charge of departments, and they aren't ready. They have plenty of starting power, but they seem to lack staying power." For example, the job cycle of some young business beginners goes somewhat like this:

1. Enthusiasm for job, firm, and bosses
2. Enthusiasm cools
3. Criticism surmounts enthusiasm

4. Dissatisfaction sets in
5. Slipshod attitude toward job begins
6. Quits or is fired

Perhaps the lack of staying power is because, until they finish school, young people make a change about every six months. A new term opens, a vacation period begins, or they graduate from one class into the next every few months of the year. But business progress is marked by no such abrupt changes; it comes quietly and steadily. So, when you begin to be restless without due cause, strive with all your might to develop staying power. It may be all you need to push you up very shortly onto the next rung of the ladder.

Perhaps, as you read, you are wondering how you will know whether or not you are making progress. Don't worry. If you are not criticized for errors, you may know your work is satisfactory. Your best gauge of success will not be a lot of praise but the nonexistence of blame. And then, there are those twin glories—promotion and a larger pay check!

## QUESTIONS

1. Can beginners because of their youth and inexperience expect special consideration from employers?
2. What, in addition to skills, will you need on your first job?
3. Why must employees strictly observe office regulations as to punctuality in arriving at work? as to a specified lunch hour?
4. What businesslike habits will help you make good? What character traits win an employer's confidence?
5. Why is the first day on a new job different from other working days? Why does the fact that the position is your first one make a good beginning especially important to you?
6. Why is it important to remember the names of people you meet in business?
7. On a new job, will you adjust yourself to conditions as you find them, or will you expect the employer to adjust everything to suit you?
8. Should you talk about office business on the outside? What about discussing with other employees information you acquire in the day's work?
9. Why do employers prefer cheerful employees? Can the habit of turning up the corners of your mouth be cultivated?
10. If you think you know of a better way of doing something, should you insist that your new employer change to your method?
11. When you work in an office, are you expected to do any odd jobs that may come up?
12. Is it ethical to use office supplies, especially stamps, for personal use?

## TOPICS FOR DISCUSSION

1. Discuss whether on your first job it is advisable to excuse yourself for any slowness or mistakes by saying

    a. "I can't be expected to know everything."
    b. "I'm sorry. I see what was wrong, and I will correct it."
    c. "This is all new to me. I need time to learn."

2. What character traits will be most helpful in getting you through the difficult period of adjustment to your first job?

3. Many students who are capable of doing better work are satisfied to slide through school with a "C" average. Discuss what such young people will need to do when they encounter the "A" requirement of the business world.

4. Discuss the advantages of beginning in a routine job. The disadvantages.

5. If you find your first job not nearly so interesting as you expected it to be, will you

    a. Quit and look for another job?
    b. Revise your ideas and adjust to the work?
    c. Study on the outside and equip yourself for a more congenial office position?

    Be prepared to give sound reasons for your choice.

6. Suppose a personal friend calls you at the office to make a luncheon date. The call comes when you are receiving instructions from your supervisor. What will you say to your friend? Will you later discourage this friend from telephoning you at the office?

7. If you are a smoker and go to work for a company that has a "no smoking" rule, would you feel justified in "sneaking" one now and then, especially if you saw older employees doing so?

8. Some beginners are credited with thinking that office work is *play* and of conducting themselves as if it were. Others expect working to be *fun* and are disappointed when it is not. You sometimes hear business spoken of as a *game*. Do you think these terms are correct as applied to business?

9. How can you use your first job as a means of appraising your vocational assets? In relation to your career plan, why is your second job more important than your first?

10. Julia Kelly is private secretary to the president of a corporation. Her friends say of her, "You could know Julia for years and never know anything about her boss's business." Do you think this same discretion is necessary in a minor typing, clerical, or stenographic position? Should a PBX operator be closemouthed about what she hears over the wire? Why?

# PROJECTS

1. Suppose you have been engaged to go to work next Monday morning as a stenographer-clerk. In anticipation of your first day, make a memo covering

   a. Questions you may need to ask about your work
   b. Information you should get about office regulations
   c. Warnings against pitfalls for which you should be on the lookout

2. Based on your knowledge of yourself and of your attitude toward work at home and in school, rate yourself on the first three questions asked on page 243. Allow 33⅓ points for each question. If you fall below 25 on any of the three questions, how will you go about improving yourself in these traits in advance of going to work?

3. Prepare a 500-word paper enlarging on the following statement in the text: "But for six months or a little longer, let these be your objectives: be as useful as possible, and get valuable experience just where you are."

4. Gather all the information you can about payroll deductions. If you cannot get accurate information elsewhere about deductions for income tax, go the office of the Internal Revenue Department in your city, and ask for a booklet on this subject. Then figure what the monthly deduction will be if your salary is $275 a month. What will it be if you receive $300 a month? Also get information about the deduction marked F.I.C.A. What do these letters stand for? Figure what this deduction will take from the above-mentioned salaries. If you live in a state where salary deductions are made for disability insurance or unemployment insurance, find out what per cent of your salary this will be, and figure the amount that will be deducted from a salary of $250 and one of $300 a month. What is left after these deductions is called take-home pay. Be prepared to present to the class your information on the salary deductions, to discuss the reason for each of them, and to explain what is meant by take-home pay.

5. Write a short paper on the subject of personal telephone calls (incoming and outgoing) on a business phone. Present the employer's point of view first, giving his reason for limiting calls to emergencies. Then present what you think may be the point of view of some employees. Lastly, give your opinion.

CHAPTER 10

# Getting Along with Others

By this time, you have doubtless realized there is much more to making good than just knowing how to be useful in a business office. In the last chapter, you had a glimpse of how such things as gossiping and making dates on the office phone can be a setback to your career. Now let's go a step farther and consider the art of getting along with those with whom you work. For it is often the human relationships in business that make or break you—the daily give and take between employer and employee, between one worker and another.

If we could all be as impersonal as the typewriters and adding machines, how simple business life would be! But how very dull, too! Conditions being what they are, I sometimes wonder if the typewriter keys don't feel the nervous tension, the strain, the hurt feelings, the jealousies—the whole emotional undercurrent.

The remedy for most cases of office nerves is, of course, the mastering of a personal technique for getting along with all these other people who are working under the same nervous tension. If you are to succeed in a job, you have to get along with your superiors, your equals, and those below you in the ranks. Fortunately, it is a technique that can be cultivated.

Let's agree that the first step in getting along with others is a sincere wish to do so, and an earnest effort in that direction. This simple rule seems so obvious I almost apologize for mentioning it. However, there are many well-trained, able, and conscientious employees who would go far but for the fact that they are disagreeable, tactless, and—worst of all—rather proud of not going out of their way to get along with anyone. Some of these unfortunates, given half a chance, ride roughshod over everybody. Others sulk over imaginary hurts. Still others snap at anyone who speaks to them about the work in hand. They are so unpleasant that no one speaks to them about anything else, and only about the work when that can't be avoided.

True, we all know some grouches who got ahead. We've all had to work under them at times. But in my experience they are the exceptions. Who knows? Maybe they weren't always grouches. Maybe they let something on the way to the top sour them.

If all office misfits could only be detected before they are hired, a lot of grief could be avoided. Sometimes, they are weeded out in the first interview. A very competent woman who does the hiring for a corporation told me that she always looks for signs of non-co-operation. "But how can you find this out in an interview?" I asked. "It's easy," she answered. "When a beginner has a chip on his shoulder about his school or our requirements, or anything else, I know he won't be able to work with other people. So I reject him. I also reject the experienced applicant who says he left his last job because he didn't like the way they did things. I know he'd want to reorganize us, which would get him into trouble right away."

### Let's Take a Look at Management

Getting along with others is a two-way street. The most amiable and willing employees will seldom accomplish all they are capable of, unless the management meets them halfway. Whether a noticeable trend toward better employer-employee relations signifies that employers have become more generous, or whether the changes have been forced on them with the times, does not greatly concern us. The changes themselves do concern us. Here are some of the advantages that management now generally offers to salaried employees: a policy of promotion from within, a short work week, longer vacations with pay, time and one-half for overtime, pension plans, group insurance, and prepaid medical and hospitalization services. These, along with social security and unemployment insurance based on Federal laws, assure both present and future benefits to working people.

Instead of taking all these things for granted as their right, incoming employees need to realize that management has provided the setting and the men and women who play the leading roles. It is up to those chosen to play the minor roles to learn their parts and perform them well. By so doing, they may eventually play leads themselves, there or elsewhere. The stage directions are, "Smile. Appear to like your job and the other characters."

### Who Is Your Boss?

Earlier you were told that you would be expected to get along with your superiors, which is another word for employer or boss. I've used the plural because there usually will be more than one person over you.

The words "employer" and "boss" as I use them here do not necessarily mean the head of the firm. If you go to work in a very large
organization, you may never have any contact with the owner or head
of the firm or even of the office. The Big Boss may be an impressive,
well-dressed personage who hurries in and out of his private office and
of whom the employees speak with bated breath. We might call him
the invisible boss. However, his general ideas, expressed through his
business methods and his personnel, will be influencing your life and
actions hourly. Your immediate and visible boss may be the head of a
department or a minor executive who is in charge of a few persons,
including you. Anyone over you, from whom you take orders, is your
boss. If the system requires that instructions be given you by a number
of persons, you can plan on having that many bosses. Each of them
may be a different type of person. This involves your adjusting yourself to their several personalities. With each, you must put your best
foot forward, as though each were the only one to be considered. If
you please this collective boss, you are a success. And, of course, you
will please him; that is what you are training for right now.

The following bit, clipped from a New York City newspaper, indicates how large "the boss" looms in the life of the working girl.

ASSORTED PHRASES PUZZLE LISTENER

"Wotta punk that guy is." "Some slave driver, I'll say." "Easygoing but
kinda daffy." "Tightwad." These and other adjectives and phrases tossed
about the group of girls around a luncheon table were rather confusing to
the listener who did not know the subject matter of this descriptive discussion. Before long, however, the problem was settled. A high-pitched voice
raised itself above the babble: "Oh, my boss—he's the most charming dictator
in the world. That is, I mean he dictates his letters in the most adorable
way."

This suggests a few types of bosses, but there are many more. There
is the cranky boss, the untidy boss, the ailing boss, the lazy boss, the
bossy boss, and the absent-minded boss, to mention a few. But even
in a volume given entirely to a description of bosses, you might not
find the employers you may draw in the business lottery. For, of course,
no two employers are alike, and you have to be quick of wit and deft
of hand in adapting yourself to the one for whom you work. It's up
to you to study the persons you work under and to classify them in
your own mind as well as you can. You'll have to be very diplomatic
to adjust to all of them. But if you are the student of human nature I
hope you may be, you will be able to figure out how best to get along
with each of them.

## Don't Avoid a Woman Boss

While the woman boss may be any or all of these types, she deserves a paragraph of her own because both young men and women have such strange ideas about working for her. In my own experience as an employer and as an executive, I have learned that very few men can take orders from a woman. I suppose it is their inborn sense of masculine superiority that makes them either disobedient or bossy when under the direction of a woman. They are sure she must be incompetent, and so they try to dominate her and often treat her with insufferable arrogance.

It is all right for men to avoid working for women. They can, usually, since women employers are in the minority. But when girls insist they want to work for men only, the matter becomes serious—for them. Dr. Lillian Gilbreth, talking before the Transcription Supervisors' Association of New York City, had this to say:

One thing which I feel is very fine is the fact that these girls who are coming into centralized departments are working for women and having a happy experience, finding them fair, interested, balanced people for whom to work.

I made a test of some four hundred young girls studying secretarial work not long ago. One of the things I asked them was whether they would prefer to work for a man or a woman, or were indifferent. About five were indifferent; all the rest wanted to work for a man. There were some very human and commendable reasons, I have no doubt, in a great many of their minds, though I think a good many of them were subconscious and perhaps would have been denied, had I put them. But it seemed to surprise these young women when I said that if they refused to work for women, they were closing doors of opportunity for women like themselves. It seemed never to have occurred to them that if the right kind of trained girls went into business and said they didn't want a woman boss, organizations would have good reason to question the advisability of promoting women into executive positions.

Actually, when girls go into a department "manned" by women, they find it a big help to have an understanding woman fighting their battles for them. But they hate to admit it. An experienced and very able girl, who became secretary to a woman physician in charge of a large sanitarium, told me how she loved this job—how much responsibility she had, and so on. "You like working for a woman, then?" I ventured to ask. "Oh," she replied quickly, "Dr. Smith is exceptional."

Don't misunderstand me. All women employers are not admirable any more than are all male bosses. The only woman I ever worked for, who owned her own business, broke practically all the rules that govern

high-grade enterprises. But I have worked also under women supervisors whom I could admire without qualification.

### Give the Boss a Break

In getting along with superiors and, specifically, bosses, there are a
few general rules—things often learned by trial and error. Your attitude in relation to interest, enthusiasm, co-operation, and loyalty will
help you mightily. A little good old-fashioned respect and deference
will add to your score. Keeping your mind on your work and striving
to keep up both the required pace and the quality standard are all-
important. These things help to keep any boss in a good humor. If he
is pleased with the way you handle your work, half the battle is won.
But when something out of the routine comes up and you receive special instructions, don't argue about them. Get whatever information
you need, and get busy. Never mind if you know a better way, or a
short cut—or at least think you do. Forget it, and do the work the way
you are told.

One night at dinner I sat next to a woman who has a national reputation as director of home economics for a chain grocery organization.
We were talking about the trying experience of dismissing employees.

"When I have to fire an employee, I always tell her why," she said,
"although it makes her hate me, and I'm not sure it does any good.
But I do it because it took me five years to find out why I once lost a
good job in which I knew my work was satisfactory. My business life
would have been easier if I had known earlier why I was let out."

"Why did you lose your job?" I asked.

"Because I argued. I used to argue when I was told to do a job a
certain way, if I thought I knew a better way. Then, if I couldn't argue
my superior out of doing it his way, I went at it hammer and tongs to
prove him wrong. I was sincere, of course, in thinking I was right. But
not until I became an executive and saw the same attitude reflected in
my own department did I see that I myself had done what annoyed me
in my own employees."

*You Can't Order the Boss Around.* Here is another story along the
same lines. An experienced legal stenographer in a Government office
in Washington, D. C., was sent by her supervisor to help one of the
lawyers get out some special work on a Saturday morning. As the hours
slipped by and the lawyer, still busy with his notes, was not yet ready
to dictate, she grew restless. Finally she said, "If we are going to get
this work out by noon, we'll have to get at it." And then there were
fireworks! Fortunately for the stenographer, her supervisor could and
did stand between her and instant dismissal. But another young woman

was assigned to do that piece of work, since the lawyer refused to deal with an employee who presumed to dictate to him. To say that the first stenographer lacked tact is to put it mildly.

Did you notice that little word "tact," which just slipped in? It is a mighty word when it comes to dealing with bosses of all kinds. What will you do, for instance, when you find yourself awaiting instructions from a minor executive who doesn't know how to pass work on to assistants? I say minor, because important executives are where they are because they have made a success of knowing how to instruct the persons under them. But if you work under one of those persons who think nobody can do things as well as he can, and you allow him to do everything for himself, there will be no job for you. So that won't do. You will have to win his confidence and show him you can take responsibility off his shoulders. And the only means of doing that is to do everything perfectly, exactly as he wishes it. If your patience holds out—and your tact—you can win him over. Probably, he will never give you credit for what you do on your own. But never mind that, for you have been adding to your own future success.

**Complete Instructions a Safeguard.** At times, your boss will be a less meticulous person, with a slapdash method of giving instructions. Then what you need is not so much patience as inspiration. This type of executive is often a brilliant man with fine ideas, but he can't be bothered with the tiresome details of carrying them out. He'll back you to the limit of all you want to do, if you show a talent for putting his ideas into smooth operation. Unless the system in the office calls for written instructions, I advise you, when dealing with this broad-gestured executive, always to make notes on what you are told to do. Make these gifted men, who usually give only partial instructions, clarify their orders before you set to work. They won't like it, perhaps. They may even put you off with "Oh, you know what to do." But tactfully stick to your point until you are sure of what they want. Then check your own end of it carefully. Regardless of how effervescent your boss may be, win a reputation for letting no errors get by you, and the job is yours for keeps. You have not only succeeded in getting along with a difficult person, but you have supplemented his brainy imagination with your own good common sense—an unbeatable combination.

This type of boss also will probably take complete credit for his successful ideas. But, being the sort he is, he won't blame you for any failures. Before one of his skyrockets has proved itself a dud he will have launched another, which in its brilliance will dim the past.

**Study Your Chief.** Let us suppose you are a beginner and that you go to work in a small office where you take orders from "the Chief" himself. You will need to know a great deal about handling a very busy and perhaps worried man. For the responsibilities of men who own their own businesses are very taxing. Although your day may be full to bursting, you cannot complain, since his is too. It may even be that he is the type of man who thinks you're not doing anything unless you seem hurried and overworked. So you must always be busy, yet able to take on all the added duties and responsibilities that may be passed along to you.

If you are the only employee, or perhaps one of two or three, you will probably have to do many personal things for your chief. He may ask you to make his railroad reservations for him, buy his presents for him, telephone messages to his home and club. And, if he is a bachelor, he may ask you to make all his purchases for him. These personal duties are usually listed as secretarial. But in a small office, the stenographer often has to take them on. Even when a man's wife thinks "the girl in the office" is a secretary for the entire family and asks her to do shopping in her noon hour, there is no use protesting. A part of the business of getting along with the boss is to be agreeable and helpful, even to the extent of accommodating his wife. Just be glad if the man has a good disposition. He could very easily be cranky or petulant and vent his temper on the office force as well as impose unduly on their time and energy.

*You Must Put Up with the Boss's Moods.* Sometimes, after speaking before a group of business girls, one of them will say to me, "You tell us our shortcomings in business, but you let the employer go scot-free. Isn't he ever at fault?" Indeed he is, often. But there's nothing we can do about it. Unfortunately, the man who pays the salaries can be as disagreeable as he chooses. Because he can hire and fire, you have to take a king-can-do-no-wrong attitude toward him. He can fire you for an outburst of temper, but can indulge his own rages at will. You have your choice of putting up with these privileged moods or retiring to private life.

Of course, you could get another job, but you'd be certain to meet with another problem of personality adjustment. You might even get another bad-tempered boss. A manufacturer for whom I supplied considerable office help when I was in employment-agency work phoned me to explain why he had not hired the stenographer I had sent for an interview. "I asked her why she left her last job, and she said, 'Because the man I worked for had a bad temper.' 'Then this is no place for you,' I told her. 'I have a bit of a temper myself!'" It seems that, on the spot, this employer staged an exhibition for the applicant. He had been annoyed at something one of his employees had done or neglected to do that morning. So he got that person on the phone and bawled him out. "Before I had finished, your little stenographer had fled," he told me. "I apologized to the man I had called down," he added, "for I wouldn't have been so violent if I hadn't wanted to give that girl a lesson."

## GOOD BUSINESS MANNERS KEEP OFFICE RELATIONS SMOOTH

There is such a thing as business etiquette for bosses, office managers, and supervisors, as well as for those who work under them. One of the basic rules is, *never criticize an employee in the presence of someone else*. On a number of occasions, I have upheld the action of an employee when we were with an interested outsider or another member of the office force. As soon as I was alone with the person who had made the mistake, I explained to him where he had been at fault. Employees appreciate this kind of fairness; it is their due, but I regret to say they do not always get it.

Even though you may go to work for a rude boss, your good business manners can do much to lubricate the employer-employee relationship. And your own poise will help a great deal. A quiet, restrained, courteous manner will often have the effect of calming a highly nervous and irritable person. Such a little thing as saying "Good morning" pleasantly does something to start the day right. There are men who boast they never say "Good morning," but don't take that too seriously. Casually greet them, if it is convenient, but don't annoy them by waiting for a reply. "Thank you" is a courteous response that does wonders in smoothing dispositions. You should not have much occasion to use "please" with your employer, but it does help with fellow workers.

*Be Reserved with Your Superiors.* Many times, the pleasant relationship between employer and employee is spoiled by the overly personal attitude of one or both. Girls ask me whether they should ever discuss their personal problems and activities with the boss. Others complain they work for "nosy" employers who keep quizzing them about their personal affairs. In either case, it seems much better to have one's relationships at the office entirely separate from one's private life. I am not speaking of "dating" with the boss—that much-overworked and overrated movie situation which is seldom met in real life. I'm talking about telling him your most intimate troubles in an effort to better your standing with him. The less your superiors know about your home life and your outside personal affairs, the better for you. In most instances, they will not pry into these matters if you do not open the subject. When they do, you can be so noncommittal as to be discouraging.

Men often become good friends with their superiors in an impersonal way that never extends to their private lives. It seems harder for girls to achieve this detachment, but when they can it is appreciated. "Do you know that girl has worked for me for two years, and I know nothing whatever about her," has been said to me by many employers in open admiration of young women who were reserved about themselves and their home life.

## You and Your Fellow Workers

Now that you've had a preview of what is involved in getting along with the boss and anyone else over you, let's see how best to get along with employees on your own level. Later in this chapter, we shall discuss office friendships and romances—the personal relationships that are often difficult, sometimes rewarding. What you do about those is left, more or less, to your own good judgment. You don't have to make personal friends of your business associates or become emotionally involved with any of them, unless you wish to do so. But you can't dodge the constant daily contacts with them as you go about your work. The good disposition we hope you have will be needed every hour of every day, if you are to do your part in that necessary procedure of "getting along with others."

As a beginner, going into an office where everyone but you has worked for weeks, months, or even years, you will be wise to keep your ears and eyes open, and your mouth shut. It will not take long for you to discover the employees who are workers, those who are drones, and those whose business conduct you admire most. In your earliest days on a job, you will stick closely to those persons who give you your first instructions and who assign your work to you. A friendly, but not familiar, manner toward them and the workers of your own age and business level will help you over your first hurdles. As you get your bearings and are no longer so dependent on your one or more bosses, the test of how well you can get along with others will begin.

*Don't Forget "Please" and "Thank You."* In addition to asking your supervisor about things you are not sure of in connection with your work, there will be times when you need to speak to a co-worker about a puzzling minor matter. Liberal use of "please" and "thank you" will smooth your way in such a situation, but do not overdo either. Be prepared for someone who is not your supervisor telling you that you are doing something incorrectly. For instance, you may be told to file correspondence, and without knowing it, you are putting letters in the file for a preceding quarter of the year, whereas they belong in the current-quarter file. The person who calls your attention to a mistake of this sort is doing you and the office a favor—and saving you a reprimand. You should not resent this. Also, suggestions will be made

*Ewing Galloway*

It's fun being a part of a smooth-running
business organization. The employees—you—
make the surroundings pleasant or unpleasant.

for shorter and easier ways of performing tasks new to you but routine
to the experienced. Accept these proposals pleasantly, try them out, and
if they work, adopt them.

You will get much helpful co-operation from the other employees
if you show appreciation of their efforts to aid you. On the other hand,
if you are touchy and show by your attitude that you'd rather do
things alone, you may be left to do just that. I need not tell you that
your receptiveness will invite poor as well as good advice. But learning
to discern what is practicable is valuable experience in itself.

*Consideration for Others.* Getting along with others takes both time
and effort, and you may have to exert most of the effort yourself. To
earn the respect of your fellow workers, you must do your own job
well. This means not only turning out the work assigned to you, but as
soon as possible, taking full responsibility for doing it yourself and not

depending on others to help out. It means keeping to a schedule and getting your work out on time, so others will not be inconvenienced. And since you wish to be treated with consideration, be certain that you show consideration for those about you. Your ready understanding of others will be appreciated. Suppose, for instance, that the person at the next desk, usually friendly and helpful, suddenly seems hostile. You ask yourself, "What have I done to offend him?" and can think of nothing. Toward the end of a day that is trying for both of you, the fact comes out that there is sickness in his home, and that he has been too worried even to be conscious of your presence. How glad you will be if you did not say sharp things to him.

*Co-operation.* In the next chapter, co-operation in business and the lack of it are discussed at some length. However, I cannot talk about your office-hours relations with your fellow workers without saying something here about the basic ingredient—co-operation. The unwillingness of so many secretaries and stenographers to do anything beyond what they considered their regular duties was largely responsible for the establishment of central stenographic departments in large offices. There were too many prima donnas saying, "That's not my work, let someone else do it." Management became fed up with this attitude, and put a supervisor in charge of groups of stenographers, with instructions to keep them busy at whatever work needed to be done. You will be sized up on your willingness to help out in emergencies. Be agreeable. Don't plead that you are too busy to take on your share of this extra work. Get busy and do it. Also, if you find yourself with even fifteen minutes of free time, with all your work caught up, go to your supervisor, and ask if there is anything else you can do. You'll be surprised at the reception this offer will receive, because it is so seldom made.

*The Workers Below You.* Before you know it, a day will come when new employees will be hired by your employer, and you will no longer be the freshman. You won't be supervising them, but remember how others who knew the routine helped you get started. Now is your opportunity to pass along to other confused beginners the tips about office procedures which made your first days easier.

It seems far off to you now, but if you are a success in business, you may someday be put in charge of a few, or many, other office workers. Then comes the supreme test of how well you get along with others. There's an old saying in the business world, "Make friends of those below you on your way up, for you'll meet the same people coming down." You who are truly going places in business will need the good will of those who work under you. They can help you, or knife you, and they will, depending on how you treated them. You can browbeat them, perhaps, but you will be wise not to. If you have been generous in admitting the ability of others and have been glad to see them advanced, your reward will come in the boosts you will get from those who can't keep up with you, but who like and admire you.

## Go Slowly in Forming Office Friendships

When you are with other members of the office force, away from the actual work, it is a good idea to say little about your private affairs. During rest periods and the lunch hour, you will exchange experiences, talk about the last movie you saw, and what will be on television that night. Unless you wish to be more personal, you need not, and it may be better if you are not. After all, it is none of their business whether or not you are "going steady." You will hear some tall tales, both true and fabricated, but you don't need to match them. Everyone appreciates a smiling listener.

Beginners are likely to think that to get along they must at once get chummy with all the other employees. Nothing could be further from the truth. You will be fortunate if, in your entire business life, you make three or four real friends who work where you do. For, after all, the same rules should hold in business as apply in any other situation. Friends should be chosen because of mutual tastes and interests. Unless you have something more in common than the happenings of the business day, you are likely to find the companionship of office mates unstimulating, if not tiresome.

And don't worry about holding aloof. In the long run, it will do your status in the office no harm. You must, of course, be pleasant at all times. But the thing to do is to ask no favors and stand on your own feet. If you are criticized for not getting chummy, what of it? Until you are very sure you want to mix socially with the office crowd, a little criticism is easier to bear than the difficulty of getting out of a situation that becomes more undesirable the deeper you get into it.

Unless you go to work for a brand-new company, you will find definite semisocial customs already established in any office you enter. For instance, the male members of the firm may give a stag luncheon and a gift whenever one of the men is leaving. And the girls may give bridal showers and baby showers and even a housewarming when one of the group moves into a new home. If it is customary for everyone to contribute on these and similar occasions, you should do so without question. If you do not wish to go to any or all of these affairs, you can always have a previous engagement. That standing date may come in handy if and when you are asked to go home to dinner with one of your office associates. Better decline if you have nothing in common with your would-be hostess but office personalities, which are better not discussed. If you accept, you will have to return the courtesy or be labeled a social boor.

### FORMALITY IS GOOD FORM IN OFFICES

As for first names—don't rush that either. Even though you hear others in the office being called by their first names, you need not join the practice at once. Wait until someone calls you by your first name; then, if you like, reciprocate. A certain formality as to names is preferable during office hours. Even though you call your equals by their first names, you should always say Miss Blank and Mr. Blank when you address them or speak of them in the presence of callers or clients.

Often, social customs spill over into the business world. Present social usage permits the immediate use of first names when strangers meet at a party, barbecue, or similar social affair. It seems sensible, as when teenagers are introduced to each other by their first names only. Business is not quite that informal. Usually, a new employee is taken around and introduced to everyone in the department, and sometimes to everybody in the entire office. The first and last names of both parties are generally used, as "Mary McDaniel, this is Ann Summers, our new file clerk." Only when Ann meets the top executive, if she does, would the introduction be "Mr. Scott, this is Ann Summers, our new file clerk." Mary and Ann before long will be calling each other by their first names, and Ann's several bosses will doubtless call her Ann after a day or so, but Ann, or any other beginner, will not call an executive by his first name— ever.

Many executives proudly state that "our employees are just like one big family." If you go to work for such a man, there will be times when you will mix socially with all your fellow workers. A firm with this policy usually gives an annual picnic or a dance or two during the winter. And there is almost certain to be a Christmas party. Of course, you go and have a good time. On these occasions, executives and subordinates meet on a friendly social basis. Just remember that Cinderella's coach turns back into a pumpkin when she enters the office the next morning. If the boss has seemed your Prince Charming, or the boss's daughter your Lady Fair, during the evening, neither of them expects you to remember it. *They* won't.

### CONDUCT AN OFFICE ROMANCE DISCREETLY

Virtually everything I have said about office friendships applies equally to office romances. Girls still go to business hoping they will "meet someone." Sometimes they do. But, having observed for years various budding, prospering, and blighted office romances, I believe it is much better to do your dancing and dating with someone who works somewhere else. If for any reason a romance curdles on you, how much easier it is to handle the ensuing unpleasantness if your discarded love is not working at the desk next to yours. But if you must date from your office, keep still about it. Chattering about what "he said" and "I said" and "she said" can make a lot of trouble and often writes "the end" to a romantic chapter.

One business girl complained to me that a young man from the firm where she worked took her to the movies quite often, but he asked her to say nothing about it at the office. She resented what appeared to her as rather an uncomplimentary secrecy. But she felt better about it when I assured her that he showed excellent judgment and real chivalry in wanting to protect their friendship from gossip both innocent and malicious.

## A SENSE OF HUMOR AND OTHER OFFICE VIRTUES

A sense of humor does more to help you understand and adjust yourself to all sorts of people than any other single trait. Whether or not it is an asset that can be acquired, if you are without it, is something I cannot tell you. Once I sat at dinner next to a university professor who assured me he was developing a sense of humor in his small daughter. Here was his method. In the professor's household, the last one dressed each morning was an "Inkie." At first, little Dorothy wept when she was an Inkie and laughed gleefully at Daddy when he was one. But before long Dorothy learned to laugh at herself when the Inkie joke turned against her. Although this system might not produce a genuine sense of humor, the professor had the right idea, since the test of a sense of humor is the ability to laugh when the joke is on oneself.

Office life is sometimes a strain on your sense of humor. Suppose, after you have built up a picture of your future business life centered around a hero-boss, you find yourself working for a man who fails in all your hopeful requirements. Worse still, you are disappointed in your work. And even your pay check doesn't stretch as far as you expected. Can you see anything funny in the contrast between your high hopes and the reality? If you can stand that test and go right ahead, undaunted, even smiling, you may rest assured you have an honest-to-goodness sense of humor.

Early in this chapter, I remarked that getting along with others is an art that can be cultivated. I sincerely believe this to be true. For one thing, each of us can make a real effort to mind his own business. You have no idea what a difference this one thing will make in your relations with other people until you try it. Make it a rule to let your friends and acquaintances in business broadcast their own personal affairs, if they wish, and discipline yourself to silence. Remember that a habit of reticence is one of the virtues that leads to highly prized confidential positions and to executive rank. And what about cutting out complaints in the interest of developing more pleasant relationships? By working on simple, everyday problems like these, you will soon acquire a reputation for having tact. And you will deserve it. Tactful persons are usually well liked, too, I've observed.

## QUESTIONS

1. Why is it important for office employees to learn to get along with others?
2. Is it more important to get along well with the executives in your firm than with the office force?
3. To what extent are office friendships desirable?
4. Do you think you would mind working for a woman boss?
5. Would you consider that you were making a door mat of yourself if you showed deference to your boss?
6. Why do written instructions from some bosses make for better employer-employee relations?
7. When should first names not be used around the office?
8. Why does a "chip on the shoulder," which shows up in an interview, indicate that an applicant won't be able to get along with others in the office?
9. Is it a good idea for a young man or woman, newly employed in a large office, to begin "dating" with someone from the office?
10. If they do, should the matter be mentioned at the office? If not, why not?

## ARE THESE STATEMENTS TRUE OR FALSE?

1. All bosses should make an effort to get along with the people that work under them.
2. You don't have to put up with a boss who has a mean disposition. Tell him off.
3. All women bosses are not to be admired—only some of them.
4. Never give in, if you are right on a point. Keep on arguing with your boss. He will respect you for it.
5. Get all the dates you can with other members of the office force. Then give the details of your "evenings out" to the rest of the girls and boys in the office. It will show how popular you are.
6. Tact is one of the best traits an office employee can have.

## TOPICS FOR DISCUSSION

1. When you have a job, why isn't it enough that you do good work? Why should you have to go out of your way to get along with everybody?

2. Do you think an employee is foolish to express a willingness to do more work than his job calls for? What about the employee who looks around for something else to do when he has spare time?

3. When someone of your own rank in business is un-co-operative, will you

   a. Call him down?
   b. Complain to your chief?
   c. Accept it and make the best of a bad situation?
   d. Speak quietly to your fellow worker, hoping this will remedy the situation?

   If the last answer is your solution, what will you do if the quiet criticism only makes him angry?

4. Fred Brewer went to work for the Smith-Jones Manufacturing Company, which employed a large office force. It was a shock to Fred to see how much grumbling there was among the older employees. There seemed to be a feud between them and the newer employees. Fred thought that much of the dissatisfaction had grown out of resentment based on jealousy because younger men had been promoted over senior employees. At lunch hour in the employees' dining room, Fred was forced to listen to disgruntled discussions and bickering. "Why can't they get along with each other?" he asked himself. Apparently Fred was expected to take sides, but he was not going to do that. If you were in a similar situation, would you

   a. Be noncommittal and say as little as possible?
   b. Listen to both factions and try to judge which side is right?
   c. Report the situation to a senior member of the firm whom you know?
   d. Avoid the issue by eating lunch elsewhere?
   e. Speak up and tell the older employees they don't know what they're talking about?

   Can you suggest better ways for spending the lunch hour?

5. Discuss why the majority of young women want to work for men. In earlier chapters, you learned that the correspondence work in many large offices is directed by women supervisors. Carried to its logical conclusion, how will the prejudice against women bosses affect the future careers of girls who enter business?

6. Discuss the generally accepted rule in business—*Don't argue with superiors or tell them what to do.* Why is this unwritten law necessary to secure smooth-running relationships?

7. Imagine that instead of the hero-boss of your dreams you find yourself working for a bad-tempered man. What will you do if he constantly bawls you out both in private and before others, calls you uncomplimentary names, and even swears at you?

8. Suppose you are a stenographer in a small firm where there is no one to plan your work. You take dictation from three executives. Ordinarily, by organizing your time, all goes well. However, when the business suddenly becomes more active, each of your bosses wants his letters got out first. Discuss how you can handle the situation.

9. What will you do if, on your first day on a new job, one of the older employees asks you to lunch? If you refuse, how can you do it so as not to be thought rude or perhaps make an enemy?

## PROJECTS

1. Write a short paper explaining why you would or would not like to work for a woman boss.

2. List some of the things that, as a beginning employee, you might wish to ask another employee to explain to you rather than ask your supervisor. Be prepared to prove your point to the class.

3. In this chapter, the following items are listed as showing a trend on the part of management to improve working conditions and to maintain the health and happiness of their employees.

   a. Policy of promotion from within
   b. Short work week
   c. Longer vacations with pay
   d. Time and one-half for overtime
   e. Pension plans
   f. Group insurance
   g. Prepaid medical and hospital services

   Choose two of these items, and write a 500-word paper explaining the help these benefits are to office workers.

4. Talk with an employed member of your family or a friend who works, and find out how many bosses this person has. Also, if you can get the information, find out what different duties the employee has under each of them, and how he gets along with all of them.

# CHAPTER 11

# Attitudes in Business

One hears a great deal these days about "attitudes." You may be very much liked for your attitudes, or hated, criticized, and even ostracized because of them. They're that important. Your general attitude toward your job, your employer, and other employees is as vital to your progress as how well you do the work. And how right or wrong your attitudes are not only determines how well you get along with the personnel but also affects your increases in salary. Knowing how business feels on this point, placement bureaus are now going back to school records. They find that, good or bad, the all-important behavior traits usually exist during student days.

## Your Attitude in School Counts

While I was doing employment interviewing, I frequently telephoned business schools to inquire about recent graduates. The school's verdict was a great help to me when I was considering a young man or woman for a job. When the reply was, "Our teachers found Mary Brown very co-operative and adaptable," or "David Owen was both reliable and even tempered when here," I felt very safe in sending them out on interviews. And how regretfully I ceased to try to place an applicant about whose attitudes I had been forewarned.

One private business school I know has the word "attitude" printed on the student record forms used by its placement bureau. I asked the placement director whether she judged the graduates' attitudes in her interviews with them or relied on the teachers for information. "Their school records are valuable, of course," she replied. "But you'd be surprised how much the young people unconsciously reveal when they come to me, just before they are graduated, to talk about jobs. The student who is alert, eager, and co-operative shows it in his whole bearing, no matter how little he says. He or she gets a rating of 'good.' But if a student is indifferent, lackadaisical, and uninterested during the interview, I naturally write 'poor.' Everything else falls in between with a 'fair.' "

Your school and your placement bureau will do everything they can to help you. *Their* attitude toward *you* is co-operative in the extreme. But they are powerless to help you if you don't give them good material with which to work.

### You Are Being Watched and Judged

Your attitude toward business is important. But it is something about which a personnel director says nothing at the time you are employed. You will be told what your duties are to be, and usually the office rules will be explained to you. But no one will say to you, "Unless your attitude is good, you won't last long here." It is assumed that you have the right attitudes. Nonetheless you are on trial in this respect. Approval will bring no pats on the back from your superiors, and disapproval may bring dismissal without warning. Those on your own level are watching you, too. If they feel you need to change your attitudes, they will often find a way to make you conform to their group standards.

An excellent example of mass action to bring a fellow employee into line appeared in a business magazine, under the heading of "Operation Chlorophyll." [1]

It seems that one woman in an office of a Chicago manufacturing company didn't take the beneficial effects of soap and water too seriously. Her presence constituted a direct attack on the sensitive noses of her co-workers. They complained to the supervisor, who didn't know how to handle the issue.

The girls then took matters into their own hands—putting chlorophyll candles on their desks and open bottles of cologne in front of the fans. Their heavy-handed bantering got out of control, however, and the personnel director had to step in with a resounding reprimand for all.

### Loafing on the Job

Perhaps you are wondering what an undesirable attitude consists of. Let me illustrate. The popular indoor sport of loafing on the job is a poor attitude. The world seems to be full of persons of low energy or inborn laziness who slide through life with a minimum of effort. When they arrive on the business scene, their chief concern seems to be to see how little work they can do and still hold the job. Often, this attitude is deliberate, but I think it is also at times unconscious. If the culprit is

[1] *The Management Review*, February, 1953.

so fortunate as to hold a job under a superior with a great deal of perception and is willing to try to correct his faults, his job is saved for him. But as a rule, there is no one to pamper business babies of this type.

I once engaged a young man to write publicity articles. He was regularly employed as a reporter on a morning newspaper, and what I paid him was so much extra money for him. Shortly after he began to work for me, his writing began to deteriorate, and I was puzzled as to the cause. Because I knew him to be a good writer, I tried to be patient and see whether his work would not come back to normal. But one day I entered the office just in time to hear him say to another employee, "This story isn't very good, but I guess it will get by her all right." It didn't.

*"Time Is Money."* One form of "getting by" is stealing time. There are offices that are so considerate in allowing time out that the employees abuse their privileges. In an organization where the stenographers were leniently handled, each girl had adopted the practice of taking off a half to a full day every week. They had found they could get away with this, and they were doing it. A new office manager soon cut their two-hour lunch periods and their days off.

My prize experience with time stealing was the case of a copy writer who, because he occasionally did some night work, imposed on his privileges to the limit regarding his morning hours. One day, I happened to observe that he arrived for work about ten, went to his private office, typed busily for a few minutes, and then left. I asked the operator if he had said where he was going and when he would be back. "Oh," she answered, "I'm sure Mr. Erwin went out to breakfast. He usually does about this time." I was curious to know what copy he could produce so quickly and discovered he had started a poem entitled "Dawn Comes to the City." We had a little talk that resulted in our mutual agreement that he might better observe the dawn from his home or from someone else's office thereafter.

The easiest way to check whether you are acquiring the time-stealing habit is to ask yourself these pertinent questions:

Am I doing all the job requires?
Am I willing to do more than my share of a co-operative task?
Am I ever satisfied with slipshod work?
Am I looking around for more work to fill my spare time, or am I trying to drag out my work to kill time?

Honest answers to these and similar questions will quickly reassure you or warn you as to where you stand.

## CO-OPERATION IS VALUED

Another unfortunate attitude met frequently in business is "That's not my work." Whenever there is an extra piece of work, such as typing a thousand envelopes to send out a form letter, there is someone who will say huffily, "That's not my work. I was employed to be Mr. Hunt's secretary." How much better to take the point of view that every least thing you can do to help the business that is paying your salary not only makes you more valuable as an employee but furthers your own business education and skill. Never mind how mechanical and uninteresting the task is.

I know a brilliant woman who for many years until she retired was assistant to the manager of a large importing house. She began her career as a saleswoman. Whenever there was a difficult or disagreeable job to be done that nobody wanted, she had a habit of saying, "Oh, let me do that." Her interest and enthusiasm for learning everything pertaining to the business carried her to the top in a very short time. I have known both young men and women to make good full-time jobs out of part-time work by digging up and doing tasks that other employees were side-stepping. Business is quick to recognize and, whenever it can, to reward such initiative.

University business offices tell me they have a great deal of trouble on this point of co-operation. Administrators feel that everyone is on the payroll of the university itself and should do any work that will be of benefit to the corporate employer. However, many university office employees resent such requirements and feel justified in maintaining that they are working for certain individuals or for a specified department. This attitude is, of course, the exact opposite of the willingness to work that is expected in business, be it educational or otherwise.

Sometimes, to be co-operative, an employee must unselfishly put personal plans aside for the good of the organization as a whole. In a large office, where I worked under civil service, a young stenographer, whom we will call Doris Hughes, was put to this test and failed her teammates. Doris had a variety of duties, the least of which was taking dictation from the assistant manager and from me. She spent several hours each day in the business office, assisting a hard-working accountant. She was responsible for statistical work that had to be kept up daily for a monthly report. And she was a working understudy to the head file clerk. November was a busy month in that office, and the Friday following Thanksgiving was the worst day of all. It was an established rule that no one was to take that day off. Although several of us wished to spend the holiday week end with relatives at a distance, in our code it

*Reproduced by permission. Lever Brothers Company, New York*

Your work is what earns your pay.

was not sporting to ask for the day and by doing so overburden others with our work.

Not so, Doris, who wanted to go on Friday to the wedding of a cousin, 200 miles away. Doris knew that if she asked for Friday she wouldn't get it, but if she were out all week she could automatically be absent Friday. So Doris fell back on tears, saying "My family comes first." The manager was finally melted into saying she could take the entire week. But Doris was the conversation piece at lunch and rest period all week, as those whose work she had increased struggled along. On her return, nothing was said about her lack of co-operation; but, because she let everybody else down, Doris has probably found that she cannot get co-operation from that office force when she needs it.

Have you ever met the employee who shrugs his shoulders and says, "I should worry, I'm not being paid to kill myself"? After you get into the business world, you will find one of his type in at least every second office. If it is a young woman, she is likely to be a charmer who is much more interested in her dates and her outside successes than in whether she makes good on her job. Her sole interest in her work is her pay check. Her identical twin, as far as attitude goes, is the employee who complains, "I wish the work would slack up." Somewhat shortsighted, surely, since when the work lets up there will be fewer employees.

Everyone has met the "know-it-alls." These people, regardless of their status in business, object to taking orders from anyone. They overlook the first rule of business: *You are only as important as your job, and you must take orders from anyone in the office who is over you in authority.* Some of these individuals know so much that they even object to taking orders from the boss himself. Not long ago, near me was a group of young girls, apparently on their first jobs. One very pretty girl remarked that she had quit that day.

"Why?" the others chorused.

"We didn't get along. Mr. Smith was too bossy."

"But wasn't he the boss?" one girl asked.

"Oh, yes," the quitter said, "but he was unreasonable. I was out three days last week, but I had told him in advance. Today, I said I was going to take Tuesday off, and he said, 'Please make up your mind whether you want to work or not.' " So she had decided she didn't want to work —there. The silence of her friends showed that they disapproved of her attitude.

### Sensitiveness and Moodiness Not Wanted

Many persons who are much too sensitive are thrust into business offices. Unless they make a quick adjustment, they are likely to have a hard time. Their feelings are always being hurt. Someone is advanced over them; a special piece of work is assigned to someone else; somebody gives a party to which they are not asked or confides a juicy bit of gossip to another member of the office force and leaves them out. Or they do what they think is an outstanding piece of work, and no one compliments them on it. They are constantly looking for offense, and naturally they find plenty. Business is a rough-and-ready place, and a busy place, too. No one takes time to stop and soothe the injuries to pride, self-love, and vanity that he may have thoughtlessly caused. The sooner these sensitive persons snap out of their easily wounded attitude, the sooner they will regard the business world as a thrilling and exciting place, and the happier they will be.

Then there is the moody person, whose feelings are up one day and down the next. Often, he illustrates the high cost of feeling low. If you are cursed with such a temperament, begin now to discipline yourself. After you go to work, it is rather late to learn, even by bitter experience, that moodiness is most unwelcome in offices. The staff is the well-oiled machinery that keeps a business moving smoothly, and as a cog in the machine, you too must keep well oiled and running evenly; otherwise, you will be discarded for a better "part."

## "Yessers" and Clock Watchers Seldom Go Far

There are many other types of persons whose attitude in business is deplorable. One is the "yes man." Though it is flattering, even to executives, to be agreed with, an overdose of yessing becomes a great bore. To succeed, you have to grow with the job, and to be eternally yessing someone does not aid your mental growth. And how can a "yes man" ever learn to make decisions of his own, which he must learn to do if he wants to become an executive.

As a final example of an undesirable attitude, there is the clock watcher. I've known office workers who got cricks in their necks turning around to look at the clock. A "clock-eyed" person should try to get a desk where he can see a clock head on. Then his great interest in the passing of time might go unobserved by the heads of the firm who are buying his time. For, not unreasonably, the owner of a business is not sympathetic with the point of view of the employee who lives through the day piecemeal, counting the minutes until his morning relief, then yawning until noon, with a repeat performance from 1 p.m. until 5 p.m., when he is the first one out the door.

Another type of clock watcher begins putting his work away about four o'clock every afternoon to be ready to leave the office at the stroke of five. If he expressed it in words, he could not more plainly say he doesn't care whether he has a job or not. Actually, many times he knows only too well that the loss of his job would have dire consequences. But it never occurs to the "clock-eyed" that there is anything wrong with his skimping on time. If you pointed it out to him, he'd say, "What are a few minutes at the end of the day?" Actually, these few minutes, day in and day out, add up to more than a full day's work a month. One wonders how he would like to be docked a day's pay for such a practice.

Out of a typical office, a young woman with a delightful sense of humor wrote the following, under the title of "Clock-watchers." [2]

What's worse than a clock-watcher? A clock-watcher-watcher. In my office, where dozens of women work, both young and old, the young girls (who were hired for their sprightly energy and promise of future value to the firm) drag in late and pallid, uncover their typewriters, sigh, yawn, glance at the clock, and then group at the water cooler to giggle over last night's dates and the oh-so-darling dresses they're going to buy on their lunch hour.

[2] Gladys Guilford Scott, in *Today's Secretary*, March, 1954.

Meanwhile there are the old "girls" (who were hired for their seriousness, their experienced know-how, and their responsible sense of follow-through). Are the old girls doing the work that the young ones are neglecting?
Don't be silly! Of course not.

Why, it takes every bit of *their* time to watch the young ones watching the clock and to gather in their own little group to gossip about how the young ones gossip.

Between the giggles and titters at the cooler, and the ominous hostile buzz of the older group in the opposite corner, who's doing the work?

What's that, boss? Who did you say ought to stop watching the clock-watcher-watchers watching the clock-watchers watch the clock?

Who did you say ought to stop gossiping about the way the gossipers are gossiping about the gossips?

Who did you say ought to buckle down to business?

Who—*me!*

The nation's largest employer, Uncle Sam, rebelled once against the early-quitting practice of many Government employees. In a circular sent to the various Government offices in Washington, D. C., the Comptroller General said:

It is observed, that some of our employees stop work before official quitting time, apparently for the purpose of making themselves ready to leave the building exactly when the bell rings. It is a rule of this office that all employees shall be at their stations of duty at the time set for work to begin and render seven hours of faithful service.

However, there's something to be said for the employee's point of view. In one of our states, the Department of Employment decided that its employees were not making the most of the first half hour of the workday and the last half hour. Orders were issued that in all state employment offices interviews were to be scheduled starting at 8 a.m. and also for the half hour between 4:30 and 5 p.m., time that had previously been used to organize the day's work and to close it. Regardless of their already heavy interviewing schedules, all interviewers were now required to talk to applicants for jobs or for unemployment insurance from the moment the office opened until it closed, except during the noon hour. I have not heard whether this practice was continued indefinitely, but all the interviewers felt imposed on, because they were also responsible for desk work, which under such a continuous interviewing program they could not handle during work hours.

## SUBSTITUTE RIGHT ATTITUDES FOR WRONG ATTITUDES

For every poor attitude, there is a good one that goes far to win success. Perhaps the best of these is interest. Not only interest in your work, but interest in life in general and a friendly but not too personal interest in those about you. And along with interest goes enthusiasm. Both of these must be at an even tempo that can be maintained. It is of no use to start off with the greatest interest and enthusiasm and, after a short time, slow down. These qualities are like typing and dictation speeds—they must be sustained day in and day out. Many beginners find this difficult after the novelty has worn off. They become restless, and distant fields look greener. They are sure a different kind of job somewhere else would hold their interest and enthusiasm much better.

*You Can Create Enthusiasm for Your Job.* Taking an interest in, and creating enthusiasm for, the job you have can do more toward making the work interesting than anything else I know. This definitely is one attitude that can be cultivated. When your family and friends ask you how you like the new job, say, "It's swell," even if in your heart it seems a bit dreary at the moment. Tell them the good things you find in the job and, surprisingly, you will soon see more things to praise. When you are interested in everything about you, you automatically become a more interesting person yourself. You actually extend your personality. And interest creates interest. Soon you will find yourself reading articles about business in general and gathering information that will be of great value to you in your job.

The brother of a friend of mine went to work in the sales department of an engineering firm several years ago. Shortly after he had started, he told his sister there would never be any opportunity for him with this organization. He explained that all the other salesmen said so, and certainly they ought to know. "Most of them who have been there for years and years are getting about the same salary they started with." My friend, who was an experienced businesswoman, told her young brother to stop listening to the complainers. "Of course, they haven't got anywhere," she said. "No one ever does who spends all his time condemning the company for which he works. It's a good job. Keep an alert, interested attitude, and you'll get somewhere right over their heads." Her prophecy proved true, for by changing his attitude, her brother made rapid strides and became assistant sales manager within a very few years.

Many successful business people are now and then interviewed by reporters and asked what, in their opinion, led to their success. To this question, I have answered that I knew where I wanted to go (had a plan), was prepared by my education for the work I wanted (advertising), and got some lucky breaks. At the top of the list of traits, or attitudes, that I felt had been my strongest points I always put *a capacity for sustained enthusiasm.* Probably, I was born with that quality, for

I don't recall working to cultivate it. I found that, after rebuffs, disappointments, and near failures, being able to go back the next day and tackle the same old job, still liking it, still interested, and still determined to solve the problems involved, helped mightily.

*Be on the Winning Team with Management.* No doubt, when we were discussing undesirable attitudes, you noticed that many of them expressed the very opposite of co-operation. Anyone who loafs on the job, who refuses to do work because it is not, strictly speaking, *his* work, or who feels too good for the job is certainly not co-operative. You know what happens in football or baseball if there is no teamwork. In business, just as in athletics, you have to play the game to win—and teamwork helps. What team are you going to choose? Will you join those who are discontented with their work? Or will you join those who see a future for themselves in loyal teamwork with the management?

I often wonder why so many employees regard the management of business as their natural enemy. Office supervisors tell me that, although they wish to help employees to advance, they often find a barrier has been erected between them by the workers themselves. Some employees seem to believe it is impossible for the heads of business to have the workers' welfare at heart. So, without waiting to find out about the situation in their firm, they take the attitude of being "ag'in the government" from the day they go to work. There is, of course, a managerial point of view, which of necessity is different from that of the employees. The responsibility of payrolls to meet, rent to pay, and work to be completed on time and done well, regardless of whether the business is making a profit, creates burdens that few employees would be willing to shoulder themselves.

A little imagination about such things will give you an appreciation of the problems of the employers for whom you work. And imagination transformed into co-operation will pay dividends to both you and the business. You can be co-operative by being thankful every day that you have work for which you are paid well and regularly. You can show this gratitude by pleasantly giving a full day's work for a full day's pay. You can be co-operative by subordinating your own opinions about how the business should be run. You can be co-operative by doing without complaint the things the management asks you to do for the good of the buisness as a whole. That's what teamwork in business means.

*You and Your Teammates.* Co-operation with the office force is just as helpful to your future as co-operation with the management. Take the matter of vacation schedules as an example. Sometimes, vacation periods are left for the employees to arrange among themselves, subject to the approval of the management. It is customary, naturally, for heads of departments to have first choice and then on down the line. In large offices, the employees are often asked for their vacation requests early in the spring. Then depending on each person's work, the management makes up a schedule so that someone who knows each employee's tasks will be on hand to take these over during that person's vacation. Every effort is made to give employees the weeks they ask for, since often they wish to be off at the same time as members of their families who work elsewhere. But adjustments have to be made, and there are inevitable disappointments when certain individuals cannot be spared for the period they requested.

But sometimes co-operation is conspicuous because of its absence. For instance, a friend who is advertising manager in a furniture store said to me, "I can't do what I had planned to on my vacation this year, because one of my artists insists on going at the only time I could conveniently carry out my plan." I was amazed at a subordinate's taking such an attitude and said so. "I held that girl's job for her when she was ill last spring," my friend replied. "But I'm all through now. If she can't co-operate any better than that, I'll replace her as soon as it is convenient." That is the way it is in business. Nothing may be said when you fail to co-operate, but the circumstances are remembered and tell against you in the end.

## CULTIVATE A CHEERFUL, RELAXED, BUT IMPERSONAL ATTITUDE

There's an antidote for the poison of moodiness. It is: Cultivate a cheerful and pleasant attitude. And one way to do that is to smile more. Simple, isn't it? But let me warn you, the smile must be genuine. Some girls assume an affected smile that is merely annoying and deceives no one. A friend who is in charge of the personnel in a large law firm once interviewed a legal stenographer who smiled throughout their fifteen-minute conversation. The interviewer liked everything about the applicant except her smile.

When she called the girl's last employer before making a final decision, my friend was told, "Eileen's all right, if you can stand the smile." Good legal stenographers were scarce, so the personnel manager hired the smiling Eileen, though with some misgivings. A month or so later, my friend suddenly realized that the perpetual smile had vanished, and that now when Eileen smiled it was because there was something to smile about. In a follow-up interview to check on how Eileen was getting along, how she liked her work, and so on, this experienced personnel manager made an interesting discovery. Eileen was happy in her work, she had been assured that she had made good, and that she was liked.

She felt secure—and the forced smile, caused, it now seemed, by sheer nervousness, was gone.

*Be Strictly Impersonal from Nine to Five.* An impersonal attitude in business is a trait valued by employers. For the most part, this means not injecting the personal into business relationships. Any display of emotion during business hours is very bad form. Regardless of how much you may be worried about outside personal matters, you must not show it while on the job. Neither must you let your likes and dislikes of persons or types of work interfere with your daily output. Business expects everyone to do his work with a strictly objective point of view. Nor does business care to have employees attracting attention to themselves by bursts of temperament, hilarity, or conspicuous dress. In fact, personal idiosyncrasies of all kinds, however minor, are frowned on because they create a disturbing element, and business seeks to maintain a calm routine throughout each workday. You can understand that such an atmosphere works for the benefit of all by minimizing the possibility of frayed nerves and tired brains.

*Take Criticism with a Smile.* To be able to take constructive criticism with a smile is one of the business attitudes to cultivate, if you are not fortunate enough to have that ability already. An employer who is an editor said to me, "I fear I am going to have to get a new secretary. The one I have is wonderful as far as her work goes, but she can't take criticism. I have to spend five or ten minutes figuring out how to tell her that the punctuation in a letter is incorrect. Unless I am very polite about it, she sulks. Punctuation is either right or it isn't, and I must have a secretary to whom I can say 'this punctuation is wrong,' and have her correct it pleasantly with no further ado." There it is again, storm clouds gathering for an employee who is as yet entirely unaware that anything is wrong.

But there is even more to it than taking deserved or constructive criticism calmly. Many times in business, criticism is unwarranted. Not every executive is a fair person, and many are not above taking out on a subordinate some hang-over of disagreeableness developed, perhaps, when his senior in command took it out on him. Unfortunately, there is nothing you can do about executive bad temper. You have to be able to take it, but you can't return it in kind.

### BE LOYAL ABOVE ALL OR QUIT

Need I tell you that a loyal attitude toward the firm for which you work is a cardinal virtue? It doesn't matter in the least whether you privately think the firm worthy of loyalty. As long as you work there, you must be deaf, dumb, and blind to its weaknesses. Or at the very least, be dumb. Sometimes, it is difficult to be loyal, to believe that everything the management does is right, and to say so when called on for comment. For the employer is not always right or even admirable. Sometimes, you know this from things you learn through your work. As a bookkeeper, for instance, you might be asked to falsify a tax statement. What to do?

I have heard of businesses that thought more of an employee who, under such circumstances, stood up for what he thought was right, and I have known of cases where the protester was dismissed for not carrying out orders for dishonest work. For such a reason, a young teacher lost an administrative position in which he had distinguished himself. His county superintendent wished him to accept a salary for supplementary teaching in one school, even though he did not teach, so that she might divert his administrative salary to political uses. Meanwhile, he would continue working in her office, but would not be officially listed on her staff. When he refused, she branded him un-co-operative, not wishing to reveal why she was dismissing him. Since he did not think it chivalrous to expose dishonesty in a woman, he had difficulty in finding another job. But truth does prevail, and eventually the young educator's record was cleared.

If you should find yourself in a position where you feel you cannot give your employer unstinted loyalty, you would do better to look for another job at the first opportunity. Life is too short to waste much of it working for a firm of which you cannot speak well, or that you cannot honestly admire. Since you should not "bite the hand that feeds you," keep still until such time as you can secure employment with a business that is worthy of your admiration and loyalty. But be sure you do not take the word of disgruntled employees for dishonest practices that may not exist. Wait until you know positively that things are not right before you put yourself out of a job. You may find valid reasons at times for separating yourself from a payroll, but you will meet with very little dishonesty in employers. In a long business career, I ran into such dishonesty only once. It was a genteel racket operating as a philanthropy, and I blamed myself for not seeing through it before I accepted the employment.

## QUESTIONS

1. Does attitude count before you go to work? in school? at home?
2. Can a student whose attitude in school is un-co-operative suddenly change after he goes to work?

3. Name some undesirable attitudes that hamper office workers. Name the opposites of these attitudes.
4. Is "getting by" the same thing as "loafing on the job"? Is it the same thing as stealing time?
5. What is wrong with beginning to put your work away a half hour before closing time? What attitude does this express?
6. Has a moody person any right to inflict his hurt feelings and his changeable temperament on his fellow workers?
7. Do you think the "know-it-all" would be liked by his superiors? his equals? those below him? How would each of these groups regard the "yes man"?
8. What attitude should a beginner take when his work is criticized?
9. Do all employers deserve the loyalty they expect?
10. What does teamwork in business mean?
11. What is wrong with being a clock watcher?
12. What is meant by the term "business babies" as used in this chapter? Does it suggest an attitude? If so, what attitude?
13. Why shouldn't one "yes" the boss? Isn't that "getting along" with him?

## TOPICS FOR DISCUSSION

1. What does the expression, "Be strictly impersonal from nine to five," mean? Discuss how being impersonal would affect a person's actions during a hard day in the office.
2. Under what circumstances would an employee have good reason for quitting his job? Find examples in this book or among your acquaintances where employees have been justified in quitting.
3. Check yourself and your attitudes in school by answering the questions on page 267. When you are an employee, would your attitudes as shown by this check be any different than they are in school? If undesirable attitudes were revealed in your replies to the questions, what can you do to change them before you enter business?
4. Do you think an employer has a right to expect all the co-operation, loyalty, interest, unselfishness, and enthusiasm that this chapter says he demands? Be prepared to discuss whether an employee is paid for the work done, his attitude while doing it, or a combination of both.
5. Explain what is meant by the following statements:

   a. "Her attitude is excellent."
   b. "I don't like his attitude."

6. Discuss whether it is ever permissible to say, "That is not my work," or "I was not hired to do that." Would the fact that you are already overworked make a difference?
7. Discuss whether you could be loyal to an employer whose business practices you have learned are dishonest.

8. Some employees excuse their loafing on the job by saying, "Well, after all, what is my small salary to a big firm like this?" Discuss the attitude of such employees.
9. Explain what is meant by an impersonal attitude. Is an objective point of view the same thing?

## SUPPLY THE MISSING WORDS IN THESE SENTENCES

1. Mary lost her job because, although she was given every chance to do so, she showed no willingness to (?).
2. If you can't speak well of your employer—in other words, be (?)—you'd better quit.
3. Anne's work was all right, but what she needed, if she was to be liked in the office, was to (?) more.
4. Jerry takes the attitude that the boss is buying his (?), not the work he turns out. But if he were sincere, Jerry would realize that he isn't even giving the employer his money's worth in (?), because he is always (?) on the job.
5. There is no (?) near Henry's desk, but he manages to see one by going for a drink of water a dozen times a day.

## PROJECTS

1. Teamwork is another term for co-operation. Write a 500-word paper showing why teamwork is as necessary in an office as on the football field.
2. Write a brief paper on loyalty. Explain what is meant by the word as it is used in business and why such a high value is placed on it by employers.
3. Taking "Office Friendships" as your theme, prepare to give a class talk covering the following points:

   a. Congeniality of tastes and interests as the basis of true friendship anywhere
   b. Office friendships too often based merely on the fact of working in the same place
   c. Inadvisability of having all one's friends among one's office associates
   d. Difficulty of maintaining impersonal relationships during business hours when on a too-personal basis after hours

4. Suppose that you are ambitious and desire to use your ability to the utmost. But you find yourself hampered by working under an executive who cannot delegate work. Write what steps you would take to win his confidence, convince him that you can be helpful to him, and ease his heavy load.

# CHAPTER 12

# Dress and Grooming on the Job

In addition to attitudes, which are under the surface, you must also consider the importance of your outward appearance, on which so much depends. In an earlier chapter you were told that appearance counts 75 per cent in *getting* a job. Now I am going to add that appearance counts at least 25 per cent in *keeping* a job.

Once you have won that precious job for which you are now training, values will shift. Your prospective employer, who in the interview judged you largely by your appearance, will now judge you by your ability and the attitudes we have been discussing. But make no mistake—the way you look, day in and day out, will count tremendously! That goes for young men quite as much as for young women. And let me remark in passing, that, although this chapter will deal largely with feminine dress and grooming, young men need not think it can be skipped. There is much here of masculine interest, too, for the underlying principles of correct dress and grooming apply to men and women alike.

### Appearance Is Important to Your Career

"What are the prime qualifications of a successful secretary?" The Katherine Gibbs School put this question to hundreds of employers. From their answers, this important Eastern secretarial school compiled the following list of conspicuous qualifications:

| | | |
|---|---|---|
| Native intelligence | Good background | Good health |
| Adaptability | Good personal appearance | Well-modulated voice |
| | | Technical excellence |

Native intelligence we are born with, and background is thrust on us. The other requirements are within our power to perfect—especially appearance. But first you must know just what business means by "a good appearance."

*Don't Slump after Getting a Job.* Virtually everything we said in Chapter 6 on appearance in applying for a job holds true after you have a job. But it seems to need repeating, for some young people become careless once they have been placed on a payroll. One night I sat at dinner next to the employment manager of one of New York City's foremost financial institutions. We had been talking about office personnel problems when he suddenly asked, "What can I do with young people who let down after they begin to work?" He explained that all too often employees look smart and immaculate when they apply for positions, but start wearing old sweaters and old trousers or skirts as soon as they are sure of their jobs. "I hate to be hard on them," he went on to say, "but nothing short of reading the riot act seems to do any good."

I can see little excuse for retrogressing in this way. And it is retrogression! These young men and women understood well enough the importance of making a good appearance for an interview. They should look at their business life as a continuous interview, for they certainly are still, and always will be, under inspection.

Here is a little skit entitled, "Appearance—Your Greatest Asset," which I have sometimes presented when asked to dramatize scenes from office life. The stage is set as a private office, and I play the role of personnel director of a manufacturing firm. I receive a telephone call from one of the executives of the company.

VOICE: Is this the personnel office? I want to tell you we're going to have to fire Miss Green.

PERSONNEL DIRECTOR: (*Laughing*) Yes, this is "Personnel." What's the matter with her, Mr. Davis?

VOICE: Everything. She comes to work looking like something the cat dragged in.

PERSONNEL DIRECTOR: Oh, surely everything can't be wrong, Mr. Davis. She looked all right when I employed her six months ago. She can't have gone entirely to pieces in that short time. Besides, her work is all right, I know.

VOICE: Well, yes. I have no complaint about her work. But I have to raise the window when she's in my office taking dictation. And last week I took cold, and...

PERSONNEL DIRECTOR: Oh, I am sorry, Mr. Davis. But don't do anything until I talk with her. I'll send for her right away and see what I can do.

Helen Green is sent for and appears in a none-too-clean sweater, soiled low-heeled sport shoes, and a sloppy wool skirt. (At this point, the audience usually gasps, or someone giggles self-consciously, and I know Helen Green's type is recognized.)

PERSONNEL DIRECTOR: Good morning, Miss Green. Won't you sit down?

GREEN: (*Lifelessly*) Good morning.

PERSONNEL DIRECTOR: Miss Green, I'm sorry to have to tell you there's been a complaint from one of our executives about your appearance. One of the men, whose dictation you take, says you look far from neat, and also he questions whether your personal grooming is all that it should be.

GREEN: I'm sorry, I——

PERSONNEL DIRECTOR: So am I, Miss Green. It is always difficult for me to tell anyone these things. But frankly, I am afraid unless we work together and act quickly you may be asked to leave. The situation has become serious for you.

GREEN: What shall I do? I don't want to lose my job.

PERSONNEL DIRECTOR: Of course, you don't. It would be a shame. And so unnecessary, because your work is very satisfactory. I wonder if you realize what a nervous strain office work is and how very careful all of us have to be, not only to bathe daily, but to use a deodorant regularly.

GREEN: Probably I have been careless.

PERSONNEL DIRECTOR: I'm sure that is all that is wrong, but that can be enough. Where do you live, Miss Green?

GREEN: A few blocks from here.

PERSONNEL DIRECTOR: Haven't you something at home that is more appropriate to wear to work than what you have on?

GREEN: Yes, but I've been saving it.

PERSONNEL DIRECTOR: What for? You may have only been saving it to wear when you go looking for another job. Why not go home and change? Then come back and let me see how you look. And fix your hair and face a bit, too, while you're about it.

When Helen returns to the stage dressed perfectly in a simple dark dress, and properly groomed, the audience usually gives her a hand. I don't blame them, for the contrast is striking. Such dealing with a situation by a personnel director might be rather drastic, but I've known it to be done. And I needn't tell you that it works. But as I explain to Helen Green in our closing lines, not all personnel directors are interested enough in holding a job for an employee to go to all that trouble. More often they'll say nothing, but at the first opportunity will replace the employee with a more personable individual.

*Your Appearance Is Being Watched.* If a careless appearance and inadequate grooming make it difficult to hold a job, what do you suppose they do when it comes to promotion? Let me tell you a story with a happy ending. Jean Allen was an experienced legal stenographer in a large law firm that chose its secretaries from the stenographic squad.

She was very capable. When the secretary of one of the partners left to be married, Jean was slated to take her place. But the personnel director knew that this partner was fastidious and Jean was not. However, she had faith in Jean and was most anxious for her to make good, not only for the sake of the substantial increase in salary, but for the recognition that the promotion meant.

So, difficult though it was, this kindly personnel director called Jean into her office and had a heart-to-heart talk with her. Among other things, she said, "I don't suppose you realize it, but there is a slight odor about your person. It may be that your clothes need cleaning. I can't tell you what causes it, but I advise you to find out before you go on this new job." Furthermore, she suggested to Jean that for the better position she should learn to dress the part of a private secretary. She would need to wear smarter clothes, a more becoming make-up, and a better hairdo. Then Jean was given the afternoon off, and various shops were suggested where she could find suitable clothes, advice on make-up, and an expert hairdresser.

As Jean left her supervisor's office, it began to dawn on her that, in the nicest possible way, she had been told to revolutionize her habits of grooming and her style of dress. Being intelligent, she obeyed implicitly, and when she showed up the following morning as Mr. Day's new secretary, none of the executives recognized her. The other employees complimented her so much that Jean didn't know whether to be happier over her changed appearance or her promotion. From then on, things went better and better for Jean. She said she felt like a new person. And her rather reluctant fiancé seemed to think she was one. Soon plans were afoot for her long-deferred marriage, and Jean was "promoted" again—this time to a life job.

The rules for correct business dress for both young men and young women when job hunting have been summed up in Chapter 6. Now we must go into further detail; for it is one thing to get together a single satisfactory outfit to wear for interviews, but quite another to plan a well-chosen and well-budgeted business wardrobe.

### WHAT TO WEAR TO WORK

The first rule you must conform to is more formality in clothes. Gone are the days when the careless comfort of school and college informality governed your daytime dress. Fortunately for you, department stores and specialty shops are well stocked with smart and correct clothes for business wear at prices you can afford. Your chief problem is to choose a wardrobe that will be most becoming and most practical for you.

*Magazines to Assist You.* Girls will find helpful information and advice on business dress in several magazines devoted to the interests of career and college girls. Recommended are *Glamour, Mademoiselle, Seventeen,* and *Today's Secretary.* The last named, in case you do not know of it, is published by the Gregg Publishing Division, McGraw-Hill Book Company, Inc., and in addition to articles and style suggestions, each issue contains several pages in shorthand and the story of an outstanding secretary. All these magazines cater to young girls—those heading for business, those already in it, or as in the case of *Mademoiselle,* the young married businesswoman who is also running a home. Consult these magazines regularly for their many articles of value in connection with your working life, and especially for their pages on dress and grooming. You will get many ideas for your clothes purchases, ideas that are usable because the clothes illustrated are priced for your income. You will also get advance news on fashion trends that can save you money.

The experience of Elva Bruce illustrates the value of knowing fashion forecasts. Elva was in the market for a good suit, and was delighted when she found one on sale, reduced from $85 to $38.95. Within a month, however, Elva was both sadder and wiser. Skirts were lengthened a good six inches, and Elva couldn't wear the skirt to her lovely new suit. The moral is that if Elva had been following the style magazines she would have read hints, if not prophecies, of the coming change in the length of skirts. In fact, she would have been saved the $20 it cost her to buy new material and have a skirt made to wear with the jacket. Every time she wore her mismatched "mistake," Elva realized that every bargain doesn't save money and determined then and there to keep herself informed on fashion trends.

There are not so many sources of clothes information for young men as for young women. But fortunately for them, men's styles don't change so radically or so suddenly. *Esquire* and some of the other magazines for men supply style news, and ideas can be got from the men's-wear windows in department stores and specialty shops, as well as from the stores' newspaper advertisements.

*Preferred Colors for Business Wear.* For men and women alike, black, navy, brown, and gray are the best colors for business. For men, there is no deviation from the rule. Women may include all shades of blue and gray, the popular beiges, and not-too-bright greens. A bright topcoat to wear to work with any of the above shades will vary the monotony and help out after business hours. However, even for office wear with the preferred dark colors, women can add a dash of color with accessories, while men can do the same with well-chosen ties. Young men office workers will do well to observe what junior executives wear in shirts, collars, ties, and socks. The chances are that they will see no gaudily striped shirts or collegiate socks.

Many people consider the sales force in stores the best-dressed group in business. Have you any idea why this is so? It is because they are required by store dress regulations to wear conservative clothes, generally black or navy. This makes sense, for these colors detract least from the merchandise to be sold. Although some stores have relaxed their dress regulations considerably in recent years, black and navy are usually the prescribed colors to be worn by women from November to March. During the summer months, most stores allow the girls to wear white or pastel shades. Store salesmen wear suits of conservative pattern and color, and may choose dark blue, brown, or dark shades of gray—never green! Sport coats, slacks, and casual-type shoes are taboo. In summer, the men may wear suits of the new synthetic fabrics or the always good Palm Beach cloth, provided they keep within the color limits allowed in the summer dress regulations. Overdressing by either men or women is condemned by store rules. Women are not encouraged in overdoing costume jewelry, except in the department where it is sold.

But too great regimentation seems also to be frowned on. I recall an amusing case of this in a large department store where the men's-wear buyer was overheard calling down his entire staff of salesmen. Through a coincidence, they had all worn navy suits to work that day. These were his words: "A little early in the morning for all to be going out dinner dancing at the hotels, isn't it, gentlemen? Or maybe we have here a bunch of undertakers getting ready for the funeral. Let's break up the schedule, and some of you wear browns or grays—so the public will know we sell something besides blue."

Several banks have told me they have adopted what amounts to dress regulations by asking their women employees to wear black during the winter months. When such a drastic rule is made, it shows that too many women have been guilty of poor taste in their choice of business clothes, with the result that everyone must share in the reprimand. Smart women often choose black as a base because it is so easy to brighten up with color, and because the same black suit or dress can, with a change of accessories, do double duty for business and after-hours dates. There's magic in a costume that can go to business with a black hat and simple accessories and be transformed by means of a frivolous hat and gay accessories!

## CORRECT SUMMER DRESS

Though you may think it a hard rule, you will find that the best-dressed women, whether in business or in town shopping, prefer dark clothes even in summer. This, of course, does not mean that light shades and white are not allowable. It is merely an indication that women who dress well realize the advantage of cool, dark clothes as against too-wrinkled light ones in hot, dusty city life. If, however, you are in a position to wear white and pastel colors *and keep them immaculate,* either by frequent laundering or dry cleaning, you may, of course, do so.

If you choose dresses or suits made of any of the new synthetic materials that are so cool and practical because they are uncrushable and don't show soil easily, be sure they do not have a house-dress look. You should, of course, also assure yourself they will wash or clean well. Most of them do.

Young men just starting out may find the problem of keeping cool and well dressed more difficult. It is allowable in all offices to remove your coat provided you are not wearing suspenders. A well-tailored shirt, smart tie, and good belt are always considered good grooming in hot weather. But such a practice presupposes, of course, that your shirt is fresh and unwrinkled every day.

*Avoid Clothes That Are Too Revealing.* Need I say that, in general, business frowns on too-tight sweaters and too-thin blouses? Much of the complaint about sweaters is caused by girls wearing them without proper foundation garments, or without any. Sweaters of the right type, worn by the right person, are allowed in most offices. Slip-on sweaters should be worn only as blouses, with suits. A two-piece knitted suit, on a neat figure, wins compliments from fellow workers, but even she who wears a size 12 must wear a girdle and a bra, if and when she wears knits.

As a matter of fact, business girls should always wear girdles and bras or all-in-one foundation garments. A friend of mine who is in charge of an office force had to ask a very large and manifestly un-corseted stenographer to buy herself some sort of restraining garment, because her appearance in the office was creating comment. "That's what my family has been telling me," the offender replied. "But I haven't been able to find anything I could be comfortable in, in this hot weather."

"Neither have I," countered the not-so-slim supervisor. "But that is beside the point. Whether or not we are comfortable, we have to wear girdles and bras or their equivalent in the office, winter *and* summer."

The too-transparent blouse is in just as poor taste as the too-revealing sweater. I know offices where the girls have been told that these all-revealing blouses must not be worn. Here's a case in point. An ex-Wave, who is assistant personnel director in a large bank, told me that she always interviews a girl whose year of probation on office machines is over and who is about to be transferred to the main floor. "During this probationary period, when they work in an upstairs office, their appearance doesn't matter so much," she explained. "But when they are to work where they will be in view of the bank's officers and its depositors, they must look right. One of the chief things I have to warn them against is the transparent blouse." Good taste also dictates that the uniforms worn by medical secretaries and dental assistants be of material heavy enough not to be transparent. The reason? In their offices they meet the public.

## WARDROBE PLANNING

The best-dressed women in business wear suits, because they are correct in the office, look well on the street, and can go places after five. Suits now come in many different weights of material; so, if you are suit-minded, you can have a suit for every season. Nubby wool, flannel, jersey, part wool, rayon, silk, acetate, linen, cotton, and new synthetic materials are now available in practical two-piece outfits. With some of these, you will not need to wear a blouse. The simply cut tailored suit does not go out of style, always looks trim and businesslike, and lends itself to many changes of blouses and accessories. Be careful to select suit syles and colors that are becoming to you, and you need never worry about how you look when on the office scene. To be sure, there will be cleaning bills, but what of it? The long wear you will get from your suits will more than offset the cleaning cost. And you will find it economical to buy one or two good-quality more expensive suits rather than several poor-quality inexpensive ones. If extreme youth is one of your problems on your first job, nothing will so add to your dignity and poise as wearing a suit.

*The Basic Dress.* While many young women wear suits to business with great success, there are others whose first choice is a basic dress. Career girls aren't so rich that they can have one wardrobe for work and another for after hours. Designers understand this, and every season fashion provides countless around-the-clock models that are both appropriate and inexpensive—in other words, basic dresses. By basic is meant a dress that is very simple in style but not strictly tailored. It is completely feminine, for it may have tucks or fullness in both blouse and skirt, should these be the fashion. If flared skirts are being worn, it

*Celanese Corporation of America*

A tailored suit is always suitable for office wear.

will have one, but skirts must be street length. Its sleeves, too, will vary with the current mode, but there will always be some sleeve. The neckline is invariably the sort that permits many different changes in scarves or jewelry. A basic dress may be any dark, rich color that fits your color scheme, but it is more likely to be black or navy. Its material can be crepe, rayon, acetate, jersey, or wool, or any suitable synthetic material, but not velvet or taffeta when used for business.

The reason this type of dress is my first love for employed women is because it can go so many places besides the office. You can multiply, add, and subtract with your basic outfit. From Monday through Friday, changes of neckwear, chiefly scarves and simple clips, will give your boss the impression you've worn a fresh and different dress every day. Among women, this routine will give you a reputation for knowing clothes. And when you go direct from the office to a date, a dressier scarf or the addition of costume jewelry will be as enlivening as though you had made a complete change. Your basic dress can even star at a party. Pearls at the neck, matching earrings, a smart, snug hat, and a small bag will lift it right up into the Sunday-night supper and cocktail-party class. Yet your budget will itemize "one dress." What the accessories cost will depend on your cleverness as a shopper, or with the needle.

*A Tailored Dress.* After you have bought your basic dress and its accessories, it is then quite right to make your second purchase a tailored dress. There is nothing nicer for steady wear. But realize that such a dress will have a limited use, and consider its value to your dress plan as a whole. There's that word "plan" again! We seem to have had plenty of use for it in this study. But never more than in relation to dress. For the real secret of being well dressed on a moderate income is to have a well-thought-out plan.

The first requisite of a dress plan is a basic color scheme that you will stick to for several years. In that way, you can double in accessories over a long period. You get the idea? Planning, planning all the time. Looking ahead, replacing the worn-outs with something that fits in with what you have already and freshens up your entire wardrobe. Someone has said that planning a year's wardrobe at a time will save 50 per cent. I don't know whether the saving is that great, but I do know that anyone who adopts a plan and sticks to it can be beautifully and suitably dressed on a reasonably small expenditure. Besides, it's fun. Moreover, this method keeps you out of the sad plight of the girl who buys something special for a date and then has nothing to wear to work. Of what joy a floor-length dance frock that wastes its charm in your clothes closet when you need dresses for work and working dresses that can date too?

*Avoid Fads and Too-Bright Colors.* Fads are not for the wardrobe of the budget-minded business girl. You have to develop an instinct for detecting and avoiding those high fashions that in six weeks will be as dead as last year's dance tunes. You have to cultivate an eye for the more conservatively styled clothes that will go on in good repute for several seasons. It is best, too, to choose clothes of good material that will last and look well as long as you choose to wear them. Buying good materials, although they may cost more at the outset, is economy in the long run.

Of course, this kind of planning takes quiet thought and fortitude. You can't just dash into a shop and pick something off a rack. First, you must work out what you need, then go window shopping, or read the fashion magazines for ideas that fit in with your plan, and finally, knowing what you want and how much you can afford to pay, go into a shop with the firm intention of sticking to your choice regardless of the blandishments of salespeople. Remember, not for you the "darling" something you don't need that has "just come in" or is reduced to "practically nothing"! Young businesswomen all over the country are being cleverly strong-minded about their clothes, and their smart appearance at work and at play is proof that it pays. Why not be one of these smart young women?

You may get a great deal of wrong advice at times from people who are looking out for their own interests. I am reminded of a fashion show I once attended in a Midwestern specialty shop. The stylist at the microphone began by saying she was going to show mainly separate skirts and shirts because these were "ideal for office wear." The first outfit shown consisted of a bright-red flannel shirt and a Kelly green wool skirt. "Fireman's red," said the announcer. "If you can't attract the boss's attention any other way, do it with color." After that she showed gay red and yellow plaids and more bright skirts and sweaters. All of them were charmingly suitable for wear at ski lodges, but not one of them would have done anything for a business girl but get her in wrong with the management and brand her as devoid of good taste in office dress.

If you like bright colors, wear them to accent your dark clothes during business hours. The best place, however, for a business girl to indulge a love for reds, yellows, and Kelly green is in play clothes. Perhaps you ask, "Why not in evening dresses?" That depends on how much you go formal. If you have only one or two evening dresses and wear them often, you will get very tired of gaudy gaiety. And those who see you often may wish you'd get something besides that shocking-pink number. No, even for gala nights on the business girl's calendar, black, white, and pastel shades wear best.

### SMART SHOPPING AND EMERGENCY PLANNING

But suppose things go against you, and for a time you can't spend money for a planned wardrobe. Illness in the family or heavy dental bills of your own sometimes ruin your budget. Yet, to hold the job, you must look well. I'll tell you what one courageous and smart young businesswoman I know did in such an emergency. She went to the basement of a good department store and tried on dresses that went with her current coat. Then she bought the simplest and most becoming of the lot—a dress that she knew she could transform into something that would look much more expensive. She knew enough about sewing and remodeling to understand how much she could undertake in that direction.

When she got the dress home, she ripped off all the superfluous bows and gimcracks. In addition she ripped apart seams that were puckered and ran them up again on the machine. The dress needed refitting, and a friend did this for her. The cheap stitching that showed she took out and replaced with new fine stitching. The hem she put in by hand.

When the remodeling was done, my friend added a new belt and a clip. It takes taste and imagination to do this sort of thing well, but the results can be miraculous.

*You Can Keep Within Your Price Range.* Few of you will need to copy the economies of my ingenious young friend with the sewing machine. Nor do you need to buy the most expensive dress or coat shown you. It goes without saying that anyone on a beginner's salary cannot buy the higher priced clothes of a woman executive. In fact, you would be criticized by your fellow workers if you dressed beyond your salary scale. You will find in a later chapter a budget prepared by a leading secretarial school for its graduates. Following the budget is a list of suggested clothing purchases, showing what a girl on a starting salary of $260 a month can get with the standard 15 per cent allotted to clothing. These suggestions should be helpful to you in working out your early expenditures for dress. When you know what you need and what you can afford, you will find a wide choice of suits, dresses, and "separates" in your local department stores. If you are petite and can wear half sizes, you will get many a bargain in the junior-miss section. In addition to the department stores, you will find, in virtually all cities, small shops that specialize in low-priced dresses appropriate for office wear. Young men of college age, by shopping in the "prep" or college section of the boys' department, can find similar values.

There are many other ways of saving money besides putting it in the bank. One of them is watching the newspapers for the "special purchase" sales of the better stores. Merchandise for these sales has been bought in quantity for such a special event, and is usually up to date in style, color, and fabric. When you can find just what you want in such a sale you will often save as much as 20 per cent. You will also see seasonal clearance sales advertised, with savings from 50 to 75 per cent. Frequently coats, suits, and dresses of good quality are to be found in these sales, but you must be cautious about patronizing this type of sale. Store buyers make good in their jobs by clearing out high-style merchandise while it is still in demand and before newer styles come in. If you are not aware of coming fashion trends, you can easily wind up with a "lemon" instead of getting a worth-while bargain.

Some young men and women are strong-minded enough to put aside money for clothes they plan to buy months hence. Others find a charge account at a good store a better method, as this enables them to pick up things at sales or to buy a costume, complete with accessories, at one time and pay for it over two or three months. In many stores, there is a special arrangement for young business people, called "a budget account." Both of these plans are all right. The thing to do is to experiment until you find which works better for you. If charge accounts are too great a temptation to spend, you will do better to follow the sterling rule of paying cash.

I hope the young men are still with us in studying this chapter. For, as I said in the beginning, the same problems, and the need for solutions, exist for them, too. If you have a place to store it through the summer, you can often buy an excellent overcoat in July or August for $15 less than you will be able to in the late fall. Should you work in a hot climate, by all means get an unlined wool gabardine, or a Palm Beach suit, or one of the Dacron or Orlon and wool mixtures for summer wear. Buy as good a one as you can afford, and make it last several summers. It will, if you take care of it. In this way, you will not only be more comfortable, but you will save your other suits. Clothes that you perspire in during the hot months are that much less fit for wear in the autumn.

### SELECT PROPER FOOTWEAR

If you will observe the type of shoes worn by the best-dressed business girls in cities throughout the country, you will see that most of them wear pumps. Oxfords are equally correct. The height of the heel is a matter of individual preference and comfort, but a medium heel is the most appropriate in the office. Evening shoes, strapped sandals, or spike-heeled dress shoes should never go to business. That they sometimes do is evidence of the wearer's poor taste. Men err less than women in the choice of suitable shoes. No man wears his patent-leather dress shoes with tweeds, nor sport shoes with evening clothes. Brown Oxfords, which go with business suits, are his choice for office wear.

One way to cut the cost of shoes is to take meticulous care of them. Heels should be straightened the moment they begin to run over. This will help your shoes to keep their shape and last longer. Moreover, run-over heels are a mark against good grooming. Using shoe trees keeps your shoes looking good and prolongs their life. Suede shoes require constant brushing, and calf shoes must be polished often, to look right. And shoelaces should never be allowed to get soiled, frayed, or shabby.

As for stockings—nylons, of course, in the preferred shades for the changing seasons. Medium-weight nylon hose look and wear best for daytime use. Save the sheers to go to your after-hours engagements. Men are very critical about crooked stocking seams, so always check the straightness of yours before you leave home. Fresh stockings every day means washing them out each night. There's economy as well as daintiness in this practice, for when perspiration is not allowed to remain in them, stockings wear much longer.

## CARE MAKES CLOTHES LAST

The care and maintenance of clothing is even more important than the care of shoes and stockings. Dry cleaning is necessary, regardless of its cost, and it must occupy an important place in the budget of every business person. Offices are dirty places, but that is no excuse for wearing soiled clothing to work. Some spots can be easily removed at home, but usually it is safer and cheaper to let the cleaner handle them. It's no economy to ruin a dress or suit to save a cleaner's bill.

Everything washable must be washed constantly. Young men have to allow more for laundry in the summer because of increased perspiration. I hope the day will come when men will be allowed to be more comfortable in hot weather. But wherever good form requires them to keep on their coats, keep them on they must! Women employees should not undertake to wear white unless they are willing to pay the price. White accessories and white gloves must be washed every time they are worn.

Frequent pressing of both men's and women's clothes is necessary to good grooming. This you can learn to do yourself. Fortunately, manufacturers, with the aid of science, are bringing out more and more new fabrics that are both crease resistant and dirt resistant. These good-looking new materials launder easily and require little or no pressing. Some dresses can be semipressed by hanging them in the bathroom with the hot water running. But this is only an emergency measure. It is a good plan to put clothes on hangers the minute you take them off. Repeatedly letting them lie on a chair for even a short time will eventually ruin their shape. When you take clothes off is a good time to let them air (on hangers) before you put them in your closet. The airing will take out some of the wrinkles. Before you put your clothes away, brush them well. A clothesbrush in the office, too, is a great help.

These are little niceties of grooming that young people are inclined to overlook. But when you go to work, the meticulous care of your person and your clothes is a "must" that you will have to observe if you are to hold your place in the keen competition you will meet.

## PERSONAL GROOMING IMPORTANT

Good grooming is an all-embracing subject that is receiving much attention these days. Good-grooming clinics and institutes are being established in many cities, and high schools and colleges are introducing courses in grooming, because it was discovered that poorly groomed individuals were finding it difficult to make a satisfactory adjustment to business and to social life.

The care of your clothing, your shoes and stockings—all your wearables—is part of a good-grooming program. Certainly, unless you are eternally laundering and cleaning your under and outer garments—pressing, mending, and otherwise keeping them shipshape, you won't have that cared-for look that is a priceless advantage in your personal as well as your business relationships. We have discussed these first, when perhaps they should have followed our present subject, *personal hygiene*—the care of the body. For the most thoughtfully selected and correct outfit for business would be wasted if worn by a person obviously in need of a bath. Being well groomed at all times means working constantly at it. That tubbed-and-scrubbed look that makes even the plainest person attractive isn't achieved with hit-or-miss bathing and shampooing. Nothing short of a grooming schedule, strictly adhered to, will produce this result. The dividends, regular and extra, that one receives for the time invested are often a surprise to the new recruit. The person who already has the daily bath and deodorant habit takes his grooming routine in stride, much as he accepts his early acquired skill in handling a knife and fork. To him, the reward for constant watchfulness of his person is the feeling that he has of health, well-being, and self-confidence.

Next to the daily bath, the most important "do" in grooming is the regular use of a deodorant. To be *immaculate* instead of *unwanted*, many persons have to use a deodorant every day—even twice a day. Others, checking themselves as carefully, find that applying a deodorant or a nonperspirant every few days or even once a week is sufficient. The important thing is that everyone must be eternally on guard, so as not to have the slightest hint of body odor, popularly known as B.O.

Personnel directors and office managers are beset by the problem of employees who, because of careless grooming, are unconsciously offending their co-workers. When I was engaged in employment work in California, we had such a situation in our office. The offender was a charming girl—our head file clerk. All of us liked Maizie, but those who worked near her complained of the odor of perspiration. The office manager asked me to handle the matter for him, and after some thought, I decided on an approach. During the morning, I called the employees, singly, into my private office. To each of them I said much the same thing: "There have been complaints that the odor of perspiration in the outer office is very noticeable. Mr. Winters (our office manager) has suggested that all of us recheck our bathing schedule and increase our use of deodorants. May we count on your co-operation?"

By using this procedure, Maizie was not singled out or embarrassed.

The plan was successful, as I learned the next day, for one by one the girls came to me and whispered, "Mrs. MacGibbon, it worked."

Among the "don'ts" of grooming is the use of perfume. Usually, the devotee of the perfume flask either has the habit or thinks it adds allure. Check allure outside when you enter office life! Heavy perfume is offensive to many people, with executives foremost in the group. That drop of perfume on the lobe of your left ear may intrigue the boy friend, but it is likely to irritate the man whose dictation you take. Also, consider how some lesser lights, especially men, must feel when they are surrounded all day long, and well-nigh overpowered, as they try to work in the midst of the conflicting scents of all the girls' favorite perfumes. A light application of toilet water is about all you should indulge in for office hours.

*Posture Counts, Too.* Perhaps posture should not be called grooming, but a person could be very clean, neat, and well groomed, and lose much of the effect by poor posture. The rules for correct posture are very simple, but it takes constant thought to get results. "Stand tall," is one rule. "Abdomen flat," is another. "Tail in," is a third. When you have straightened out your back by getting yourself thus lined up, it is easy to hold your head erect, and your shoulders will be where they belong. Then walk with your toes parallel. When at your typewriter, sit well back in your chair. Reach forward by swinging from your hips. Your posture and your figure will be ruined if you hunch your shoulders and duck your head when you are typing. When walking, breathe deeply, and expand your chest. This will improve your health and make you appear a more vibrant person.

"A lot of hard work," you say. Certainly. That fresh-from-the-bandbox look is not achieved without effort. But when you have acquired it, you can forget yourself, knowing that you look your best.

*Hands and Nails Require Care.* When you do office work, your hands are conspicuous. And they get very soiled as you file, handle carbons, and often use leaky pens. In many offices, there is only cold water in the dressing rooms, but even so you must wash your hands frequently during the day. Your own toilet soap and a small bottle of hand lotion in a desk drawer will help keep your hands in condition, if you will use them. I suppose our male readers would scorn such beauty aids in the office, but they might use hand cream at night, as I advise you girls to do.

Your nails must be well manicured at all times. After you have carefully manicured your nails, you may wish to buff them to a high, natural polish. If you prefer the liquid polishes, light shades are acceptable during business hours. But regardless of what shade you use, remember that the polish must be in perfect condition. Chipped and peeling polish is unforgivable. While most bosses have become resigned to bright nail polish, they cringe at the sight of overlong, talonlike claws. I understand that inch-long fingernails originated in China where they were worn by men of wealth to show that they did not work with their hands. Since you work all the time with your hands, you should not, and doubtless will not, adopt this sometime fad.

It should not be necessary to condemn bright polish on toenails, but alas, many girls who enjoy wearing open-toed shoes can't resist doing a paint job on the toes that show. Red toenails may enhance a beach costume, but on the job they are extremely revolting to most bosses. Speaking of beaches reminds me of a reprimand I felt forced to give to a capable girl who was my secretary for four years. The office was located in a beach town, where open-toed sandals and red toenails were the order of the day, even on the streets. But when Mary wore them to work I told her, "Regardless of how the town dresses, please bear in mind that a certain amount of dignity is required of us because we represent the state." Mary agreed with me that, just then, her feet were no credit to our unseen employer.

*Daily Care of Hair—a Good-Grooming Must.* Let's hope you are one of those lucky persons whose mother taught you early that, to have beautiful hair, you must give it one hundred strokes every day with a stiff brush. In case you didn't learn that beauty secret when barely big enough to wield a brush, now is a good time to start the twice-a-day brushing. There's no better way to have healthy, shining hair. Even when you girls have permanents and beauty-parlor "sets," your hair should be brushed often, and reset, if necessary. You had better learn now to set pin curls, for you will have to do it often to keep your hair looking as it should every day at the office. Of course, brushing and frequent shampooing of the hair are as important for men as for women. Fortunately, correct feminine hair styling for business wear is not hard to achieve. A simple hairdress that is easy to keep in order, and becoming to you, should also be appropriate for business hours. A long bob, reaching midway down the shoulders, though at times popular for evening affairs, is never a suitable hairdo to wear to work. If you must keep your hair long for your social life, pin it up neatly for office hours. Girls should learn to use a rear-view mirror, for it is astonishing how many of them dress their hair in front and not in back. One last caution. During business hours, forgo girlish flowers, clips, and bows in your hair. They are as out of place as a floor-length evening gown would be.

Before we leave the subject of hair, I must share with you a little poem by Norman Jaffray that once appeared in the *New York Herald Tribune*.

## WOMAN'S CROWNING LIABILITY

Of all the things that vex
The fair, the harried sex,
No trouble can compare
With woman's crop of hair.
Uneasy lies the brow
That wears this crown, I vow,
For woman's vaunted stubble
Provides no end of trouble:
It's full of snarls and rats;
It won't go under hats;
No cap invented yet
Prevents its getting wet;
It must be clipped each week

By the approved technique;
Its various moods require
Long hours beneath the drier;
It threatens any day
To turn a noisome gray;
And when milady deigns
To dally with her swains,
Their spirits suffer drouth
When hair gets in their mouth.
Not love preoccupies
Her deep, her troubled eyes;
It is her hair, they'll find,
That's really on her mind.

*Make-up Should Look Natural.* The "do's" of make-up, I think, are more important than the "don'ts." For while good taste forbids the use of too much make-up, good sense suggests that the right make-up

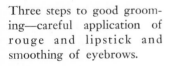

Three steps to good grooming—careful application of rouge and lipstick and smoothing of eyebrows.

*Courtesy Helena Rubenstein, Inc.*

is important. You should look as natural and as healthy as possible. If you will turn back to Chapter 6, you will find there suggestions for make-up that are just as valuable on the job as in getting the job. Whatever make-up you wear to the office should be carefully applied at home and freshened or repaired, as need be, at noon or during rest periods. Getting out your make-up kit and boldly or stealthily dabbing on powder or applying lipstick is frowned on by higher-ups. Such a practice suggests that your mind is on your looks rather than on your work.

So dress as well as you can afford, and see to it that you are well groomed. Then forget yourself and your clothes. Nervous mannerisms can spoil all your effort, if you let them. The hair-patters and shoulder-strap-twitchers show a lack of the poise that business considers desirable.

## QUESTIONS

1. After you go to work, has appearance the same importance as when you were looking for a job?
2. What other qualities now come to the fore?
3. Can you afford to become slack in your dress and grooming after you have a job?
4. Do you think excellent work can offset careless dress and uncleanliness?
5. Can you wear the same clothes to work that you wore when job hunting?
6. Name the colors generally approved for business wear for men and women alike. How can business people use color to liven up their office clothes? Must dark colors be worn in summer, or are light colors and white permissible?
7. Is it a better plan for beginning workers to buy

   a. High fashions that are good only for the present season?
   b. Conservative styles that can be worn indefinitely?

8. Why is taking care of your clothes an important part of being well dressed? Name some of the simple things you now do to keep your clothes in good condition. Name some that you have not done but that you intend to begin to do as part of your preparation for business life.
9. Is it allowable to wear perfume to business?
10. Do employers approve of red toenails?
11. Is it considered good form to wear elaborate costume jewelry, including earrings, to work?
12. Should a stout woman wear sweaters or knitted dresses to business?
13. Under what circumstances is it permissible for women to remove suit jackets in the office? for men to remove their coats?
14. Is it in good taste for women to wear transparent blouses when they expect to remove their jackets?

15. What is the one unbreakable rule regarding women's white accessories and men's linen?
16. Is it allowable for women to apply make-up at their desks in view of the office force?

## WHAT IS WRONG WITH THESE STATEMENTS?

1. If you are not good looking, there is nothing you can do to achieve a good appearance.
2. All employees slump in appearance as soon as they get jobs.
3. Office managers are not particular about the appearance of those who work under them.
4. The best-dressed women in stores, banks, and other places of business never wear black.
5. A basic dress is a dressy afternoon frock.
6. If a salesperson tells you a dress or suit is becoming, you should buy it.
7. Planning your wardrobe for a year will not save you money, but it will save time.
8. Fireman's red worn by a stenographer is sure to impress an employer favorably.
9. Those on small beginning salaries should not be expected to dress appropriately.
10. A young man is foolish to buy an overcoat in the summer.
11. Girls save money by buying one pair of stockings at a time.
12. Since her dates are more important than her job, a business girl should put more money into evening clothes than into office clothes.
13. Having the good taste to dress correctly in the office seldom helps win promotion.

## TOPICS FOR DISCUSSION

1. Give the reasons why employers wish to be surrounded by well-dressed, immaculately groomed employees.
2. Discuss how posture helps a person make a good appearance. Explain what "stand tall" means.
3. Discuss the prospects of the young man or woman who dresses suitably to get a job, but becomes careless after going to work.
4. What is the advantage of buying clothing according to a plan as compared with buying whatever you see that you like?
5. How many office outfits do you think you will need when you first go to work? Why do you need more than one, if you do? What is the advantage of keeping everything in one color scheme?
6. Explain what a basic dress is, and why it is recommended as the first purchase a stenographer or typist should make after she gets a job.

7. Executives expect a young woman in the lowest salary brackets to be as appropriately dressed and as well groomed as the women in higher salaried positions. Should a beginner on a small salary

a. Go in debt to buy clothes?
b. Disregard the management's wishes?
c. Buy appropriate dresses at prices she can afford?

8. Discuss the advantage to a girl of wearing suits to work. What are the disadvantages, if any?

## PROJECTS

1. *For Men Students.* In Chapter 14, you will find a clothes budget based on an annual expenditure of $360. Turn to it, and study it. Assume that you have had eight months' wear out of the clothes listed there. Plan replacements over a three months' period, beginning in December. Do not spend over $75.

2. *For Women Students.* Plan an expenditure over a three months' period that will complete and correct a basic wardrobe that now contains:

Shabby blue topcoat                    Blue hat (felt)
Good gray crepe basic dress            Good green wool dress
Pair good brown shoes                  Pair blue gloves
  (classic pumps)                      Blue bag

Do not spend over $75. Assume that it is December, and plan to buy certain things at January sales. Explain your reasons for each purchase planned.

3. *All Students.* Starting with the job-getting outfit you assembled as a work exercise in Chapter 6, build it into a suitable wardrobe for wear on a beginning job. Make a list of what you will need to complete such a wardrobe.

4. *Women Students.* Assume that you have bought a black basic dress and wish to add accessories to it that will afford changes for office wear three times a week. List your selection of accessories. Also list accessories you would use with the dress to make it suitable for wear to

a. A Sunday-night supper party
b. Church

CHAPTER 13

# Stepping Up to a Better Job

Now you are making good on your job, and you know something about the importance of making a well-groomed and well-dressed appearance. We shall suppose your employers are watching you with approval. They think you have what it takes for promotion, and certainly promotion is highly desirable! What can you do to speed up that step up?

Often, making good on a job and stepping up to a better one turn out to be one and the same thing. You may work along for months or even years, doing your best work each day but feeling like little more than a busy bee. And then suddenly new horizons open. You find yourself singled out to fill a vacancy, or perhaps even a new job is created for you. It is all very breath-taking and exciting. You have been doing better work than you realized! Those over you have been aware of it, and now they reward you. You have outgrown your old job and are now ready for the next step, though perhaps you have been too close to the picture to see what has been happening to you. Let me illustrate with a story told me by the head of a Midwestern school for secretaries.

## A Promotion Without the Tag

Lois Quinn had been working for about three years and was pretty discouraged. She felt she wasn't getting anywhere. Her disappointment was the more keen because one of her friends had made outstanding progress in another firm. So one evening, Lois called on her school principal and discussed the situation with her. Together they analyzed the two companies for which Lois and her friend worked. It appeared that Lois was working for the more conservative of the two, and apparently their policy was to move slowly in the matter of promotions. Obviously, Lois was making good, for she had received several small increases in salary. Her teacher was at a loss to tell her how to improve her situation beyond patiently plugging on. However, just as she was leaving, Lois mentioned her assistant.

"You have an assistant?" the principal asked.

"Oh, yes, they gave me a girl to break in on some of the routine work. That was about three months ago," Lois replied.

"And you're worrying about whether there is a future there for you? You may not have been given a new title or a sizable raise in salary, but when an employer gives you an assistant to free you from routine work, you can be certain there are definite promotional plans afoot for you. Congratulations! You're already on your way."

### TRY TO BECOME INDISPENSABLE

Let us now consider the positive qualities that will help you win promotion. It goes without saying that, if you are going to stay with a firm and work up in it, you must make yourself indispensable as soon as possible. Obviously, one way to accomplish this is to become someone's right hand—an assistant who relieves an overworked executive of burdensome detail. In a small business where you have an opportunity to show what you can do right from the start, you sometimes become indispensable very quickly. This is why many young people with marked executive ability are happiest in a small business where they are given a variety and multiplicity of duties.

*Do High-Quality Work.* In large organizations, you get no such chance to become an extra pair of eyes, hands, and feet for someone who needs to delegate all the odd jobs he can. So you must find another way to make yourself indispensable. Perhaps, you can produce such a high quality of work that it will be noticed by others. I recall the case of a young woman in an advertising agency who set out to make the copy she typed look exceptionally attractive. She succeeded so well that soon all the copy writers were asking that she type their copy because her work gave them and the agency's clients a better idea of how the advertisements would look in type.

*Be a Quantity Producer.* Other people make themselves invaluable because of the quantity of work they can turn out—with quality not overlooked, of course. This is especially true of shipping clerks, order clerks, and others in whose work time is an important factor. It may well be true of filing clerks also, since in their job countless papers must be handled daily if the files are to be instantly useful and up to the minute.

You may think it hopeless, especially in many of the beginning routine jobs of business, to establish a reputation for doing something better than anyone else in your office. But it is not. You'd be surprised how often an executive says, "I simply couldn't get along without John. Why he can . . ." and he launches forth in praise of an employee who can turn out some routine job in record time and perfect shape with a minimum of instruction.

*Save Executives' Time.* Some young people become almost indispensable because they think of ways to save executives' time. A man in a high position in an automobile-parts manufacturing company told me he had such a secretary. Without any prompting, she sorted his mail into three sections. It was as simple as a, b, c—only she called it "1, 2, 3," like this:

1. You don't need to bother. I have taken care of these.
2. You should know about, but the office manager can take care of them.
3. You should take care of these.

Looks simple enough, doesn't it? But no other secretary had ever devised such a timesaver for him. Because there was fundamentally sound organization in this little plan, it actually saved the executive hours of time formerly spent in unnecessary reading of mail and freed him for constructive work. No wonder he boasted about his perfect secretary!

The same businessman told me of a case in marked contrast to this. A dealer had written to say he must have a certain part immediately. "The people are touring, are tied up here, and are charging their hotel bills to us. Please rush it!" the harassed dealer ended his letter. The executive, greatly rushed himself, said to a stenographer who was substituting for his secretary: "Have this part sent out at once, and send him a letter, airmail, that it's coming. You can sign it. I won't be back in time." The next day he found this carbon on his desk: "We are very sorry to hear of your troubles. No doubt, you will hear from us shortly." The fur flew. The telegraph wires hummed. And the stenographer lost her job.

*Be a Good Housekeeper.* The business world is well sprinkled with indispensable secretaries who have become such because they first proved their ability to handle detail unerringly in lesser positions. Men do not, as a sex, like to be bothered with detail and are glad to entrust it to others as fast as this can safely be done. It was feminine capacity for looking after the housekeeping end of business that brought women into offices, and the same good trait has made this work almost exclusively theirs.

Sometimes, a secretary extends her capacity for handling infinite detail until it includes looking after her boss's well-being. At a tea given by the Stenographers' Club in St. Louis, I talked with two young women who were secretaries to a lumberman and a brewer, respectively. In recounting the things they did to make themselves especially useful to their employers—the little things that were most appreciated —one said, "When my chief comes in looking as if he had had a late night, I put a row of aspirin tablets on a tray beside his thermos of fresh water, which I also always provide." The second said: "Ditto. Only it's a different remedy I leave handy." Another bit of "business" that one of these secretaries found useful was to keep an eye on where her boss put things. "He buzzes for me to find everything in his desk," she explained "It makes a hit if I can find things more quickly than he can."

It is a common occurrence that a good secretary climbs with her boss. She helps him make good, and when he soars to greater heights in his firm, or elsewhere, she goes right along with him at a sizable salary boost. I'd be willing to wager that those two secretaries will go along with their bosses. They will, if their work is equal to their understanding of their employers.

### LEARN TO TAKE ON RESPONSIBILITY

Most secretaries reach that goal because they have been able to take responsibility in lower positions. Many head bookkeepers grow out of accurate assistant bookkeepers, who often step up still higher to the job of auditor or comptroller. Business is ever on the lookout for young men who can be trained for important executive positions. In the clerical end of business, also, there is advancement for those who are able to see more than mere routine in the tasks before them. The fact of such promotions is a matter of daily record. What we are concerned with is the "how" of this ladder-climbing act. I wish I could give you a definite rule!

Different people get on in different ways and at different levels. The very differences that exist between individuals, as well as between opportunities, are factors in advancement. But all advancement has one thing as a prerequisite, and that is successful performance in a previous job. As in the Army, promotion from the ranks of business is likely to be won on merit. That is why, in an earlier chapter, I stressed the importance of forgetting promotion at the start and concentrating on showing what you can do in the job you have.

*Too-Early Efforts Unwise.* Even the beginner must be able to take some responsibility. Just seeing each task through to a successful conclusion is a test of your ability to shoulder responsibility. But beware of assuming responsibility before you are ready for it or have the necessary background of experience. Responsibility implies the making of

Business is quick to promote those who have
earned advancement and who show promise of
increased value to the firm.

decisions, and executives do not care to have subordinates deciding
things that it is not their job to decide.

I am reminded of a case of too much assurance. In an advertising
agency on the Pacific Coast, a capable young woman had been working
for several months on a temporary basis as assistant in the production
department. Her duties were confined to detail. For a long time, the
production manager had been hoping that this skillful assistant would
be put on a permanent basis and had so recommended. During his absence, the recommendation went through. But alas! It was the signal
for the assistant to start various innovations of her own that were only
half thought out. The other executives with whom she came in contact
suffered in silence and avoided her as much as possible, waiting for the
return of her immediate chief. When the production manager returned
from his vacation he dismissed the too-self-confident girl. It took him
several days to countermand the incorrect orders she had issued to
artists, photoengravers, and printers and get his department back to
normal.

*Wisdom Urges Caution.* Perhaps, you are wondering how you can ever learn to take responsibility if you don't make a try at it. Suppose that, with one or two minor positions to your credit, you are breaking in on a new job. One day in the absence of your superior you answer the telephone. The man on the wire says, "This is Ben Brown of the Anchor Roofing Company. Regarding that order of wallboard you just delivered. We find we need only half of it. Send your truck over, and take the rest back."

What will you do? Try to handle it as your chief would, or merely be as efficient as possible without committing yourself? The latter course by all means. To say "We'll send for it" or "That's a noncancelable order" would be to exceed your authority, even if you know what the firm's policy is in such situations. Not until you have been directly instructed to handle such emergencies should you take the initiative. How then are you going to show your ability to take responsibility? By using tact and judgment. Instead of merely saying: "Mr. Davis is out. Please call him later," you might say something like this: "I'm sorry, Mr. Brown, but Mr. Davis is out. I'll give him your message, and he'll call you as soon as he comes back. No one else has the authority to have the trucks pick up merchandise that has been delivered on order."

By such a reply, you have built up the importance of your chief, and you have made it clear to Mr. Brown that perhaps he can't return that wallboard. If he can, he will be doubly pleased, and grateful to Mr. Davis. Getting the facts and passing them on promptly and correctly is your first job and a good lesson in the taking of responsibility. Making decisions will come later.

*Avoid Carelessness.* Carelessness and taking responsibility never dovetail. One beginner I know had this unhappy experience. An executive dictated a telegram and said, "Send it night letter." When Gladys typed the telegram, she marked it correctly against the NL at the top of the telegraph form. But the executive changed the wording, necessitating the retyping of the message. This time Gladys neglected to check it "night letter," and the telegraph company assumed it should go as a straight message. When the item showed up on the Western Union bill at $27.65, Gladys received a well-deserved reprimand.

*Some Don't Want Responsibility.* Some people like responsibility, and others shun it. You have seen this happen in school. There are boys and girls who can always be counted on to run the class, to put on shows, and to organize other activities. You may say that John and Marie are born leaders or that they have marked executive ability. Both are probably true. John and Marie, and their like, stand out because the majority of the students are just as well pleased to be followers. The same thing is seen in business, and perhaps it is a good thing that this is so. It leaves the field clear for the ambitious and the capable. But remember that leaders must have something to lead. There would never be an army or a theatrical production—to mention obvious examples— if there were no soldiers for officers to lead or cast to support the star. And there would be no business to transact if there were no subordinates to grease the wheels of routine and keep the work rolling through the filling of orders.

A young woman who operates a training school for a business-machine manufacturer in New York City tells me she finds very few, out of the 1,700 employees she instructs and places each year, who want to take responsibility. Her job is to give specific training in the operation of her company's machines to the employees of firms that are installing these machines and to a few young businesswomen. Although she accepts only a small percentage of the latter who apply for training, she says even this carefully chosen group are for the most part responsibility dodgers. Too often, when my friend has a chance to place an operator in a better position with more salary, the girl declines. She is well satisfied where she is. To take on responsibility sometimes means staying after five. This type of worker prefers a definite quitting time to making more money.

## LISTEN FOR OPPORTUNITY'S HONK

But this book is written for ambitious young people. So let's look at some of the ways in which opportunity may come to you in business. Someone has said that opportunity no longer comes to the door and knocks. It merely drives up to the curb and honks. So you must be listening, or even half out the window watching, all ready to jump in and close the door.

Often, opportunity steals up without so much as a honk. One day, you are asked rather casually to supervise the work of someone else. Some of the best positions in the field of office work lie in supervising, and they are practically without exception filled from the ranks. So, if you are, with no warning, requested to stay for a few minutes after work to instruct a new employee on operating the switchboard, or on the filing system, or on some other phase of clerical work with which you are familiar, take the assignment without a murmur. Believe me, you can afford to forget your date with the hairdresser or the handball game at the "Y." This lucky break is more likely to occur in a small office, for in a large office the work is likely to be centralized, with a supervisor taking care of such things. But in a small office, you can begin to prepare for supervising work there as the business grows, or elsewhere in a larger office later on.

After a talk I gave to business girls in a Southern city, Ruth Hill came to me and said that she worked in the local offices of a Northern industrialist and had recently been asked to supervise the work of fourteen typists and stenographers. "I am not at all interested in that kind of work," Ruth told me. "Shall I ask them to report to me every morning what they did the day before?" she queried.

Apparently, the executive in charge of the office had given Ruth no instructions, but had assumed that she would know what to do. Nor had he explained to her that this was decidedly a step up for her. Ruth had never heard of a stenographic pool, and since the central stenographic bureau by any name had not penetrated her city, she was at a loss to know what had happened to her and what to do with her new responsibilities. I did my best to show her that opportunity had not only honked, but had picked her up and started off with her. Although I have not heard the outcome, I hope Ruth had the executive ability her chief credited her with having, and that she profited from the literature I sent her, telling how such departments are organized and operated.

Sometimes, the supervising jobs are in the bookkeeping department. Suppose you are working on the books, and at the end of the year, they put you in charge of getting out the annual report and give you an assistant. Will you complain because the responsibility for this important work has been given you? I hope not. It is opportunity honking at your door.

*Routes to Personnel Work.* If you are a young woman and the day comes when you are asked to interview some prospective employees, opportunity has rolled up to your door in a shining new twelve-cylinder wonder! What may look like just another odd job given to you because everyone else is busy may be the open door to your future career. Why? Because the position of personnel director is among the best of executive positions open to women, and that first request to interview applicants marks you as a trusted employee and indicates that your firm thinks you may have the necessary qualifications for handling people. Carefully as I have checked the position of personnel director, from San Francisco to New York City, I have yet to find a woman in charge of office personnel who had not got her training on the job. Business seldom brings in trained personnel people from the outside to do the employing of its office force. The office personnel director, as I have met her in her clubs in New York, Chicago, and elsewhere, has come up through being first a stenographer, then a secretary or sometimes a head stenographer. Consequently, she knows what each job requires in skills, character traits, and personality. And what may be equally important, she knows her firm's preferences.

So, if you have a chance at interviewing even one employee, snap it up. And be sure you pick a good one. For if your choice makes good, your score will go up, and soon you will be asked to interview others. When this happens, your cue is to begin to study personnel work on the side. Theory plus practice is all-important.

### Good Work and Knowledge Really Make the Lucky Break

But sometimes promotion comes not through opportunities to do new kinds of work, but through what seems to be a "lucky break." An automobile dealer told me how he had lost a valued secretary because luck was on her side. An important visiting executive asked the dealer to lend him a stenographer to take some letters. The dealer called his own secretary. The letters were dictated, and in a short time back they came, perfectly typed, correctly spelled—in every way model letters. The visiting executive was so impressed that he said to the dealer, "I need a secretary in Detroit, and if you have no objection, I'd like to employ yours." Since the request came from his principal, the dealer could not refuse. "What a break!" he said, telling me the story. "Out of 20,000 employees of this company, my secretary, in another city, got the chance to show the Big Boss what she could do."

Again, there are times when promotion comes not so much through what you are doing as through a knowledge of something else. John Whitaker, after graduating from an American university, studied art for two years in Paris. When John returned home, he took the only job he could get—timekeeper in a large manufacturing firm in Chicago. His employers had a number of French customers, and one day a party of them arrived unexpectedly at the Chicago plant. They could speak no English, and there was considerable flurry in the executive office. "Get someone who can speak French, and send him in here right away," the word went out. A foreman who knew John spoke French sent him to the office immediately. John was introduced to the visitors and was instructed to show them not only the plant but the city as well, with plenty of money to fulfill the order. John made such a hit that, later, when the visitors called on the president of the company in New York City, they told him about the courteous young man who had acted as their tireless guide. At once, the president wrote to Chicago to know why such a young man was only a timekeeper.

Not long afterward, another group of French customers came over. Having heard so much about his courtesy to their fellow countrymen, they asked that John be allowed to show them about. This established

John as a valuable employee. Officials of the company say he is going places in their organization. It was John's good fortune that, plus being a courteous and well-educated young man, he spoke French fluently. Otherwise, he might never have come to the attention of the heads of the business.

### PROMOTION IN YOUR SPECIAL TYPE OF WORK

But sometimes promotion does not come suddenly or spectacularly. It may come through merely placing on your already overburdened shoulders more of the type of work that you've been doing. More responsibility right where you are! Well, that is all right, too. Maybe your career is to be carved out by your advancement in the kind of work you are doing—bookkeeping, stenographic, or clerical. There are outstanding jobs ahead in your special type of work, and as you gradually learn to do more things in this field, you will shorten the distance between your beginning job and the top positions.

Some very good managerial positions grow out of the faithful performance of office duties. The majority of these, with titles and substantial salaries, go to the male workers in the department. For the number of organizations that prefer men as head clerks, office managers, and department heads far exceeds those that promote women to these positions. But you still have such a chance in some business firms.

### CREATING AN ORIGINAL JOB WITH A FUTURE

More and more clever young women are using shorthand as an entering wedge to the field of their choice and are developing interesting original jobs for themselves. Here is a good example of what I mean.

*The Radio and Television Route.* Leone Aiken graduated from an Eastern college for women and returned to her home in the Middle West. She was determined to work in radio, although not at all sure just where. She applied for work at the broadcasting stations in her home town and then branched out to a job hunt in New York City. But as she said, "They just laughed at me." For Leone had nothing to offer but her eagerness to work in radio, her knowledge of writing. and her lovely speaking voice. Alas, the woods are full of attractive girls with these unproved qualifications. So Leone returned once more to her home town. In desperation, she went to the head of an excellent business school for girls. "I guess I'll have to take a business course, but it's radio I want," she told the director of admissions.

"Maybe we can help you get into radio through shorthand," the director encouraged her. "Along with secretarial courses, we give several months' training in any specific field a student elects. You might like to choose advertising, so that you could learn something about radio and how to write commercials. You would get some of the vocabulary, too, which would help you later, if we are able to get you a position taking dictation from an executive for a broadcasting company."

This was so encouraging to Leone that she took a tuck in her career plan. For almost nine months, she concentrated on shorthand and type-writing and everything she could learn about radio. With her training over, Leone went up like a rocket. She had something to offer now. Before long, through the school placement bureau, she became secretary to the program director of a radio station. This gave her a chance to learn how programs were put together. Soon she was filling in for her chief when he had more programs to prepare than he could get on the air on time. Presently, Leone began to suggest ideas for educational programs on subjects in which she was especially informed. Today, Leone's office door carries the title of Educational Director, and she is an important factor in Station ZZZ's reputation for excellent programs. This is a true story, though neither "Leone Aiken" nor "ZZZ" is listed in any directory.

## INITIATIVE AN ASSET FOR THE CLIMBER

Among other assets, Leone had initiative, which is necessary along with the ability to take responsibility, if you are to step up into a better job. But as with assuming responsibility, you have to be careful not to use too much initiative until you have learned a firm's policies as well as how to perform many tasks. Otherwise, you might be a self-starter going into reverse. Of what avail to start in the wrong direction or to start the wrong things?

However, the error is far more often a lack of initiative than a pre-mature abundance of it. When I was on a speaking trip before audiences of career girls in the Central States, a very interesting young woman told me, among other things: "I've been for ten years in the office of a big rubber company here, and I've watched them come and go. One thing I never have been able to figure out is how seemingly intelligent girls can sit down right in the midst of a thousand things crying to be done and see nothing to do. They actually fold their hands in idleness and wait to be told what to do next." Though I could not explain the lack of interest of the idlers, I could very well understand why this young woman had held her job and progressed.

*Interest and Enthusiasm.* Of course, initiative is the natural comple-ment of interest and enthusiasm—those two qualities that are almost certain indications of success ahead. But it is one thing to do the more or less routine things that anyone with a spark of interest can see need to be done, and another thing to make constructive suggestions for improving your own work or the work in general. So, having interest and enthusiasm, strive to cultivate a mental attitude that will develop initiative. But be sure not to neglect the wholesome brake on impetuosity—caution. In your great enthusiasm to be useful, you are likely to rush in headlong before you have won the confidence of others in your good judgment, or even before your ideas are well thought out. That is why you cannot be allowed to initiate things before you have become seasoned in business generally and in your own work specifically. A wise woman I once knew often said, "A right thing done in the right way at the wrong time can be as disastrous as the wrong thing."

*Presenting Creative Ideas.* So, while you are letting your creative mind play around with ideas that might be valuable to your employer, do not present them until you are sure you have all the kinks out of them. When you are sure you have a sound idea and that the time has come to suggest it, be equally sure you take it to the right person. Many a good idea has been lifted whole because its originator talked too exuberantly to the wrong person. It sometimes even happens that your immediate superior is not above stealing ideas and presenting them as his (or her) own brilliant contributions. When this happens, there is nothing you can do about it. I mention this, not to discourage you, but to warn you to keep still about your creative ideas until such time as you yourself can take them to the top—or its equivalent.

*Encouraging Initiative.* In order that employees with original ideas may get a fair opportunity to present them without interference, some businesses provide question boxes in which to place anonymous or signed suggestions for improving the service, the product, or general relations both inside and outside the firm. When the heads of a business think highly of any such suggestions, they seek out the men and women who offered them. In spite of the many harebrained ideas I have seen suggested, my experience leads me to believe that alert executives keep their eyes and ears open for constructive ideas from even the newest and lowliest employee. I know a young woman whose suggestions put in a box in a department store got her from behind the counter into the advertising department where she most wished to work.

*When Ideas Are Discouraged.* Let's suppose you think you have *the big idea* for a new product that the company could manufacture or a new way of advertising to attract wide attention. You suggest it in person or via the box route, and nothing happens. Shall you go on, trying to get your idea recognized? Not if you are wise. Forget your dream child for the time being, anyway. The test of your interest and enthusiasm lies in your ability to take a beating of this sort and come up smiling. You would have to do this even if ideas were your stock in trade, as in the advertising business. So don't let disappointment sour you on your job when your work is, after all, specifically office work. The firm probably has chemists or other specialists to work out new products, and advertising experts to create its advertising ideas. Why not devote your efforts to winning distinction in your own special field? By the law of growth from within, your chances are far greater in your own specialty than outside it, unless you are in the wrong field.

Your inability to put across a fundamentally sound idea connected with your own work may indicate that there is something wrong with the setup beyond your power to correct. If, after careful thought, you see this clearly and feel that your future there is limited, you have a legitimate reason for quietly beginning to look about for another job in a more progressive organization.

A young man I know found his work in the display department of a high-grade specialty shop greatly hampered by the lack of organization. Also, he found it hard to endure the constant nightwork necessitated by the slack methods of his superior. So he tried to suggest to the head of his department ways to systematize the work with less overtime (for which they were not paid) and equally good results. His chief told the young man his job was to trim windows, not to plan the running of the department. "This kind of work can't be organized," was his alibi for his own lack of executive ability. There was nothing to do, if my young friend wanted to keep his job, but confine his initiative within the limits of his own work and refrain from criticism or suggestion as to the management of the department. Before long, being ambitious, he looked for a job where sound executive planning and sensible delegation of work gave him a better opportunity to progress with his creative ideas for display.

## How Employers React to Ambition

Business sometimes is a bit wary of ambitious employees for the reason that they are inclined to put on too heavy pressure. Perhaps, they have taken too much to heart the saying that no one is interested in you but yourself and therefore feel the necessity to push themselves forward. But business has a different point of view. The personnel director of an Eastern broadcasting company says that too persistent employees are a nuisance, that they are inclined to be restless in their jobs and, in consequence, make trouble. Then too, I have met employers who say frankly that they prefer to employ those who are not too ambitious. It is more comfortable for the business not to be constantly making adjustments in personnel and payroll. And more economical, too. I regret to say there are businesses whose policy is always to pay as low salaries as they can get away with and never allow anyone to advance very far. It is all right to start with such firms for the sake of experience. But, if you are ambitious, having acquired what you need, you will have to go elsewhere to be paid for it.

*Glamour Magazine* [1] conducted a survey among employers and secretaries to find out what each group thought of the secretary and her work. The employers to whom questionnaires were sent were chosen from the membership of the American Management Association. The secretaries questioned were members of the National Association of Secretaries and of the Seraphic Secretaries of America, and worked either for executives or administrative personnel in business firms or in professional offices. Among other things, *Glamour* wanted to know whether these employers frowned on ambition in their secretaries. Here is what was found out.

When we asked them whether they were opposed to hiring a secretary who considered the job a steppingstone to another job in the company, the large majority of employers said *no*. The most often stated reasons for this reaction were:

> Ambition is desirable
> More ambition means better performance
> Good to have a goal
> Everyone has a right to strive, hope, and work to better herself

But when *Glamour* asked the secretaries their reasons for working, the magazine had to report that "very few mentioned any feeling that secretarial work is a steppingstone to other jobs. This indicates that there might be a tendency on the part of a large proportion of secretaries to lose sight of the type of ambition that their employers are looking for, *or* that they might not be willing to pay the price of the extra responsibilities, *or* that their bosses do not get across to their secretaries the fact that they welcome ambition."

### CHANGING JOBS TO GET UP FASTER

It is impossible to lay down general rules for quitting one job in the hope of getting another with better promotional possibilities. All I can say is, "Think things through." By keeping mentally alert to what is going on around you and viewing your situation objectively, you should know whether it is wise to begin looking around for something else.

[1] Glamour's Secretarial Survey. Copyright, 1950. New York: The Conde Nast Publications, Inc.

You should also know *when* to do this. You will, of course, consider your present employer in making any change. You owe the present job something. The question is how much?

Employees who are afraid to leave fairly good positions when jobs are scarce become more independent when office workers are in demand. The high salary scale that is paid beginners when employers are unable to get experienced office help has rankled many faithful secretaries, stenographers, and bookkeepers, who have seen recent graduates with unproved skills hired at only five dollars a week less than they are getting after working, say, five years. Employment agencies in New York, Chicago, and other cities tell me that in their files are excellent applicants who quit because their employers refused to give them substantial raises. These experienced office workers were asking for well over $400 a month, based on what they felt they were worth as compared with what employers were paying boys and girls who had never worked. But the agencies were not able to get such fancy salaries for experienced workers and most of them, after several weeks of unemployment, were having to accept about the same salaries they had been getting.

## STUDY THE BUSINESS AND STANDARDS OF YOUR FIRM

You can easily see that there is more to this matter of stepping up than merely doing your best work from day to day. You are going to have to use your mind as well as your skills. The first day you go to work is none too soon to begin studying the business in which you find yourself. Get together the company's advertising and anything else you can, and inform yourself about the business that from now on will be your meal ticket. Absorb all the printed information available, as it usually will be more accurate than what other employees tell you. Also study the organization itself. This is the right way to get a true picture of the firm and of your place in it. No matter how small your job may be, it is actually an important one. If this were not so, the job would have been eliminated, and you would not have been hired.

You can often learn much by observing the working habits of other employees who have progressed from junior positions such as yours. And sometimes you can learn a great deal about the standards of your employer by appraising the employees as a whole. If the routine is smooth and quiet without undue supervision, you may be sure you are working for a businesslike organization. Evidently, they prefer to employ high-grade workers who give a full day's work without prodding—and they get it.

If, on the other hand, you find yourself in an office filled with loudmouthed individuals who loaf on the job unless under constant supervision, you may be equally sure that your employer is being imposed on by indifferent employees. To get anywhere in such a setup, you will have to accept unpopularity with "the gang." You will be forced to do good work independently of them, on the chance that someone in authority will notice you and appreciate the difference. Unless this happens before too long and you see a better-than-average job for yourself there, you'd be justified in leaving. Anyway, you might never be happy working with that kind of employee. You know that "like attracts like," and it is a good idea, whenever possible, to get into an organization staffed with employees who have much the same standards and manners as your own.

### Find Out about Promotional Policies

Should you decide, after some months of combined work and observation, that you are working for a firm you would like to stay with, try to find out its promotional policy. You will not, of course, expect immediate promotion, but it is important to your future that you know what you must do to get ahead and how far you can go. Find out the answers to the following questions:

How long have some of these young people been working for the company?
Have they been advanced?
Are they stuck at the same jobs they began with?
From what group are the junior executives drawn?
Who reach secretarial positions?
Do the better jobs go to those within the organization?
Do key positions go to persons brought in from the outside?

These are vital questions to you, for, unless they can be answered to your satisfaction, your chance for advancement is slim, and you should know it.

*Promotion from Within.* I am glad to say that promotion from within is becoming more and more the accepted policy among business organizations. In working for a small business where one has direct contact with the heads of the firm, promotion is greatly simplified for those who make good. In a big organization, you may never meet anyone higher than the head of your department or the personnel director who hired you. These individuals act according to rules laid down by those above them, and although they may recommend you for promotion, the final decision does not always rest with them. Therefore, it is important that you find out, before you've been too long on the job, whether, if neces-

ary, you will be given training for more responsible work and the
opportunity to advance when you make good.

If you find you are with an organization that to the best of its ability
considers the promotional possibilities of its employees at the time it
elects them, you are fortunate. For then you can write the name of this
firm into your career plan and begin to prepare yourself, on and off the
job, to realize your ambitions.

*Progressive Bank Plans Employees' Promotion.* The training of employees is very expensive. When an employer has paid an employee
while learning a job and paid a higher priced person to train him, the
employer has an investment in that trainee. The only way that the
investment can be made to pay off is by retaining the employee, and to
keep him, the employer needs to show him that advancement is possible. Because of this, enlightened employers are giving serious thought
to promotional plans.

I have before me such a plan worked out by a Pacific Coast bank that
has several hundred employees. While a firm of management consultants
assisted in working out what the president of the bank calls their "personnel program," it is evident that members of the bank's staff put in
considerable overtime doing the necessary spadework. First, every employee was asked to write a description of his job, giving his duties and
responsibilities in detail. When completed, these were turned over to
a committee of bank employees, who, acting as job analysts, prepared a
detailed job specification for each of the thirty-one different jobs in
the bank. Depending on its importance, each job was then assigned a
grade, and the salary worth of each job in each of the job grades was
determined.

To be sure that the salary set for each job was in line with the salaries
paid for comparable work by other employing firms, a salary survey
was conducted for the bank by the management consultants. Thirteen
banks in all were checked, four in San Francisco, four in Los Angeles,
three in Seattle, and two in Portland. Ten companies of other types
were also contacted, and information obtained as to salaries paid by
them for similar work. In this group were insurance companies, manufacturers, steamship companies, a major oil corporation, a brokerage
business, and a lithograph firm. Based on this information, a salary
schedule was prepared showing a minimum and a maximum salary for
each job grade, with several steps between in each grade, thus providing
for orderly promotions.

As a result of this survey, each of the bank's employees was advised
of the title assigned his job, the grade of the job, and the salary scale for
that grade. At the same time, a plan was inaugurated for salary increases

based on performance ratings. Under this plan, each employee is rated periodically by his supervisor, on both *job* standards and *bank* standards. As I examine this printed form, I note that there are four degrees of accomplishment for each standard. Under job standards, for instance, the performance of the employee is rated on job knowledge, judgment, human relations (manners and co-operation), quality of work, and quantity of work. Under bank standards, his performance is rated for dependability, adaptability, industriousness, initiative, resourcefulness, and general attitude.

I wish that space permitted giving you the breakdown under some of these headings, so you could see how much in line they are with the qualities we have discussed in previous chapters. One under bank standards must suffice. For instance, under *adaptability*, the person doing the rating must consider the following questions in grading the employee:

Does he readily adapt himself to difficult personalities and situations?
Does he get along well with others?
Does he readily adjust his thinking to new methods and procedures, and assist management in making them work?

After the rater has completed the form, he is required to discuss it in a desk interview with the employee. In this way, the employee can be aided in improving his work so that he can be advanced.

Performance rating is certain to be adopted more widely. If you work for a firm that uses this procedure, you are fortunate, for your good work will be noticed and reported to the top personnel.

*Promotion from Without.* If you observe that in your firm the really good jobs go to outsiders, my advice is to begin to look around for something else. You will notice I said "observe." Beware of listening to office gossip as to company policy in this important matter. After you have worked there for six or eight months, if you are still not sure of the promotional policy, have a talk with the office manager or the personnel director. Ask this executive frankly what your chances are of getting ahead with this firm. He will usually answer you with equal frankness.

When I was an account executive in a national advertising agency, we had to go outside to get someone qualified to be both private secretary and office manager. Because it was a small organization, the president's secretary was also in charge of six or seven stenographers and a telephone-receptionist. When the young woman who had held this position for several years left to be married, the heads of the business realized that none of the stenographers was qualified to take over her job. The commodity in that business was *words*. All the executives were college graduates who had specialized in English, and the president was not only highly educated but had worked on a New York newspaper and wrote plays on the side. His vocabulary taxed the knowledge of the best-qualified secretaries backed up by an unabridged edition of *Webster's Dictionary*. Regardless of their unfitness for the job, each of the six stenographers expected to be promoted into it.

Because I was the only woman executive, I was asked to find someone for the position. My recommendation was Margery Adams, a young woman with a college degree and several years of good secretarial experience. Margery had never supervised anyone, but she had a wealth of common sense and a rare humor that I thought would see her through. She needed and used an abundance of both before she had that office organized. When Margery arrived to take over, she found the atmosphere fairly ablaze with ill will toward her. Before the first day was over, she had picked out the ringleader and led her into the quiet library to talk things over.

"I understand you say you will not work under me," Margery said to the stenographer. "Is that correct?"

"Yes," was the grudging answer. "I'm going to quit."

"Then you had better leave tonight," said Margery, shaking inside, but hiding her nervousness. "You see, I have been put in charge here, and if you stay you will have to work under me. But before you go, there is one thing I want made clear. You had a chance at this job. The heads of the business knew your work, and if they had wanted you, they would have given the job to you. I had never heard of this firm or the position until I was asked to come for an interview. You have no quarrel with me. You have a good job, and I hope you will stay."

She did, but the budding office manager had to dismiss one of the other stenographers before the rest surrendered to the fact that she was in charge.

## LEARN FACTS ABOUT THE BUSINESS AND ITS EXECUTIVES

A study of the business in which you are working will quite naturally increase your interest in it. For even the most dry-as-dust organization has its romantic past—the dreams of its founders, their early, courageous struggles, and the difficulties they have surmounted. You will gradually pick up fascinating bits of past history that, pieced together, will form a colorful picture and lead you to a better understanding of the present, and even the future, of the firm. And since you are expected to be a loyal employee, you should have an intelligent loyalty that knows what you are upholding. Certainly, when outsiders ask you general questions, you should be able to give a more satisfying answer than "I don't know."

While you are acquiring these facts, it would be a good plan also to learn all you can about the officers of the company—not in a gossipy way, but something about them as individuals and about their ideas. For example:

What position do they hold in the community?
Are they looked on as having broad views on labor? on wages? on unions?
Is their management of the business progressive?
Is the firm making money under their management?

Sometimes, you will glean this information from reading the daily newspapers. For if you work for a firm whose stock is listed and whose top executives are quoted on business conditions or are interviewed regarding their careers, many of the things you should know will be news.

This business you work for is not the only one of its kind in existence. Your next step is to find out how your employer ranks among his competitors. Something about this particular type of business as a whole is also valuable information. Such inquiry may help to provide the steps to the promotion you desire.

Suppose, for instance, you have gone to work in the offices of a retail furniture company. You are thrilled to find that the firm has been in business for nearly a century and that the founder was a cabinetmaker of repute. Some of his exquisite pieces of handicraft are in the state capitol, you hear, and how you long to see them! Will you leave it at that? Or will you begin to read up on furniture in your spare time, so that when you hear someone speak of a "cabriole," you will know what is meant? Under such circumstances, you will get a great deal of enjoyment and information if you attend a night course in interior decorating and learn something about woods, textiles, and period furniture.

Real estate, food manufacturing, electrotyping, publishing—whatever the business—each has its rich background, the study of which you can pursue with infinite pleasure and profit.

*Executives Appreciate This Interest.* Such study will often do a lot for you with your superiors. Many executives will be more interested in helping you get ahead if they see you are sufficiently interested in their business to study it in your spare time. These men and women will go out of their way to answer questions and explain their business to an eager employee who evinces a desire to learn more than the immediate demands of his (or her) particular job. But be sure that your interest is genuine.

I recall an occasion when I hopefully engaged a new stenographer who had majored in economics in college. My work at that time consisted of planning and directing the advertising and merchandising for a household product that was sold nationally in grocery stores. When I engaged Hope Andrews, I thought she would be especially helpful because, since she was an economics major, she would be interested in seeing the processes of distribution actually at work. So we spent several hours going through my records of product information. I explained what happened to our household cleaner from the time it left the factory, tracing it through the hands of the broker, jobber, chain store, and independent retailer until it arrived on the homemaker's kitchen shelf. I went over our newspaper and magazine advertising with Hope, giving her a capsule edition of a course in merchandising.

At the time, she showed sufficient interest to keep me at my gratuitous effort. But I soon realized from her work and her attitude that she had actually been bored to tears. She asked no further questions and made mistakes that showed she did not care whether she knew a broker from a jobber. In that office, it was the policy to increase the pay of new stenographers after six months. But when this time came, Hope's work was no better than it had been the first day. Three months later, the question of an increase for her came up again, and still no improvement to warrant a raise. At this point, Hope decided there was no future for her in our office, and the office decided Hope was not promotional material, so she was permitted to "resign." The future was there, as the next incumbent quickly realized. But Hope was one of those persons who could not be bothered to acquire background knowledge that would make her valuable to the firm for which she worked.

The owner of a successful business school in the Middle West feels that this study of the business in which a girl is engaged is so important that she urges her graduates to spend at least one night a month at the public library. "Go to the business-research section," she tells them, "and read the trade papers in your field. Improve both your knowledge and your vocabulary. Keep your eyes open for new things in this line of business. Be up to date and informed." I can think of no wiser advice to beginners.

## Learn the Underlying Principles of Business

But the study of your own business and the field in general is only a beginning! To be really intelligent, you must know the general principles underlying the structure of business. Your father and other male relatives may be professional people; hence, the home talk you hear may not be along business lines. In that case, more than if you have a trade background, you should take a general interest in business as such. You are fortunate if you have studied economics, because you will then have the theory of much you will now meet in practice.

*Night Study Recommended.* Banking, finance, and investment, marketing and distribution, selling and advertising, social security, taxation, labor problems, and the difference between gross income and net profit are all topics with which you should have at least a bowing acquaintance. Night school, preferably at the university level, is a reservoir of such knowledge. If night classes are not available, there are books on all these subjects. You will be surprised, perhaps, to find that their authors make many of them as good reading as any mystery or love story. I venture to say that, no matter what subject you choose, you will find it presented by modern writers in a manner to hold your interest. And even if you are neither study-minded nor book-minded, you can and should read regularly the financial pages of a good metropolitan newspaper.

*Newspapers Keep You Informed.* If you have not already done so, begin to read the editorials of newspapers as well as the front-page news. Now that you are going to be a part of the busy world and not a mere observer or ornament, you will need to be fully informed on every aspect of the times. Listen to your boss's general conversation, and you will soon realize how politics may affect his business and your job. You must grasp the meaning to you of the passage of certain laws in Washington or the effect of electing a certain man to office. And don't think you can afford to say, "Politics doesn't mean a thing to me." It can mean everything, as many citizens learn for the first time during a war. Government, through Selective Service, tax legislation, the Office of Price Administration, and other bureaus, touched intimately the lives of everyone during World War II.

### GOING INTO BUSINESS FOR YOURSELF

But maybe you have been indifferent as to what you get out of a job because you plan to go into business for yourself. "I'll be my own boss," you say. This is the illusion that leads so many to seek happiness and success, not through working for others, but for themselves. I say "illusion," for the truth is that the owner of a business has as many bosses as he has customers. And sometimes they are harder to deal with than the pepperiest employer ever dared to be. And as for hours! A sixteen-hour day is nothing when you work for yourself.

A business of your own is certainly not to be thought of by beginners.

Running a business calls for knowledge not only of the line of business you undertake, but of fundamental business practices. This can be got only through experience—and plenty of it. Therefore, my advice to beginners who think they'll start their own businesses because they can't find jobs to their liking is, "Get your experience on somebody else's money."

There is nothing wrong with having an eventual business of your own as the goal in a career plan. But it should be something to look forward to and to save for, not an escape from unemployment, unpleasant working conditions, or trying bosses. That many people do start their own business ill-advisedly is indicated by the records of failures for small businesses. Statistics show that two-thirds of the failures are due to beginners' handicaps.

If your own name over a shop is your ambition, tuck your dream away for some years to come. Don't be tempted to get it out and dust it off until you have reached the top in your field on someone else's payroll.

When all is said and done, the most important thing in getting ahead is that you desire to do so. If your ambition is of the start-stop-start-stop variety, your progress is bound to be slow. Spurts of ambition do not make the grade. But if you have a clear idea of where you want to go, and if you watch for the green light, you are far more likely to hit a highway with less traffic to slow you down. So keep your hand on the wheel and your foot on the gas and *go!*

## QUESTIONS

1. How can saving an employer's time help you to advance?
2. Why is making yourself indispensable the first step in getting ahead?
3. What are the dangers to a beginner of taking responsibility too soon?
4. Name several higher types of positions that often go to women who have proved their ability to take responsibility.
5. When some office employees run out of work, they wait in idleness until they are told what to do. What negative trait does this indicate?
6. Can interest and enthusiasm be cultivated? how?
7. If you present a good idea to your firm and it is turned down, should you

   a. Sulk about it?
   b. Keep still and forget the occurrence?
   c. Quit and tell everybody why?

8. Do all employers like to have ambitious people working for them?

9. Why is it important to find out early what the promotional policies of your employer are?

10. Once you have a job, why is a background knowledge of the business as essential as your skills in getting ahead?

## TOPICS FOR DISCUSSION

1. Discuss the relationship between making good on the job and stepping up to a better one.

2. Discuss why it is impossible to state a definite rule whereby everyone can step up the ladder to success.

3. Do you think an indifferent person would be likely to have initiative? Can he develop it? Express your ideas on this subject.

4. What part does turning out quality work play in making an employee indispensable? Granted that employers are impressed by quantity production, should quality of work be slighted to turn out quantity?

5. Discuss the figure of speech, "Opportunity no longer comes to the door and knocks. It merely drives up to the curb and honks." Carry the figure on to cover what happens after one gets into the car.

6. Discuss various ways in which supervising positions can open up. Personnel positions.

7. Do you agree with the statement in the text, "Carelessness and taking responsibility never dovetail"? Do you know of any careless people who you think could be entrusted with responsibility?

8. Suppose you have what you think are excellent ideas for improving the product, the service, or the office methods of the firm you work for. What will you need to bear in mind in planning to present them to the organization?

9. Based on your present knowledge of the business world, which of the following possibilities expresses what you wish most from your business life?

  a. Easy work
  b. An interesting job
  c. Pleasant surroundings
  d. Work with congenial people
  e. A good salary, regardless of working conditions
  f. Prestige in the business world
  g. Security

10. Discuss why a beginner should get experience in his chosen field before going into business for himself.

11. Discuss the advantage to a beginner of going to work for a firm that has a policy of promotion from within.

12. Do you think that following an organized plan of study should help an ambitious employee win advancement?

# PROJECTS

1. With respect to the expression "business housekeepers," list some duties of the office worker that correspond to home duties. In preparing this list, do not limit yourself to the illustrations given in this chapter.

2. Suppose you are a stenographer in the offices of an airplane factory. Make an outline showing how you would proceed to

   a. Study your own firm.

   b. Study the industry as a whole.

   c. Become informed on political and economic conditions affecting the entire industry and the business you work for.

   d. Become informed on the probable effect on the industry of wartime advances in aviation.

3. Read the editorial page of your newspaper for several days. Report on articles of importance to office workers. If any national or world events occur that directly affect business, be prepared to show how and why this is, and whether or not it would affect employees.

4. For three years, Virginia Smith had been secretary-stenographer for the Owens Building Supply Company. Everything pointed to the fact that Virginia had made herself indispensable to the heads of the firm, but she had not received many raises. Virginia, feeling that they could not get along without her, decided that she would force the issue by threatening to quit unless she was paid more. Mr. Owens told Virginia he could not afford to pay her more, so she quit. When Virginia began looking for another job, she found she could not get a better salary than she had been receiving. After two weeks, Virginia called on Mr. Owens and asked him to take her back at her old salary. But the position was filled.

   Write your opinion of Virginia's handling of her problem. Where did she make her first mistake?

5. Many employees are stuck, year after year, in the same job. Often, they blame the office manager for their not being promoted. Sometimes they quit, go to work somewhere else, and the same thing happens there. Briefly, here are some of the reasons those employees don't advance. Study them, and write a 500-word paper, stating what the person should do to get ahead. Let's say there are different reasons for each person. No one person would have all these faults.

   a. Mary's skills aren't good enough for her to hold anything but a minor job.

   b. John is a timid soul and shows no initiative. He doesn't see things that need to be done. He hasn't much ambition, and he is out a good deal because of sickness.

   c. Anne is more interested in her outside life than in her job. She is popular, has lots of dates, and thinks she may be lucky enough to marry someone who can support her.

CHAPTER 14

# Managing Your Income

When you first go to work, you will be earning money regularly for the first time in your life, and will want to learn, I hope, how to live on your income. This should be the first promise you make yourself, because much of your future success on and off the job may depend on it.

If your beginning salary is small and you do not live at home, you may need to make a considerable adjustment to be able to live on what you earn. Such an achievement will greatly help in advancing your career plans. Moreover, you will be a free agent, able to take a not-so-well-paying job, if you wish, provided that it has future possibilities.

From your first working day, you will see around you many who are mismanaging their incomes in one way or another. Some, regardless of how much they earn or how near they are to payday, will always be broke. They may have anticipated their salaries by going into debt, or been improvident or extravagant. Others, who fritter away their money on odds and ends or expensive lunches, may try to borrow from you to tide them over till payday. Their frequent failure to repay is further evidence of their scrambled finances.

## PLAN TO AVOID DEBT

At the risk of being thought old-fashioned, I should warn you that your peace of mind will be destroyed by worry if you get into debt, and your efficiency will suffer in consequence. It may take Spartan self-control to resist the temptation to spend your hard-earned money recklessly. You often hear the defense, "It's my own money—I ought to be able to spend it the way I want to!"

You will be able to spend your own money as you want to and have something to show for it if you will adopt a well-thought-out program covering your personal income and outgo. My suggestion is that you establish a policy and begin keeping to it the very first day you become employed. Waiting even a week or two is dangerous, considering the lure of easy credit. It is much harder to get out of debt than it is to get in, as countless young employees have discovered.

**Don't Overestimate Your Salary.** Even though you have worked during one or more vacations, the money you earned was scarcely enough to send you on a buying spree. What you would do with those earnings was doubtless planned well in advance—as the buying of your fall clothes or generous spending money for the football season ahead. From these transactions, you undoubtedly got some experience in handling money, but since you did not then take on the responsibility for your own support for the year, it was not quite the same as earning a steady salary, month in and month out.

Depending on the economic situation of the period when you start to work, your beginning salary will be from $225 to, say, $275 a month. In prospect, this seems to you like a lot of money. Unless you have been an active member of your family's finance committee, you probably have no idea what it costs to run your parents' home, nor what it has cost to keep you in the manner to which you have become accustomed. Quite possibly you have never had so much money of your own, all at once, as you'll receive in your first pay check. Don't let it burn a hole in your pocket, and don't let this sudden affluence go to your head.

As I was working out what you would do with your pay check, my morning newspaper supplied an apt couplet, on the editorial page.

> "Of pay checks the essence
> Is quick evanescence."

Truer words were never spoken, or perhaps I should say written.

**Estimate Your Expenses.** First, list your income. This will be your take-home pay, which is what is left after your employer has deducted for the withholding (income) tax and social security. Then, list your actual living expenses for the same period as the pay check—one week, two weeks, or a month. (Employers have different pay periods, but most of them are now weekly or bimonthly.) The main item here is room and board, whether you pay for these at home or in a boardinghouse, or your rent and food cost if you share an apartment with a working friend. To this, you will add the cost of lunches and daily transportation to and from work.

Those expenses are "musts," and they will take a sizable slice out of your check. Other expenses, not so definite but equally certain, are for personal upkeep—laundry, dry cleaning, drugs, toilet articles and cosmetics for young women, and the equivalent in soap, shaving supplies, tooth paste, and deodorants for young men. There are other items that

*Consumer Education Department,*
*Household Finance Corporation*

The wise use of money requires careful planning.
One way of checking your spending is by using
a budget.

belong in this listing, as you will discover, but the ones I mention are so vital for your good grooming that I urge you not to skimp on them. When you have arrived at an approximate total of your living expenses, plus important sundries, you can begin to think about what you will spend for other things, such as clothes.

Our budget for beginning employees, shown on page 334, allows 15 per cent for clothing. This, on a monthly salary of $260 is $39 a month. When you need a suit, coat, or overcoat, you will need to restrict your clothing expenditures for several months so as to have enough cash to buy a good item that will last for several years. Each month, 5 per cent of your salary, or more, should be put into savings of some kind. In your plan for making your salary go as far as possible, allot something to recreation. You are certainly entitled to a little fun out of your first and later pay checks. The better you plan your essential spending, the more generous you can be in what you allow yourself for the movies or theater, a week-end trip with friends, and books, magazines, and newspapers.

Keep this rough estimate of your necessary expenses, and check your expenditures against it for several months at least. You may wish to keep a cash account, jotting down what you spend each day, and allocating it to your budget so you will know just where your money goes. Remember that keeping accounts is looking backward, while budget making is looking forward—looking into the future and anticipating possible needs. Hence, budgeting is more important than accounting for every penny you spend.

You may have to talk firmly to yourself before you are willing to accept the budgeting idea. For budgets take little account of personal indulgences or "I-simply-must-haves." The advantage of budgeting is that it helps you face facts, forces you to realize that if you indulge yourself in one classification some other item will have to suffer, or you will find yourself going without enough food or getting into debt. Also, budgeting will help you to discover how to live as comfortably as possible on what you earn.

*Middle Ground Recommended.* Perhaps you think too much fuss is being made over what you do with the money you earn. Could be. There is, however, a definite purpose in the unsought advice you will get from this chapter and from any course on money management you take in school or college. By showing you the middle road through what can be a tangle of personal finances, we hope to help you avoid the extremes, which are (1) being utterly irresponsible about money, and (2) thinking of nothing but money.

If you follow the first course, you will have possessions—and money troubles without end. Following the second course will bring frequent unhappiness, because you will never be satisfied with what you earn. Become a tightwad, and you will close the door to many pleasant friendships, and your family relations, too, will suffer. When you know how to spend wisely, you will get more for your money, you will enjoy what your earnings buy, and you will have a future very different from that of those foolish young people you will read about later in this chapter.

## DON'T BE TAKEN IN BY TOO-EASY CREDIT

Debt can sneak up on you in friendly guise. Many stores that specialize in charge or installment accounts offer liberal credit to anyone who is employed. While the amount of credit allowed an individual is supposed to be based on his salary, when several stores grant full credit, a person can easily spend his entire salary in advance of earning it, and no store will stop him—then. This practice makes it all too easy for young people who have not yet learned how to handle money to charge beyond their means. What happens when the inexperienced beginner takes advantage of this too-generous credit? He soon finds that the amount left over after living expenses are paid does not go far when divided among his numerous creditors. Then the dunning begins. Letters, collectors, and threats make life miserable for the debt-burdened one. Often, his employer is notified of the indebtedness, which certainly does not help employer-employee relationships. For nothing more quickly discredits an employee with the heads of a business than to have the details of his mismanaged personal finances brought to their attention.

**Creditors Can Garnishee Salaries.** In many states, creditors are permitted to garnishee the employee's salary. This means they can attach your salary and force your employer to pay a portion of it direct to them. Having your salary or a good part of it withheld is bad enough, but the frequent alternative of borrowing from a loan shark at exorbitant interest is worse yet. In fact, borrowing from Peter to pay Paul often creates a far more difficult situation. Phony finance companies whose advertising sounds so helpful exist only to take advantage of the people who get themselves into jams. Not only are their interest rates out of all proportion to the sum borrowed, but often, owing to the ignorance of the borrower, they collect indefinitely.

LEGITIMATE CHARGE ACCOUNTS

Of course, I am not speaking against legitimate charge accounts with reputable firms, except to urge you to be careful not to buy beyond your ability to pay within the required period, usually a month. If you open a charge account with any store, you are immediately listed with the Retail Merchants' Association in your town. Thereafter, your ability to pay can be checked on by any other store, even in another city, when you apply for credit. You can see how important it is to keep your credit good, since you will always be judged by it.

**Don't Mortgage Your Future.** Apart from the value of good credit, it is risky to run up bills that will swamp you for months ahead. Under such circumstances, an unexpected illness, an accident, or the sudden loss of your job would put you in a serious predicament. I know a case in point.

On his first job after leaving college, James Powell earned $60 a week, but he spent on a $100-a-week scale. For years, James had looked forward to the time when he could have a bachelor apartment in New York City. So his first move after getting a job was to sign an apartment lease. Then he bought furniture on a lease account. Jim at once opened several charge accounts at Fifth Avenue stores, because this was part of the picture he had envisioned for himself. Among other things, he charged an $85 dinner suit, and a $15 bottle of perfume for his sister. Doing the town night life often made Jim late with the rent. Friends who dropped in for cocktails nonchalantly used the telephone, and soon there was an unpaid telephone bill, with the company threatening to discontinue the service.

The implications of all this had not yet dawned on Jim when he received his notice from the draft board. But the day James was drafted, all he had to show for his first six months' work was an unbreakable lease, some half-paid-for furniture, and overdue bills from companies that were no longer so polite as when he was opening the accounts.

Fortunately, James was able to sublet his apartment to people who also took over the furniture and paid him enough to settle most of his other debts. His family squared up the rest, not without acid comment on his colorful start in life. When discharged from the Army, James determined it would be the simple life for him as a civilian. "I'm going on practically a cash-and-carry system this time," he said, and he meant it.

### INSTALLMENT BUYING A FORM OF DEBT

Notice that James took advantage of the attractive-sounding offers of installment buying. He was one of many who, through this alluring plan, spend their money far in advance of earning it. In an apartment building where I once lived, the manager was trying to help a young couple in the house work out their financial problems. "That little bride comes in every day with skimpy-looking paper bags. I am sure those two aren't eating enough, or properly," she said. And she was right. It developed that the young man had a reasonably good job with the telephone company. His salary was $250 a month before tax deductions, which meant that he actually took home $217. After they had paid their rent and made the payments on their furniture and the car, they had only $67 left—on which to eat, clothe themselves, and keep their car going! The young wife tried to make food money stretch—in the poorest possible way—with delicatessen buying. But neither she nor her husband could be made to see that it was the car that put everything else out of balance. "We have to have a car," they protested. "All our friends have. If we didn't, what would we do week ends?" Eventually, they decided to move to a cheaper apartment and keep up their front on the highway.

Here is an even sadder tale. I have a friend who was once the answer to prayer of every installment salesman. Angela loved things for her home, and, when the salesmen showed her how easily she could have an automatic washing machine, an ironer, a vacuum cleaner, and a new refrigerator, she signed the contracts. What was $3 or $5 a week on this and $10 on that? Now, Angela and her husband were buying their home, their furniture, and a car, also on deferred payments. And between them they had signed away the husband's salary for several years to come. The few unmarked dollars a week left had to be doled out, bit by bit, for their most pressing cash necessities. But the contracts were signed, and there was nothing to be done except for Angela to cut down on every item of their living and for her husband to keep working to meet the payments.

One day, a brush fire burned block after block of the suburb in which they lived. Everything went, except the car. But according to the lease contracts, Angela and her husband had to go on paying for the house and everything in it quite as if nothing had happened. All that summer, they lived in a tent on the edge of town, laboriously whittling away at their mountain of debt. In the fall, Angela went to work, and they moved back into town. But it was a long time before this couple became solvent again. Their home has been run on a cash basis ever since.

Forgive me for painting such a gloomy picture. But it is better to be forewarned against easy credit than to be taken in by the beautiful mirage, unaware of the tragedy its deception can hold in store.

*Paying Cash—Out of Date?* I have a newspaper clipping that shows a smiling young man who is public-relations director for the credit bureau of a medium-sized California city. The article says that this gentleman will address the Junior Chamber of Commerce on the topic, "Cash on the Barrelhead, Thing of the Past." No doubt, the dinner speaker encouraged the "Jaycees" to forget cash payment as old-fashioned and tie themselves up with installment contracts, that being the modern way of going into debt. He may not have mentioned that item of "carrying charges," which is the high interest rate one pays for this type of credit. The enthusiastic purchaser on "easy terms" never seems to notice that this increases the price he pays for his car, house, television set, garbage-disposal unit—and so on.

### BUDGETING KEEPS YOU SOLVENT

As suggested earlier, the most approved solution to managing your personal finances is to work according to a budget. Every young business person I know, who has become smart at salary stretching without debt or worry, budgets expenditures either actually or in effect. One young stenographer whom I have known since her business-school days never ceases to arouse my wonder and admiration. As a result of both good taste and careful planning, Elizabeth is always perfectly dressed.

She has a small apartment of her own and adds lovely furnishings, bit by bit. Yet, if extras pop up, such as a wedding gift or a baby shower, Elizabeth does her part smilingly. Of course, she has learned to do without. I suggested once that we go to the ballet when it was playing for a few days in our city. "I'd love it," said Elizabeth, "but I'm saving for a new office dress, so this month I can't spend anything for entertainment." She didn't mope about missing the ballet, either, though Elizabeth's secret sorrow is that she couldn't be a dancer. What a wife that girl will make for some young businessman! She will stretch his money so far his head will swim with his surprising affluence.

There are budgets and budgets. I suggest you look up some of them in the library to get the general idea. You will find that most of them are designed for household use and are based on family life. It may be that a budget compiled by business girls and reflecting the actual distribution of their earnings is more difficult to find. Such a project could be profitably undertaken by any group of employed girls who wish to make their salaries go further by spending according to plan. The results of such a study would be most helpful to those who assembled the figures and to thousands of other young people who work and live on what they earn.

The budget shown on page 334 was compiled by a widely known school for secretaries for use in a class on Career Orientation. In lending me this budget for your use, the owner of the school wrote, "We use the figure of $260 a month, a typical salary for an exceptional beginner or a capable girl with one year's good experience. This salary figure is not a median or a minimum; it simply represents the kind of salary figure at which we place our graduates who have the qualifications described." Knowing this school as I do, I am satisfied that the budget herewith presented is based on the best of the standard budgets, adapted to the needs of business girls who, as graduates, have related their experiences to understanding teachers.

Although this budget was compiled for graduates from a girls' school, it will work just as well for young men who are starting out in the business world. Obviously, your starting or continuing salary will depend not only on your qualifications but on the geographical location of your work. Generally speaking, salaries are lower in the Southern States and in smaller cities and towns throughout the country in the belief that living costs are lower there.

**Board and Room.** Let us analyze this budget in a few particulars. You will doubtless think that the estimated cost given here for board and room should be labeled "living at home," and that it must be based on one's having a generous family. I think so, too. But the amount shown is about one-third of the salary, and theoretically that is what board and room should cost. Where a person lives away from home, the cost of a shared room and two meals a day is usually estimated at from $15 to $18 weekly. In some larger cities, however, it would be difficult to get satisfactory board and room for that figure. When the allotted 32 per cent does not cover board and room, it will be necessary to dip into the 5 per cent savings fund or trim the 17 per cent personal-upkeep allowance to take care of the increased cost-of-living expenses. In case your salary is less than $260, it is probable that both savings and personal upkeep will suffer until a raise makes it possible to bring expenses back to the proper percentage.

### BUDGET FOR EMPLOYED GIRL[1]

Computed on base salary of $260 a month with income tax deduction for one individual. The figures are not exact computations.

| INCOME | PERCENTAGE | MONTHLY | SEMI-MONTHLY |
|---|---|---|---|
| *Totals* | 100% | $260 | $130 |
| *Deductions* (one exemption) | | | |
| Withholding tax | 14% | $ 36.40 | $ 18.20 |
| F.I.C.A.* | 3% | 7.80 | 3.90 |
| C.E.T.† | 1% | 2.60 | 1.30 |
| | 18% | $ 46.80 | $ 23.40 |
| Take-home pay | 82% | $213.20 | $106.60 |
| *Room and Board* | 30% | 78 | |
| *Personal Upkeep* | 20% | 52 | |
| Includes: | | | |
| Laundry and cleaning | | | |
| Cosmetics-hair | | | |
| Recreation (movies, bowling, parties, etc.) | | | |
| Reading material | | | |
| *Clothing* | 15% | 39 | |
| *Lunch and Carfare* | 13% | 33.80 | |
| *Miscellaneous* (including your state income tax) | 4% | 10.40 | |

Savings plan will begin with the first increase in salary.

* Federal Insurance Contributions Act (Social Security).

† City Earnings Tax (levied in a number of large cities).

*A Car Wrecks a Budget.* You may be one of those persons who feel that they cannot live without keeping a car. If so, you scanned the budget in vain for that item. One of the first shocks of living on what you earn will probably be the discovery that your salary will not provide all the things you had when you lived with your family, and a car may be one of these. For obviously, out of a salary of $200 a month

[1] Reproduced by permission of Margaret A. Hickey, Director, Miss Hickey's School for Secretaries, St. Louis, Missouri.

or less, you could not purchase even a considerably used car or maintain one. In case you already own a car, you will have to decide what items on your budget you will eliminate to keep the car on the highway. My advice is to let a pleasure car wait until you are earning enough to operate one on a reasonable allowance that takes care of insurance, garage, repairs, gas, and oil. Otherwise, the pleasure will be doubtful. Experienced motorists will not drive a car one mile unless it is fully covered by insurance, and certainly young business people should not take the financial risks involved in driving an unprotected car.

Of course, if a car is your only means of getting to work, you would have to deduct from other classifications in your budget and throw in your carfare allowance besides. Even so, you would have such difficulties in remaining solvent that, unless you could arrange for another employee with a car to taxi you to and from work daily, you might find it better to get a more accessible job.

## ALL EMPLOYEES SHOULD SAVE SOMETHING

Even though it may seem to you that it is impossible to save on a salary of $250 or even $300 a month, you should try to do so. Otherwise, you may find yourself in an emergency without any reserve funds. An accident or a sudden illness, with income halted and expenses increased, is a disheartening experience unless you have some money saved. Our Yankee President, Calvin Coolidge, had the right idea on saving when he said: "There are three maxims which have made New England great. 'Use it up. Make it do. Do without.'" I suggest that you make this your motto.

*Saving for Special Things.* Perhaps, a more attractive way to be saving is to save for something you want. Saving for a radio, a television set, a vacation trip, or a fur coat is a safer way to acquire such things than on the installment plan. For one thing, if misfortune catches up with you, you will have money on hand that can be used. But with better luck, when you have had the fun of the thing you were saving for, you can plunge into another saving project with zest and anticipation. Presently, you will come to enjoy saving not only for extras, but for your future.

*Savings Banks and Savings Bonds.* There are all sorts of ways to save. The rate of interest paid by savings banks is not high, but the method is convenient, and your savings up to $10,000 are guaranteed by our Government. When you are saving for something and will want to withdraw some cash, a savings account in a nearby bank will probably be best for you. Interest will be paid on money left in your account for six months or longer, and you can draw out all or part of your deposits

*The Chase National Bank of the City of New York*

The bank not only helps you by keeping your
money safe, but it can also offer sound advice on
savings and investments.

at any time. Regardless of what other types of long-range saving plans
you adopt, I recommend your starting an account with a savings bank
as your first adventure in saving. Maybe you've had such an account
while in school, in which case as soon as you have a regular salary, you
can put new life into the old bankbook.

For a saving plan that looks to the future, there is nothing better than
Government bonds. They are the best investment on earth, for when
you buy these bonds you are really lending money to your Government, and your investment is as safe as the United States Treasury.
Also, when the bonds mature, in 7¾ years, you will receive more than
savings-bank interest. Virtually all employers have established a plan
whereby a deduction can be made from the employees' pay checks and
applied toward the purchase of Government bonds. You authorize
your employer to make a stated deduction from each of your pay

checks. The amount taken out will be shown on your check stub each payday, and when enough has been deducted to buy a bond, the employing firm will have a bank send you the bond you have purchased. This is the only kind of installment buying I recommend to you in your early working life. Actually, it isn't that, for, in fact, you are saving something each week, or every two weeks, until there is enough to buy the bond outright. You may not know what you will use your bonds for, after ten or more years, but it will be heartening to feel that you are accumulating money toward the purchase at some later day of a home, a European trip, or even a fine new car.

***Insurance Is One Way of Saving.*** Many people find life insurance an excellent way to save for the future, meanwhile enjoying protection for their dependents. Having insurance premiums to meet monthly, quarterly, or semiannually forces you to put aside a stated sum to be ready with your payments.

For young men, especially, it is a good idea to take out a straight life insurance or term insurance policy while youth is on your side. The rate you pay is very low on account of your age, because the insurance companies expect you to live a long time. Assuming you are not married, you would name a parent, sister, or brother as your beneficiary, changing the policy over to your wife when you marry. In this way, you have the continued benefit of the low rate on this policy for the rest of your life. If you are subject to the draft, and serve your shift in one of the armed services, you will be entitled to take out National Service Life Insurance under the Government plan. The rates for this insurance are low, and you will do well to continue such a policy after you are again in civilian life.

There are other forms of insurance worth investigating, if that type of saving attracts you. For instance a twenty- or thirty-payment life insurance policy, while more expensive than straight life or term insurance, gives you protection for a dependent, and, in twenty or thirty years will pay *you* the face value of the policy. Many persons take little pleasure in saving for something from which they will not benefit. In this type of policy, you are your own beneficiary.

Whether or not you realize it, the payments deducted from your salary for social security are the best kind of insurance—contributory social insurance operated by the United States Government. Under the Social Security Act, employers and wage earners contribute equally to a trust fund, out of which benefits are paid. You become eligible for monthly insurance payments at the age of sixty-five if you have received, in covered jobs, a certain minimum amount of pay in each of a specified number of calendar quarters. If the wage earner dies before reaching age sixty-five, his dependents are eligible for monthly or lump-sum insurance payments, or if he has no family, a lump sum may be paid toward funeral expenses. These things seem far away now, but each month's payment toward later security should add to your peace of mind.

## SCHOOLS AND HOMES TEACH MONEY MANAGEMENT

You are fortunate if in your home or school, or both, you have been taught how to handle money. More and more schools are giving courses that cover such things as budgeting, life insurance, the use of credit, and the purchase of homes. The purpose of these courses is to help young people learn to control their spending and prepare them for the much greater money responsibility they will meet when earning a salary. What is sometimes called "money sense" usually has to be acquired. Probably a better term for it is "money management," which can be taught in the home long before children reach high school age. I know of one father who announced a nickel-carrying contest to his three small sons. The boy who won the prize for carrying his nickel longest learned sales resistance so well that by his twenty-first birthday he had saved a thousand dollars. Not all in nickels, I presume.

At an all-day conference held at the University of Pennsylvania, some forty teachers met with representatives of the Institute of Life Insurance to discuss the teaching of money management in the nation's high schools. A serious problem reported at the meeting was the "easy-come, easy-go" attitude toward money that some teachers thought was developing among many teen-agers. The reasons given for this attitude were plentiful jobs and the fact that most high school boys face military service after graduation. The answer to the problem, according to the teachers, is to help the boys make plans for the future and to teach them to look beyond both graduation and military service. By doing this, it is thought that a student can be made to see that the realization of a long-range plan may depend on how well he manages his money now.

Teaching a boy or girl a simple system of keeping track of money can pay dividends in the form of being able to buy something that is very much wanted. A case in point is the problem that now occupies the minds of a large part of the nation's young people—how to own a car of one's own. Some sober before-the-fact examination of how much it costs to run an automobile is necessary before parents should allow the car to be bought.

The account of this conference did not say whether the close relationship between budgeting and marriage was a topic for discussion.

It should have been, for working out a budget and sticking to it is excellent training for wedding bells. Young people who hope to be married will greatly increase their chances of happiness if they have trained themselves to handle money intelligently. It takes fortitude, discipline, and self-sacrifice to live within one's income, however large or small, and these are virtues that, especially when related to spending and saving, are all-important to successful married life.

*Gambling Is a Losing Game.* All this is in direct contrast to the "get something for nothing" idea. But petty gambling brings more heartaches than winnings. Slot machines, pinball games, the races, lotteries, and sweepstakes keep some people in a state of delirious expectation and usually deep debt. Only those who can afford to lose can afford to gamble. Employers rightly become suspicious of employees who are known to be gamblers. Moreover, all employees who handle money have to be bonded. And bonding companies have an uncanny way of finding out about employees' private lives and habits.

## DRESSING ON A CLOTHES BUDGET

But let us turn from wise saving for a brighter tomorrow to wise spending for a brighter today. To most of you, this will probably mean clothes. And since being well dressed is a business asset, let us see how well we can figure it out.

When, earlier in this chapter, you studied the budget for an employed girl, you noticed, no doubt, that 15 per cent was allowed for clothes, and that this amounted to $39 a month, or $468 a year. Many of you girls probably wondered how you could dress on that sum. If you have been clothing yourself on an allowance while in school, you will not be staggered by this budget figure. Some parents wisely give their children the experience of dressing themselves out of an allowance during high school days, so they will learn early how to plan and save for the things they need most. In case you have been doing that, you will know a good deal about the cost of wearing apparel and will be able to shift into the careful spending of your own-earned clothes money without too much difficulty. But if you have not had to keep your clothes buying within set limits, now is the time to start. Let's hope you have a well-stocked clothes closet when you go to work, and that your party things are already supplied.

For, regardless of the demands of your social life, you will now have to put business clothes first—at least until you have acquired enough things suitable for office wear. That is why in Chapter 12 I recommended a basic dress as your first purchase after you go to work, and explained how you could make that dress double for informal after-hours dates by changes of accessories. Unless you already have a simple dress that is more tailored than your basic dress, your second purchase should be a dress of this type. If the basic dress is black or navy, as recommended, the tailored frock can be a brighter blue, or if your coat is black, the dress can be a dark green or burgundy. You will have to stick closely to one color scheme to hold down the cost of coats and accessories. With these two dresses, you at least have a change while they take turns at the cleaners. However, I hope you already have one or two other suitable dresses to give these an occasional rest. If you have a tailored suit, you can rest your dresses by wearing the suit to work, say, one day a week. Your budget, if carefully manipulated, will permit your buying a blouse now and then, so you can change your suit appearance by wearing different-colored blouses. Usually, a suit jacket is kept on in an office, except during warm weather, and your blouses can be sleeveless if you will be sure not to remove the jacket. But if your office is overheated, and you will have to be seen in blouse and skirt for part of the day, buy only blouses with some kind of sleeve. While tailored blouses with long sleeves look more businesslike, they soil quickly. A three-quarter sleeve or one just above the elbow is in good taste and generally acceptable. But no transparent or frilly blouses, please!

What a business wardrobe—simple as it may be—will cost, with the shoes, hose, bags, gloves, and any other accessories that you will need, is hard to estimate, because prices differ according to locality and the general price trend. Of course, you will be buying a wardrobe based on use for two, three, or even four years, adding several major articles each year, in your color scheme, so that they will harmonize with what you already have. Girls and women with almost unlimited money to spend for clothes plan this way; so why shouldn't thrifty business girls do likewise? You can be glad you won't have to spend much for hats; that is, you won't if you live in a fairly small city. In large cities, I have observed, hats are worn as much as ever. In the smaller communities, I know young businesswomen who have had to buy or borrow hats to wear to a wedding. Boys and men are permitted to go hatless if they wish, even in large cities, but the best-dressed men wear hats.

To show you that you can dress reasonably well on an annual dress budget of $450, I shall suggest one based on average costs. We assume that you have a fair wardrobe to start with. Each of you will undoubtedly carry over from school days enough clothes to wear around home and some that are just right for your social life. I am hoping you have one or two outfits suitable to wear to work, as a start. Your budget will need that extra help.

FIRST-YEAR CLOTHING BUDGET FOR BUSINESS GIRLS
Based on 15 per cent of $3,000

| | |
|---|---:|
| 1 basic dress | $ 25.00 |
| 1 tailored dress | 22.00 |
| 12 pairs nylon hose | 14.00 |
| 3 pairs shoes | 50.00 |
| 1 fairly dressy blouse | 12.50 |
| 2 tailored blouses | 10.00 |
| 1 coat | 75.00 |
| 2 handbags | 18.50 |
| 1 wool suit | 60.00 |
| 2 hats | 10.00 |
| 3 summer dresses or suits (cotton) | 60.00 |
| Accessories, as scarves, jewelry | 20.00 |
| 2 girdles | 10.00 |
| 3 slips | 16.00 |
| 2 pairs pajamas, or 2 nightgowns | 10.00 |
| 2 pairs gloves | 9.00 |
| Miscellaneous lingerie | 28.00 |
| | $450.00 |

You will have to save for several months to make your major purchases, especially the coat. In your second year, you should have a
raise, after which your 15 per cent should put you in the clear. Then
you will be able to be more generous with yourself in both your business and after-hours wardrobes.

## A Clothes Budget for Young Men, Too

And now for the young men. Although their clothes problem is less
complicated than that of the girls, their expenditures for clothing call
for just as much thought. Since the same general budgeting rule of
15 per cent for clothing should be followed, the budget given below
is based on 15 per cent of a salary of $250 a month. The costs quoted
are approximate. You may find them slightly higher, or even somewhat
lower, in your home city.

We shall assume that you already possess many of the items listed.
Nevertheless, to get off to a good start, you should plan to include or
replace the items shown here at your earliest convenience, during your
first year of employment. It goes without saying that any money saved
on the purchase prices listed here may be used for other necessary expenditures. Note also that climatic conditions in your part of the
country will determine how you spend some of your money. For instance, seasonal clothing changes are necessary in the East, while a
lightweight summer suit is not essential in the Far West. Your first

year's clothes spending should run something like this, based on 15 per cent of $3,000.

### CLOTHES FOR OFFICE WEAR FOR BUSINESSMEN

| | |
|---|---:|
| 1 wool suit (winter) | $ 55.00 |
| 1 light weight suit (spring and fall) | 45.00 |
| 1 summer suit | 35.00 |
| 1 topcoat (with wool lining for winter) | 65.00 |
| 1 hat | 10.00 |
| 2 pairs shoes | 45.00 |
| 6 pairs socks | 9.00 |
| 6 shirts | 26.00 |
| 6 pairs shorts | 8.00 |
| 6 undershirts | 6.00 |
| 3 ties | 6.00 |
| Accessories, as belt, jewelry | 8.00 |
| 1 light weight raincoat | 25.00 |
| | $343.00 |

### CLOTHES FOR LEISURE

| | |
|---|---:|
| 1 sport coat | 35.00 |
| 1 pair slacks | 16.00 |
| 2 sport shirts | 10.00 |
| 1 slip-on sweater | 12.00 |
| 1 coat-style sweater | 14.00 |
| 2 pairs pajamas | 10.00 |
| 1 pair loafers | 10.00 |
| | $107.00 |
| | $450.00 |

Where bargains are concerned, the same watchfulness recommended to young women is suggested for young men. Shop wisely, and don't be taken in by the sharp salesman who tries to high-pressure you with, "Why it's the latest thing. It's what they're all wearing now!" And don't forget that where quality merchandise is concerned it is often thrifty to put five or ten dollars more into an item that is to last you several years. The old saying, "You get just what you pay for," always remains true.

### A RAISE WILL HELP THE BUDGET

Of course, there is nothing that will help out your budget so much as an increase in salary. Perhaps you have felt for some time that you were doing work that entitled you to more, but the all-important raise has not come. Shall you ask for it? If so, how?

I am reminded of a young man just starting out in the business world who was given a position by a family friend, more or less out of good will. The lad's work was selling roofing material. He rushed about for a month or six weeks, covering much territory but bringing in few orders. His living expenses, however, were beyond his income. At the end of his six weeks' initiation, he asked the head of the firm for more money. "I can't possibly live on what I'm making," he said conclusively. "Would ten dollars a month more help you out?" "I'll say it would!" "All right, we'll make it that," his employer promised. "But I think you'd better begin looking around for something else. Your sales don't indicate you're very well suited to this type of work." The sequel of this story is that, when the young man looked around, all he could find was a job that paid a third less than he was getting before the family friend increased his salary. And his parents insisted that he live on it until he learned to adjust his standard of living to his income.

**You Earn the Raise First.** The fact that you need more money is not a reason for asking for a raise. Everyone always needs more income, or could use it. The reason must be better than that. Neither does a person ask for a raise simply because someone else doing similar work gets more. You are not supposed to know what the other employees are paid. A friend of mine who is in charge of 150 employees in a large office says, "Employees must be worth more money for some time before they get it. First they must prove their worth over a period of time through greatly increased services. Demonstrated ability comes first—then increases."

This same office manager, along with several other men and women in like positions, told me of their current salary headache. Because of the scarcity of acceptable beginners and the competition among employers for their services, business firms have been forced to pay high starting salaries. This often results in recent graduates starting at weekly salaries that are only five or six dollars a week less than the salaries paid competent employees after several years' service. Naturally, this creates dissatisfaction among the seasoned workers and causes them to ask for increases that will bring their salaries proportionately higher than those paid to beginners. While personnel directors and office managers see the injustice in the salary situation created when help is scarce, and sympathize with those adversely affected by it, they are powerless to alter the salary scale. "The business simply can't afford to pay everybody at the same rate we are having to pay beginners," they say.

**Find Out Your Firm's Salary Policy.** Many business firms have a definite policy regarding salary increases and a stated time, once or twice a year, for reviewing them. When you have worked for such a firm and fulfilled their requirements as to length of service and satisfactory work, you will get your raise along with the other eligibles. If you have met the requirements and are overlooked at the regular increase period, you have a right to ask why.

But perhaps your firm has no such fixed policy. Then you have to be brave and take your request to headquarters. Be sure you have all the facts well thought out and are prepared to prove your right to an advance in pay. Only your increased value to the business in both quality and quantity production is a sound reason for asking for more money.

**Get on the Productive Side.** You may be doing work that you feel is worth considerably more money to your firm, but you will be unwise in asking for an increase unless you know the business is making a good profit. Bear in mind that all office work is on the nonproductive side of business and is counted as part of the overhead. It is actually a service department—necessary, but producing no income. The sales force has to bring in the money with which to pay the stenographic, bookkeeping, and clerical salaries. It is more difficult for an office worker to justify an increase in salary than it is for employees who are on the productive side of business. Since this is so, you should not expect employers to be willing to pay sky-high salaries for this type of work. If your income is to rise substantially, you will have to show ability a little beyond mere service-department requirements. One way is to increase your output in whatever job you are in, accept more responsibility, and do such outstanding work that you will attract attention to your executive ability. With an eye out for a junior executive position in some other department, such as advertising, selling, or transportation, you may be able to co-ordinate your career plan and your promotional objective—and presto! you have the raise!

## QUESTIONS

1. Do office workers, as a rule, handle their personal finances in a business-like manner?
2. Why is it important that young people just starting in business learn to manage their incomes intelligently?
3. When does the text suggest that you should adopt a well-thought-out program regarding your personal income and outgo?
4. Mention several ways in which a business beginner can become badly in debt almost before he is aware of what is happening.
5. Can an employee hide his financial difficulties from his employer indefinitely? Why not?
6. Mention the circumstances under which the use of a charge account with a good store is desirable. When is the use of installment buying proper?

7. Why is budgeting offered as the remedy for financial mismanagement?
8. Apart from keeping him solvent, what does conscientious budgeting do for the budgeteer?
9. What, besides immediate protection for dependents, do you gain by taking out life insurance when you are young?
10. How much do you think a beginner on $35 a week should allow himself daily for lunch? What can he get for that amount? Would this be an adequate lunch?

## TOPICS FOR DISCUSSION

1. The following advertisement appeared in a New York City newspaper:

> Young man who gets paid on Monday and is broke by Wednesday would like to exchange small loans with young man who gets paid on Wednesday and is broke by Monday.

Discuss systematic borrowing as a solution for the financial problems of office workers.

2. Young people usually have to work for a number of years before they earn as much as their school and college allowances or the equivalent of the living provided at home. Discuss how you think youthful employees can bridge this gap and adjust their living to their salaries.

3. Discuss the advantages and disadvantages to the beginning worker of easy credit.

4. Agnes Wood earns $60 a week after taxes. She lives at home and pays $18 a week for board and room. Her lunches cost $6 a week, and transportation averages $3 a week. Agnes figures she has $33 a week to do with as she pleases. On this assumption Agnes buys a fur coat on the installment plan and signs a contract to pay $22 a week for twenty weeks. Agnes thinks she is staying well within her present salary. What expenses has she failed to figure on? What will happen if she cannot meet the terms of her contract after twelve weeks?

5. Talk with some of your young friends who are working, and find out what per cent of their salaries they spend for personal upkeep. How much of this goes for vacation? what for dentistry?

If they spend more than 15 per cent for clothes, do you think they are justified? why? On what items do they cut to get more for personal upkeep and clothes?

Do they pay cash? run charge accounts? If the latter, do they have thirty, sixty, or ninety days to pay? Does this credit help them with their personal financing?

6. Discuss the advantages of sticking closely to a budget as compared with the policy of spending as you go. Which method requires the greater mental effort? Which brings the greater peace of mind?

7. Turn to the clothes budget for young men earning $250 a month,

shown on page 342. Suppose you are earning this salary. Do you think that you could work out a satisfactory business wardrobe without exceeding 15 per cent of your annual salary? Would you change any items in the plans suggested here? If so, state what substitutions you would make, and why.

8. If you feel that you could not dress sufficiently well for business on 15 per cent of $250 a month, what readjustments of your budget would you make to get more for clothes? Justify this shifting of funds by proving that you could manage the other items for less than the budget allots to them.

9. Explain what the following terms mean, as used in this chapter: an attachment on your salary; phony finance companies; budgeteers; borrowing from Peter to pay Paul; mortgaging your future; garnishee; legitimate charge accounts; buying on the installment plan; loan sharks.

    Also explain the following related terms not used in this chapter, but which you see in a daily paper: lease account; investigate before you invest; lessor; lessee.

10. Have you found it easier to save for something you want, such as a radio, a television set, a car, or a vacation, than just to save on general principle? What is the difference?

## PROJECTS

1. Assume that you are earning $60 a week, or the equivalent monthly salary of $260. Using the Budget for the Employed Girl given in this chapter, make an itemized account of one month's expenditures for the different classifications.

    Before doing this, check costs in your community and see whether they correspond favorably with those used in compiling this budget. For instance, can you get board and room in your city for what this budget allows for food and shelter? If not, readjust the budget, allowing more for this major item and taking it away from funds allotted elsewhere. Be prepared to give reasons for your change.

    You will observe that there is no allowance in this budget for medical care or drugs. If you should need to spend money for these things, out of what fund would you draw? Should you be laying aside money for such possible emergencies?

2. Many young people who like privacy are intrigued with the idea of living alone as soon as they are on their own. A secretary who earns $250 a month says that bugeting has taught her she cannot afford to operate an apartment by herself. When she tried it out, spending $100 a month for rent, she either had to eat sketchily or she had no new clothes. Based on the $250 budget given in this chapter, figure out how the total budget is unbalanced by stepping up the item of shelter to $100 a month. What classifications would you cut if you spent over 40

per cent of your income for rent? How would the strain be eased if three young men or three young businesswomen shared an apartment for which they paid $125?

3. Do you believe that every income producer should save something out of each pay check? Or do you think the low-salaried worker can safely put off saving until he is earning enough to have something left over for saving? If so, how will he determine when the time to begin to save has arrived? Do you think 5 per cent is too much to save? What do you think is the best plan for saving—a savings-bank account, insurance, or some other form of investment? Write your ideas, and present them to the class.

4. If you wanted a raise, would you go to the boss and tell him that you

   a. Can't live on your present salary (giving reasons)?
   b. Are doing work that is worth more (and prove it)?
   c. Are discouraged because your work is evidently not appreciated?
   d. Will quit unless you are given more money?

5. Why is there a limit beyond which office salaries cannot be raised? What is the answer to this for the ambitious young person who is worth more money and is willing to concentrate all his abilities and effort on earning more?

6. Find out the laundry and dry-cleaning charges in your city. Figure what allowance you will need to make for these items in your budget in order to present the neat appearance that business requires. Young men find that the laundering of shirts is a considerable item; whereas young women who launder many of their things at home spend more for dry cleaning than men do.

7. Write a 500-word paper on "The Advantage to an Office Worker of Keeping His Credit Good."

# CHAPTER 15

# Personality in Business

Many employers declare that personality is the quality that gets the job. Apparently, it is often the deciding factor in an employment interview. With several applicants from whom to choose, it is only natural that the employer should select the one whose personality is most pleasing to him.

This being so, how important it is that young people about to start job hunting should find out what employers mean by personality. If I can give you a few tips now, you will still have time to take inventory of your personality assets and liabilities and to start cultivating this mysterious something that is so much in demand and that is so difficult to define.

First, let's do a little eavesdropping in an employment agency. The time is nine o'clock any morning, and the telephones are busy with calls from employers asking that applicants be sent them for interviewing. Or perhaps they are reporting decisions on those applicants interviewed the day before.

## WANTED: AN ATTRACTIVE PERSONALITY

The first employer says, "Send me a stenographer with an attractive personality." You notice that he mentions this before describing the job. The next request is for "a young man with a clean-cut personality." The third call is from a personnel director who says, "I'd like to interview typists who can do fifty or more words a minute. But don't send anyone who hasn't a pleasing personality." Then an office manager rings up to say, "We don't like that girl you sent over yesterday. She lacks personality."

Before noon, there are calls for a PBX operator with a "telephone personality" and a Comptometer operator with a "nice personality." Just as you are leaving, an irate man on the line says, "I wouldn't have that bookkeeper around. He may know his stuff, but he has a 'disagreeable personality.' "

*Is Personality Largely Appearance?* It is quite evident that business is looking for personality, you decide. But what do they mean by the word? You ask the employment agency whether it is appearance that is wanted. "Not entirely," the interviewer tells you. "Appearance counts a lot, of course, but what these employers want goes deeper than the surface. It's hard to define."

*Personality Not Mere Charm.* "Maybe they want charm," you suggest hopefully, because you've heard that word used interchangeably with personality. But apparently that's not the answer, for the interviewer fairly bristles as she says: "I should say not! If there is one thing business doesn't want it is employees exuding charm all over the place. They have enough troubles without that."

*Employers Want Appearance Plus.* Let's say, then, that in prospective employees business is looking for personality factors, which are appearance *plus* something else. The experience of Jane Doane illustrates my point.

Jane had just completed a commercial course in high school when her family moved to another city. This made Jane doubly timid about looking for work, since she could now have no help from her school, and she knew no one in the city to which her family had moved. However, Jane's uncle wrote from New York to some business friends of his, and through them Jane was introduced to a good employment agency. In this way, something of Jane's background became known, and she was sent to be interviewed by one of the agency's most exacting clients.

Jane made a good impression on the personnel director, which won her an interview with the vice-president, who finally passed on everybody. Jane's good grooming and good manners, plus what he had been told about her, counted greatly in her favor. But she looked very young, the executive told her. "I come from a young-looking family," said Jane, which showed she was quick thinking.

"If I give you this job as typist, do you think you could dress so you appear older?" the vice-president asked before he committed himself. "I don't want them to think I'm hiring babies around here. Have you any black clothes?"

Jane said she hadn't, but she would be glad to get some. The executive then suggested that Jane and her mother meet their personnel director downtown next day and select suitable office clothes for Jane —not at the firm's expense, I regret to say. And so young Jane got her first lesson in what to wear for business. With the aid of her mother and the personnel director, she was outfitted in two neat blue dresses. The next time she goes to look for a job—which will not be soon, I'm told—Jane will know better than to wear a schoolgirl's outfit. Her clothes almost lost her that job, Jane says. But her personality got it for her, for Jane was the tenth girl to be interviewed.

On the Pacific Coast, I heard of another case in which a young woman got a job solely through her personality. The virtually indispensable secretary to a bank president was retiring, and the bank needed an outstanding young woman in this position. The work was easy, and any of the other stenographers in the bank could have done it; but none of them met the personality requirements. Those secretaries who sit outside a bank president's private office are usually seen by the public, and must look attractive, be gracious in their manners, and be exceedingly tactful in meeting callers. But this is not all. They must be highly intelligent and equal to handling any situation that may arise at their strategic outpost.

The president and several directors interviewed eight or nine applicants without success. Just as they despaired of getting the type they wanted, somebody said he knew somebody who knew Margery Kenny. So Margery Kenny was called in from her minor job on a small magazine. When Margery entered the room and spoke, both the president and a director who was present knew that she had the poise and intelligence they were looking for. They felt sure she could handle visitors and grace the outer office besides. So personality helped Margery to skip several rungs of her experience ladder.

*Appearance Can Be Deceptive.* Sometimes, an employer puts so much stress on personality that he overlooks other things for which personality is not a substitute. Ability, for instance. An amusing story is told of a Midwestern businessman who turned down ten stenographic applicants and employed the eleventh because she had the personality he was visualizing. But after a few days, her inefficiency was too much for him. "That girl can't read her notes, and she can't spell," he complained to the employment agency. "She's got my work all balled up. What do you mean sending me anybody so dumb?"

But the employment agent was not to be browbeaten. "Don't blame me!" she said. "The first person I send out is always the best one I have right then to fill the specifications. If she, or one or two others, isn't acceptable, I know an employer is looking for a certain type of personality. All I can do then is to keep on sending applicants, hoping to hit on the type he has in mind. The first one I sent you was my choice; the eleventh was yours."

*Personality Not Prettiness.* That employers are wary of the beauty-conscious applicant is indicated by a story an employer told me. He was looking for a young woman with an attractive personality to fill a stenographic vacancy. In Amy Rogers, he thought he had found her. He was just about to say, "All right, Miss Rogers, we'll consider the position yours," when Amy wrecked her chances. All she did was raise her hand and daintily stroke a well-arched eyebrow. This employer had had plenty of experience with girls who made up at their desks, and he knew that they spent far too much time in the dressing room fixing their hair and faces. "Right then I decided less beauty and more work was what I wanted," he told me. "Personality isn't prettiness anyway. Sometimes, a young woman who is quite plain has an exceptionally attractive personality." I agreed with him. Very often a plain girl can and does compensate for her lack of beauty by enriching her personality and making her clothes and grooming work for her.

*Social Graces Not Wanted.* And if beauty is not personality, neither are charm and social graces. At least they are not considered so in business. Frances Maule in an article written for *The Independent Woman* has this to say:

An office is no place for the exercise of witching charm or the display of social graces. A woman who is used to gathering bouquets as the life of the party is likely to find herself receiving brickbats if she starts trying to be the life of the office.

## Wanted: A Clean-cut Personality

Along with the rather wide search for male stenographers and secretaries, of which I spoke in an earlier chapter, go specific personality requirements. Employment agencies tell me that "clean-cut" is one of the descriptive adjectives most used by employers. Yet none of them knows just what this nice-sounding hyphenated adjective means. I take it that the expression is used to define faultless grooming as well as correct dress, and yet I am sure its implications do not stop there. Business is certainly not looking for "Fancy Dans." It wants that clean-cut young man to be something of the collegiate type at its best in dress and grooming. It wants him to be alert and interested in everything about him and not to register boredom. It would appreciate a grain of humility and an ounce of deference in his attitude. In an interview, the young male applicant is being sized up right then as a possible future executive, and his personality must stand up under this appraisal.

*Appearance Plays Its Part.* A young friend of mine who has done considerable selling tells me that he got his first sales job in an unusual way. Waiting to be interviewed for holiday work in a metropolitan department store, he was once singled out from a long line of applicants. He heard those ahead of him being told, "We're not taking anybody on. Sorry." So his hopes were low indeed. Judge his surprise when someone tapped him on the shoulder and said, "Come this way." He was ushered into an adjoining office, and even though inexperienced, he was hired to sell in the men's furnishings department. They told him he had the right personality for that work. He thought he had been singled out because he was especially well dressed and well groomed on that occasion. But no doubt, without his knowing it, he was that "clean-cut" type so in demand.

A year or so later, when this young man was selling materials to the building trades, his sales manager told him he was dressed too well for the job. "You mustn't attract attention by your clothes," the sales executive said. "You'll do better to look like everyone else, about as ordinary as the men you are calling on. Let your personality shine in the sale itself –rather than in your appearance." These stories suggest that there is no established success pattern in personality.

A DEFINITION OF PERSONALITY

So far, I have avoided giving any definitions of personality. But I think the illustrations cited make it clear that, for our purposes, we can consider that *personality is the physical and mental make-up that distinguishes one person from another.* The words "personality" and "individuality" are often used interchangeably, and I believe it will simplify our discussion if we so regard them. But let us be very sure we understand what is meant. Again quoting Frances Maule, let us remember that personality is not "unbridled individuality running riot all over the place. In business, personality means control—and above all, the ability to keep those aspects of your personality that have no relation to your work strictly tucked away during office hours."

*The Basis of Individuality.* Individuality—that which makes each of us unique—is God given. Part of the great mystery of all nature is that there are no duplicates. In his factories, man turns out hundreds, thousands, and even millions of duplicates. But not so in the great universe. No two leaves are just alike. If you doubt it, try to find twin leaves. And no two snowflakes are just alike. You will discover under a microscope that, among the myriad beautiful geometric designs of snowflakes, each is utterly different from its companion. And so it is with people. Even identical twins, more nearly alike than any other persons, have different characteristics.

*Be Your Individual Self.* So, when you are considering how to improve your personality for business, the first and most important thing I urge on you is *be your individual self.* Surrounded as you are by mass education, reading, and entertainment—not to mention the school-day phobia of "everybody's doing it"—the tendency is to flatten out into a standardized pattern. Fight this for all you are worth. Dig deep into the self that is individually yours. Try to understand it better, and then undertake the needed improvements so that this "you" will be increasingly admirable from within and without. In my observation, there is everything to be said against acquiring personality by imitation and nothing to be said for it. At best, the imitation can be only skin deep. Even then, the mask acquired seldom goes with anything else the copy-cat possesses—voice, way of living, or occupation. The timid lad who tries to copy the backslapping salesman whom he so admires is not likely to be a success in the role. Yet if he would stick to his own type and individuality and bring out the best in them, he might well become outstanding in his own right.

But when I say, "Be yourself. Be individual," I do not mean to suggest that you be arty or Bohemian. There is a great difference between emphasizing a genuine individual personality and taking on artificial poses. Perhaps I should say, "Find yourself." For when you discover that best self which is fundamentally *you* and are satisfied increasingly to express it, calmly and quietly, you will have a personality that will be recognized as genuinely fine. Let me warn you, you have a life-work ahead of you. But in the doing, you will find life interesting and worth while.

## Don't Imitate Glamorous Personalities

Many books and articles on personality development recommend imitating someone you admire. Perhaps this explains the many imitators of current movie stars. There is nothing new in this tendency. I remember Hollywood during the days when Mary Pickford was affectionately known as "America's sweetheart." Both Los Angeles and Hollywood were filled with imitation Marys from all over the country. Some of them, with their corkscrew curls, managed to look almost like their pattern, but I never heard that it got them into the movies or anywhere else. I have known Olivia de Havilland and her sister Joan Fontaine since they were little girls. Neither of these girls has ever imitated anyone. Their opportunities for success came largely because they were distinctly individual. Daring to be more and more themselves is an ever-expanding creed with each of them.

When speaking before a group of salespeople in a Pittsburgh department store on "The Selling Personality," I was asked by the management to suggest several motion-picture stars as ideals for employees to imitate. But I refused on the ground that such spectacular personalities —even if they could be found and reproduced in quantity—would not necessarily be good salespeople. However, this request was exceptional. The truth is that business is not looking for glamorous movie personalities to perform the unglamorous duties of stenographers, mail clerks, or salespersons. Neither does business demand showy personalities in employees who meet the public at reception and information desks, or at service counters that in many offices divide the help from the customers or clients. Here is a story, told me by an interviewer in a state employment office in Connecticut, that illustrates how imitation can work against you when you are looking for a job. The time was June, and the waiting room was filled each morning with recent young graduates applying for office work. "I can't tell them apart," the interviewer said. "They are all dressed alike. They wear their hair the same way. And they all chew gum with identical gusto. I register them and do the best I can for them, but the truth is not one of them makes the slightest impression on me. The next morning I look out, and apparently the same girls are waiting again. But no! I ask their names and find that these are not yesterday's applicants, but more just like them."

These New England girls, like students all over the country, were either following the latest school fad in dress or imitating the most popular girl in their class. Whichever it was, each girl had lost her precious individuality. Although not permanently serious, since they would later snap out of it, the regimentation was temporarily serious. For if they had no individuality with which to interest an employment agency, it is certain they would make no better impression on an employer who interviewed them.

Earlier it was suggested that you choose as your ideal someone in your office whose appearance is conservative and correct. This is very different from imitating a flashy personality. You must learn to be selective. When starting in business, you may need guidance in conforming to the accepted standards of dress and conduct. If you are keenly alert, always on the lookout for ways to improve yourself, you will find many good ideas you can use. By the time you have adapted these ideas to fit your needs, they will have become your own.

## AN ATTRACTIVE BUSINESS PERSONALITY CAN BE YOURS

You can attain a desirable business personality partly by conscious effort. The suggestions offered in this chapter will give you a basis on which to begin. Also, you can gain through observing those about you. Watch how they adjust to the general standard, and profit by their triumphs and failures.

Good habits and attitudes help unconsciously. Much of your success in achieving a satisfactory business personality will come about unconsciously. As you work to establish the right attitudes and habits of businesslike conduct, your personality will develop, too. For when your attitudes and habits on the job are good, they result in very much the type of personality that business wants. You need not fear this personality will be an affectation, any more than curbing your temper or closing your ears to gossip will be.

As you grow with your job, you will find that your office personality becomes *you* from nine o'clock to five. Eventually, it will be as much a part of you as your office clothes and just as easy to get into at the proper time. Or you may come to enjoy having a dual personality and to like the business "you" so much that you will voluntarily seek to explore its possibilities further. But be assured that, whether or not the real you likes that other "you," the effort you make to train it in the way it should go will enrich the personality you think of as your true self. Then you'll be a well-integrated, socially adjusted pair.

Fortunately for us all, personality can be improved. Many junior colleges, commercial high schools, and private business schools now give courses in personal development to help students adjust themselves to business requirements. These courses sometimes stress character development and often do much to aid students in analyzing themselves. Also, such courses afford teachers an opportunity to suggest the changing of habits. Where an understanding teacher or counselor is available for private conferences, he can make suggestions or give constructive criticisms that may be the means of correcting attitudes and peculiarities that could prove fatal in business.

**You Do Most of the Work Yourself.** Before you can improve your personality, you must see what is wrong, and admit it to yourself. All the courses and counseling in the world are so much wasted effort unless you face up to your need for self-improvement and self-discipline. You must be willing to go to work on your personality faults. No one else can do this for you. Some of your shortcomings are certain to be bad habits and attitudes. Study these lists, and check the items that you should correct.

POOR HABITS

1. Biting fingernails
2. Humming or whistling while others are working or reading
3. Chewing gum
4. Picking nose
5. Not enough shampoos and showers
6. Dirty hands and nails
7. Oversleeping and being late to school or work
8. Too-late hours on week nights
9. Wearing soiled clothing
10. Not using deodorant

POOR ATTITUDES

1. Self-pity
2. Complaining
3. Criticizing family and friends
4. Losing your temper
5. Being rude
6. Carrying tales
7. Being self-centered
8. Considering all your actions perfect
9. Being disrespectful
10. Boasting and bragging

It has been said that the best way to get rid of a bad habit is to replace it with a good one. Good luck to you!

Before you become discouraged at the prospect of fighting a lone battle with your worst self, realize that reinforcements are close at hand. Your best friends, when they know of your efforts, will co-operate with you. Your parents, too, when they see that you are sincerely trying, will encourage and aid you. A well-known psychologist has said, "The development of personality depends on learning to do an increasing number of things for and with people." Tests have shown the truth of this statement. In a survey of 4,000 high school students, it was found that athletes almost always rated tops in personality, while students with the best scholastic standing might or might not rate high. The same tests showed that girls and boys who had spent two or more summers in camp usually got high scores, whereas one summer in camp failed to register. Such findings seem to prove the psychologist's point, that doing things for and with people tends to improve the individual's personality.

For many young people, community activities in camp, learning to play bridge, or joining a tennis club are much easier methods of self-improvement than plugging away at character traits. Some of both kinds of discipline are probably the ideal system. Gains made in either will help your business personality as well as with your after-hours self. In other words, personality must start with the inner person and grow outward.

## What the Employer Seeks in Personality

The average employer has done a good job of arriving at a sum total of this thing called personality. Observation of the adjustment that his employees make or fail to make has caused him to seek in his office force practically all the characteristics we have defined as desirable personality traits.

Suppose we check them off once more. *Appearance*—about which I have said so much—looms large as a personality factor in business. And everyone can improve his or her appearance. *Character* is watched for in interviews, and your character is judged by what you say and even more by whether or not it shines through your face and manner. For the employer knows that where there is visible character, there is likely to be honesty, industry, and loyalty. *Individuality* that is restrained by common sense is desired by the kind of employer for whom you would like to work. *Emotional stability* and *balance* are rated high by this employer, though he may not use these words. He will say he wants only those on his payroll who can get along with others. Whether you are a good mixer after hours does not concern him. But during business hours, he wishes you to have certain qualities that enable you to adjust to those above and below you, as well as to your equals. The employer may not know how to name the personality requirements for the jobs he lists with employment agencies, but he knows what he is looking for and is able to recognize these qualities when he talks with applicants.

## YOUR PERSONALITY FROM NINE TO FIVE

There seems to be a more generally accepted personality pattern for holding a job than for getting one. Here it is: *During business hours most employers want their employees to be dignified and formal, without sacrificing naturalness, and pleasantly impersonal and unobtrusive, without being negative. Also, they expect unfailing courtesy, alertness, and order.*

It may seem to you that there would be a total lack of individuality in a large group of employees if all of them achieved the ideal personality I have just outlined. I assure you this is not the case. That unique gift of individuality everyone possesses makes each person's interpretation of a business personality distinctly his own. Business does not want human rubber stamps, any more than it wants prima donnas or screen heroes.

*Personality Adjustments in Business.* But let's take a close-up of personality on the job. Here personality is on trial. Can the individual conform? He may have the personality requirements for getting a job and know how to do the work. But if he can't adjust himself to the conditions or the personalities he meets, he is headed for failure. Sometimes, an inventory of his personality will set him on the right track.

And sometimes, a quick rightabout-face is imperative. This is especially true of experienced workers who find that each new job demands some personality adjustment.

To illustrate: A man may have worked for a very formal type of organization where the personality requirements were such that he found he could adjust himself without much difficulty. Then a change of jobs puts him into a rough-and-ready firm that likes everyone to be hail fellow well met. Regardless of whether this standard is akin to his real self, he has to conform. If he is not able to do so, the whisper soon starts: "He won't last long. He doesn't fit in here."

Many young women ask me what to do when they find themselves in such a situation. They say their employers consider them too formal. I assure them that formality is the rule and they have met only the exception that proves it. All they can do, however, is to adjust themselves as best they can. Then, if the informality is too uncongenial, they can keep their eyes open for another job.

*Those Who Understand Themselves Conform Best.* How easily you accept the personality requirements of business may depend on the degree to which you have analyzed and understand yourself. Those poised individuals who have analyzed their personalities and found their places in the scheme of things usually make the necessary adaptation with little difficulty. Although acting the part that business requires of them may really be a form of acting, they are sufficiently well balanced to fit into the business machine without being crushed in the process.

*A Feeling of Inferiority.* But on every hand, we see employees who have trouble making the necessary personality adjustments. Often, everybody around them knows what is wrong, but they blunder blindly on. Let us consider a few undesirable personality traits. First, there is the old bugaboo, the feeling of inferiority. This may make its possessor too timid, shy, or fearful to function adequately in business.

Take Beatrice Bowen, an able assistant bookkeeper, as an example. Beatrice had such a poor opinion of herself that she quaked internally with timidity. She really suffered when her duties necessitated her working closely with other people in the office. Beatrice meant to meet everybody halfway and hold up her end, and she thought she was doing it. But no one could read her mind, and her standoffishness caused her to be thought un-co-operative. For a time, Beatrice's feeling of inferiority reacted against her and prevented her advancement. But like the heroines in the magazine advertisements, she overheard a remark that tipped her off to what was the matter. There was nothing wrong with Beatrice's intelligence, however. When she realized that she must do something to overcome the discomfort she felt with other people, she took a course in public speaking, followed by joining a club where she had to express herself now and then, and corrected the trouble. Now Beatrice is a well-adjusted girl with a most acceptable business personality.

But sometimes, a feeling of inferiority acts in just the opposite way. I have seen it produce strutters and boasters in business, especially in men of small stature who, because they were in positions of authority, could bully men they could not combat physically. In the lower salary brackets, this trait sometimes manifests itself as in the case of Muriel Johnstone. Muriel is a good-looking, neatly dressed office girl, who talks all the time. Her chatter is annoying to other workers. Frequent pleas to "pipe down" do no good. Muriel is not aware of it, but she talks to cover up a sense of inferiority. She is nervous and self-conscious when the room is quiet. Muriel hasn't learned to live with herself and her own thoughts, either at home or at work. She hasn't analyzed herself and found out her undesirable traits; therefore, she doesn't know how or what to change. In consequence, she has not inspired those over her to promote her into more responsible work. So Muriel remains an office girl.

*False Superiority Hinders Progress.* Another unfortunate personality trait is manifested by the person who thinks he is too good to associate with his office mates. Sometimes, this superior attitude is due to a difference in social position or to his having a better education than others of the staff or even of the management. Again, the fault may be found in the person who has held a better position and feels the present job a step down. Perhaps you recall that the conceited child in school usually had it taken out of him by other children. And the same is true of a superiority complex when it enters business. If for any reason you feel superior, get busy and overcome this trait, which will get you nowhere and may cause you much unhappiness. Certainly, it is ten times harder for a snob to advance than it is for a sincere, steady worker who mixes with kindliness and appreciation among his fellow workers.

*Bad Dispositions Are a Drawback.* Bad dispositions loom large among personality traits that often hold back able persons. The office worker who loses his temper is considered a liability in business. His office-hours personality is poor because he cannot be counted on to be agreeable and self-controlled. Since he cannot manage himself emotionally, those above him are not inclined to promote him, for they doubt his ability to handle others. Although an occasional brilliant hothead reaches a top position, the business woods are full of men and women who have blocked their own futures because they have antagonized everyone above, around, and below them. Business makes short work of those who indulge their tempers or their temperaments. If it does not dismiss them, it is likely to give them a life sentence at the rock pile of insignificant detail.

*Negative Personality Hampers Owner.* Sometimes, the personality defect is nothing so definite as a bad temper. Young people for whom the business world seems too dull are dead weight in an office. And alas, there are enough of them for employers to classify them as an undesirable type. The young woman who never smiles and has no interest in the beehive activities around her, even though she does her work well, is given a low personality rating. The young man who goes through the motions of his job in a shuffling, listless manner isn't worth a salary, even if his job is only running the envelope sealer. Such young people are completely negative—human zeros.

There is the story of Henrietta Holden. Even her "Good morning" was so grave, it amounted to a rebuke that descended on employer and fellow worker alike. She carried out orders with a fidelity that was priceless, but with a disinterest that was infuriating. The Christmas bonus that made the office delirious with joy put no sparkle in her eye or gladness in her voice. Her boss broke his arm and carried it in a sling for six weeks; his son carried the ball sixty yards to a touchdown; the water system burst and flooded the files; the wife of the youngest executive presented him with an heir; and the firm landed a million dollar contract. All these things required direct action from Henrietta, and her brain and hands were busy with their details, but she might have been an automaton for all the outward interest she manifested. When she was threatened with the loss of her job because she was so "wooden," Henrietta came to life with an astonished protest, begged for a second chance, and got it. Now her good deed for the day is showing interest in someone or something, in making her voice warm and cordial, in praising the efficiency of the new air-cooling system, in consoling the boss on his poor golf score or the greenest typist for the slowness of her first week's work. In other words, Henrietta is transforming herself into an interested and interesting human being.

*Positive Personality Wins.* As opposed to the negative personality, we find the positive personality, which often sweeps everything before it. For example, there was Eddie, an elevator boy in a department store. Eddie had a high school education and no particular training, but his agreeable, efficient manner of handling himself, his passengers, and the other employees brought him to the attention of the store executives. He conformed and fitted in, or he would not have been the subject of such favorable comment as this:

"That Eddie's quite a boy."

"Yes, he has a lot of personality. Everybody likes him."

"He's very sure of himself."

"But he's not cocky."

"Too bad to keep him on a dead-end job."

"Don't worry, Eddie can't be sidetracked. Besides, I hear there are plans for him."

"Is that so? I'm glad. He's a good kid."

The upshot of all this was that the superintendent who did the employing had a talk with Eddie about his future.

"You have the personality for selling," the superintendent said. "Would you like to try it?"

But Eddie, being a positive person had his own ideas. He wanted to go into office work. So, while he continued saying "Third floor" and "Going up" for seven or eight months longer, Eddie studied business subjects at night. As soon as he had mastered typing and gained some knowledge of bookkeeping, he was promoted into the store office as a general clerk. It was Eddie's likable, well-rounded personality that got him his chance. Although the war interrupted his progress, Eddie is now doing executive work in the accounting end of the business. Note that Eddie had a plan, stuck to it, and achieved his career goal.

## THE MISUSE OF PERSONALITY

The advantage of having or cultivating a genuinely good personality has been stressed throughout this chapter. But a storm warning must be posted. The business and the social world swarm with men and women who, though endowed by nature with wonderful personalities, misuse their birthright. There is a wide range between the coyly smiling stenographer who gets others to do her work and the smooth operator who, with the greatest ease, gets his phony checks cashed. But they are brothers and sisters under the skin.

*Don't Be Like These Foolish Young People.* Take the case of Carol Hilton, who looked the part of the perfect stenographer headed for a top secretarial job. From childhood, Carol was a "personality kid," with everyone, including her parents and her teachers, encouraging her to "use" her charming personality. She learned to believe early in life that the world was her oyster, ready to yield its pearl at her slightest demand. Carol had no difficulty getting a good start in business, because everyone was "so helpful." She was always the first girl sent out by an employment agency because she seemed to possess the ideal business personality. And Carol never let an agency down—she always got the job. Furthermore, she did it without taking any of those boring performance tests. When an interviewer asked about her skills, Carol would say convincingly, "Don't worry about my shorthand and typing. Mr. Edwards (mentioning her last employer) will tell you how good I am."

During the first few weeks on any job, Carol devoted herself to "getting in good" with everybody, from the office boy to the president of the firm. They all liked her, and some said, "We were lucky to get such a swell gal." The charm of her presence was so all-enveloping that the poor quality of her work went unnoticed. When it became apparent that she was behind in her work, Carol glibly alibied, "I'm so sorry. I just haven't had time since Mr. Smith got back from New York with all those new contracts." So by executive order other girls were assigned to help Carol catch up. Thus the "getting by" routine was successfully launched. From then on, everything went according to her plan, with much of her work done by others. It took her sudden illness and absence from the office to reveal what her "charming personality" had concealed. Her files were in a mess, her notebook showed that important letters were still not transcribed, telephone messages had died on the pad; and, according to the office grapevine, there was evidence that she was conspiring to take over the spot of private secretary to the Big Boss.

On her next visit to the employment agency, Carol turned on the charm and remarked, "Confidentially, they were a stuffy lot, and those women were cats. I was planning to leave, anyway, because I didn't like working in that end of town. Haven't you a position in a bank uptown? I'd love that."

If this book were about salesmen instead of office workers, many stories could be told of people who live by their personalities. They are to be found in various businesses; and, if you let them, they will be glad to sell you "the finest TV set money can buy, at this ridiculously low price. And no money down!" They also perform in shyster brokerage firms to sell you "this certified oil stock that won't cost you a fraction of its real value." Sometimes, you find them in used-car lots, ready to sell you "a good, clean car that has had only one owner." Or, if you prefer, his brother will sell you a set of books you'll never read. No matter how honest he looks and sounds, don't be taken in by this slick approach.

But back to the office scene, where you are certain to meet the counterpart of this character. He is a specialist at getting you and the others to pull his chestnuts out of the fire. Any morning at 9:05, you'll hear him on the phone saying, "Come on, Jeanie, be a good girl, and tell the boss I'm sick and can't make it today. You'd do that for an old pal now, wouldn't you, honey? Sure, you would. You're a good kid."

Another situation that often develops involves money—your money, to be precise. The employee who misuses his personality in this way thinks nothing of borrowing a "quick five or ten" from you or anyone else. But by the time this glib operator finishes telling you that touching story—or simply takes it for granted that you exist to accommodate him —you've been taken! If you doubt this, because this person seems such a "nice guy" or "swell gal," you'll think differently when you find out how long it takes to get your money back.

You may have little need of the advice on improving your personality given earlier in this chapter. Indeed, you may be one of those gifted persons born with a near-perfect personality. If so, you are to be congratulated—and forewarned. You will be tempted at times to use this gift selfishly in your own interests. Instead, recognize the true worth of your individuality, and employ it legitimately.

## A Working Definition of Personality

And now a word about that *whole* personality. There are many definitions of personality, several of which have been discussed here. One that I like is from a standard dictionary. "Personality: the sum of one's qualities of body, mind, and character that makes one human being different from another." John Dewey, the dean of American philosophers, is said to have defined personality as "the sum total of tendencies to respond." Consider this definition carefully. You will discover that those who respond to no stimuli are the negative personalities. They lack interests. Those who respond to undesirable stimuli become twisted in their values, and their lives are wasted and unproductive of good. The worst of these become criminals.

In contrast, think of the most interesting person you know. You will readily recognize in him a wide range of response. He responds to the stimulus of beauty everywhere—in nature, in art and literature, in friendship and family life. His horizon is broadened by the stimulus of travel, and his acute social consciousness causes him to respond to the best in everyone he meets. His interests are ever expanding because his "tendencies to respond" know no limit.

You can do no better than to adopt as your own this working rule for developing personality. Every small gain you make in widening your responses will enrich your life and extend your sphere of usefulness in business and elsewhere. You will attract others to you because you will have, in greater or less degree, that major gift of a fine personality—the ability to make those in your presence feel strong, capable, and refreshed.

## QUESTIONS

1. Other things being equal, why is personality often the deciding factor in employment interviews?
2. Why is it important that you begin taking an inventory of your personality assets before you leave school?
3. What do you think is meant by a "telephone personality"?
4. Is charm the same thing as personality?
5. Can personality take the place of real ability?
6. Why would personality be thought so important in selecting a secretary for a bank president? Would it be as important in choosing a clerical worker?
7. Do employers consider beauty an indispensable part of an attractive personality in women employees?
8. Is the prima donna or the movie hero type of personality what business is looking for?
9. Is there a set personality pattern for men in business? for women?
10. Do employers encourage employees in a display of individuality during business hours?
11. Can personality be changed overnight? Can someone else develop your personality for you by telling you what needs to be done?
12. When a person has acquired an acceptable business personality, can he go through his entire working life without making further adjustments?
13. Can a person improve his business personality by watching those about him? Will he learn as much from observing the failures as from the successes? If so, why? If not, why not?
14. When employers seek an attractive personality, is it good looks they want?
15. To have a "clean-cut" personality must a young man look like a "Fancy Dan"?
16. Is surface personality a reliable indication of real ability?
17. To develop your personality, is it advisable to imitate a favorite movie star?
18. Can a person who expresses complete indifference to everything have a good business personality?
19. Is a positive personality necessarily an aggressive one?

## TOPICS FOR DISCUSSION

1. Explain what you think is meant by a "pleasing" personality in women and a "clean-cut" personality in men.
2. Discuss what is meant by a personality that fits the job. Is the same type of personality needed in a receptionist as in a file clerk? In a salesman, as in an accountant?

Discuss the different personality qualifications of the four occupations just mentioned.

3. Business wants employees who can

   a. Get along with others
   b. Control their emotions
   c. Demonstrate such qualities as agreeableness, industriousness, leadership, resourcefulness, and a capacity for teamwork

   Discuss whether all these qualifications can be considered personality traits. Also, to what degree they can be cultivated.

4. Do you think the words "personality" and "individuality" can be used interchangeably?

5. Discuss personality from the point of view that it consists largely of

   a. Appearance
   b. Character traits
   c. Good habits
   d. Emotional stability and balance
   e. Ability to interest and influence others

6. To cultivate a desirable personality, should you

   a. Read self-help books?
   b. Think more of other people's wishes and comfort?
   c. Take a course in personal development?
   d. Work constantly at improving your character traits?
   e. Try to replace bad habits with good ones?
   f. Learn to be better dressed and groomed?

   If you think a combination of these procedures would be better than any one, state which combination you think would be most effective, and why.

7. Suppose you were timid and felt that you should overcome this stumbling block. How would you go about it?

   If your chief personality problem were a bad temper, how would you try to overcome it?

8. If self-analysis reveals that your personality is negative, what can you do to become a more positive person?

   If you have a feeling of inferiority or superiority, what can you do to get rid of this handicap?

9. A leading dramatic teacher has said that vitality and courage are among the most important ingredients of a fine personality. She adds that any aspirant for stage or screen success must have perseverance and energy far above the average.

   Do you think these qualities are needed to the same extent by business beginners? Discuss how vitality and courage would be helpful in getting a job and in making good on it. If these qualities are lacking, how can they be acquired?

10. Consider the definition of business personality as given on page 357. If all employees in an office are successful in expressing this personality pattern from nine to five, will they lose their individuality?

## PROJECTS

*Self-test of Personality Traits*

1. So that you may make a preliminary estimate of qualities certain to be important in your business life, here is a scale by which you can rate yourself. These are personality traits stressed by employers. If you have not yet been employed, you can base your self-judgment only on how you have rated in school and home life when these characteristics have been in evidence.

   Consider 5 as high and 3 as average. Grade yourself as fairly and honestly as you can.

| TRAITS | RANK IN RELATION TO OTHER ADULTS | | | | |
|---|---|---|---|---|---|
| | 5<br>80-100% | 4<br>60-80% | 3<br>40-60% | 2<br>20-40% | 1<br>0-20% |
| Am I—sincere<br>enthusiastic<br>interested<br>tactful<br>alert<br>cheerful<br>friendly<br>loyal<br>sympathetic<br>patient<br>honest<br>impersonal<br>pleasing | | | | | |
| Have I—initiative<br>a sense of humor<br>charity<br>understanding<br>an agreeable disposition | | | | | |

This type of analysis can be carried further by adding other qualities equally pertinent to success in office work.

2. Write a 500-word paper on the following topic: It is his goal in life that molds a man's personality.

3. Two men go into the same bank on the same day, applying for automobile loans. Both are granted loans. The first man is a smooth talker, who assures the bank official that he will have the loan paid off in half the time. The second borrower makes no such flowery promises, is businesslike in his approach, and makes all his later payments promptly on the date agreed on. The first individual defaults on his payments, and his car is repossessed.

   *a.* Explain to the class how the first man may have misused his personality.

   *b.* If you or your family have been taken in by one of the types of smooth talkers mentioned in the text, describe that experience briefly.

CHAPTER 16

# Successful Living

If you have made use of the suggestions given in the previous chapters, you are well forward in your approach to business. You have made a plan for your business life and plotted a course toward a job. You have also learned something about how to organize yourself on a job and how to plan a wardrobe for a job. And you have been given an idea of how to budget. There is one more important step to take—the organization of your personal life, apart from your business life. For no matter how well planned the steps toward your business objectives, if your personal affairs are without organization, you may fail to achieve successful living.

"Will I have to live my job twenty-four hours a day?" you ask. Certainly not. But what you do with the remaining sixteen has a direct bearing on the success of your eight working hours.

## OUTSIDE LIVING IS EMPLOYER'S CONCERN

You will remember that I told you in the chapter on interviewing that a prospective employer would ask you questions about your living and your interests outside the office. These questions are not an impertinence. By your answers, an employer often can judge whether you are a playboy or a young woman who lives only for dates; whether your health is sound or whether you will be absent frequently through illness. These last two conditions are especially important. Many business organizations now require that all incoming employees pass a physical examination. One Midwestern industrial organization asks on its application blank, "Do you object to taking a physical examination annually?" All office and factory employees of this company undergo a physical examination once a year. If they fail to pass it satisfactorily, they do not remain on the payroll, unless the condition found can be easily remedied.

368

Whatever preliminary checkup business makes regarding your health or your personal life is the result of costly experience. Business firms have had to endure indifferent, lazy, and un-co-operative employees for a long time. On the other hand, they have always recognized the worth of the dependable. Often, the difference between these two groups is only a matter of the way they live. Probably, there are many who might never have become classified in the first group if they had realized the need of organizing their outside lives.

*Eight Hours' Sleep for Workers.* Once you have entered business, if you mean to stay, you can't burn the candle at both ends. No one is physically able to keep late hours every night and be wide awake on the job at eight or nine the next morning. You may be able to stand it for a while, but sooner or later you will begin to show the strain. Nervousness, listlessness, yawns, and nods over your work will creep up on you. But more damaging still to your success are the errors that will crop up in your work because you are not alert. These are signs that you need more sleep.

Eight hours' sleep should be the minimum for everyone who works. A little fun during the week is good relaxation, but eleven o'clock should be the deadline for bedtime. If you confine your late dates to Friday and Saturday nights, you will feel so fit that getting up on workdays won't be hard at all.

The able men and women who do the hiring and firing in business realize better than anyone else what a good plan it is to save your health in your twenties because you'll need it in your thirties. A seasoned personnel director well knows that many of the causes for dismissal and failure to be promoted are the result of lack of self-organization. Carelessness, tardiness, and absence for causes other than illness are often due to insufficient sleep. Lack of ambition and lack of initiative can easily follow when you have no physical "pep" day after day. Actually, although some people become unfit for work because of actual illnesses, there are many who unfit themselves by unwise living.

*Marathon Dressers Often Lose Out.* And don't sleep in the morning until you have time only to throw on your clothes, gulp some coffee, and dash for the office. Your whole day will go better if you allow time to bathe, dress, breakfast, and make your transportation connections without hurry. Don't start the day wrong by arriving at the office breathless, flushed, and full of apologies.

Believe me, I am serious when I say that the marathon dressers who clock their speed aren't nearly so smart as they think. A Chicago department-store buyer told me how such a practice sometimes works out. "Promotions usually come unexpectedly," she said. "Somebody drops out of the department, and without warning I am asked to recommend a young woman to fill the position. Naturally, I suggest someone whose work merits the advance. Invariably I'm told, 'Send her up. We want to take a look at her.' Then, woe betide the woman if she got up too late that morning to dress her hair properly, or if she was out so late the night before that she neglected to put on a fresh blouse. Nothing I can say about her work will act as a smoke screen for her untidy appearance, and a better-groomed applicant gets the promotion." I have seen much the same thing happen in offices.

## THREE WELL-BALANCED MEALS A DAY

In self-organization for successful living, another simple rule of life is three well-balanced meals a day—meals, eaten at regular times. The young woman who lunches daily on a soda cannot keep up with her ambitions for herself or the demands of her job. The young man who stays in bed until he has only time for a cup of coffee has no fuel to keep him going until lunch, and his work inevitably suffers. That same boy would never dream of starting out in his car without making sure he had gas in the tank.

Doctors point out that, since we do our heaviest and best work in the morning hours, all of us need large satisfying breakfasts. Many office workers who once had the "fruit juice and coffee" habit, and who have added cereal and eggs in some form, wonder how they ever got through a day's work with such a poor start. Present-day medical knowledge of what it takes to keep the human machine in top running order is so widely publicized that there is little excuse for not being informed on what your food intake should be. The starches that so many of us love are flash-in-the-pan energy that burns up quickly. But the good old proteins—milk, cheese, fish, meat, and eggs—are the steady-burning flame. They stay with us and see us through. Of course, we also require the fruits and vegetables that provide the needed vitamins and minerals. Get them, plus starches and proteins, in proper proportions, and you have the well-balanced diet that makes for success and health both on and off the job. Though good, wholesome food may seem to be costly in the budget, there's no thrift in economizing in that item to buy clothes or records. I have known young people who, though they were late finding it out, were actually suffering from anemia or malnutrition, due to skimping on food. What good the television set or the almost-new car for which they have tied up their food money for months ahead, if they have no health with which to enjoy these possessions? And what about the doctor bills that usually result from such false economy?

*Unorganized Eating Habits.* To show you what unorganized eating habits can do to you and your future, let me tell you the story of David Grier, a fine lad who had no idea what trouble he was piling up for himself. On leaving college, David got a beginner's job with excellent prospects for advancement. Although he had had no specific training, his personality and general education inspired a good firm to start him in clerical work, headed for a junior executive job. David was living away from home, and after a few trials, he labeled boardinghouses as "too gossipy." So he moved to a delightful studio room overlooking a garden, where he could be alone. This upset his living budget, for the room cost nearly half of his monthly wage. However, he laughed off this extravagance by planning to cook his own meals.

David was six feet tall and required plenty of fuel. What he knew about cooking could be put in a thimble. But, with the daring of the uninitiated, he started out. The house where David had his studio possessed a community kitchen. It was the custom for the first tenant up in the morning to make coffee and toast for the rest of them. "Swell," thought David. "One meal to the good." And he didn't bother to add eggs or cereal to this meager start. His lunch was equally poor, since the only eating place near his work was a restaurant where the fare did not agree with him. At night, his chances for preparing proper food were still slim, because the married couples took over the community kitchen until nearly nine o'clock. So David's meals grew more and more inadequate and irregular.

But that was not all. David was a confirmed "stayer-upper." In the house with the garden, there were interesting people with whom David liked to talk. And talk they did, night after night, until one or two o'clock seemed normal bedtime.

David grew more and more dissatisfied with his job and disliked getting up early to go to work. He complained about his employer and his co-workers. Any doctor would have told him he was not thinking straight because he needed more sleep and better food. Nothing makes for discontent quite so much as an abused body. David finally told his employers he needed a rest and would have to go to the country. They tried to persuade him to remain and dangled a sound future before his eyes. But David had lost sight of his good fortune and opportunity in this business, and so he quit. His undernourished body and his over-stimulated mind had rebelled, and he was not far from the truth when he said he was worn out and ill.

It was several years before David got another job with so assured a future and an equal salary. However, by the time he went into the Army, David had become well organized and was on his way to success. His

Your leisure time is important, too, in developing
a well-rounded personality.

three years in the Army built up his health, taught him discipline, and
in many ways helped to correct any lurking effects of his early mistakes.
David now plans his living to help, not hinder, his business progress.

### YOU CAN'T DO WITHOUT EXERCISE

As part of your regime for successful living, you should not neglect
fresh air and exercise. Tennis, golf, swimming, and other sports over
the week end are a big help in keeping you physically and mentally fit.
Walking at least part of the way to and from work is another excellent
way to keep in form. Occasional week ends spent in active sports or
an annual vacation cooking in the sun are not enough. Find out what
forms of exercise suit you best and keep them up faithfully, if it is only
ten-minute setting-up exercises every morning before an open window.
But daily exercise in the fresh air is the thing that counts. For those
office jobs, where you sit all day, recreation of an outdoor active type
brings rewards. However, suppose you have a job where you are on
your feet all day, walking from place to place as in many department-

store jobs. Then, the chances are you'll want to pick something like sailing, that is, if you have a friend who owns a sailing craft. Bowling, archery, trapshooting, or rifle marksmanship will give you fresh air and be easy on your arches. Of course, the spectator sports are fun and often thrilling. You can make football, baseball, basketball, or all three a part of your recreational and social pattern.

Another factor of great importance to success is emotional stability. For life consists of much more than physical habits, however good they may be. Emotional stability is closely associated with a well-balanced life. This means good living habits, with work and fun in proper proportion. Another place to use your ability to plan!

## WHAT DO YOU OWE THE JOB?

If you are a young woman who keeps house for yourself, your husband, or your dependents, be sure that you do not allow your domestic program to limit your strength for your office hours. I once had a secretary who started her housekeeping day at five-thirty each morning. Monday, she cleaned. Tuesday, she washed. Wednesday, she ironed. Thursday, she cleaned again. Friday, she cooked in anticipation of her regular custom of having Friday-night dinner guests. Saturday, she got her home ready for the week end. Each morning, she had done half a day's work before she began her office work, and by noon she was exhausted.

Often, my homemaking secretary came to the office dressed for a social evening, rather than in business clothes, so that she would be ready at night to put a company dinner on the table. At noon, she shopped for the parties she gave and often neglected her own lunch. Eventually, her home life absorbed her time and attention to such an extent that I had to ask her to leave. It is this type of employee that makes one ask, "Doesn't she realize she owes *something* to the job?" Earlier, we spoke of those beginners who think that all they owe to their jobs is their presence for so many hours, five days a week. But the employer has a right to expect his employees to concentrate on their work while they are doing it—not to be thinking constantly of their after-hours interests and counting the minutes until closing time. He has a right to expect them to have healthy bodies and clear, well-organized minds, so that they will be efficient in their work. The Greeks had a word for it—"a sound mind in a sound body." Beyond these two things, the employer is justified in asking that his employees do their best to earn their salaries. A surprisingly large number of people never consider that simple fact. They seem to think that the world owes them a living and is paying it to them through an employer.

## What Do You Want Out of Life?

What do you want out of life? Perhaps I hear you answer: "Enough money to get along. To do a little traveling, maybe. Or to go on to college. Enough to buy a home—later on. It doesn't have to be a million." From that reply, it would seem that you count success in terms of money—you think that by making enough money you can buy the things you want out of life. That's a generally accepted belief. The American conception of *success* is often based on how prosperous you appear, what model and make of car you drive, how expensive a house you own, and how important a position you hold in the business world. True, those things are evidence of a certain kind of success. Hoodlums and gangsters can qualify as successful, if all that matters is the outward sign—getting and spending money. By bringing to your work the best you have to give, you should be able to earn enough to satisfy your normal wants. You may have greater gifts—and greater luck—so that you will acquire more than you need of this world's goods.

My question goes deeper than the getting and spending of money. For somewhere along the main line of life's railroad, you will run into problems that cannot be solved by money. If you have developed that inner, finer you—the person who *really lives*—you will have something that mere money can never give you. To many people, money is a means of idleness. When they have made enough money to fulfill their ambition of not working, they vegetate, grow fat, and die, shortly. Others, especially those who "come into money" while they are young, find a quick way to kill themselves in idle dissipation. Money hasn't been, for them, the means of successful living. Pardon me, if I seem to have taken to the soapbox when, instead of lecturing, I really want to urge you to begin thinking about *what kind of person you want to be.*

## Will Life and the Job Bore You?

It may seem to you, as you look forward to your working life, that a good job and a steady income with some chance for advancement will fulfill your fondest dreams. But many of you, after the novelty of working has worn off, will wonder at the lost glitter of those dreams. Inevitably comes a time when most of us ask ourselves, "What's it all about?" After four or five years of routine, we get fed up. "What am I getting out of life? All I do is work, go home, go to bed, get up, and go to work again. A little fun now and then, but nothing exciting. What's the answer?"

The answer lies within yourself. How much you get out of life depends on you. Boredom comes from within. And no one need ever be bored for five minutes! If you want life to turn cartwheels for you, you must widen your stage by enriching your experience. And you can do it, regardless of where you may be in your personal development. Your reward will come to you in countless ways. For one thing, living a richer life outside your work often makes you more promotable in your work. Or an awakened outlook through study and expanded interests may lead you to see more clearly your capabilities as a worker. If this clearer vision shows you that another employer could make better use of your ability than your present one, you will have the courage to tackle selling your services elsewhere. Once out of your mental rut, you will go on preparing for a still better job or even an entirely different job whose possibilities you had never imagined until now.

*Educate Yourself.* I constantly meet people who feel inferior because of the lack of a college education. Business-school students frequently ask me, "Isn't it true that the best office jobs go to those who have college degrees?" No, it is not true. In very few businesses do the office employees need more general education than they can get in a four-year academic high school course. The broad general background that a college education should supply is not needed by the rank-and-file office worker. It is more of a personal than a business asset, except in those businesses or professions where the actual work is on the collegiate level, as in law, education, medicine, and various technical lines.

But if you wanted to go to college and couldn't, there is still no reason why you cannot obtain a college education or its equivalent. Get busy now, and work for a degree through evening classes or correspondence courses in university extension. Today, anyone can have a college education who is willing to pay the price in time, effort, and the sacrifice of other interests.

However, if college holds little or no interest for you, don't feel guilty. What you want may be smaller doses of broadening culture, which you can certainly get without the six-year night-class grind. Adult-education courses cover everything from arts and crafts (painting, leatherwork, pottery, and woodworking) to commercial subjects that may aid you on your job. Or university extension courses will give you many subjects you will enjoy, such as drama, languages, writing, psychology—with many of the courses good for university credit, if you wish.

*Art and Music.* But why limit your self-education to evening classes? Try making some week-end visits to museums and art galleries for pleasure and inspiration. If you are a week-end painter or an amateur photographer, such jaunts to the galleries are a "must." Perhaps music appeals to you more. Remember that no one is born with cultivated tastes. Such things must be acquired. If your musical ear is at present attuned only to cowboy music, you can look forward to progressing through semiclassical music and on to symphonies and operas. Perhaps, such a highly trained ear will never be yours, but you can start by trying your ear on a little classical music, now and then, to get the feel of it. However, if "long hair" music has no appeal, leave it for now, promising yourself you'll try a concert sometime in the future. You might enjoy it more at a later time.

*Reading Good Literature.* While art and music are subjects that you will seek out in your program of self-education, another great interest lies even closer at hand. All you have to do is open a book. The whole world of history, science—and above all, literature—lies before you. Through the public library or your own purchase of books, embark on this adventure. If you have that priceless gift—intellectual curiosity—your education will be a continuing process. You will be delving into new subjects all your life. Everything you see and hear will challenge you to learn about it through reading or observation. Nothing can prevent you from being educated in the best sense.

However, if you are among those who have not yet discovered the joy in books, and if reading seems a dull way to spend time, I suggest that you begin with fiction. Start by reading some of the current best sellers that are reviewed in your newspaper or in the magazines. Or ask a librarian to suggest the titles of some of the good novels that have been out for several years and are still being read. The good ones last, and the reading of books that survive their best-seller popularity is more worth while. One book will lead to another, and you will discover authors that you like so much you want to read their earlier works. If you have not read the great classics, dip back into some of them, and in addition to spellbinding stories, you will learn about life in a different day and a different world. Forget that you started out to educate yourself, or to fill in the gaps in your education. Here is pure enjoyment. You have discovered a source of happiness that could not be bought, and that nothing can take from you.

*Travel Is Educational.* Travel, too, is educational—and it is also a lot of fun. Many working people set aside a certain sum each month—budget it, if you like—for a trip to some faraway place. In the meantime, they read up on the trip itself, the country they are to visit, the art objects and the historical sites they are to see. So they get a double pleasure from saving. But interesting as foreign travel is, you don't have to wait until you can spend considerable time and money on a long trip. Get out and see your own country. It is a great experience to drive or

Travel is educational—and fun. Thousands of
office workers make annual "excursions" to all
parts of the country.

go by train across these wonderful United States. Seeing and talking with
people in other states and sections of our country is an experience you'll
never forget. When the names of states and cities seen or heard in the
news bring pictures of them to your mind—real, not imaginary pictures
—you will be a broader-minded, better-informed person. And a more
interesting one, too.

One young woman I know, Marge Murdock, the first year she
worked, fulfilled her dream to travel beyond the borders of her native
state. Through much self-sacrifice, she saved $200 from her small salary
and was able to spend her first two-week vacation exploring two
nearby states. It was well she did, for Marge married the next year,
and her growing family has tied her to the home acre ever since. But
I am sure that when the children are old enough to be taken on trips,
and her husband can be persuaded, Marge will continue her traveling.
There's something about that "travel bug"—once you're infected with
it—there seems to be no cure but more of the same.

Often, the disease breaks out mildly in the form of armchair travel. You read a book about Mexico, let us say. And you can't be satisfied until you see that fascinating country that lies so close at hand. Somehow you manage to accumulate enough money for the trip, and you spend a wonderful vacation getting there by ship and possibly home by plane. After that, every vacation means a trip somewhere—and don't say it can't be done. The PBX operator in an office where I once worked was determined to see the world. Elizabeth was a thrifty soul, and it took her only a few years to save enough to take a European trip, *modestly*, if one may use the word in connection with anything so wonderful as going to Europe. Elizabeth went "off season," and so took advantage of lower transportation and hotel rates. When she reached England, a travel bureau put her in touch with three other persons—a dentist and his wife and a beauty operator—who were going to the same places, and they made up a party. The dentist rented a car, and they shared a motor trip through the Alps to Italy. Doesn't that make you long to do what these adventurous working people did? You can, you know. It means making a travel plan, much as you made a career plan earlier. Then, it means stiffening your backbone to resist the temptation to spend your money on trifles that will get you nowhere. You intend to spend your money going somewhere!

A word of caution about travel. Don't undertake it to get away from an unpleasant situation that you haven't been able to lick. Travel is an expensive way to find out that you can't run away from anything, including yourself. You'll find the unsolved problems tumbling out of your suitcase the moment you begin to unpack. They went right along with you!

### Cultivate "Awareness"

Let me introduce you to a word you have not met, so far, in this book. Back of everything said here about self-education, self-organization, and self-improvement lies the word "awareness." To become aware of everything about you is like listening through your eyes and your mind. You see beauty in the simplest things in nature—a field of wild flowers, or a tiny violet peeping up in the garden. You look out on the world around you as if you were seeing it for the first time, as indeed you are. Unless you can see the people and the scenes close at hand, with an understanding mind and heart, you won't see below the surface when you travel, and so you will miss the best part of your visit to other states and countries.

Perhaps, the way to illustrate what I mean by "awareness" is to tell you that men who have been at war learned it there. For them, each minute, each hour, each day had to be lived to the fullest, because there might not be another day. What they actually saw may have been dreary enough, but they appreciated being able to see and be a part of their surroundings. And the almost blood-brother friendships that developed among "buddies" were in part due to their sharing and understanding each other's awareness. You are more fortunate because you are not under the threat of death in battle while finding this "awareness." Try looking out on the world some morning with a new approach, listening, seeing, and above all *feeling*, and you may discover awareness for yourself. Once you have found it, never let it go.

## How Is Your Hobby Horsepower?

A hobby may be what you need to give your life that extra something. Maybe several hobbies, who knows. It is fashionable now, and sensible, too, to have a hobby. So, if you haven't one already, you might begin to look them over. They may be classified as (1) doing things, (2) making things, (3) acquiring things, and (4) learning things. Previously, we mentioned music and art as fields of interest you might like to explore. Either of them, cultivated as hobbies, would start under number four—"learning things." But before long, you'd find yourself working at them under number one—"doing things." Two of the greatest exponents of week-end painting are Winston Churchill and Dwight D. Eisenhower. These two busy men, burdened with far more than their own personal problems, have found relaxation through this hobby. And their pictures are good, too, though neither ever studied painting.

If you are in quest of a hobby, you may find suggestions in the newspapers, since hobbies have become news. Finding your particular hobby can be as much fun as the hobby itself. And remember hobbies *are* for fun, for recreation. If they are not, they may become just another kind of work, and then the whole benefit and idea are lost.

I have recommended hobbies because they fill spare time, provide intellectual and emotional outlets, and make you a better employee. But the right kind of hobby does a great deal more. It makes a specialist of you. And any specialist who really knows his stuff is a worth-while person—someone in whom people are interested. If your hobby is a game or sport that you engage in with others, it will make you a better mixer and extend your social life. And if you go in for an adventurous hobby like birdbanding, in the pursuit of which you climb lofty cliffs and trees, and perhaps attach metal bands to the legs of eaglets, you will be written up in the magazines.

*Hobbies Sometimes Shape Vocations.* Some hobbies lead not only into fascinating bypaths, but often develop into lucrative vocations.

One business girl I know made a hobby of heraldry. This led her to full-time work, looking up the family trees of the pedigree-minded. Soon she was making water-color sketches of each client's coat of arms to go with his neatly typed genealogy. Eventually, her heraldic work grew to such proportions that it paid her better than her stenographic job, and almost without trying, she had an established, interesting business of her own.

I am told that the largest manufacturer of playground equipment in the United States was a broker when he began making slides and sand-boxes for his two small sons. He constructed them so cleverly, with a minimum number of sharp corners to get bumped on, that soon his friends begged him to make slides for their children. And so to Big Business!

A hobby of mine that took a vocational turn was business etiquette. It grew and aroused so much interest that I gave up a good executive job in an advertising agency and set out traveling 100,000 miles, talking to present and future business girls about manners, dress, and conduct in a business office. Even as you read, you are getting a further development of what began as the small hobby of collecting facts about a variety of tragic, funny, serious, or frivolous business situations and how to handle them. My hobby led to the writing of my first book, *Manners in Business*, which became a best seller when written up in *Time Magazine*. And it compelled me to write this textbook, to tell you how to fit yourself for business. You never can tell where your hobbyhorse will take you.

***Don't Let Your Hobbyhorse Ride You.*** One thing to guard against, where hobbies are concerned, is letting your hobby dominate your life or your conversation. Some people get so enthusiastic about their hobbies that they talk of nothing else. Stamp collecting may be all-absorbing to you, but it can be very boring if you talk about it incessantly to friends whose only interest in stamps is to put them on letters. The amateur photographer has, for him, a wonderful hobby that takes him out of doors—and may keep him broke. But after the guests at a party have looked at his color slides with interest, they don't relish spending the rest of the evening hearing him expound on the technicalities of projection. I believe this is called "inflating one's ego at the other fellow's expense." But whatever you call it, there is no better way to lose friends than to let your hobbyhorse run wild.

And the same overinterest in a hobby can wreck a person's job. An executive in a railway company told me about one of his men secretaries whose hobby was playing in a band. Harry's mind seemed to be more taken up with his saxophone than with his work. And all day long the telephone rang, calling him on matters connected with that band. Finally, Harry's boss said, "It's your job or the band—make your choice." Harry trimmed down on the band, which after all wasn't feeding him.

## MAKING AND KEEPING FRIENDS

You may or may not need a hobby, but there's no question that you—like everyone else—need friends. There's a saying, "The only way to have a friend is to be one." So, while you're looking yourself over with a view to reorganizing some departments of your life, take a look at your mental file of friends. Is it a fat file, bulging with names, and brought up to date? Or is it a thin file, and perhaps not even a current file? Do you take time to keep up with your old friends? Do you call them up and suggest doing something or going some place together? Or do you wait for them to make the first move? If you wait and they make no move, are you hurt because you are left out? How long since you've made a new friend? If you haven't made any new friends lately, is it your fault? Do you really want friends? They take time, and thought—which you might prefer to spend on yourself. You can't be self-centered and expect other people to care about you.

By "making friends," I don't mean getting chummy with everyone you meet. Friends should be collected, much as you might collect valuable items connected with a hobby. Real friendship is based on having common interests—places you and your friend like to go to together, things you like to do together or talk about when you are with each other. When you have friends of that sort, you may not see them for months, or years. But when you meet again, you take up the friendship from where you left off, just as if you had not been separated. Money or possessions don't enter into this kind of friendship. One of you may have more than the other, but the one with the least never feels it, for he knows that the warmth of his friendship makes up for his not being able always to keep even with his friend in, say, occasional treats. Close friends are always careful not to become involved financially, for they know the truth of the saying, "It's a rare friendship that can survive a short-range money transaction."

However, there are other problems connected with friendship, one of which is how to meet other persons whose interests and tastes are similar to your own. "What are you going to do when you are working in a strange city and have no chance to meet people outside of business?" a young woman asked me not long ago. The answer is to join a club. The Y.M.C.A., the Y.W.C.A., and young peoples' church organizations welcome newcomers and have brought congenial friends to many. In most large cities, there are girls' clubs where business girls can live happily and inexpensively, where normal good times with other young women are the rule, and parties to which young men are invited are the high lights. Young men away from home often find living at the Y.M.C.A. a means of making friends. There, too, they can swim daily and enjoy other recreations. In many communities, there are organizations, such as hiking clubs, to which anyone will be admitted who can present the necessary character credentials.

Then, too, there are groups based solely on the interest of those who belong—such as amateur theatricals, puppet productions, and glee clubs. If you don't know how to make a contact with such a group, watch the newspapers, and when you learn where and when the group meets, go to one of their meetings, and introduce yourself. Many times they are looking for a girl who can act the part of "maid" in the next play, or for a lad with a good bass voice. Also, the adult-education or university-extension classes mentioned earlier can bring you in touch with young people who like the same things, and you may find yourself dropping into a drugstore afterward to join with others in a gab-fest about the evening's lecture.

*Be a Friend to Yourself.* There's one person closer to you than a brother—yourself. No matter what interests you have, nor how many friends, in the last analysis it is yourself you have to live with. You'll understand yourself better, and get along better with yourself, if you learn to enjoy being alone. I think it was the poet Wordsworth who said, "The world is too much with us." And he lived before radio and television had invaded our homes, making privacy hard to get. Not only do those voices coming through the air bring entertainment, but they bring national and world problems to our minds. Much of this is part of that important thing, "keeping posted," but you have to be strong-minded enough to tune out now and then, and find a moment of quiet in which to get acquainted with your inner self. Surrounded all day with people who work where you do, and living with your family, it may be that the subway or bus ride to and from work will be your only safety valve. If so, practice being alone in a crowd. Don't always sit and talk with an acquaintance. You and your friend-who-is-yourself need to be alone once in a while.

## You and the English Language

You were told early in this book that, if you work in the correspondence side of business, the English language is the backbone of your success. Now I want to tell you how much it can mean in your social life. When you set out to improve yourself through reading, or traveling, your constant companion will be the language you read and speak. Test out your *awareness to words*. Listen to the words you and others use when speaking. How pleasing is your speech? When you open your mouth and begin to speak, you tell an observing, or shall I say a listening, person everything about yourself. Your choice of words, your diction, the smooth or the rasping quality of your voice, all speak loudly for or against you as a person. You may have an accent that tells in your first spoken sentence what part of the country you come from. While your accent may be charming, instead of something to get rid of, you probably have other mannerisms of speech that won't charm anyone. A high-pitched voice, for instance. Or one so low that you can't be heard. Listen to yourself. Or have a record made of your speech. You may not like what you hear.

If you belong to a club, there will be times when you will want to make a motion or speak for or against something the members are voting on. Can you stand up and say what you want to say, clearly and to the point? Or do you start every sentence with "Well—"? If you don't, you are 100 per cent better than most amateurs. On the radio quiz programs, as in any gathering, the average speaker, "the man on the street," can't start off with anything but "W-e-l-l-." And when he gets going a bit further, that "uh" keeps—uh—interrupting, as he—uh—gropes for words. Dropping the "well's" and the "uh's," and learning to speak well, extemporaneously, will increase your self-confidence and open up new social and business contacts for you. My recommendation is *not* one of these guaranteed-to-win-friends-and-influence-people courses, but a plain, everyday public-speaking class, such as those offered through the school department in any city or town. Studying public speaking will improve your reading, also. It makes you more conscious of words and sentences, their construction and meaning. You may become so interested in self-expression through speaking that you will tackle expressing yourself through writing. Then you will have not a hobby but a lifelong study. Success to you.

## THE RESPONSIBILITY OF CITIZENSHIP

Every Christmas for years, the newspapers, and now radio and television, repeat the classic reply that an editor once wrote to a little girl named Virginia, when she asked him if there was a Santa Claus. On a recent Christmas broadcast, a girl named Marcia received a reply to a letter in which she asked questions more difficult to answer. "What do you think the United States will be in 1962? What is your opinion of world affairs today?" Marcia wrote to Benjamin F. Fairless, Chairman of the Board of the United States Steel Corporation, because her father works for that company and she wanted to use Mr. Fairless's reply in her civics class. Here is a portion of it:

I think the best advice I can offer you is to say that you must believe in America and its future and work hard to further its progress. You must never doubt for a moment that we have a great country which has count-less opportunities for young people like yourself. I would prefer not to discuss world affairs except to say that it may seem to you that the world is filled with uncertainties and difficult problems. Well, you are correct. It is. But remember, every generation has its serious problems, and your generation is no exception.

Today, we in America are the hope of the free world, and you and your classmates—along with the thousands of other students across the nation—are the hope of this country. Now to live up to this responsibility you should take part in your school and community activities and show an active interest in your local and national governments. By doing this, you will add real meaning to your belief and faith in our country.

No young American's life can be well rounded until he or she begins to take the responsibilities of citizenship into account. Remember, the good American way of life is the result of the individual thought and action of the millions of men and women who have cast their votes since our country became the United States. The America of tomorrow depends on what you do about it today. It may even be that the world of tomorrow depends on how young America thinks and acts.

Young America won the fighting part of a costly war. It has since proved its gallantry in an even harder war—harder because, for many reasons, the war it fought along with the United Nations in Korea could not be brought to victory on the battlefield. Out of this tried-and-true young America must come the leaders who will guide the nation into the second half of a century unsurpassed for importance in all history. An enduring peace can be achieved only through wise and strong leadership and an intelligent, informed citizenry.

"What can I do?" you ask. Much. You can register to vote as soon as you are twenty-one. You can take an intelligent interest in municipal, state, and national elections and express your convictions through your vote. You can keep informed on both domestic and international issues, many of which are closely bound up with the problems of peace. A position of world leadership has been imposed on the United States, not only through our military might, but through our industrial strength, unsurpassed wealth, and democratic ideals. This means that each of us is now not only an American citizen but a citizen of the world. As such, we must strive to know and understand other peoples. Within our own borders, we must actively discourage discrimination

National Association of Manufacturers

Your career lies before you. Which route will
you take?

against any person or group because of race, color, or creed. As President Eisenhower so aptly stated:

The supreme belief of our society is in the dignity and freedom of the individual. To the respect of that dignity, to the defense of that freedom, all effort is pledged. . . . This sovereign faith of ours . . . is infinitely more than a dry and lifeless philosophic doctrine. It is the nerve and the fiber of our very laws . . . the very source of the greatness and the genius of America.

## BEGIN NOW TO FORM YOUR PHILOSOPHY OF LIFE

In addition to all your interests, you may feel strongly the need for a philosophy of life. It may seem to you that you are not living fully until you have opened up your spiritual windows. If you deplore the inattention to spiritual qualities that is prevalent in this age, by all means do something about it. Do not rest until you find something outside yourself to which you can turn.

Different individuals find the answer to this deep need in varying ways. Some find it in religion. Others turn to an ideal of truth. Still others find help in contemplating the order and the beauty of the universe. Many stumble along until middle age before they find the answer that satisfies them.

As a starter to guide you, perhaps there is no better philosophy than that which follows the Golden Rule. This means kindliness, generosity, and forbearance, remembering always that each individual has a right to his own way of life and his own point of view. Whatever philosophy you evolve for yourself as you experience life, you will never have to discard kindliness and tolerance as a fixed principle of conduct. The organized brutality of war, which ridiculed these simple, homely virtues, was unable to dim them. More than ever we know that character *is* worth working for. To become a well-organized, stable person is the great responsibility life places on each of us. Our happiness depends on this self-organization, and so does our *real* success.

## QUESTIONS

1. Are employers concerned about how their employees spend their time after leaving work? If so, why?
2. Why do many firms now insist that all incoming employees take a physical examination?
3. Why is it not advisable to be a last-minute riser in the morning?
4. Do you think that a married woman who works in an office is justified in putting her home duties first? If not, why not?
5. Why is daily exercise in the open air especially recommended for office workers?
6. Will a few summer week ends at the beach or occasional participation in winter sports put you in physical shape for the whole year?
7. Should hobbies be closely related to one's work?
8. Do you consider weaving or modeling in clay the best types of hobby for office workers? If not, suggest some other hobbies you think would be better.
9. Why does a hobby make you a more interesting person?
10. If you can't afford to travel, should you consider the reading of travel books a waste of time?
11. How can young working people away from home make friends? Do they need friends, or should a good job be enough?
12. What are the most usual methods of outside study among young business people?
13. Is it possible for a person who works eight hours a day to get a college education? What does such a program call for besides time and study?

14. Why is it important that every young American should take his responsibilities of citizenship seriously? Why should he register and vote?
15. If your boss told you how he wanted you to vote, would you feel that you had to follow his instructions? If not, why not?
16. Should religion be discussed around the office? If not, why not?
17. Do you think that successful living off the job will help to make for success on the job?

## TOPICS FOR DISCUSSION

1. A personnel director spoke for many employers when she said, "What business wants is the right person living at his (or her) best at all times." Do you think this is asking too much of employees?
2. Explain what has caused employers to become so particular about the health and living habits of their employees.
3. When an employee organizes his outside life so as to live more fully, who gains most from this organization—the individual or the employer?
4. Discuss what relationship eight hours of sleep and three well-balanced meals a day bear to one's success on the job.

   In developing this idea, take into consideration those employees who burn the candle at both ends and eat with little regard for their bodily requirements.
5. Name several hobbies in which you are interested. Discuss whether any of them would fit into your life if you were a bookkeeper. Also, if you were a receptionist, meeting people all day.
6. Discuss why it is important that hobbies be play.
7. Discuss what a well-chosen hobby might have done for David Grier. Do you think that joining a club and meeting young people his own age might have brought about a better organization of David's outside life and fitted him to hold his job?
8. Do you agree with the statement, "When one goes too far in recreation it becomes dissipation"?
9. Discuss the statement in this chapter, "The America of tomorrow depends on what you do about it today." Can young people neglect their duties as citizens and expect to have a democracy that will work? Can they safely leave to politicians the responsibility of safeguarding their rights as citizens? Why is it imperative that young people take an active interest in political and economic problems?

## PROJECTS

1. Assume that you have a stenographic position at which you work five days a week. Your office hours are from eight to five. It takes you half an hour to reach your office. You live at home and have a pleasant circle of friends. Your salary is $70 a week.

Work out a time schedule for the hours you spend away from the office. State what time you will get up, what time you will go to bed, at what hours you will eat. Allow time for exercise, hobbies, fun with friends, and some educational pursuits. This schedule should show how you will spend your Saturdays and Sundays as well as your evenings.

2. Plan a talk for class on the advantage of having not just one hobbyhorse but a whole stable full. Cover the question of whether one's hobbies should be related, or whether contrasting ones should be chosen for greater variety. Mention some hobbies that could easily grow out of others.

3. Although that may not be their original purpose, some hobbies have vocational possibilities. List five interests that could grow into full-time jobs. Have you a leisure-time pursuit that might someday develop into an occupation? If so, trace the necessary stages of study, working at your hobby, and perfecting your skill before you could expect to earn a living at it.

4. Through travel, Helen Whitlock has made herself an interesting and stimulating person. Although Helen has only a two-week vacation each year, she plans trips that can be made within that time. Right now, Helen is reading up on Yucatan and saving her money to go there. She owns many books on the relics of the Mayan civilization and can speak interestingly of the excavations at Chichen Itzá. Even if Helen never makes this trip, the preparation for it has broadened her.

Select a place you would like to visit. Find out what the trip would cost and how long it would take. List the available books that would give you the needed information to get the most out of the trip. Be prepared to talk about this proposed trip to the class.

5. Get from the public library a list of good modern fiction, including several historical novels. These books should be chosen to interest members of the class who read a number of books each year, and to attract those who may not yet have found joy in reading. Make a selection from this list. Read the book, and prepare a brief review for class. Bring a copy of the list to class, also.

6. In this chapter, the statement is made that knowing the English language and using it easily and well will help you socially. This is not expanded in the text. Think this through, and write a brief paper explaining how this ability to express yourself in words would make your conversation more interesting

a. At a dinner party
b. When talking with older people
c. In table talk in your own home

7. By discussing the subject of the novel you have just finished reading, explain how you would combine your reading and your ability to express yourself.

# Bibliography

## Job Getting and Job Success

Backer, Esther R., and Richard L. Lawrence. *Success and Satisfaction in Your Office Job.* New York, Harper & Brothers, 1954.

Battista, O. A. *Commonscience in Everyday Life.* Milwaukee, The Bruce Publishing Company, 1960.

Bell, Mary, and Rae Abrams. *Business Behavior.* Cincinnati, South-Western Publishing Co., 1956.

Bliven, Bruce, Jr. *The Wonderful Writing Machine.* New York, Random House, 1954.

Burke, Marylin C. *The Executive Secretary.* New York, Doubleday & Company, Inc., 1959.

Burt, Jesse C. *Your Vocational Adventure.* Nashville, Abingdon Press, 1959.

Coggswell, Harry. *Find A Career in Advertising.* New York, G. P. Putnam's Sons, 1960.

Cromwell, Floyd. *Success in the World of Work,* Third Edition. Bloomington, Illinois, McKnight & McKnight Publishing Co., 1955.

Delano, Margaret. *How to be a Top Secretary.* New York, Tupper and Love, Inc., 1954.

Ferrari, Erma Paul. *Careers for You.* Nashville, Abingdon Press, 1954.

Forsee, Aylesa. *American Women Who Scored Firsts.* Philadelphia, Macrae Smith Co., 1958.

Forsee, Aylesa. *Women Who Reached for Tomorrow.* Philadelphia, Macrae Smith Co., 1960.

Galus, Henry S. *Charting Your Course.* Philadelphia, Macrae Smith Co., 1957.

Gemmill, Henry, and Bernard Kilgore. *Do You Belong in Journalism?* New York, Appleton-Century-Crofts, Inc., (Whiteside), 1959.

Gerth, Josephine H. *Highways to Jobs for Women.* New York, William Morrow & Co., Inc., 1948.

Hatch, Raymond N. *You and Your Future.* Bloomington, Illinois, McKnight & McKnight Publishing Co., 1955.

Hatch, Raymond N. *Exploring Occupations*, Third Edition. Bloomington, Illinois, McKnight & McKnight Publishing Co., 1955.

Hill, Napoleon, and W. Clement Stone. *Success Through a Positive Mental Attitude*. Chicago, Combined Registry Company, 1959.

Kitson, Harry Dexter. *I Find My Vocation*, Fourth Edition. New York, McGraw-Hill Book Company, Inc., 1954.

Larison, R. H. *How to Get and Hold the Job You Want*. New York, Lomhman's Green, 1950.

Master, Robert V. *How They Got Their Start*. New York, Sterling Publishing Company, 1958.

Maule, Frances. *Executive Careers for Women*. New York, Harper & Brothers, 1957.

Myers, George E., Gladys M. Little, and Sarah A. Robinson. *Planning Your Future*, Fourth Edition. New York, McGraw-Hill Book Co., Inc., 1953.

Reilly, William J. *Career Planning for High School Students*. New York, Harper & Brothers, 1953.

Robinson, Clark. *Making the Most of School and Life*. New York, The Macmillan Co., 1952.

Scott, Judith Unger. *Cues for Careers*. Philadelphia, Macrae Smith Co., 1954.

Sifferd, Calvin S. *Selecting an Occupation*, Second Edition. Bloomington, Illinois, McKnight & McKnight Publishing Co., 1953.

Simmons, Harry. *How to Get Ahead in Modern Business*. Englewood Cliffs, New Jersey, Prentice-Hall, Inc., 1953.

Smith, Frances. *Find A Career in Education*. New York, G. P. Putnam's Sons, 1960.

Smith, Leonard J. *Career Planning*. New York, Harper & Brothers, 1959.

Thorndike, Robert L., and Elizabeth Hagen. *Ten Thousand Careers*. New York, John Wiley and Sons, Inc., 1959.

Westervelt, Virginia Veeder. *Choosing a Career in a Changing World*. New York, G. P. Putnam's Sons, 1959.

## Manners—Business and Social

Beery, Mary. *Manners Made Easy*, Second Edition. New York, McGraw-Hill Book Co., Inc., 1954.

Carson, Byrta. *How You Look and Dress*, Third Edition. New York, McGraw-Hill Book Co., Inc., 1959.

Free, Anne R. *Social Usage*. New York, Appleton-Century-Crofts, Inc., 1960.

Kaufman, S. Jay. *How to Arrange a Public Function*. New York, David McKay Co., Inc., 1953.

MacGibbon, Elizabeth Gregg. *Manners in Business*, Second Edition. New York, The Macmillan Co., 1954.

Scott, Judith Unger. *Manners for Moderns*. Philadelphia, Macrae Smith Co., 1949.

Shaw, Carolyn Hagner. *Modern Manners*. New York, E. P. Dutton & Co.,
Inc., 1959.

Stephenson, Margaret. *As Others Like You*, Third Edition. Bloomington,
Illinois, McKnight & McKnight Publishing Co., 1957.

Stephenson, Margaret. *Good Manners, The Magic Key*. Bloomington, Illinois, McKnight & McKnight Publishing Co., 1959.

Stratton, Dorothy C., and Helen B. Schleman. *Your Best Foot Forward*,
Revised Edition. New York, McGraw-Hill Book Co., Inc., 1955.

Vanderbilt, Amy. *Amy Vanderbilt's Complete Book of Etiquette*. New
York, Doubleday & Company, Inc., 1958.

## Books and Business Background

Archer, Fred C., Raymond Brecker, and John C. Frakes. *General Office
Practice*. New York, Gregg Publishing Division, McGraw-Hill Book Co.,
Inc., 1958.

Carlson, Paul A., Hamden L. Forkner, and Lewis D. Boynton. *20th Century Bookkeeping and Accounting*, 21st Edition. Cincinnati, South-Western Publishing Co., 1958.

Cox, Homer L. *Coping With Correspondence*. New York, Sterling Publishing Co., Inc., 1950.

Ernest, John A., and George M. DaVall. *Salesmanship Fundamentals*, Second Edition. New York, Gregg Publishing Division, McGraw-Hill Book
Co., Inc., 1959.

Felter, Emma K., and Marie Reynolds. *Basic Clerical Practice*, Second Edition. New York, Gregg Publishing Division, McGraw-Hill Book Co.,
Inc., 1959.

Freeman, M. Herbert, J Marshall Hanna, and Gilbert Kahn. *Bookkeeping
and Accounting Simplified*, Second Edition. New York, Gregg Publishing
Division, McGraw-Hill Book Co., Inc., 1958.

Gilmartin, John G. *Building Your Vocabulary*, Second Edition. Englewood
Cliffs, New Jersey, Prentice-Hall, Inc., 1957.

Glos, R. E., and H. A. Baker. *Introduction to Business*, Fourth Edition.
Cincinnati, South-Western Publishing Co., 1959.

Gough, Vera. *You're the Speaker*. New York, Whiteside, Inc., 1954.

Gregg, John Robert, Albert C. Fries, Margaret Rowe, and Dorothy L.
Travis. *Applied Secretarial Practice*, Fourth Edition. New York, Gregg
Publishing Division, McGraw-Hill Book Co., Inc., 1957.

Kirk, John G., Maurice L. Crawford, and Mark H. Quay. *General Clerical
Procedures*, Third Edition. Englewood Cliffs, New Jersey, Prentice-Hall,
Inc., 1959.

Price, Ray G., Vernon A. Musselman, and Edwin E. Weeks: *General Business for Everyday Living*, Second Edition. New York, Gregg Publishing
Division, McGraw-Hill Book Co., Inc., 1960.

Richert, G. Henry. *Retailing Principles and Practice*, Third Edition. New York, Gregg Publishing Division, McGraw-Hill Book Co., Inc., 1954.

Sherwood, J. F., A. B. Carson, and Clem Boling. *College Accounting*, Sixth Edition. Cincinnati, South-Western Publishing Co., 1957.

Shilt, Bernard A., and William Harmon Wilson. *Business Principles and Management*, Third Edition. Cincinnati, South-Western Publishing Co., 1954.

Strony, Madeline, and M. Emily Greenaway. *The Secretary At Work*, Second Edition. New York, Gregg Publishing Division, McGraw-Hill Book Co., Inc., 1958.

Tonne, Herbert A., and Sidney Simon, and Esby C. McGill. *Business Principles, Organization and Management*. New York, Gregg Publishing Division, McGraw-Hill Book Co., Inc., 1958.

Whitcomb, Helen, and John Whitcomb. *Strictly for Secretaries*. New York, Whittlesey House, McGraw-Hill Book Co., Inc., 1957.

Williams, C. B., and J. Ball. *Effective Business Writing*, Second Edition. New York, The Ronald Press Company, 1953.

## Office Reference Books

Anderson, Ruth I., Lura Lynn Straub, and E. Dana Gibson. *Word Finder*. Englewood Cliffs, New Jersey, Prentice-Hall, Inc., 1960.

Beamer, Esther Kihn, J Marshall Hanna, and Estelle L. Popham. *Effective Secretarial Practice*, Third Edition. Cincinnati, South-Western Publishing Co., 1956.

Brauer, John C., and Richard E. Richardson. *The Dental Assistant*, Second Edition. New York, McGraw-Hill Book Co., Inc., 1960.

Bredow, Miriam. *Handbook for the Medical Secretary*, Fourth Edition. New York, Gregg Publishing Division, McGraw-Hill Book Co., Inc., 1959.

Butterfield, Wm. H. *Effective Personal Letters*. Englewood Cliffs, New Jersey, Prentice-Hall, Inc., 1951.

Coffin, Kenneth B., and R. Forest Coldwell. *The Medical Secretary*. New York, The Macmillan Co., 1959.

Fernald, James C. *English Grammar Simplified*. New York, Funk & Wagnalls Co., 1957.

Gavin, Ruth E., and E. Lillian Hutchinson. *Reference Manual for Stenographers and Typists*, Third Edition. New York, Gregg Publishing Division, McGraw-Hill Book Co., Inc., 1961.

Hutchinson, Lois Irene. *Standard Handbook for Secretaries*, Seventh Edition. New York, Gregg Publishing Division, McGraw-Hill Book Co., Inc., 1956.

Kahn, Gilbert, Theodore Yerian, and Jeffrey R. Stewart, Jr. *Progressive Filing*, Seventh Edition. New York, Gregg Publishing Division, McGraw-Hill Book Co., Inc., 1961.

Leslie, Louis A. *20,000 Words—Spelled, Divided and Accented for Quick Reference*, Fourth Edition. New York, Gregg Publishing Division, Mc-Graw-Hill Book Co., Inc., 1959.

Mayo, Lucy Graves. *Communication Handbook for Secretaries: A Guide to Effective Writing and Speaking*. New York, Gregg Publishing Division, McGraw-Hill Book Co., Inc., 1958.

Menning, J. H., and C. W. Wilkinson. *Writing Business Letters*. Homewood, Illinois, Richard D. Irwin, Inc., 1959.

Miller, Bessie May. *Legal Secretary's Complete Handbook*. Englewood Cliffs, New Jersey, Prentice-Hall, Inc., 1953.

Miller, Bessie May. *Private Secretary's Encyclopedia Dictionary*. Englewood Cliffs, New Jersey, Prentice-Hall, Inc., 1958.

Murphey, Robert W. *How and Where to Look It Up*. New York, McGraw-Hill Book Co., Inc., 1958.

Perrin, Porter G. *Writer's Guide and Index to English*, Third Edition. Chicago, Scott, Foresman & Company, 1959.

Stewart, Marie M., E. Lillian Hutchinson, Frank W. Lanham, and Kenneth Zimmer. *Business English and Communication*, Second Edition. New York, Gregg Publishing Division, McGraw-Hill Book Co., Inc., 1961.

Taintor, Sarah A., and Kate M. Monro. *Secretary's Handbook*, Eighth Edition. New York, The Macmillan Co., 1958.

Tressler, J. C., and Maurice C. Lippman. *Business English in Action*. Boston, D. C. Heath & Company, 1957.

Watson, William Eichler. *Standard Book of Letter Writing and Correct Social Forms*. Englewood Cliffs, New Jersey, Prentice-Hall, Inc., 1958.

*Webster's New Collegiate Dictionary*. Massachusetts, G. & C. Merriam Co., 1956.

Woolley, Edwin C., Franklin W. Scott, and Frederick Bracher. *College Handbook of Composition*, Sixth Edition. Boston, D. C. Heath & Company, 1958.

## Personality and Personal Success

Billet, Roy O., and Wendell Yeo. *Growing Up*. Boston, D. C. Heath & Company, 1959.

Bonner, E. *Personality*. New York, The Ronald Press Company, 1961.

Byrne, Brendan. *Three Weeks to a Better Memory*. Philadelphia, Holt, Rinehart and Winston, Inc., 1951.

Daly, Maureen. *What's Your P.Q.?* New York, Dodd, Mead & Co., 1952.

Emmett, E. R. *Thinking Clearly*. New York, Longmans, Green, & Co., Inc., 1960.

Ferrari, Erma Paul. *A Teenager's Guide to Personal Success*. Nashville, 1957.

Harsh, C. M., and H. G. Schrikel. *Personality*, Second Edition. New York, The Ronald Press Company, 1959.

Jones, J. Curtis. *On Being Your Best*. New York, The Macmillan Co., 1950.

Lachar, Rhoda. *You Are Unlimited*. Chicago, Follett Publishing Company, 1952.

Laird, Donald A., and Eleanor C. Laird. *Practical Business Psychology*, Third Edition. New York, Gregg Publishing Division, McGraw-Hill Book Co., Inc., 1961.

Lane, Janet. *Your Carriage, Madam*, Second Edition. New York, John Wiley and Sons, Inc., 1947.

Leeper, Robert Ward, and Peter Madison. *Toward Understanding Human Personalities*. New York, Appleton-Century-Crofts, Inc., 1959.

Nutley, Grace Stuart. *How to Carry on a Conversation*. New York, Sterling Publishing Co., Inc., 1959.

Pierce, Wellington G. *This is the Life*. Boston, D. C. Heath & Company, 1951.

Reid, Lillian N. *Personality and Etiquette*, Revised Edition. Boston, D. C. Heath & Company, 1950.

Robinson, Clark. *Making the Most of School and Life*. New York, The Macmillan Co., 1952.

Scott, Judith Unger. *Pattern for Personality*. Philadelphia, Macrae Smith Co., 1951.

Sferra, Adam G., Mary Elizabeth Wright, and Louis A. Rice. *Personality and Human Relations*, Second Edition. New York, Gregg Publishing Division, McGraw-Hill Book Co., 1961.

Shacter, Helen. *Understanding Ourselves*, Second Edition. Bloomington, Illinois, McKnight & McKnight Publishing Co., 1952.

Uris, Dorothy. *Everybody's Book of Better Speaking*. New York, David McKay Co., Inc., 1960.

Wilson, Everett B., and Sylvia B. Wright. *Getting Along With People in Business*. New York, Funk & Wagnalls Co., 1950.

# Index

33632